The Logic of Number

The Logic of Number

Neil Tennant

Great Clarendon Street, Oxford, OX2 6DP,
United Kingdom

Oxford University Press is a department of the University of Oxford.
It furthers the University's objective of excellence in research, scholarship,
and education by publishing worldwide. Oxford is a registered trade mark of
Oxford University Press in the UK and in certain other countries

First Edition published in 2022

Published in the United States of America by Oxford University Press
198 Madison Avenue, New York, NY 10016, United States of America

British Library Cataloguing in Publication Data
Data available

Library of Congress Control Number: 2021950477

ISBN 978–0–19–284667–9

DOI: 10.1093/oso/9780192846679.001.0001

Printed and bound in the UK by
TJ Books Limited

In grateful acknowledgment of the enduring influence of my high school teachers of mathematics:

John ('Cabbage') Strachan†
of Maritzburg College, Pietermaritzburg, South Africa; and
Alex ('The Bang') Gunther† *and Sanderson ('Sandy') Smith,*
both of The Cate School, Carpinteria, California

Die ganzen Zahlen hat der liebe Gott gemacht, alles andere ist Menschenwerk.

God made the whole numbers, all else is the work of humankind.

—Leopold Kronecker, as quoted in Weber [1891–2], at p. 19; from a lecture by Kronecker to the Berliner Naturforscher-Versammlung in 1886.

But if God gave us the natural numbers, and humankind has done all the rest, it's been a less than thorough job so far.

Contents

Acknowledgments

This monograph has been brewing over many years, with much of its material slowly accumulating without being sent off in discrete packages to learned journals. Some of the historical material about logicism, though, did find its way into my 2013 survey article 'Logicism and neo-logicism' in the *Stanford Encyclopedia of Philosophy*. I am grateful to the Editor for permission to re-use that material here. The proof of the Non-Compossibility Theorem first appeared in my 2010 article 'Deductive v. Expressive Power: a Pre-Gödelian Predicament', in the *Journal of Philosophy*.

For helpful correspondence about historical or conceptual matters, thanks are owed to Patricia Blanchette, John Burgess, Michael Detlefsen[†], Marcus Giaquinto, Ivor Grattan-Guinness[†], Richard Heck, Paolo Mancosu, Adrian Mathias, Charles David McCarty[†], Colin McLarty, Michael Potter, Michael Rathjen, George Schumm, Jamie Tappenden, Robert Thomas, and Mark Wilson; and for translational matters to Steven Boer, Philip Ebert, Julia Jorati, Ulrich Kohlenbach, Volker Peckhaus, and Peter Schroeder-Heister. The work in various earlier drafts or presentations has benefited from fruitful discussions with, and helpful comments from, my own teachers, colleagues, and students past and present: Ethan Brauer, Julian Cole, Roy Cook, Steven Dalglish, Jason DeWitt, Salvatore Florio, Harvey Friedman, Erich Jones, Robert Kraut, Kenneth Manders, Peter Milne, Alex Oliver, Marco Panza, Michael Potter, Patrick Reeder, Ian Rumfitt, Richard Samuels, Stewart Shapiro, Timothy Smiley, Matthew Souba, Damon Stanley, and Alan Weir. Naturally the author is solely responsible for any errors that remain.

I have also benefited from the bracing exchanges on the moderated email list on foundations of mathematics, run initially by Steven Simpson, and later by Martin Davis at fom@cs.nyu.edu. Although I have enjoyed too many off-line exchanges to be able to acknowledge them all here, I ought to make particular mention of the late Solomon Feferman, and of Akihiro Kanamori, Moshé Machover, and Wilfried Sieg.

My final note of thanks goes to Peter Momtchiloff and Henry Clarke at Oxford University Press, for their editorial support and their help with perfecting final copy.

Earlier versions of parts of this work have had the benefit of being presented for critical scrutiny at various academic gatherings. Very often comments from members in an audience can make the writer aware of a possible fallacy, an unconsidered perspective, an anticipation of one's views, or thematic connections one had not noticed. If, dear reader, you have not been named so far, please know that I am grateful to you for whatever help you might have rendered at the following meetings: Colloquium of the Ohio State Interdisciplinary Project on Emergence of Number, 2019; Workshop on 'Logics of Consequence: Logical Inferentialism, Defeasible Reasoning and Transitivity', Concordia University, Montreal, 2017; Logica Symposium 2016, organized by the Institute of Philosophy, Academy of Sciences of the Czech Republic, Hejnice; Logic Group, University of Cambridge, 2016; Buffalo Logic Colloquium, SUNY at Buffalo, 2015; Conference on Truth Pluralism and Logical Pluralism, University of Connecticut, 2015; Workshop 'No Ifs, Ands Or Buts', Departments of Linguistics and Philosophy, Ohio State, 2015; Workshop on the Semantics of Cardinals, Departments of Linguistics and Philosophy, Ohio State, 2014; Midwest Workshops in Philosophy of Mathematics XVII, XIV, VIII, and VI, Notre Dame; Workshop 'Proofs that and proofs why', Institut d'Histoire et Philosophie des Sciences, Paris, 2013; 60th Parallel Workshop on Proof Theory and Constructivism, Stockholm, 2013; Kline Workshop on A Priori Knowledge, University of Missouri, 2013; Philosophy of Mathematics Special Interest Group of the Mathematical Association of America (POMSIGMAA), Lexington, 2012; Workshop on Reverse Mathematics, University of Chicago, 2009; NYU Conference on Philosophy of Mathematics, 2009; Workshop and AMS Special Session on Constructive Mathematics, Boca Raton, Florida, 2009; Pittsburgh Fellowship Reunion Conference, Athens, Ohio, 2008; Logic Program, Indiana University, 2006; Arché Abstraction Weekend: Tennant's Philosophy of Mathematics, at the University of St. Andrews, 2004; Workshop on 'Negation in constructive logic', Department of Philosophy, Dresden University of Technology, 2004.

Part I

Natural Logicism

Chapter 1

What is Natural Logicism?

Abstract

Natural Logicism is a new species of logicism. It is based on Gentzenian rules of natural deduction, including ones governing logico-mathematical expressions that Gentzen himself did not treat. Natural Logicism could be developed for any branch of mathematics. The aim would be to determine how much of its foundation is 'logical', or analytic; and in what sense the objects dealt with might be logical objects. Here the focus is on Natural Logicism for the numbers. The two main traditional aims of logicism are pursued. The numbers are shown to be 'logical objects', and deeper principles about them are formulated from which one can then deduce as theorems the usual 'first principles' that mathematicians lay down. This requires that one develop the free logic for number-abstraction operators (natural, rational, and real). The logical treatment of these operators can be called 'single-barreled abstractionism'. It is an important advance on, and is in contrast with, the 'double-barreled' abstractionism of other neo-Fregeans. Another contrast with these others is that the underlying logic employed—Core Logic—is not only free but also constructive and relevant. An important methodological condition of adequacy is imposed on the natural logicist account: it must show how the different kinds of number are applicable in our wider thought and talk about the world.

This work aims to set out a philosophy, foundation, and methodology for mathematics that can best be described as 'natural logicist'. It is what logicists might have arrived at, had they enjoyed the benefits of Gerhard Gentzen's inferential methods of *natural* deduction for *logic*. Mathematical content, we contend, is best captured by inferential rules, arguably of a logical kind. They are set out in a natural deduction format, and govern a primitive vocabulary of expressions. These belong to a variety of syntactic types. They include both logical operators and logico-mathematical constants, functions, operators and predicates. The objects of each mathematical theory—for example, numbers in the case of arithmetic; points, lines and planes in the case of geometry—are to be treated as *sui generis*. The task is then to find suitable rules of inference governing the basic functions, sorts (or kinds), and relations characteristic of the different mathematical domains.

It is a fascinating and controversial question whether for certain kinds of math-

The Logic of Number. Neil Tennant, Oxford University Press. © Neil Tennant 2022.
DOI: 10.1093/oso/9780192846679.003.0001

ematical entities—in particular, the natural numbers—a case can be made for regarding them as logical objects, and our basic knowledge about them as logical in its provenance. One main aim of Natural Logicism is to furnish some technical criteria to help answer such questions. This work, as its title makes clear, confines itself to Natural Logicism about the numbers—natural, rational and real. These are the main areas for which, thus far, any kind of logicism has been proposed in the past. The theories in question form part of what German-speaking scholars called *Arithmetik*. The reader will recall that the subtitle of Gottlob Frege's famous *Begriffsschrift* (Frege [1879]) was 'eine der *arithmetischen* nachgebildete Formelsprache des reinen Denkens' [emphasis added].

This does not mean, however, that the same approach would be inappropriately, or unprofitably, extended to yet other branches of mathematics, such as various geometries, the differential and integral calculus, and set theory. This author believes, on the basis of investigations both completed and ongoing, that it can be. Its extension to these other branches will, however, have to be deferred to a subsequent volume.

The author's own version of logicism about the natural numbers was called Constructive Logicism, in Tennant [1987b] (henceforth: *AR&L*).[1] That treatment will be advanced further here in Part II, in a more polished and complete form. In Part III we extend that logicist treatment to the rational numbers. Finally, in Part IV we investigate the difficult and delicate question of the extent to which the real continuum is 'purely logical' in nature. We shall push our developed techniques as far as possible in search of a satisfying logicist treatment; but we shall finally concede an important role to our *a priori* geometric intuition in the genesis of our grasp of the real numbers.

It is clear that in assessing any kind of logicism about mathematics, we need to attend to how, exactly, logic serves mathematics (and perhaps, even, vice versa). There are two ways that logic does so.

1. Logic provides formal proofs that 'regiment' the informal proofs of ordinary mathematics.

2. (More ambitious, hence controversial:) Logic furnishes definitions of the primitive concepts of mathematics, allowing one to derive the mathematician's 'first principles' (the axioms, or postulates of the branch in question) as results within logic itself.

With (1), Logic is being pursued as proof theory. Subscribing to (1) hardly qualifies one as a logicist, though. Hilbert, after all, was a formalist about mathematics, not a logicist, and he certainly subscribed to (1). All logicists, however, must subscribe to (1). It is a necessary, but by no means sufficient, commitment on the part of any thinker who is to qualify as a logicist. That said, what a logician

[1] This is the appropriate point at which to advise the reader that, apart from *AR&L*, all references to the author's own works will be by date only. All works by others will continue to be cited by both name and date.

qua logicist does with formal proofs and the rules of inference that generate them can be of the utmost importance. Logic itself does not come in 'one size that fits all'. In precisely delineating all the logical rules of inference to which one may resort when formalizing mathematical proofs, and nontrivially deriving conventional mathematical axioms in different branches of mathematics, the would-be logicist logician can make the most of the under-appreciated resources that logic itself (especially: proof theory) is able to offer.

With (2), one passes from logic proper to logicism, which is a specific philosophical account of the nature of (certain parts of) mathematical knowledge and its objects. We shall discuss (1) and (2) in reverse order.

Logicism in its original and most ambitious form is the philosophical and foundational doctrine that all the truth of *Arithmetik* is a species of logical truth and that all *arithmetische* objects are logical objects. Logicism maintains that Logic (in some suitably general and powerful sense that will have to be defined) is capable of furnishing definitions of the primitive concepts of this main branch of mathematics. These definitions allow one to derive the mathematician's 'first principles' of number theory as results within logic itself. The logicist is therefore purporting to uncover a deeper source of justification for these 'first principles' than just that they seem obvious or self-evident to mathematicians working in the branch of mathematics in question, or that they have been enshrined as axiomatic or postulational within the tradition of informal rigor in mathematics. The original logicists wanted to be able to claim with appropriate justification that the truths of this branch of mathematics can be revealed as analytic in Kant's sense; or, more appropriately and accurately: in the sense of 'analytic' explicated by Frege, who stressed the need to adhere to only logical laws and definitions in one's derivations of the mathematical results in question.

In more contemporary terminology: these results are true solely by virtue of the meanings of the linguistic expressions involved. To this, the Natural Logicist would add: those meanings, moreover, are conferred by rules of inference governing the introduction and elimination of suitably 'dominant' occurrences of the expressions in question—occurrences in conclusions (in the case of introduction rules) and occurrences in major premises (in the case of elimination rules).

Another consequence of a logicist view is that mathematical certainty (in *Arithmetik*, at least) partakes of certainty about logical truth. The same holds for necessity: this kind of mathematical necessity partakes of the necessity of logical truth. This holds, however, only to the extent that the mathematical statements in question are within the scope of the logicism that one has succeeded in developing. (Logicist though he was about *Arithmetik*, Frege did not espouse logicism about geometry. In his view, Euclidean geometry was synthetic *a priori*.)

One advantage of Natural Logicism as a new kind of logicism regarding mathematics in general is (as already signaled above) that its methods can be used to determine to what extent the truths in a particular branch of mathematics might be logical in their provenance. So it is more nuanced and discerning than logicism in its original and ambitious form, even when confined to number theory. Considerable interest attaches to the question whether the methods of Natural Logicism can be extended to other branches of mathematics besides *Arithmetik*—even if only to reveal how extensive a part of another such branch (if not all of it) is logical in its provenance.

In the course of laying a natural-logicist foundation for each mathematical discipline, it has proved imperative also to achieve clarity about the norms of logical inference within a *free logic with abstraction operators*. A free logic is one that can deal with non-denoting but grammatically well-formed singular terms. (See p. 11 ff. for how certain ones of our basic inference rules need to be reframed for free logic.) The present author has dealt successively with the description operator, the number-abstraction operator, and the set-abstraction operator.[2] With the appropriate free logic formulated, one can turn one's attention to the concepts and operations specific to each mathematical discipline in turn. We can briefly mention three examples in this connection.

First, a logical investigation of orderly pairing affords a logicist treatment of addition and multiplication in arithmetic.[3]

Second, a natural-deduction investigation of the incidence operators in projective geometry affords a logicist treatment of the foundations of that discipline within which its famous Principle of Duality is beautifully clarified.[4]

Third, a natural-deduction investigation of functions *sui generis* (and not by way of set-theoretical surrogacy) leads to an elegant treatment of derivatives of real functions, which hews to the basic intuitions of the student of calculus.

Let us consider now the logical aims of Natural Logicism. The main one is to regiment rigorously but faithfully mathematical reasoning in all the different branches of mathematics. One does this by using a system of appropriate natural-deduction rules. This, as already remarked, is what justifies calling this version of logicism 'natural'. One's formal proofs must be structural homologues of the informally rigorous proofs that one finds in peer-reviewed mathematical texts. The formal proofs must employ formal analogues of all the defined notions that mathematicians have devised, and for which they have supplied the special abbreviatory notations that have become part of the *lingua franca* of their mathematical disciplines.

The natural logicist therefore has to attend carefully to what is really 'built in' to any defined concept. This is in addition to uncovering what one's usual 'first principles' happen to be for one's mathematical reasoning, and investigating whether these 'first' principles can themselves be derived logically from even deeper foundations. The logical formalism supplied must 'carve informal proofs at their joints'. (Thus, logical regimentation is a form of anatomization of these

[2]See [1978], ch. 7, for natural-deduction rules for the description operator and the set-abstraction operator. Natural-deduction rules for the number-abstraction operator were given in *AR&L*. The rules for the set-abstraction operator are stated (and used) in this work in Chapter 24.

[3]See [2009].

[4]Exactly how this is so is explained in Chapter 4, p. 42.

bodies of intellectual work.) By reflecting their own informally rigorous proofs back to them, in their perfected formal versions, the natural logicist should be able to motivate practicing mathematicians to engage more readily in the study of formal proofs. Synergies between natural logicists and practising mathematicians could very well lead to the formulation of proof-search strategies in automated or interactive theorem-proving that are tailored to the branch of mathematics in question.

There are also some philosophical payoffs to be had, besides those of 'cognitive prosthetics' in proof-search. One can address the issue of analytic *versus* synthetic truth in mathematics with sharper tools at one's disposal. And, on the mathematical side: occasionally one will detect a deeply hidden fallacy in even the best extant texts, as the perfecting formal proof takes shape and it turns out that there are logical gaps that the informal reasoning—perhaps, say, because of some inadvertently over-specific feature of a geometrical diagram—had kept hidden from the original author of the informal proof.[5]

It might be objected that there are some prima-facie problems for the pursuit of the main logical aims of Natural Logicism described above. Here we mention the two most important ones. We shall provide quick but appropriate rebuttals, and supply some further comments on matters arising.

1. The natural logicist will have to introduce an indefinite number of 'pasigraphically primitive' expressions (for all the defined terms).

Rebuttal: Here the natural logicist is merely keeping pace with the mathematician who is formulating new and interesting concepts, and introducing new notations (pasigraphs) for them. The natural logicist is just mirroring the continuing development of informal mathematics, with its ever-increasing stock of defined concepts, and 'single-symbol' notations for them. (These notations can of course involve parameters—think of $a \subseteq b$ for the subset relation, or $\mathcal{P}(a)$ for the power-set operation, in set theory based on $\in$ as its only 'extralogical' expression.) The alleged problem is mitigated, indeed eliminated, by the fact that these defined concepts are always finite in number.[6]

2. The sheer attention to detail that would be involved in thus 'perfecting' mathematical texts might be off-putting to [all/nearly all/most/many/several/ a few... ?] mathematicians and/or foundationalists.

Rebuttal: Welcome to the task of fully Fregean and Gentzenian foundations. At least it affords a prospect of gainful employment for logicians undertaking to do what logicians ought to do—which is to clarify the structure of mathematical

[5]This has been the author's own experience in regimenting a proof in projective geometry (of Desargues' Theorem) by none other than Coxeter. But the details would make for too long a digression.

[6]For an example of how pasigraphs can be usefully deployed, the reader could take a look at the Digression on inferentialist formulation of geometrical axioms, on p. 272 ff. We treat pasigraphs in set theory in [forthcoming].

reasoning at the most refined possible level of symbolic detail.[7] Ultimately, of course, one would expect to exploit computerization for the great bulk of this sort of work. But the intelligent design of efficient proof-search algorithms calls for advanced proof-theoretical insights and understanding.[8]

Let us venture more here in response to the prima-facie problem (1) above. As any working mathematician knows, mathematical reasoning involves widespread use of defined notions. Their definitions need to be 'unpacked' by appropriate logical inferences when those defined notions come into play. The defined concepts should be manageable, fruitful, and of wide application. But, most importantly from the logical point of view: they should help one to 'atomicize' the reasoning. What is meant by this can be explained as follows.

Definitions typically capture logically complex notions and represent them with new lexical primitives (symbolizing the definienda).[9] By choosing definitions arranged in a well-founded partial ordering, or 'pyramid' of compilation of the right 'logical density', it becomes possible to regiment mathematical reasoning by means of formal proofs in which virtually all the sentences that occur appear to be 'atomic'. Here is a very simple example. In order to prove that t is a subset of u, it suffices (given the definition of the subset relation) to find a proof whose overall structure is

$$\dfrac{\dfrac{}{a \in t}{}^{(i)} \quad \vdots \quad a \in u}{t \subseteq u}{}^{(i)} \; .$$

At this outer layer, at least, the sentences involved appear to be atomic, thanks to the inferential rules (here, in particular, the introduction rule) adopted for the pasigraph '... ⊆ ...'.

Particular care should be taken to identify and explicitly mention the various parameters on which a defined concept depends. This calls for a considerable

---

[7]With regard to this avowed aim, we shall clearly have to go about matters more effectively than did Peano. Ernst Snapper wryly wrote (Snapper [1979], p. 214)

> ... even the great Peano had mistaken ideas about the real purpose of formalization. He published one of his most important discoveries in differential equations in a formalized language (very similar to a first order language) with the result that nobody read it until some charitable soul translated the article into common German.

[8]This is the case even with computational proof-search in decidable propositional logics. See [1992].

[9]These lexical primitives are what we have called 'pasigraphs' above. They can be function-signs, such as the power-set operation $\mathcal{P}(\;)$ or the union-operation $\cup(\;)$ in set theory; or predicates, such as the binary '... ⊆ ...', again in set theory. The reader will easily supply a host of other familiar pasigraphs from different branches of mathematics, representing concepts that enjoy logically complex definitions in terms of the chosen primitive expressions of the branch in question.

degree of self-discipline on the part of the would-be formalizer of mathematical reasoning.

Such rules pin down the concepts in question. This is what justifies use of the label 'logicism'. Judicious choices of definitions, in which the definienda are furnished with introduction and elimination rules, enable one to minimize the logical complexity of sentences appearing in the formal proofs provided as regimentations of passages of informal mathematical reasoning. This will be in evidence in Part II, where we derive the Dedekind–Peano postulates for arithmetic using our primitive rules of inference governing the variable-binding term-forming operator # ('the number of'), the one-place function s ('the successor of') and the name 0 ('zero').

The early forms of logicism tended to obscure the virtues of the 'homologizing' kind of logical rigor just described (in the regimentation of mathematical proofs), both because the required formal systems of proof had yet to be developed, and because those early forms were tied to a quite orthogonal project. This was the project of trying to furnish an all-embracing, over-arching theory of classes or theory of types. The universe of discourse of the sought unifying theory, it was hoped, would accommodate (through appropriate surrogates) all the various kinds of mathematical objects that different mathematical theories are 'about'.

This Fregean and Russellian bent (see Chapter 2 for more on this) had the consequence that Logicism, as a philosophy of mathematics, and a provider of foundations for it, appeared to be over-ambitious. Yet Logicism can and should be prosecuted without any concern for the unification of mathematics via class theory or set theory or category theory or the theory of types (to name the most important 'unifying theories' on offer). A logicism worthy of the name could confine itself to simply making existing proofs in the main corpora of rigorous[10] but informal mathematics, perfectly rigorous because completely formal and symbolic.

This methodological constraint forces one to make judicious choices of lemmas interpolated between one's mathematical axioms and the theorems that one seeks to derive from them. It obliges one also to deploy a logic that enables one to make the kind of deductive progress that is evident throughout mathematics. The standard systems of Classical Logic and Intuitionistic Logic provide a rule of 'unrestricted Cut', which is designed to ensure that proofs can be 'accumulated': if one has proved lemma φ from axioms Δ, and has also proved theorem ψ from lemma φ plus further axioms Γ, then one has *ipso facto* proved theorem ψ from the combination of axioms $\Delta \cup \Gamma$. This is the consideration that Gentzen had in mind when formulating the rule of Cut as a rule *in* his sequent calculi for these two logics:

$$\frac{\Delta : \varphi \qquad \varphi, \Gamma : \psi}{\Delta, \Gamma : \psi}\,.$$

[10]Here we mean 'rigorous' to be understood in the usual way that a well-trained mathematician understands it. All main steps are explicitly indicated. Appeals to intuition are made only when the writer and the reader can be expected to know how to eliminate them in favor of more rigorous symbolic reasoning.

It is not necessary, however, to have a rule of Cut in such an unrestricted form in order to ensure deductive progress in mathematics. Indeed, it is not necessary to have a rule of Cut at all, as part of one's logical system. All that is needed, rather, is the truth of the following statement of the *admissibility* of Cut:

> There is an effective binary operation [,] on proofs such that given any proof Π of the sequent $\Delta : \varphi$, and given any proof Σ of the sequent $\varphi, \Gamma : \psi$, the proof $[\Pi, \Sigma]$ proves either ψ or $\perp$ from (some subset of) $\Delta \cup \Gamma$ (that is, $[\Pi, \Sigma]$ proves either a sequent $\Theta : \varphi$ or a sequent $\Theta : \perp$, for some subset Θ of $\Delta \cup \Gamma$).[11]

A remarkable feature of the introduction and elimination rules for the standard logical operators is that (with the elimination rules stated in their 'parallelized' forms) one can insist that only normal-form proofs count as proofs, and still secure the truth of the displayed claim. Normality, moreover, is guaranteed by a beautifully simple expedient: major premises of eliminations must 'stand proud', with no proof-work above them. A major goal for the research program of Natural Logicism is to preserve these metalogical features of first-order Core Logic $\mathbb{C}$ (or Classical Core Logic $\mathbb{C}^+$) when we extend it by adopting our envisaged introduction and elimination rules for more peculiarly mathematical notions.[12]

This is one of the less appreciated benefits of full formalization of mathematical proofs. It enables the maturing mathematician to become aware of which steps of reasoning might be especially controversial or methodologically significant. It also sharpens the theorist's awareness of how certain reduction procedures might effect a welcome increase in the degree of constructivity or purity of a proof, or a decrease in its degree of impredicativity.[13]

All these matters have to do with the advantages of furnishing formal proofs as perfections of existing mathematical arguments that are informally rigorous but by no means as detailed, and effectively checkable, as fully formalized proofs are. The logicism in Natural Logicism is what is driving the felt need for fully formalized proofs. It was Frege's main aim in using his *Begriffsschrift* in his *Grundgesetze*—to ensure that there are absolutely no logical lacunae in his derivations of the laws of arithmetic within what he took to be a purely logical system.

In addition to this, however, there is another main aim that one can adjoin here, *pace* Frege. It is to furnish logical systems with enough primitive rules of inference to cope with all the steps that practicing mathematicians themselves take as primitive—in the sense that they recognize no need to be more explicit and detailed about the more intricate logical structures that would be revealed in the sentences they are manipulating in their inferences, if they were to 'unpack' every single defined notion embedded within them, thereby rendering the sentences in

---

[11]For fuller discussion of how this 'restricted transitivity' principle fully serves all the mathematician's needs, see [2012a] and [2017].

[12]For a detailed treatment of the Core systems, see [2017]. For the primitive rules of these systems, see p. 26 ff.

[13]In this connection see [2015].

the 'officially primitive' notation. In this connection one must also attend to what the 'basic sorts' of abstract objects are that mathematicians take themselves to be dealing with, when they reason from their first principles within any particular branch of mathematics, to the deductively much further removed theorems that they wish to prove. To take a simple example: if one is working within number theory, is one really conceiving of the natural numbers as finite von Neumann ordinals? When acolytes are introduced to number theory, are the objects of that study introduced to them as finite pure sets containing the empty set as a member, and such that of any two distinct members, one is a member of the other? We think not. It strikes us that the beginner in number theory is (quite correctly) introduced to the natural numbers as objects *sui generis*, endowed with no 'internal structure' of the kind just adverted to.

The question naturally arises, for any 'branch of mathematics', or mathematical theory T: how far might the natural-logicist approach be extended to T? Could T be laid out in its own 'native' terms, shorn of the specifically set-theoretic notions that are employed in its contemporary treatments in textbooks? Could one avoid the 'ontological riches' of a set-theoretic foundation, by helping oneself only to what is specifically needed, both conceptually and ontologically, in order to attain the results one is after? And how might one systematically characterize a certain part of any given branch of mathematics in a logicist fashion, even if one cannot succeed in giving a logicist account of the whole?

By way of tentative reply to these questions, a few more words might now be in order about the author's development of Natural Logicism so far. As the reader will see, its reach has been extended beyond the usual confines of *Arithmetik*. In this volume, however, we deal with only the naturals, the rationals, and the reals. For Natural Logicism to take shape as a program, it needed to have some logical fundamentals developed, and then to have them applied in various areas. What follows is an eclectic progress report, before we engage in earnest with the three areas of number theory to which this volume is devoted. Works cited by date alone, the reader will recall—see footnote 1 on p. 4—are by the present author.

In [1978], ch. 7, a natural-deduction system for free logic was formulated, which could accommodate the potentially non-denoting terms that occur in mathematical theorizing. When working in a free logic, one has to keep track of existential commitments and presuppositions.

We shall abbreviate $\exists x\, x = t$ to $\exists!t$, where t is any closed term (including parameters). The following are the modified and/or new rules that one uses in free logic for the quantifiers and for identity:

∀-Introduction

$$\dfrac{\dfrac{}{\exists!a}{\scriptstyle(i)} \quad \vdots \quad \varphi}{\forall x \varphi^a_x}{\scriptstyle(i)}$$

where a is ∀-parametric in the subproof

∀-Elimination

$$\frac{\forall x\varphi \quad \exists!t}{\varphi^x_t}$$

∃-Introduction

$$\frac{\varphi^x_t \quad \exists!t}{\exists x\varphi}$$

∃-Elimination

$$\frac{\exists x\varphi \qquad \begin{array}{c} \overline{\exists!a}^{(i)} \;,\; \overline{\varphi^x_a}^{(i)} \\ \vdots \\ \psi \end{array}}{\psi}{\scriptstyle (i)}$$

where a is ∃-parametric in the subproof on the right

Reflexivity of Identity

$$\frac{\exists!t}{t = t}$$

Free logic also has the following two special rules:

Rule of Atomic Denotation

$$\frac{A(\ldots t \ldots)}{\exists!t}\text{ , where } A \text{ is atomic}$$

Rule of Functional Denotation

$$\frac{\exists!f(\ldots t \ldots)}{\exists!t}$$

In *AR&L* a general account was also given of so-called 'transitional atomic logic'. With this logic one seeks to carry out one's reasoning while having as many as possible of the sentences occurring in one's proofs be atomic. A neo-logicist project was then pursued: a constructive and relevant foundation for successor arithmetic was set out, taking the number-term forming operator $\#x\Phi x$ ('the number of Φs') as primitive. Meaning-determining introduction and elimination rules for #, zero and the successor function were formulated, and the familiar Dedekind–Peano axioms for arithmetic, usually taken as the starting points for any proofs of theorems of arithmetic, were non-trivially (but with full formality) derived for the language of 0, s and #. Ontological commitment was incurred, seriatim, only to zero and successive naturals. No commitment at all was incurred to any infinite totality of numbers, or to 'the number' of any infinite totality. The treatment in *AR&L* was fully Kroneckerian—unlike that of the neo-Fregeans who had been using the double-barreled Hume's Principle

$$\text{HP} \qquad \#x\Phi x = \#x\Psi x \;\leftrightarrow\; \exists R\; Rxy[\Phi x \text{ 1-1 } \Psi y]\,.$$

One main concern in *AR&L* was to elucidate the application of natural numbers to count finite collections.

The applicability of the natural numbers is demonstrated by interdeducing (for each number n), within the foundational natural-logicist theory, the number-committal claim

$$\#x\Phi(x) = \underline{n} \quad \text{(`The number of } \Phi\text{s is } \underline{n}\text{')}$$

in which both the (closed) abstractive term $\#x\Phi(x)$ and the numeral $\underline{n}$ occur substantively—or, as a logician would say, as singular term—with the number-*non*committal claim

$$\exists_n x\Phi(x) \quad \text{(`There are exactly } n \ \Phi\text{s'),}$$

in which n occurs (in the English rendering) adjectivally.[14] The latter is any one of the familiar forms of 'numerosity claim'. These can be formulated in the language of first-order logic with identity, but without any specifically numerical expressions. See Chapter 8 for further explanation and discussion. The same project was extended, in [2009], in order to deal with addition and multiplication. The extra first-order resources affording a neo-logicist treatment of addition and multiplication were the rules for the logic of orderly pairing.

In [1997b], it was argued that the formulation of mathematical theories in terms of introduction and elimination rules for the main logico-mathematical operators furnished a principled basis for drawing an analytic/synthetic distinction within those mathematical theories. The operators in question are term-forming operators, not sentence-forming ones. Hence the natural-deduction paradigm of introduction and elimination rules (for connectives and quantifiers) had to be extended in order to deal with them.

Other neo-Fregeans at the time used 'double-barreled' abstraction principles. A double-barreled abstraction principle for an abstraction operator @ is one that takes the form

$$@(\ldots) = @(\text{---}) \leftrightarrow \text{Condition}(\ldots;\text{---}).$$

The left-hand side

$$@(\ldots) = @(\text{---})$$

is an identity statement, both of whose terms have @ dominant. The operator @ may or may not be variable-binding. The right-hand side

$$\text{Condition}(\ldots;\text{---})$$

is expressed using extralogical primitives occurring in the two terms of the identity statement, lying in the scope of those dominant occurrences of @.

In keeping with the approach that had been taken in *AR&L*—which, as already intimated, was a break from the double-barreled abstractionism then (and even

[14] As we shall see in due course, n need not even occur (except, possibly, as a subscript to a bound variable) in the first-order sentence that regiments the thought that there are exactly n Φs.

now, still) in vogue—the rules for any term-forming operator were required in [1997b] to be *single*-barreled. Single-barreled rules characterize conditions for a term-forming operator's introduction and elimination when it is dominant on one side of an identity statement, on whose other side is a most-general placeholder t for singular terms in the language. This does formal justice both to an important demand made by Frege himself, and to Quine's famous dictum 'No entity without identity'. So one seeks harmoniously balanced introduction and elimination rules for the likes of

$t = \bigsqcup x\Phi(x)$ ('t is the sum (fusion) of all individuals x such that $\Phi(x)$');
$t = \#x\Phi(x)$ ('t is the number of individuals x such that $\Phi(x)$');
$t = \iota x\Phi(x)$ ('t is the individual x such that $\Phi(x)$'); and
$t = \{x|\Phi(x)\}$ ('t is the set of all individuals x such that $\Phi(x)$').

For example, the logic of sets that is generated by such introduction and elimination rules for the set-abstraction operator $\{x|\Phi(x)\}$ yields a body of (derived) analytic results, among which is the so-called Axiom of Extensionality:

$$\forall x\forall y(\forall z(z \in x \leftrightarrow z \in y) \rightarrow x = y).$$

Such results form a body of theorizing that Quine once called 'virtual set theory'. It makes no ontological commitments; it simply explores the conceptual constraints governing identity, property-possession, and the mere possibility of set-formation. On the synthetic side would be existential claims such as 'ω exists'.[15] In [forthcoming], the natural logicist treatment of ontologically non-committal set theory is developed in complete detail.

In [2004], a general account was provided of the logic of a variety of abstraction operators, including set-abstraction. In [2012c] and [2018], the method of formulating introduction and elimination rules was applied to the fusion operator in mereology, with systematic and simplifying effects.

Given that the general method of introduction and elimination rules could be claimed to have dealt, with some measure of success, with the notions of set, number, and part-whole, the neo-Kantian question arises: could this method bear fruit when applied to geometry? Our answer to this question is positive, but will have to await development in a subsequent volume.

To anticipate: one can focus, at the outset, on the simplest and most elegant kind of geometry—synthetic projective geometry in both two and three dimensions (where 'synthetic' is used here in the geometer's sense). The logico-philosophical project just described can thereby be extended beyond the perhaps

[15] For the reader not versed in modern set theory: ω is defined to be the set of all finite von Neumann ordinals, which are the usual set-theoretic surrogates for the natural numbers. Corresponding to the natural number 0 is the empty set $\emptyset$. Corresponding to the natural number 1 is the singleton of 0, namely $\{\emptyset\}$. In general, corresponding to the natural number $n + 1$ is the set $\{0, \ldots, n\}$. In this way, the 'less than' relation $<$ among natural numbers corresponds conveniently to the relation $\in$ of set-membership. Moreover, n is the cardinal number of a set X by virtue of there being a 1-1 mapping from X onto n.

more central concerns with set, number, and the relations of parts to wholes.[16] The 'geometry of incidence' (one can think this as the 'logic of criss-crossing') can be captured with simple and elegant rules for the introduction and elimination of the 'incidence operators'. The aim is to dig more deeply than even the most rigorously-minded geometers are wont to do, in order to furnish a logical foundation that will yield conventional axiomatizations as by-products. We have found that we can proceed at first order, avoiding recourse to any higher-order or set-theoretic or mereological conceptions of geometrical entities.

Various branches of pure mathematics, such as arithmetic, different geometries, set theory etc. have been axiomatized by the pure mathematicians who practice in those fields. These mathematicians are interested first and foremost in the abstract structures formed by the mathematical objects under investigation, even when the intention is to try to characterize the structure in question up to isomorphism. Questions of applicability are usually set to one side, as are questions concerning the ultimate logical foundations of that branch of mathematics within rational thought as a whole. One of the (perhaps unintended) consequences of this 'pure isolationist' approach on the part of pure mathematicians is that axioms are chosen with a pragmatic eye to how quickly they can yield desired consequences, and how readily they will be accepted (without proof) by the intended audience. Both consistency and certainty are desiderata, to be sure; but pragmatic compromises are also struck in pursuit of both brevity of proof and power of single axioms.

This means, in the case of some of the traditional axiomatizations of different branches of geometry, that there is a trade-off between the length of axioms and their number—usually resulting in longer axioms, and fewer of them. The axioms eventually chosen serve mainly as convenient starting points for deductions, provided only that one's acolyte audience will accept them as true of the intended subject matter. There is no uncompromising concern, on the part of practicing mathematicians, to ensure that all the axioms laid down are conceptually basic, or—even better—analytic of the concepts involved. Nor is there any concern to keep the axioms within some tightly constrained syntactic class, involving, say, a minimal number of quantifier alternations.

Our natural logicist study of projective geometry on which we are here briefly reporting has departed rather self-consciously from this established precedent in mathematical axiomatization. Rather than stating axioms—which are (usually complex) sentences of a formal language—we state transitional atomic rules of inference. These are rules of inference, in natural-deduction format, in which only atomic sentences feature. Some of them may contain parameters, thereby enabling one to express existential import—but still the only sentences in view are atomic. We state a great many rules, arranged, as far as possible, in thematically coherent groups. Our basic methodological principle is: state more simply

[16] Reference was made in [1997b] at pp. 301 and 446 to an earlier stage of the work here decribed on natural foundations for projective geometry.

and more frequently, rather than less simply and less frequently. Fundamental principles of geometry should be like so many little ants, making for a supple organic whole, rather than like heavy foundation stones that are difficult to put in place.

We shall revisit projective geometry as a branch of mathematics of special interest to the natural logicist, whose logical methods can shed interesting light on the phenomenon of projective duality. That topic will be broached in due course (p. 42).

Chapter 2

Before and After Frege

Abstract

The logicizing trend of Dedekind and Frege arose in the wake of the arithmetization of analysis begun by Gauss and consummated by Weierstraß. In Kantian terms, these mathematicians and foundationalists sought to account for number theory as the product of our faculty of understanding, and not of *a priori* forms of intuition. The discussion turns to Frege's class theory and his ill-fated Basic Law V, which was prey to Russell's Paradox; and describes the later development of modern set theory as the 'carrier theory' for mathematical foundations.

The doctrine of logicism had its first glimmerings in the writings of Dedekind, but it really only came to full flowering in the work of Frege. Their combined contributions represented a culmination of the trend, by their time well under way among leading mathematicians, toward the arithmetization of real (and complex) analysis—the aforementioned *Arithmetik*. It is important to appreciate, then, that *Arithmetik* covered more than just the arithmetic of whole numbers. Frege's concept-script, as we have just emphasized, was a formula-language modeled on the increasingly rigorous mathematical language of his day. Its sentences that involved explicit (and alternating) quantifiers were finally, even if only intuitively, properly understood by the best mathematicians, as they proposed definitions of limits, derivatives, and integrals, and of notions such as continuity and uniform continuity of functions. The mathematical community had at long last achieved that degree of *Weierstraß'sche Strenge* that has been celebrated ever since. This was not confined to the arithmetic (in today's English sense) of the whole numbers 0, 1, ... Rather, it was the *Arithmetik* of Gauss and Riemann, which encompassed all of number theory up to and including complex analysis, and for which Cauchy and Weierstraß were the first to provide a rigorous foundation—at least, in the mathematicians' sense of 'rigorous', if not in the sense of the word as used by formal logicians. One frequently speaks of 'informal rigor' in the mathematicians' case, in order to underscore this contrast with the rigor sought by formal logicians.

The Logic of Number. Neil Tennant, Oxford University Press. © Neil Tennant 2022.
DOI: 10.1093/oso/9780192846679.003.0002

The logicizing trend begun by Dedekind had its roots in the even earlier works of Gauss, and of Bolzano. Analysis, they maintained, had to be 'arithmetized', i.e., de-geometrized. This mathematical trend came to maturity in the works of Cauchy and Weierstraß, and became the dominant paradigm in Western thought about the nature of mathematics. The leading idea of the arithmetizers was that the concepts and first principles of arithmetic and analysis are to be found in the human understanding, independently of its *a priori* geometric intuitions concerning any spatial or temporal continua. Arithmetic and analysis, the arithmetizers (and after them, the logicists) contended, are completely conceptual and logical in their axiomatic sources and in their deductive development. In Kantian terms (which of course were available to, and influential for, these theorizers), arithmetic and analysis are fruits of our faculty of understanding, not of our *a priori* forms of intuition.

Frege, as is well known, went in for overkill with the formal system that (so he hoped and intended) was to vindicate his logicism. He sought to unify all of arithmetic and analysis within a general theory of classes. Classes were supposed to be logical objects *par excellence*. The strategy was to define the natural numbers, say, as particular classes within a much more capacious universe of abstract, logical objects. Using the definitions, one would then derive the first principles of arithmetic (the Dedekind–Peano axioms, say) as theorems within the theory of classes; and eventually do the same for (at least) real analysis. To that end one would exploit, ultimately, only the deeper underlying axioms governing classes themselves.

Among these axioms was Frege's ill-fated Basic Law V.[1] It can be expressed (in the troublesome direction) as the following rule of inference governing concepts Φ and Ψ:

$$\frac{\forall x(\Phi x \leftrightarrow \Psi x)}{\{x|\Phi x\} = \{x|\Psi x\}} \;.$$

In words of beguiling simplicity: co-extensive concepts have identical extensions.

This allows one to derive what is today known as a principle of 'naive comprehension'. This easily deducible second-order consequence of Basic Law V says that, corresponding to any concept Φ, there exists the class of all and only those things that fall under the concept Φ. In the language of second-order logic:

$$\forall\Phi\exists X\forall y(y \in X \leftrightarrow \Phi y)\,.$$

Russell's famous paradox ensued. For Φy take $y \notin y$, expressing the concept of non-self-membership. One thereby obtains

$$\exists X\forall y(y \in X \leftrightarrow y \notin y)\,.$$

[1] As a referee has helpfully observed, Frege's actual formulation of Basic Law V involved value-ranges of functions generally. (See *Grundgesetze*, Vol. I, §20.) Concepts are just a special case—they are functions whose range is $\{T, F\}$. (See *Grundgesetze*, Vol. I, §3.) We are content here to concentrate on this special case.

Let r be such an X. So

$$\forall y(y \in r \leftrightarrow y \notin y)\,.$$

Note that r is an object within the scope of this generalization. Instantiating with respect to r, one obtains

$$r \in r \leftrightarrow r \notin r\,.$$

But one can show in short order, within a very weak propositional logic, that any statement of the form

$$A \leftrightarrow \neg A$$

is inconsistent.[2] So Frege's Basic Law V is inconsistent.

It was this simple formal discovery that occasioned the 'crisis in foundations' early in the twentieth century.

Russell offered his own solution to the problem of his paradox, in the form of his theory of types (both simple and ramified). By partitioning the universe of objects into types, or levels, he sought to avoid the vicious circularity that he had diagnosed as the underlying problem with Fregean class abstraction. According to Russell, it should be illicit to define a class C impredicatively—that is, in a way that involves generalizing about any range of individuals to which C itself would have to belong. Thus, the notion of self-membership, along with non-self-membership, could not even be deployed.[3] This has the curious effect of rehabilitating Basic Law V (at least, from Russell's point of view), and not holding it as the source of the paradox.

This Russellian constraint on class abstraction, however, meant that for many a 'class abstract' of the form 'the class of all x such that $\Phi(x)$', the existence of such a class could not be guaranteed as a matter of logic. Instead, one would have to postulate that such classes existed. And this came to be regarded as detracting from their status as would-be logical objects, and revealing them instead as no more than mathematical posits. Their existence was once again (at best) a synthetic *a priori* matter, rather than one of analytic necessity and certainty.

Exactly why such classes would have qualified as logical objects courtesy of a single immensely powerful postulate (had it been consistent), but would not so qualify if their existence has to be secured in a more piecemeal postulational fashion, has never been clear to this writer. But that was the Achilles' heel of Russellian logicism. The existential postulation present in Russell's Multiplicative Axiom (nowadays known as the Axiom of Choice), in his Axiom of Infinity, and in his Axiom of Reducibility were seen as marks of the merely mathematical, albeit against the background of a much more capacious universe of abstract objects than just the natural numbers or the real numbers themselves.

For various methodological reasons, which we shall now summarize, the theory of types fell out of favor as a foundational theory for mathematics. First,

[2] We have been using the mathematician's 'relation-slash' notation $r \notin r$ instead of the logician's 'sentence-prefix' notation $\neg(r \in r)$.

[3] See Shapiro [2000a], at p. 116, for a useful exposition of the details of Russell's reasoning here.

it was de-ramified, so as to become the simple theory of types. Then higher-order ('extended') predicate logic took over from simple type theory. Finally, a set-theoretic interpretation of extended predicate logic was given in the celebrated *Grundzüge der theoretischen Logik* of Hilbert and Ackermann. This can be found at Ch. 4, §3. 'Darstellung der Grundbegriffe der Mengenlehre im erweiterten Kalkül' of the first edition Hilbert and Ackermann [1928]. The upshot of all this was that the default logic and language of mathematical foundations became first-orderized. The first-order set theory due to Zermelo [1908] and Fraenkel [1922], now known as ZFC (in its version with the Axiom of Choice) became the overarching background theory. It aimed to characterize the cumulative hierarchy of sets, whose ever-higher ranks would accommodate extensions for erstwhile higher-order predicates. The concept of a higher-order predicate being satisfied by lower-order ones would be expressed straightforwardly at first order, by saying that the extensions of the latter, lower-order ones would form a tuple belonging to the extension of the former, higher-order one. It would just be up to the set theorist to guarantee a rich enough universe of sets for this uniform first-orderization of formerly 'typed' or 'higher-order' discourse to go through.

The aim of foundationalists favoring set theory was still to unify all of mathematics, and to provide a capacious universe of abstract objects in order to do so. All the different mathematical theories would be interpretable within set theory, upon suitable identification of 'set-theoretic surrogates' for the objects studied by those theories. So, for example, the finite von Neumann ordinals can serve as set-theoretic surrogates for the natural numbers. We do not say that the finite von Neumann ordinals are *the* set-theoretic surrogates for the natural numbers, because of the well-known 'Benacerraf point' that there are other recursive progressions within the universe of (hereditarily finite) pure sets that could serve just as well—Zermelo's finite ordinals, for example.[4]

Zermelo's set-surrogates for 0 and 1 are those of von Neumann ($\emptyset$ and $\{\emptyset\}$ respectively); whereafter, for Zermelo, each successive (finite) ordinal 'is' the singleton of its immediate predecessor. For von Neumann, by contrast, it 'is' the set of all its predecessors. And $\mathscr{P}(\omega)$, the power set of the set of natural numbers, can be the set-theoretic surrogate for the real continuum.[5]

After the profound influence of the Séminaire Nicolas Bourbaki in the early to mid-twentieth century and the 'new math' revolution that it occasioned, we are nowadays accustomed to conduct our higher mathematical thinking only (or mainly) in set-theoretical terms. But many of the 'textbook' results of advanced mathematics were formulated and proved (in accordance with the standards of informal rigor of the time) before set theory had reached maturity as the general 'carrier theory' for higher mathematics.

[4]It is worth noting that Benacerraf has since recanted his requirement that the sequence of objects chosen as the natural numbers form a recursive progression. See Benacerraf [1996].

[5]Cantor's theorem (that every set has strictly more subsets than members) has the special case that $\mathscr{P}(\omega)$ has more members than ω does, hence is uncountable—because ω itself is the gold-standard of countability.

Chapter 3

After Gentzen

Abstract

Gentzen's pioneering method of natural deduction had a considerable impact. There are important meaning-theoretic ideas underlying its design. Gentzen's rules of natural deduction afforded a clear logical distinction between constructive and non-constructive reasoning. The rules of Core Logic and its classicized extension are explained. The Core systems capture the further logical property of relevance (between premises and conclusions of proofs) that is a basic feature of all mathematical reasoning. The details of free logic are laid out. It is vital for the proper handling of various singular terms in mathematics that fail to denote. Important examples of such terms are ones formed by variable-binding operators—definite descriptive terms, number-abstraction terms, and set-abstraction terms. Rules of natural deduction are formulated, governing the introduction and elimination of these abstraction operators in the context of canonical identity statements. These are the single-barreled rules on which this study lays great stress.

Along with with the Bourbakian first-orderization of foundational theorizing using set theory, there was a momentous turn of events on the logical front. Set theory, after all, still required a system of first-order logic for its development. At long last a logical proof-system was formulated that afforded eminently faithful rigorizations of expert reasoners' deductive reasoning. It was Gentzen's system of natural deduction. It did not just provide a deducibility relation coextensive with what mathematicians could in principle rigorously but informally prove. Rather, it provided formal proofs that were structure-preserving regimentations of mathematicians' informal but (for them) sufficiently rigorous proofs. Informal proofs could be seen as homologously supplied with missing but interpolated detail, to become their fully formalized versions in the system that Gentzen provided.

That the contrast between the system of natural deduction of Gentzen [1934, 1935] and the earlier, much more artificial Frege–Hilbert systems reflects favorably on the former appears to be tacitly conceded at p. 25 in Hilbert and Ackermann [1938]—the second, 'improved' (*verbesserte*) edition of *Grundzüge der theoretischen Logik*, whose first edition appeared, as already noted, in 1928.

The Logic of Number. Neil Tennant, Oxford University Press.
DOI: 10.1093/oso/9780192846679.003.0003

There Hilbert and Ackermann wrote[1]

> We mention finally one more system, one occupying a special position, the 'calculus of natural deduction'[fn] set up by G. Gentzen, which emerged from the endeavor to make the formal derivation of formulae resemble more closely than it has until now the contentful procedure of proof that is customary, for example, in mathematics. The calculus contains no logical axioms, but only rules of inference, which specify which consequences can be drawn from given assumptions, as well as rules that deliver formulae while rendering them independent of [certain] assumptions.

It was only with Gentzen's work in the mid-1930s that researchers in foundations were equipped with formal calculi of deduction that could do real justice to the actual structure of inferential dependencies within mathematical proofs. What we have in mind here are the dependencies of conclusions both upon one's given premises (mathematical axioms), and upon assumptions that may have been made only 'for the sake of argument'. Examples of assumptions of the latter kind are *reductio* assumptions (assume φ; derive absurdity; conclude the negation $\neg\varphi$, now independently of φ); assumptions for conditional proof (assume φ; derive ψ; conclude the conditional $\varphi \rightarrow \psi$, now independently of φ); and the case-assumptions for proof-by-cases (first assume φ in order to derive θ; second, assume ψ in order to derive θ; thence conclude θ from the disjunction $\varphi \vee \psi$, the latter now independent of the case-assumption φ that appears in the first case-proof, and independent of the case-assumption ψ that appears in the second case-proof).

Looking back, it strikes one as quite extraordinary that the community of mathematical logicians took so long to discover the calculi of natural deduction (and the sequent calculi), once Frege, in 1879, had cracked the previously hidden grammatical code of multiply quantified sentences. It is extraordinary that Gödel, in 1929, could have demonstrated the completeness of first-order logic before Gentzen's natural formulation of it, when that logic was available only in the forms of the highly unnatural deductive calculi devised by Frege, by Hilbert, and by Russell and Whitehead.

The essential breakthrough of Gentzen's treatment was to treat each logical operator in isolation, with rules of its own, rules in which only that operator would

[1]This is the author's translation. Another translation is provided in Hilbert and Ackermann [1950] at p. 30. The original German is as follows.

> Wir erwähnen endlich noch als eine Sonderstellung einnehmend den von G. GENTZEN aufgestellten „Kalkül des natürlichen Schließens"[fn], der aus dem Bestreben hervorgegangen ist, das formale Ableiten von Formeln mehr als bisher dem inhaltlichen Beweisverfahren, wie es z. B. in der Mathematik üblich ist, anzugleichen. Der Kalkül enthält keine logischen Axiome, sondern nur Schlußfiguren, die angeben, welche Folgerungen aus gegebenen Annahmen gezogen werden können, sowie solche, die Formeln liefern, bei denen die Abhängigkeit von den Annahmen beseitigt ist.

explicitly feature. Moreover, the rules in question would deal only with a single occurrence (in dominant position) of the operator in question. The rule for reasoning to a conclusion with the operator dominant was called its introduction rule; while the rule for reasoning from a premise on the basis of its enjoying a dominant occurrence of the operator in question was called its elimination rule.

The introduction and elimination rules for any logical operator have to be in a certain kind of equilibrium. Once it is identified, it lends itself to an interpretation of the rules as forming the basis of an intelligible social contract between any responsible, rational, and sincere speaker, and any responsible, rational, and trusting listener.[2] The basic idea is that the introduction rule for a logical operator articulates the responsibilities on the part of asserters of a statement with that operator dominant, to have established their warrant for its assertion. Correlatively, the elimination rule spells out the entitlements on the part of the listener to extract from such a statement, and rely on, what the asserter purports to have established.

It follows that the introduction and elimination rules for a logical operator have to be in the aforementioned equilibrium, in order to maximize the social benefits of the flow of information by means of logically structured sentences. The speaker's responsibilities must be adequate unto the listener's entitlements, so that the listener does not reason rashly to any unjustified further conclusions. Put another way: the listener's entitlements (expressed by the elimination rule) must not exceed the tacit guarantees being made by the speaker (expressed by the introduction rule). One can also say that the listener's entitlements must not fall short (via the elimination rule) of the tacit guarantees actually being made by any speaker who has conformed to the requirement of the introduction rule.[3] The elimination rule must enable the listener to extract the maximum possible information from the speaker's assumed discharge of obligations imposed by the introduction rule.

The equilibrium between introduction rules and their corresponding elimination rules is explicated by the so-called reduction procedures for the logical operators. These enable one to remove from a proof any sentence occurrence that stands both as the conclusion of an application of an introduction rule and as the major premise of an application of the corresponding elimination rule. Repeated application of the reduction procedures will eventually turn the proof into one that is in so-called *normal form*—essentially, one that is not eligible for any further application of the procedures.[4]

The reduction procedure for conjunction illustrates the foregoing ideas clearly. In the case of conjunctions $A \wedge B$

(i) one who undertakes to assert $A \wedge B$ should ensure that both A and

[2]It has been Michael Dummett, especially, who has advanced this interpretation. The present author has also stressed the importance of such equilibrium for the evolution of logically structured natural languages. See [1984a] and [1987a].

[3]This point is made by Steinberger [2011].

[4]The normalization theorem is due to Prawitz. See Prawitz [1965].

B are indeed the case: for A and B are what any listener would be able logically to infer from the (major) premise $A \wedge B$.

(ii) one who hears $A \wedge B$ sincerely asserted should be able logically to infer from it both A and B: for this is information that the asserter ought to have acquired before inferring to the conclusion $A \wedge B$.

This harmony between the speaker's obligations, as in (i), and the listener's entitlements, as in (ii), is brought out by the following two-part reduction procedure for $\wedge$:[5]

$$\dfrac{\dfrac{\begin{array}{cc}\Delta & \Gamma\\ \Pi & \Sigma\\ A & B\end{array}}{A\wedge B}}{A} \quad\mapsto\quad \begin{array}{c}\Delta\\ \Pi\\ A\end{array} \qquad\qquad \dfrac{\dfrac{\begin{array}{cc}\Delta & \Gamma\\ \Pi & \Sigma\\ A & B\end{array}}{A\wedge B}}{B} \quad\mapsto\quad \begin{array}{c}\Gamma\\ \Sigma\\ B\end{array}$$

Here, Π is a proof of the conclusion A from the set Δ of premises; and Σ is a proof of the conclusion B from the set Γ of premises. The sets Δ and Γ can in general be distinct; indeed, they can be disjoint.

The unreduced proof-schema on the left in each case shows $A \wedge B$ standing both as the conclusion of ($\wedge$-I) and as the major premise of ($\wedge$-E). In other words, the operator $\wedge$ is introduced, and then immediately eliminated. The occurrence of $A \wedge B$ is 'maximal'. It forms a 'local peak'—an unsightly 'knuckle'. The reducts to the right of each arrow respectively show that one cannot thereby obtain anything that one did not already possess.

Note also that each of the reducts on the right of the arrow $\mapsto$ has either Δ or Γ as its set of undischarged assumptions. Whichever one it is, it could well be a proper subset of the overall set $\Delta \cup \Gamma$ of undischarged assumptions of the unreduced proof-complex on the left. So with the reduction procedure for $\wedge$ we learn an important lesson: reducing a proof (i.e., getting rid of a maximal sentence occurrence within it) can in general lead to a logically stronger result. This is because when Θ is a proper subset of Ξ, the argument $\Theta : \varphi$ might be a logically stronger argument than the argument $\Xi : \varphi$. It will be a logically stronger argument if one of the sentences in $(\Xi \setminus \Theta)$—that is, the set of members of Ξ that are not members of Θ—does not itself follow logically from Θ. To summarize: by dropping premises of an argument, one can produce a logically stronger argument. And applying a reduction procedure can enable one to drop premises in one's proof of an argument. So reduction is a potentially epistemically gainful operation to perform on any eligible proof, for it can produce a logically stronger result.

[5] Here, for ease of illustration, we follow Gentzen and Prawitz in using $\wedge$-E in its serial form. Elimination rules can also be stated in a parallelized form, due to Peter Schroeder-Heister. See Schroeder-Heister [1984]. For the advantages of the parallelized rules in automated proof-search, see [1992]. For their special role in analyzing the relation of relevance borne by premises to conclusions within proofs, see [2002a], [2012a], and [2015].

Quite apart from its capacity to 'rigorize' or 'regiment' informal mathematical proofs in a way that preserves, while supplying missing or suppressed details to, those proofs' overall inferential or deductive structures, the Gentzenian system of natural deduction afforded a wonderful illumination of the principled, and profound, difference between constructive and non-constructive ('strictly classical') mathematical reasoning. Basically, constructive reasoning proceeds on the basis of just the introduction and elimination rules; while strictly classical reasoning helps itself to any of the further (and less natural) rules known as the Law of Excluded Middle; Classical Dilemma; Double Negation Elimination; and Classical Reductio ad Absurdum.

Natural Logicism pursues its foundational investigations of Number without resorting to any of these added classical extras. So the logicism of the Natural Logicist is of a very pure kind. It aims to reveal the extent to which Logic alone, in its delineation of the reach of mathematical concepts, can furnish an adequate grasp of the three main kinds of number—natural, rational, and real. Indeed, the ascetic minimalism of the logic employed by the Natural Logicist is even more thorough than thus far indicated. It ought to be mentioned that the Natural Logicist eschews not only the strictly classical rules of negation but also the Absurdity Rule of Intuitionistic Logic:

$$\frac{\bot}{\varphi}$$

(also known as *Ex Falso Quodlibet*), thereby ensuring that all proofs establish their conclusions *relevantly* from their premises. The resulting constructive and relevant system (of appropriately formulated introduction and elimination rules) is what we have called the system $\mathbb{C}$ of *Core Logic*. It has been fully developed in our earlier work [2017]. Its classicized extension $\mathbb{C}^+$ provides regimentations of all the informally rigorous deductive reasoning of classical mathematics, because *the latter is thoroughly relevant*. There is no need for *Ex Falso Quodlibet* within mathematics, no matter whether it is constructive or classical.[6]

For the record, and—we should stress—for purposes internal to this study, we shall set out here the primitive rules of inference of Core Logic $\mathbb{C}$ and the additional classical primitive rules of Classical Core Logic $\mathbb{C}^+$. Note that all elimination rules are in parallelized form. Their major premises stand proud, with no non-trivial proof-work above them. This guarantees that all proofs are in normal form. Boxes appended to discharge strokes indicate that one is required to have used the indicated assumption of the subordinate proof concerned; whereas a diamond indicates that one need not have so used it. Applying a discharge rule discharges all undischarged occurrences of the indicated assumption. The rules for the quantifiers are for free logic; they were broached on p. 11 and are reprised here with ($\forall$I) and ($\exists$E) in their 'no vacuous discharge' form.

[6]This was first established in the constructive case in [1994].

RULES OF CORE LOGIC
IN NATURAL DEDUCTION AND SEQUENT FORMS

Rule	Natural deduction	Rule	Sequent form
$(\neg\mathrm{I})$	$\dfrac{\begin{matrix}\overset{(i)}{\square} \\ \varphi \\ \vdots \\ \bot\end{matrix}}{\neg\varphi}\,{}^{(i)}$	$(\neg_R)$	$\dfrac{\varphi, \Delta :}{\Delta : \neg\varphi}$
$(\neg\mathrm{E})$	$\dfrac{\neg\varphi \quad \begin{matrix}\vdots \\ \varphi\end{matrix}}{\bot}$	$(\neg_L)$	$\dfrac{\Delta : \varphi}{\neg\varphi, \Delta :}$
$(\wedge\mathrm{I})$	$\dfrac{\begin{matrix}\vdots \\ \varphi\end{matrix} \quad \begin{matrix}\vdots \\ \psi\end{matrix}}{\varphi \wedge \psi}$	$(\wedge_R)$	$\dfrac{\Delta : \varphi \qquad \Gamma : \psi}{\Delta, \Gamma : \varphi\wedge\psi}$
$(\wedge\mathrm{E})$	$\dfrac{\varphi \wedge \psi \qquad \begin{matrix}{}^{(i)}\square^{(i)} \\ \underbrace{\varphi , \psi} \\ \vdots \\ \theta\end{matrix}}{\theta}\,{}^{(i)}$	$(\wedge_L)$	$\dfrac{\Delta : \theta}{\varphi\wedge\psi, \Delta\setminus\{\varphi, \psi\} : \theta}$ where $\Delta \cap \{\varphi, \psi\} \neq \emptyset$
$(\vee\mathrm{I})$	$\dfrac{\begin{matrix}\vdots \\ \varphi\end{matrix}}{\varphi \vee \psi} \quad \dfrac{\begin{matrix}\vdots \\ \psi\end{matrix}}{\varphi \vee \psi}$	$(\vee_R)$	$\dfrac{\Delta : \varphi}{\Delta : \varphi\vee\psi} \quad \dfrac{\Delta : \psi}{\Delta : \varphi\vee\psi}$
$(\vee\mathrm{E})$	$\dfrac{\varphi \vee \psi \quad \begin{matrix}\overset{(i)}{\square} \\ \varphi \\ \vdots \\ \theta/\bot\end{matrix} \quad \begin{matrix}\overset{(i)}{\square} \\ \psi \\ \vdots \\ \theta/\bot\end{matrix}}{\theta/\bot}\,{}^{(i)}$	$(\vee_L)$	$\dfrac{\varphi, \Delta : \theta/\bot \qquad \psi, \Gamma : \theta/\bot}{\varphi\vee\psi, \Delta, \Gamma : \theta/\bot}$

(→I)(a)
$$\dfrac{\begin{array}{c}\square^{(i)} \\ \varphi \\ \vdots \\ \bot\end{array}}{\varphi \to \psi}\,(i)$$

(→I)(b)
$$\dfrac{\begin{array}{c}\lozenge^{(i)} \\ \varphi \\ \vdots \\ \psi\end{array}}{\varphi \to \psi}\,(i)$$

$(\to_R)$(a)
$$\dfrac{\Delta, \varphi \,:\,}{\Delta \,:\, \varphi \to \psi}$$

$(\to_R)$(b)
$$\dfrac{\Delta \,:\, \psi}{\Delta \backslash \{\varphi\} \,:\, \varphi \to \psi}$$

(→E)
$$\dfrac{\varphi \to \psi \qquad \begin{array}{c}\vdots \\ \varphi\end{array} \qquad \begin{array}{c}\square^{(i)} \\ \psi \\ \vdots \\ \theta\end{array}}{\theta}\,(i)$$

$(\to_L)$
$$\dfrac{\Delta \,:\, \varphi \qquad \psi, \Gamma \,:\, \theta}{\varphi \to \psi, \Delta, \Gamma \,:\, \theta}$$

(∃I)
$$\dfrac{\begin{array}{c}\vdots \\ \exists! t\end{array} \qquad \begin{array}{c}\vdots \\ \varphi^x_t\end{array}}{\exists x \varphi}$$

$(\exists_R)$
$$\dfrac{\Delta \,:\, \exists! t \qquad \Gamma \,:\, \varphi^x_t}{\Delta, \Gamma \,:\, \exists x \varphi}$$

(∃E)
$$\dfrac{\exists x \varphi^{\textcircled{a}} \qquad \begin{array}{c}\underbrace{\textcircled{a} \ldots \overset{\square^{(i)}}{\varphi^x_a}\;,\; \overset{\square^{(i)}}{\exists! a} \ldots \textcircled{a}} \\ \vdots \\ \psi^{\textcircled{a}}\end{array}}{\psi}\,(i)$$

$(\exists_L)$
$$\dfrac{\varphi^x_a, \exists! a, \Delta \,:\, \psi}{\exists x \varphi, \Delta \,:\, \psi} \quad \textcircled{a}$$

(∀I)
$$\dfrac{\begin{array}{c}\textcircled{a} \\ \vdots \\ \varphi\end{array}}{\forall x \varphi^a_x}$$

$(\forall_R)$
$$\dfrac{\exists! a, \Delta \,:\, \varphi}{\Delta \,:\, \forall x \varphi^a_x} \quad \textcircled{a}$$

(∀E)
$$\dfrac{\forall x \varphi \quad \exists! t_1 \ldots \exists! t_n \qquad \begin{array}{c}{}^{(i)}\!\!-\!\!-\cdots \square \cdots -\!\!-^{(i)} \\ \underbrace{\varphi^x_{t_1}\;,\;\ldots\;,\;\varphi^x_{t_n}} \\ \vdots \\ \theta\end{array}}{\theta}\,(i)$$

$(\forall_L)$
$$\dfrac{\Delta_1 : \exists! t_1 \;\ldots\; \Delta_n : \exists! t_n \quad \Gamma, \varphi^x_{t_1}\;,\;\ldots\;,\;\varphi^x_{t_n} : \theta}{\forall x \varphi, \Delta_1, \ldots, \Delta_n, \Gamma \,:\, \theta}$$

RULES OF CLASSICAL CORE LOGIC $\mathbb{C}^+$

In order to obtain Classical Core Logic from Core Logic, it suffices to add either Classical Reductio or Dilemma. These two strictly classical rules are interderivable in Core Logic. In each of these rules, it is the sentence φ that is its 'classical focus'. This is because the reasoner who applies the rule is presuming that φ is determinately true, or false, even though it might not be known (or indeed, even knowable) which is the case.[7]

(CR)
$$\cfrac{\cfrac{\overline{\neg\varphi}^{\,\Box\,(i)}}{\vdots}\quad}{\cfrac{\bot}{\varphi}\,(i)}$$

(CR)
$$\frac{\neg\varphi, \Delta : \emptyset}{\Delta : \varphi}$$

(Dil)
$$\frac{\begin{matrix}\overline{\varphi}^{\,\Box\,(i)} & \overline{\neg\varphi}^{\,\Box\,(i)}\\ \vdots & \vdots\\ \psi & \psi\end{matrix}}{\psi}\,(i)$$

(Dil)
$$\frac{\varphi, \Delta : \psi \quad \neg\varphi, \Gamma : \psi}{\Delta, \Gamma : \psi}$$

$$\frac{\begin{matrix}\overline{\varphi}^{\,\Box\,(i)} & \overline{\neg\varphi}^{\,\Box\,(i)}\\ \vdots & \vdots\\ \psi & \bot\end{matrix}}{\psi}\,(i)$$

$$\frac{\varphi, \Delta : \psi \quad \neg\varphi, \Gamma : \emptyset}{\Delta, \Gamma : \psi}$$

It is important to point out at this stage that the Gentzen–Prawitz tradition continued an inappropriate reliance on the standard, unfree version of first-order logic. This is the version that is based on the background assumptions that (i) the universe is non-empty, and (more importantly), (ii) every well-formed singular term denotes.

By contrast, and as will have become evident already from the framing of the quantifier rules above, the present author adopts a free logic, which can deal with languages containing non-denoting singular terms. This is of the utmost importance for the foundations of mathematics, even if one is not concerned to furnish a logicist foundation. For, extant mathematics, whether provincial (as with number

[7] See [1997b] for extended philosophical discussion of this point.

theory) or cosmopolitan (as with set theory), is rife with non-denoting, but well-formed, singular terms. One need only think of the respective examples $\frac{1}{0}$ and $\{x|x \notin x\}$ to be persuaded of this.

Regarding the example $\frac{1}{0}$, we note Dirichlet's recognition of the need to treat as non-denoting any would-be quotient terms involving 0 as their divisor. From Dirichlet [1894], §159, here is a footnote on p. 434 (author's translation):[8]

> In accordance with the concept of a quotient it will be regarded ... as self-evident that the divisor or denominator is a number distinct from zero.

And shortly thereafter, in §160, at p. 453, after speaking of the closure of any *Körper* under the rational operations of addition, subtraction, multiplication, and division, Dirichlet writes (author's translation):[9]

> Here we regard it as self-evident that the number zero can never be the denominator of a quotient; we therefore always assume in advance that a *Körper* contains at least one number distinct from zero, because otherwise it would be impossible to speak of a quotient within this system.

The conventional foundationalist clearly needs a logic that can handle singular terms that do not denote. That need is even more acute for the *logicist* foundationalist, because on a logicist approach one needs to be able to identify exactly where certain ontological commitments are carefully (and honestly) undertaken. The cavalier approach of an unfree logic renders the methodologically requisite and logically subtle discernments well-nigh impossible. Our rules for number-abstraction operators, therefore, have to be understood as laid out in the context of a *free* logic. The present author has already stressed this elsewhere,[10] and it is a major feature of the logical resources employed in this work.

The logical rules stated above, then, are the ones at the disposal of the Natural Logicist, in so far as the usual connectives and quantifiers of first-order logic are concerned. They form an important part of the *resources* of Natural Logicism. We now resume our description of its *aims*, in response to which we shall need to expand our logical resources.

---

[8]The original German is as follows:

> Dem Begriffe eines Quotienten gemäss wird es ... als selbstverständlich angesehen, dass der Divisor oder Nenner eine von Null verschiedene Zahl ist.

[9]The original German is as follows:

> Hierbei sehen wir es als selbstverständlich an, dass die Zahl Null niemals den Nenner eines Quotienten bilden kann; wir setzen deshalb auch immer voraus, dass ein Körper mindestens eine von Null verschiedene Zahl enthält, weil sonst von einem Quotienten innerhalb dieses Systems gar nicht gesprochen werden könnte.

[10]See *AR&L*, chs. 20 and 25; and [2003].

As further discussion below will flesh out, it is another main aim of Natural Logicism to reveal how the intended *applicability* of the three main kinds of number is intrinsic to the kinds of abstraction that give rise to them. It will emerge, in a perhaps surprising, but intellectually instructive way, that with *none* of them do we need to have developed *any* of their additive or multiplicative (or, more generally, algebraic) properties *at all*. All we need are the correct formulations of the appropriate *rules for abstraction* of numbers of the respective kinds—formulations whose general form is inspired, ultimately, by what Gentzen had done for the logical connectives and quantifiers.

Powerful, incisive and revolutionary though Gentzen's approach to the connectives and quantifiers has proved to be, it was, in its turn, curiously limited. It was restricted to just the universally acknowledged logical operators of first-order logic: $\neg$, $\wedge$, $\vee$, $\rightarrow$, $\exists$, and $\forall$. This restriction to first order was understandable, of course, in light of the brief history sketched above of the first-orderization of mathematical language and logic, and the emergence of first-order set theory as the foundational *lingua franca*. At exactly the same time (1934), Carnap published his *Logische Syntax der Sprache*, which offered an account of analyticity for languages in which all logico-mathematical operators could make similar contributions to the status of a sentence as analytically true (or analytically false). Carnap, however, did this by employing axiomatizations involving all the various logico-mathematical operators, co-functioning in grammatically complex axioms. His approach was therefore quite unlike that of Gentzen, which was single-operator focused.

The 1930s let the tradition fall prey to an unfortunate methodological lacuna: a failure to generalize Gentzen's approach beyond the strictly logical operators of first-order logic. Proof theory was thereby deprived of a potentially fertile agenda: an investigation of the various forms that introduction and elimination rules might take, as it addresses rule-governed expressions whose rules are not quite so neatly classifiable as introduction and elimination rules (as are those for the connectives and quantifiers). This is the case, for example, with families of 'coeval' and interdependent concepts of a nevertheless logico-mathematical kind. An excellent example of such a family (with three members) is that of the ordered pair of any two things; the first member of any ordered pair; and the second member of the same.[11]

Another novel feature of this example, and of other examples that could be given, is that the operators in question are ones that form singular terms. Gentzen, as already noted, had confined his study to sentence-forming operators. Perhaps it was Tarski's theory of truth for formalized languages[12] that deflected interest away from further development of Gentzen's essentially inferentialist approach to the meanings of logical and mathematical operators.

Apart from the usual connectives and quantifiers, certain expressions that

[11] See [2009] for further details.

[12] See Tarski [1933 in Polish].

might traditionally be thought to be peculiar to certain branches of mathematics, and indeed certain ones that can be used in *any* branch of mathematics, are the so-called 'variable-binding term-forming operators'.[13]

Among these is the famous definite-description operator

$$\iota x\Phi(x)$$

('the Φ'), whose logical behavior was first characterized by Russell [1905].

Russell himself introduced the iota only via contextual definition, and did not have it as a primitive logical expression of the formal language.[14] His contextual definition was that

$$\Psi(\iota x\Phi(x))$$

was to be read as

$$\exists x(\forall y(x = y \leftrightarrow \Phi(y)) \wedge \Psi(x))\,.$$

Note that in the latter definiens there is no grammatically well-formed term corresponding to $\iota x\Phi(x)$. This is what makes the definition a 'contextual' one, as opposed to an *explicit* or *abbreviatory* one, in which there *would be* some grammatically well-formed term corresponding to $\iota x\Phi(x)$. With a contextual definition, one is able to spell out the contribution of a definendum (here, the term $\iota x\Phi(x)$) to the truth-conditions of a sentence in which it occurs only by providing truth-conditions for some wider context—often, the whole sentence in which the term occurs—without providing any definiens term of greater complexity, of which the definiendum term is to be taken as an abbreviation. In a language with the iota featuring as a primitive operator, the last two formal sentences displayed would have to be interdeducible:

$$\Psi(\iota x\Phi(x)) \;\dashv\vdash\; \exists x(\forall y(x = y \leftrightarrow \Phi(y)) \wedge \Psi(x))\,.$$

The definite-description operator can be reckoned to the underlying logic, since it can be deployed in *any* branch of mathematics, and indeed in any kind of discourse at all. The logical rules governing it, after all, form the logic of the word 'the'—which is certainly topic-neutral.

Other variable-binding term operators used in certain branches of mathematics are the set-abstraction operator

$$\{x|\Phi(x)\}$$

[13]An early mention of these operators under the designation 'variable-binding term operators', and a clear definition of them, are to be found in Hatcher [1968], at p. 65. They are often referred to by means of the rather ungainly abbreviation 'v.b.t.o.', which we shall avoid.

[14]We ought to mention that Russell's 'iota' was an ordinary iota rotated by 180 degrees. This was in keeping with the convention, in those days, of creating logical symbols by means of half-turns of more familiar and suggestive symbols. Thus, we have ∃ for Exists, and ∀ for All. It is curious that LaTeX does not afford us the Russellian iota; we just have to make do with the ordinary one.

('the set of all Φs') and the number-abstraction operator

$$\#x\Phi(x)$$

('the number of Φs').[15] It will be part of the overall implications of Natural Logicism, however, that the latter two variable-binding term operators, like the definite-description operator, deserve places at the logical table. They are genuinely *logical* expressions, not extra-logical ones.

The rules for number-abstraction that will be furnished in this study are what we called on p. 14 *single-barreled* rules of abstraction. They characterize *variable-binding term-forming* operators, for which, in this introductory exposition, we can use the more general placeholder @. If $\varphi(x)$ is a formula with x free, then one can form the *singular term* $@x\varphi(x)$, in which no occurrences of the variable x remain free. The Gentzen–Prawitz tradition in natural deduction (and, concomitantly, in sequent calculus) did not pay any attention to the rich possibilities of logico-mathematical expression afforded by such operators. The Gentzen–Prawitz introduction and elimination rules concerned only *sentence*-forming operators (i.e., connectives and quantifiers), not *term*-forming operators.

It is obvious, however, that no sentence has @ as a dominant operator. Therefore, in order to 'get at' or 'focus on' @ in 'dominant' position, one must consider terms of the form $@x\varphi(x)$ in a *simplest possible*, and *philosophically revelatory*, canonical context. We recall Quine's dictum from p. 14: 'No entity without identity.' The single-barreled abstractionist accordingly seeks to formulate introduction and elimination rules respectively governing the drawing of conclusions, and the exploitation of major premises, of the form

$$t = @x\varphi(x)\,.$$

We shall call such sentences 'canonical identity statements'. The placeholder t within them is for *any closed singular term*—a name, a parameter, a closed functional term, or any other (closed) abstractive term. The single occurrence of @ (by newly stipulated convention, on the *right-hand* side of a canonical identity statement)[16] is what makes the rules governing @-abstraction *single-barreled* rules.

Just to give the reader a foretaste of things to come, we mention here that our main aim, in our natural-logicist study of the natural numbers (i.e., the finite counting numbers, or so-called 'whole numbers') will be to put forward (once again) appropriate single-barreled introduction and elimination rules for canonical identity statements of the form

$$t = \#x\varphi(x)\,.$$[17]

[15] Some neo-logicists use the notation $Nx\Phi x$ for 'the number of Φs'. In our estimation, '#' is a better choice than 'N', even if only because of Boolos's delightful name 'octothorpe' for it.

[16] Since identity is a symmetric relation, one could just as easily have stipulated the left-hand side—which is what makes our stipulation a *convention*!

[17] Such rules were first put forward in *AR&L*.

One could also mention at this stage, in more tantalizing if not prospective vein (at least, for the present study), that one can present an ontologically non-committal, wholly analytic, 'virtual' set theory (in Quine's sense) by laying down appropriate single-barreled introduction and elimination rules for canonical identity statements of the form

$$t = \{x|\varphi(x)\}\,.$$[18]

[18]Such rules were first put forward in [1978], at p. 172.

Chapter 4

Foundations After Gödel

Abstract

There are two fundamental *a priori* constraints furnished by work in the foundations of mathematics: the Gödelian incompleteness theorems and the Non-Compossibility theorem. One cannot axiomatize the truths of arithmetic; nor can one maximize both expressive and deductive power in any language for mathematics. The main aims of contemporary work in the foundations of mathematics are described. A contrast is drawn between providing a uniform set-theoretic foundation for all branches of mathematics as opposed to treating each branch as enjoying its own special vocabulary of primitives and treating its objects *sui generis*. Special interest attaches to the problem of establishing the consistency of any given mathematical theory. There is a linear hierarchy of consistency strengths that have been uncovered since the discovery of the Gödelian phenomena. This hierarchy has been illuminated by work in reverse mathematics (studying second-order subsystems of arithmetic), in proof theory (studying proof-theoretic ordinals), and in set theory (studying large-cardinal existence axioms).

The area of study known as 'foundations of mathematics' has always aimed to classify a wide range of mathematical theories according to their various systematic properties, and to study important relations amongst them. It has also sought a single unifying, over-arching theory that can accommodate all those more 'provincial' theories, upon suitable interpretation of the latter in the former.

In its pursuit of these aims, the field was fundamentally transformed by the work of Kurt Gödel. One talks nowadays of the 'Gödel phenomena'. First, there is the essential incompleteness of consistent mathematical theories that are sufficiently strong to represent all recursive functions on the natural numbers. Second, there is the impossibility of any such theory proving its own consistency.[1]

Gödel's incompleteness theorems shook the world of foundations as dramatically as Russell's Paradox had done almost three decades earlier. The incompleteness phenomena are now rock-hard givens. Any new tide of fashion in the Philosophy of Mathematics has to crash against them, swirl around them, and make its peace with them. They are *a priori* theoretical achievements, necessary truths

[1] See Gödel [1931].

The Logic of Number. Neil Tennant, Oxford University Press. © Neil Tennant 2022.
DOI: 10.1093/oso/9780192846679.003.0004

proved for eternity, like the irrationality of the square root of 2. They not 'mere' phenomena like the observational phenomena in a Quinean web of belief—on the 'periphery', with assignments of truth to them only ever provisional, and highly revisable. No, the borrowing of the word 'phenomena' to describe what Gödel had discovered was not in any way a conscious adaptation of Kantian terminology or empiricist prioritizations. It was, rather, intended as an acknowledgment of the revolutionary significance of the hard *a priori* truths that Gödel had established. The word 'phenomena' here derives its sense more from 'That's *phenomenal*!', as an expression of intellectual awe.

The incompleteness established by Gödel's theorems is that of (consistent) axiomatizable *theories* T in the formal first-order language of arithmetic, with 0, s, $+$ and $\times$ as its extra-logical primitives. Such incompleteness takes the form

$$\text{for some sentence } \varphi \ (T \nvdash \varphi \text{ and } T, \varphi \nvdash \bot)\,.$$

Indeed, it takes the following strongest possible form:

$$\text{for some } \Pi^0_1\text{-sentence } \varphi \ (T \nvdash \varphi \text{ and } T, \varphi \nvdash \bot)\,.^2$$

One should not lose sight of the contrastive irony that Gödel had only just before established his completeness theorem for first-order *logic*: the result that every valid argument in a first-order language admits of formal proof.[3] In today's familiar metalogical notation:

$$\text{for all sets } \Delta \text{ of sentences, for all sentences } \varphi,\ \text{ if } \Delta \models \varphi \text{ then } \Delta \vdash \varphi\,.$$

So the incompleteness of arithmetical theory is *theoretical* incompleteness, and is not to be attributed to any shortfall or deficiency in one's logical means of proof. At first order, we 'max out' in *deductive power*; but, the natural numbers forming the structure $\mathbb{N}$ that they do, we cannot effectively enumerate all the sentences $\mathbb{N}$ makes true. The set of sentences in the first-order language of arithmetic that are true in the standard model $\mathbb{N}$ is called Th($\mathbb{N}$)—'the first-order theory of $\mathbb{N}$'. Gödel's first incompleteness theorem is to the effect that no consistent and decidable set of axioms in the language of arithmetic can enable us, by means of logical proofs, to enumerate Th($\mathbb{N}$). The 'fault' lies not in our means of logical deduction (at first order), but rather in the sheer richness of *first-order* arithmetical truth.

It is well known that Gödel established his first incompleteness theorem by constructing a sentence (call it G) that 'says of itself' that it is unprovable in the formal system of arithmetic concerned. (This, in Gödel's case, was in effect the system PA of Peano arithmetic, in the garb of its treatment by Russell and

---

[2] Π^0_1-sentences are also known as sentences of 'Goldbach type'. They have the logical form $\forall n F(n)$, where the generalization is over the natural numbers, and F is an effectively decidable predicate of numbers.

[3] See Gödel [1930].

Whitehead in their theory of types in *Principia Mathematica*.) The sentence G can be understood as 'saying' this because it is interdeducible, *modulo* PA, with

$$\forall n \; n \text{ is not the Gödel-code number of a PA-proof of } \ulcorner G \urcorner .$$

The first incompleteness theorem states that, if PA is consistent, then both

$$\text{PA} \nvdash G \text{ and PA}, G \nvdash \bot .$$

This is what is meant by saying that G is *undecidable* in PA, or (equivalently) *independent* of PA.

We shall be needing, for our continuing discussion here, only the first of these non-provabilities: that of G from PA.[4]

Since PA $\nvdash G$, we are assured, for every 'standard' natural number n, of the truth-in-$\mathbb{N}$ of

$$n \text{ is not the Gödel-code number of a PA-proof of } \ulcorner G \urcorner .$$

It follows (given the meaning of the universal quantifier $\forall n$) that G is true-in-$\mathbb{N}$.

Since PA $\nvdash G$, we have in addition, by the completeness of first-order logic, the assurance that PA $\nvDash G$. That is, some model of PA falsifies G. Let $\mathcal{N}$ be such a model. We have just seen that G is true-in-$\mathbb{N}$. And isomorphic models make the same sentences true. So $\mathcal{N}$ cannot be isomorphic to $\mathbb{N}$. *A fortiori*, $\mathcal{N}$ cannot *be* $\mathbb{N}$.

$\mathcal{N}$ must contain in its domain a 'non-standard' number (call it γ) that is a counterexample, within $\mathcal{N}$, to the generalization

$$\forall n \; n \text{ is not the Gödel-code number of a PA-proof of } G .$$

That is, in the model $\mathcal{N}$, the individual γ satisfies the predicate

$$x \textit{ is} \text{ the Gödel-code number of a PA-proof of } \ulcorner G \urcorner.$$

In so doing, γ cannot be any of the standard natural numbers, all of which have to appear in $\mathcal{N}$, courtesy of the Peano axioms for zero and successor; and all of which *fail*, in $\mathcal{N}$, to satisfy the predicate just displayed. So $\mathcal{N}$ is not isomorphic to $\mathbb{N}$.

The metalogical reasoning we have undertaken here from Gödel's completeness theorem for first-order logic and his first incompleteness theorem for first-order arithmetic (as its starting points) would have been available to thinkers in the mid- to late-1930s. That reasoning employs the model-relative adaptation of Tarski's celebrated theory of truth for formalized languages, in making the move

[4] In Gödel's original paper, the assumption that PA is consistent sufficed for the proof that PA $\nvdash G$. In order to prove that PA,$G \nvdash \bot$, Gödel used the stronger assumption that PA is ω-consistent. Shortly thereafter, Rosser [1936] established the independence of a suitable G from PA using just the assumption of PA's consistency.

from G's not being provable from the axioms of PA to the existence of a model of PA that falsifies G. A thinker apprised of the consequence, just spelled out, that PA has non-standard models might think that this chastening deficiency of PA (i.e., failing to characterize the standard model $\mathbb{N}$ up to isomorphism) is the result of PA's incompleteness. Surely, the naive thought might go, this would not be the case for the *complete* theory Th($\mathbb{N}$) itself? Such a thinker might, in a brief moment of unschooled optimism, think that Th($\mathbb{N}$) (if only we could 'lay our hands on it'), would *exactly describe* the structure $\mathbb{N}$. That is, any model of Th($\mathbb{N}$) would be isomorphic to $\mathbb{N}$ itself.

This thought is seriously mistaken. The first-order theory of $\mathbb{N}$, despite being *theoretically complete*, has countable *non-standard* models—models that are not isomorphic to $\mathbb{N}$. The first-order theorizing of even a divine being apprised of Th($\mathbb{N}$) suffers from a great deficit in expressive power. It is unable to 'pin down' what is in $\mathbb{N}$ (i.e., just the whole numbers), and how things stand with them.

So the maximization of deductive power at first order is offset by a concomitant loss of expressive power (again, at first order).

How might matters stand in this regard at *second* order? The answer is: equally bleakly. To be sure, the second-order theory of Peano arithmetic has $\mathbb{N}$ as its sole model (expressive success!). This is because the Principle of Mathematical Induction is no longer an axiom schema (as it is in first-order Peano arithmetic), but is rather a single second-order axiom:

$$\forall\Phi((\Phi 0 \land \forall n(\Phi n \rightarrow \Phi sn)) \rightarrow \forall m\Phi m).$$

Let Φx take the second-order instance 'x is but finitely many steps of s away from 0'. Clearly, for this choice of Φx we have

$$\Phi 0 \land \forall n(\Phi n \rightarrow \Phi sn).$$

Hence with one step of $\rightarrow$-E we conclude

$$\forall m\Phi m.$$

That is, *everything* (in the model) is but finitely many steps of successor away from zero. In other words, the model contains only the standard natural numbers. It is the intended model $\mathbb{N}$.

But now this expressive completeness acquired upon ascending to second-order is offset by the *deductive incompleteness* of second-order logic. The logical truths at second-order are not axiomatizable. And second-order logical consequence is not compact. Moreover, there are infinite sets of second-order sentences that have no models at all (i.e., they are incoherent, or unsatisfiable) but that cannot be proved to be inconsistent.

So the maximization of expressive power at second order is offset by a concomitant loss of deductive power (again, at second order).

The question immediately arises: might this just be a contrast between languages (and possible proof systems) at first *versus* second order? Or might these two 'offsets' be symptomatic of a more general, and deeper, problem or predicament?

The answer is: *the latter.* There is an ineliminable tension between our aspiration for the greatest possible *deductive* power, and our aspiration for the greatest possible *expressive* power. The two powers are *non-compossible*. That is the extraordinary lesson of Metatheorem 1 below. The predicament that it poses is *pre-Gödelian*, both in the conceptual materials it employs and in its arrestingly simple method of proof.[5] It was only after Gödel uncovered the Gödel phenomena that this non-compossibility dawned (in the mid- to late-1930s) on the community of mathematical logicians and foundationalists (and then only concerning first-order *versus* second-order languages). But the non-compossibility can be established by an argument nowhere near as intricate as that of Gödel for his incompleteness theorems. Indeed, it could easily have been established as early as 1918 within the Göttingen school, where Hilbert, Bernays, and Ackermann had formulated all the requisite concepts. Moreover, the argument is stated in utterly general terms, so as to apply to any language whatsoever that one might contemplate using for the formalization of mathematical theorizing.

In building up to Metatheorem 1, we shall need but a few definitions.

Definition 1. *L is an* eligible language *just in case:*

- *L contains the dyadic predicate of identity ($=$);*
- *L contains the one-place connective of negation ($\neg$); and*
- *L contains* either *the existential quantifier ($\exists$)* or *a monadic predicate (which we shall symbolize as $\exists!x$) meaning 'x exists', or 'x is defined'.*

Only the latter alternative (the monadic predicate) is actually required. If 'x exists' is not primitive in L, then it can be defined by using the existential quantifier:

$$\exists!x \ \equiv_{df} \ \exists y\, y=x\,.$$

In order to formalize any branch of mathematics, one has to use an eligible language in the sense of Definition 1. This requirement is minimal in the extreme. Every formal language ever used for this purpose meets it. So does every possible extension of any such language, no matter what expressions are added: names, function signs, predicates (of any adicity and any order); variable-binding term-forming operators, such as set-abstraction, number-abstraction, or definite description; different kinds of quantifiers (binary or higher-order or infinitary or ...); modal operators; counterfactual connectives; epistemic operators; ... .

Definition 2. *Let L be an eligible language and let a be a name not in L. We define $L^a_{\neq}$ to be the set of non-identities*

$$\{\neg a=t \mid t \text{ is a term in } L\}$$

[5] See [2000] for further historical background for the result.

Definition 3. *Let L be an eligible language and let a be a name not in L. We define L^a to be the set*

$$L^a_{\neq} \cup \{\exists!a\}.$$

Metatheorem 1. *It is impossible that the following seven conditions hold:*

1. *L is an eligible language*
2. *Δ is a set of L-sentences*
3. *$\mathfrak{M}$ is an infinite L-model of Δ*
4. *every element of $\mathfrak{M}$ is denoted by some L-term*
5. *every L-model of Δ is isomorphic to $\mathfrak{M}$*
6. *S is a sound proof-system for the L-operators*
7. *for any name a not in L, if $\Delta \cup L^a$ has no model, then there is an S-proof of $\bot$ from $\Delta \cup L^a$*

For a completely detailed but conceptually simple proof of Metatheorem 1, see Appendix A.

Note that if the proof-system S is strongly complete, then (7) holds (but not conversely). So (7) represents a modest measure of deductive power. Note also that (5) is a modest measure, too, of expressive power. Metatheorem (1) therefore tells us that it is impossible simultaneously (i.e., with or for any eligible language L) to maximize both expressive and deductive power. Success in maximizing either one of them entails failure to maximize the other. This result is completely general, applying to every conceivable language L that could possibly be considered for the formalization of mathematics.

If God gave us the whole numbers (as Kronecker maintained), then She gave them to us with the Gödel phenomena built in. Moreover, God Herself could not have given us any logic, language, or conceptual system by means of which simultaneously to describe Her gift up to isomorphism, and be able, in principle, to deduce (from any decidable set of true first principles) every truth about Her gift to us—even when the expression of such truths is confined to the modest fragment of the first-order language of arithmetic.

This is the predicament in which every foundationalist and philosopher of mathematics now finds themselves. The perennial debates between nominalist and platonist, between formalist and contentualist, between classicist and constructivist, and between synthetic *a priorist* and logicist will no doubt continue. They just have to be conducted within the mutually acknowledged metalogical landscape just articulated: one containing the rocks of the Gödel phenomena, and the deep chasm of non-compossibility. And it is important to point out at this juncture that the presence of those rocks and that chasm can be established by means of reasoning wholly within Core Logic.

Let us now turn to the question of what systematic work the foundationalist can undertake, in the shadow of these two features of the logical landscape.

Given the usual 'branches' of mathematics, such as number theory, geometry (Euclidean and non-Euclidean), topology, etc., the foundationalist typically seeks to do the following:

1. identify their primitive concepts and first principles;
2. formulate a logic that applies to all of them;
3. investigate properties of theories, such as
   (a) T has a (countable) model;
   (b) T is κ-categorical, i.e., T has exactly one model, up to isomorphism, of cardinality κ;
   (c) T is complete, i.e., for every sentence φ in the language of T, either T proves φ or T refutes φ; and
   (d) T is decidable, i.e., there is an effective method for determining, given any sentence φ in the language of T, whether T proves φ;
4. investigate relationships among various theories, such as
   (a) T conservatively extends T' (with respect to a certain class of sentences);
   (b) If T is consistent, then T' is consistent;
   (c) T proves the consistency of T';
   (d) T is interpretable in T'; and
5. provide (axioms for) a unifying theory with as few primitives as possible, in which all of the theories can be interpreted.

Different branches of mathematics, as any practicing mathematician knows, are distinguished by their different stocks of basic concepts—which means that they are distinguished, in turn, by their 'extra-logical' vocabularies of primitive expressions. Illustrations follow.

First, let us mention primitive expressions of particular logico-linguistic categories, with examples drawn from different branches of mathematics. These expressions can be simple names, such as 0, 1, π, and e; function signs, such as $+$ and $\times$; and/or predicates, such as 'greater than' ($>$) and 'parallel to' ($//$). And let us not forget the classificatory, or sortal, concepts, such as '... is a natural number', '... is a real number', '... is a point', '... is a line', '... is a plane', etc., for which particular monadic predicates may be used,

Second, let us mention four different branches of mathematics, and their respective vocabularies of primitive extra-logical expressions.

1. The language of arithmetic contains the primitive expressions 0, s, +, ×, ^ (exponentiation).[6]

2. The language of three-dimensional projective geometry contains the following primitive expressions:

    - the sortal predicates '... is a point', '... is a line', '... is a plane';
    - the binary relation '... is included in (or lies on) ...'; plus
    - the incidence operators
        - the point $\pi(l, f)$ of intersection of line l and plane f
        - the point $\Pi(l, l')$ of intersection of the two co-planar lines l and l'
        - the line $\Lambda(f, f')$ of intersection of the two planes f and f'
        - the line $\lambda(p, p')$ determined by the two points p and p'
        - the plane $\Phi(l, l')$ determined by the two intersecting lines l and l'
        - the plane $\phi(l, p)$ determined by the line l and the point p not on l

    In Chapter 1 we mentioned briefly that a natural logicist treatment of projective geometry clarifies the Principle of Duality. By reference to the list here of all the primitive expressions of projective geometry, we can now offer the following clarification of how this is so.

    > Given any proof Σ of a theorem φ, the dual result φ' is proved by the dual proof Σ', obtained by merely interchanging 'point' and 'plane' (in the 3-D case), likewise interchanging the lowercase incidence operators with the corresponding uppercase incidence operators in the list above, and switching the arguments of all occurrences of the incidence relation.[7] One otherwise leaves unchanged the macro-structure of Σ (i.e., its pattern of applications of rules of inference) in thus passing to its dual Σ'. The dual of any primitive rule of inference in the natural-logicist formulation of projective geometry is itself a primitive rule. (Indeed, some rules are self-dual.) This can all be summarized in the elegant motto that the proof of the dual of any theorem is the dual of the proof of the theorem. (The two proofs are 'dual isomorphs'.)

[6]The expression a^b is more frequently rendered a^b; and the expression $a \times b$ as ab.

[7]In the 2-D case, one interchanges 'point' and 'line' within the proof Σ, interchanges appropriately different pairs in the dimensionally reduced set of incidence operators, and switches the arguments of all occurrences of the incidence relation.

3. In addition to the primitives of arithmetic, the language of real analysis calls for

    - a notation for functions: $\lambda x.f(x)$; and
    - the ordering relation $<$.

4. The language of set theory contains but one binary predicate, $\in$;[8] and, if one wishes, the set-abstraction operator $\{x| \ldots x \ldots\}$. (The latter is useful but not essential for the development of set theory.)

It is interesting to inquire about the basic concepts and the pre-set-theoretic, 'native' (not: naive!) intuitions of the mathematicians who were able to formulate and prove important results that have only subsequently acquired their predominantly set-theoretical trappings. We have in mind here not the kind of not-altogether-trustworthy geometric intuitions against which real analysis[9] (so it was thought) had to be guarded via the arithmetization undertaken by Cauchy and Weierstraß. Rather, we have in mind the analytic[10] intuitions[11] of the competent mathematician, which, when clear and distinct, betoken a thorough grasp of the mathematical concept(s) involved. A case in point would be the intuition that the natural numbers obey the Principle of Mathematical Induction. *Pace* Poincaré, we consider this intuition to be analytic, not synthetic. Its analyticity can be exhibited by furnishing the Principle of Mathematical Induction with a constructive logicist derivation using only rules that are analytic of the notions 'number of Fs', 'successor' and 'zero'.[12]

The aforementioned general inquiry, as explained in Chapter 1 (p. 11 ff.), is one on which the present author has been engaged for some time. It has led to a 'natural-logicist' reformulation of the following: arithmetic; projective geometry; Euclidean geometry; real differential calculus; the theory of higher infinities; and set theory itself[13] (as just one among other branches of higher mathematics, rather than as an all-embracing foundational theory).[14]

---

[8]We concede that it is quite extraordinary that all of mathematics can be obtained using only a single binary predicate.

[9]Here, 'analysis' is meant in the mathematical sense—the study of real numbers and functions of reals.

[10]Here, 'analytic' is meant not in the mathematical sense mentioned in footnote 9, but in the Kantian sense, as arising from the meanings of the words involved.

[11]Here, 'intuitions' is used in the sense of ordinary mathematical parlance, and not in the special Kantian sense of 'telling us something informative about the world', which Kantians regard as the contradictory of the Kantian sense of 'analytic'!

[12]See *AR&L*, ch. 25, 'On deriving the basic laws of arithmetic: or, how to Frege-Wright a Dedekind–Peano'. See also p. 126 of this work.

[13]Just as the Dedekind–Peano axioms for arithmetic are derived as non-trivial results within a deeper logicist account of number, so too the Axiom of Extensionality of set theory is derived non-trivially from the deeper principles laid down in the logicist account of the set-abstraction operator. See [2004] for details.

[14]For the most recent formulation of an ontologically non-committal system of natural-deduction rules for set theory, see [forthcoming]. The rules are also stated and used here, in Chapter 24, p. 309ff.

As remarked by Harrington, Morley, Ščedrov and Simpson in Harrington et al. [1985] at p. vii:

> ... ZFC ... is not appropriate ... for a more delicate study of the nature of mathematical proof. Standard mathematics is not inherently or peculiarly set-theoretic.

This remark was intended to set the stage for their subsequent explanation of how arresting it was that Friedman had been able to demonstrate necessary uses of abstract set theory in order to prove results in 'relatively concrete mathematical situations' (*ibid.*, p. viii). What that means, however, is that the concrete result in question (φ, say) is provable in ZFC plus some large-cardinal axiom, and in turn implies (*modulo* some weak base theory, such as EFA)[15] the consistency of ZFC plus all smaller large-cardinal axioms. If one's main concern is to calibrate the consistency strength of a particular concrete-looking conjecture φ in this way, then of course it behooves one to translate both φ and the 'native' axioms of the theory T (to which φ might or might not belong) into the language of set theory, so that the calibration can proceed. If, however, one's main concern is to clarify the logical structure of the reasoning by which all the known results of the 'native' theory have been established, then it is better to eschew the set-theoretical trappings that help only with the calibration question, and deal with T directly, natively, *sui generis*.

How can one tell whether a formal mathematical theory is consistent, or what its consistency strength is? The easiest answer is: via mutual interpretation with alternative formalizations (which can of course be set-theoretic) whose consistency strength has already been calibrated.

It is obvious that mutually interpretable theories have the same consistency strength. One of Friedman's remarkable results is that the *converse* of this holds: theories that have the same consistency strength are mutually interpretable. For exposition, see Smoryński [1985]. More recently, Friedman has written (see Friedman [2007])

> The striking observation is that one finds a remarkable linearity [of consistency strengths]. This linearity is found not only with finitely axiomatized systems ... but with the non-finitely axiomatized systems such as PA and ZFC. This is perhaps the most intriguing, thought provoking, fundamental, and deep phenomenon in the whole of the foundations of mathematics.

We turn now to a discussion of the linear ordering, by consistency strength, of various mathematical theories of interest to the foundationalist. At chapter's end on p. 48 the reader will find a table giving more details about this ordering, focusing on certain well known theories.

[15]EFA is exponential function arithmetic.

$T \approx T'$ means that the theories T and T' have the same consistency strength, in the sense that each can prove the consistency of the other, on the assumption of its own consistency.

The calibration of consistency strengths is made possible by 'uniformizing' the ontology of the mathematical theories being compared. In set theory in the Zermeloan tradition, different systems of axioms all address the 'same ontology' of hereditarily pure sets within a cumulative hierarchy. In the more recent tradition of Reverse Mathematics, developed by Friedman and Simpson, the natural numbers are taken as given (by God, if one is Kroneckerian; or by honest logicist toil, if one is a constructive logicist). They are taken to form one sort; and then the question becomes which *sets* of natural numbers one should acknowledge, as forming a second sort. The stronger the commitment on this second score, the greater (potentially, at least) is the consistency strength of one's theory. Significant though the work has been, in comparing various theories when cast in these terms, one cannot help remarking how 'unnatural' that re-formulation is, when one considers the methods of coding employed in order to define negative integers, rational numbers, real numbers, etc. out of the naturals. The reverse mathematician, like the set theorist, makes of the domain of *Arithmetik* one of individually distorted surrogates. It would seem that this has proved to be the price of providing a uniformized measure of existential-postulational strength of the theories being compared.

For the set theorist, it is a matter of postulating the existence of ever-larger cardinals; while for the reverse mathematician, it is a matter of postulating ever more inclusive ranges of instances (i.e., substitution-classes of formulae of the language) for the two axiom schemes of comprehension and of induction. It puts one in a position to show how the theories 'line up' in order of increasing strength.

The strength is of two kinds. First, there is reverse-mathematical strength, providing for proofs of ever stronger mathematical theorems—theorems that are in fact equivalent, modulo the preceding, weaker, theory, to the newly adopted instances of comprehension and induction. Second, there is consistency strength, whereby either the stronger theory is able to establish the consistency of the weaker theory, or it can be shown (within the weaker theory) that the stronger theory is conservative over the weaker theory on a certain class of sentences. It is worth noting that increases in reverse-mathematical strength *need not* be accompanied by increases in consistency strength.

An arresting clutch of theories attesting to this last point is PRA, RCA_0, WKL_0, and Σ^0_1-PA. These are ordered in increasing reverse-mathematical strength, but are all of the same consistency strength (they all have ordinal strength ω^{ω}).[16] A highly notable result in this connection is that WKL_0 is conservative over PRA on Π^0_2-sentences; and *this fact is itself provable in* PRA. Now, WKL_0 proves the Gödel–Henkin result that every consistent set of first-order sentences has a model

[16]The interested reader will find all the relevant results in Simpson [1999]. See Theorem IX.3.16, on p. 381. See also his papers Simpson [1988], [2010], and [2020].

that is countable—and that first-order logic is therefore strongly complete. This means that when we assert the strong completeness of first-order logic, we are doing so on the basis of a background mathematics *of the same consistency strength* as PRA. And PRA is of very low consistency strength—indeed, Tait [1981] argues that PRA is the best explication we have of the methodological commitments of *finitism*.

PRA is accordingly an early entry in Table 4.1. Consistency strength increases as one goes down the rows. Theories with the same consistency strength are listed on the same row, but perhaps in different columns. The columns house the different kinds of theories in question (first-order arithmetics; second-order arithmetics; higher-order arithmetics; first-order set theories; second-order set theories).

Before the reader examines the table, a word of warning is in order. The terminology 'second-order' is well established among those foundationalists who study these matters (see the upper half of the middle column below); but the label is not earned (or incurred) by quantification that is genuinely second order, that is, quantification over properties of, and/or relations among, ground-level individuals. Rather, the 'second-order' entities are ground-level entities of a second sort, so that one is really dealing with a two-sorted, first-order system. Entities of the first sort can bear the membership relation to entities of the second sort; but entities of both sorts are nevertheless ground-level individuals—as indeed sets themselves are, within the context of first-order set theory.

Sources: We draw here on Table E: Twenty Milestones on the Fundamental Series, at pp. 220–1 of Burgess [2005]; on Table I.4, Models of subsystems of Z_2, at p. 53 of Simpson [1999]; as well as on Friedman [2007]. The interested reader will also find a wealth of further information in Hajek and Pudlak [1998], Kanamori [1994], and Simpson [1999]. Table 4.1 is a summary one, highlighting the most important, and best-known, theories. There are many others that could be interpolated between various neighboring entries within this summary. But they would be of interest only to specialists with highly technical interests; and can be omitted here in the interest of surveyability. The reader will find the 'missing' theories by consulting the sources just cited.

Note: P^2 is also called Z^2 (a.k.a. *analysis*) by those working on so-called second-order subsystems of arithmetic. We use Burgess's choice of P here (after Peano) in order to avoid confusion with Zermelo set theory. We also use his superscripted minus sign on an acronym for a set theory to indicate that the Axiom of Power Sets is dropped; and his notation '$-\infty$' to mean that the Axiom of Infinity is dropped.

In thus paying homage to the formidable achievements of foundationalists in locating almost every theory of interest on the linear scale of consistency strengths, the present author nevertheless ventures to suggest that this achievement is a ladder that one is now free to kick away.

If our main aim is to illuminate the structure of mathematical reasoning itself, then a natural logicist approach is preferable by far, rather than the straitjacketing that is involved in getting all these different theories into the forms indicated by the column-headings above them. The natural logicist is prepared to treat each theory (and its objects) in a *sui generis* fashion, tailoring the formal rules for construction of proofs in a way that does analytic justice to the vast body of proofs in actual journal articles and textbooks written by, and for, the practitioners of these mathematical disciplines. Any foundationalist anxious to know the consistency strength of a theory T that holds one's interest can of course determine it by interpreting T in some T' (and interpreting T' in T), where T' is a theory that has already been calibrated by the methods we can now eschew. This is because (as Friedman has shown) sameness of consistency strength is equivalent to mutual interpretability.

Table 4.1: Linear hierarchy of consistency strengths: a summary view

1st-order arithmetics	2nd-order arithmetics	1st-order set theories
Q (Robinson arithmetic) ≈ Polynomial Function Arithmetic		
Exponential Function Arithmetic		
Superexponential Function Arithmetic		
Primitive Recursive Arithmetic	$RCA_0 \approx WKL_0$	
Q_ω (Grzegorczyk Arithmetic) ≈ $I\Sigma_1$ (Parsons Arithmetic)		
Peano Arithmetic	ACA_0	$Z^- - \infty$
	ATR_0	
	Π^1_1-CA_0 (≈ Π^1_1-Frege Arithmetic)	
	$P^2 = PA^2$ (a.k.a. Z_2, ≈ Frege Arithmetic)	$Z^- \approx ZF^-$
Higher-order arithmetics	**1st-order set theories**	**2nd-order set theories**
$P^3 = PA^3$	$ZF^- + \mathscr{P}(\omega)$	
$P^4 = PA^4$	$ZF^- + \mathscr{P}^2(\omega)$	
P^ω = PM (type theory)		
	Weak Zermelo	
	Z (Zermelo) ≈	
	ZC ≈ Z + V=L	
	KP($\mathscr{P}$)	
	ZFC ≈ ZF + V=L	NBG
		ZFC^2 = MK
	ZFC + Inaccessible	
	ZFC + Indescribable	B(ernays)
	ZFC + Measurable	
	ZFC + Woodin	
	ZFC + Rank into Itself	
	ZFC + Rank + 1 into Itself	
	NBG+V into V	
	ZFC + Reinhardt (⊥)	

Chapter 5

Logico-Genetic Theorizing

Abstract

The general features of logico-genetic theorizing are explained. The Natural Logicism advanced in this study is an example. This kind of theorizing is concerned to clarify rational beings' entitlement to various familiar species of mathematical object. A logico-genetic account must meet certain conditions of adequacy. In the case of number theory, four such conditions are proposed. The first, which is to explain the applicability of various kinds of number, is to be met by deriving all instances of a relevant Schema: Schema N for the natural numbers, Schema Q for the rationals, and Schema R for the reals. The second condition of adequacy is that it be revealed how it is that the naturals sit among the rationals as themselves again, and the rationals in turn sit among the reals as themselves again. The third and fourth conditions concern a logico-genetic account of the reals: it should reveal enough of the metaphysical nature of the reals to allow one to derive the basic laws about the real numbers; and it should reveal that there are uncountably many real numbers. A logico-genetic account can be, but does not have to be, fully logicist. It can recognize non-logical sources of intuition as providing first principles from which mathematical knowledge of suitably related objects can flow in a strictly logical fashion. Thus, for example, geometric intuition about the continuity of a line can provide first principles from which one can logically deduce basic properties of the real numbers.

The account of number on offer here, while naturally and logically bearing the label 'Natural Logicism' on the basis of what we have thus far outlined, is also an exercise in what the author would like to call *logico-genesis*. Logico-genetic theorizing in the foundations of mathematics addresses the following kind of radical problem, for any species Ξ of mathematical objects:

> Show how we are entitled to our concept of Ξs, and to the underlying presumption that there are such things as Ξs, structured in the way they must be if our mathematical theory about Ξs is to be true.

The problem is described as radical because one is not allowed to assume either familiarity with (the structure of) Ξs, or even the existence of Ξs, in explaining the entitlement in question. Rather, we have to undertake the hard work that is

The Logic of Number. Neil Tennant, Oxford University Press. © Neil Tennant 2022.
DOI: 10.1093/oso/9780192846679.003.0005

involved in 're-discovering' the fact that there are such things as Ξs, and that they are indeed structured the way our current best theories about Ξs say they are. (One says 'theories' in the plural, because so often there are many different presentations of 'the' theory—and even though these different presentations are inter-derivable.)

One is reminded here of Russell's tart remark that

> The method of "postulating" what we want has many advantages; they are the same as the advantages of theft over honest toil. Let us leave them to others and proceed with our honest toil. (Russell [1919], p. 71)

Russell was commenting on the postulation of real numbers as corresponding to arbitrary Dedekind cuts of the rationals. Against this, he extolled his own method of 'construction' of real numbers as simply the lower sections of Dedekind cuts (*ibid.*, pp. 72–3). He wrote:

> The great advantage of this method is that it requires no new assumptions, but enables us to proceed deductively from the original apparatus of logic.

But Russell's own 'original apparatus of logic' of course enjoyed a postulational logico-mathematical strength that would today be embarrassing to have to point out to him. He was referring to his theory of types, involving both the axiom of infinity and the multiplicative axiom (i.e., what is nowadays known as the axiom of choice). Today we know that this system is of much greater consistency strength than the system of real analysis.[1] It is all very well to extol the virtues of honest constructive toil over what is mistakenly perceived as postulational theft—but not when it involves wielding heavy sledgehammers to crack relatively small walnuts.

By contrast with the approaches of both Dedekind and Russell, one can conceive of a logico-genetic account as re-constructive. It takes a familiar species Ξ of mathematical objects, presumed to be available to us by way of some canonical presentation, and re-works the path of entitlement to them. Depending on the species Ξ in question, there will be conditions of adequacy that any logico-genetic account of Ξs must meet. Whether these conditions of adequacy will eliminate all but one such account is a question we do not attempt to answer here. With our choice of the reals as the Ξs in Part IV of this study, we shall be arguing that the particular geometrically-inspired account we favor is the only one, among competing extant accounts, that meets the four adequacy conditions that are to be laid out below (pp. 55 ff.). It is an open question whether there might be a more obviously logicist or arithmetizing account, avoiding any recourse to geometric intuition, that can meet our four conditions of adequacy. Certainly, no extant account of this kind does.

---

[1] See Burgess [2005].

Note that we disagree here with Crispin Wright (see Wright [2000], at p. 320), who maintains that the metaphysical and the epistemological parts[2] of the neo-logicist's project could in principle be separated out, so that one might be able to give an account of what kind of things Ξs are, without yet being able to deliver an adequate axiomatic theory of Ξs. In the view of the present author, an adequate metaphysical conception of Ξs—as given by an appropriate logico-genetic account—should furnish one with an adequate theory of Ξs. This is not to say that the metaphysical conception should be so precise that it would in principle decide the truth or falsity of any statement in the language we use to describe Ξs. Rather, it is to say that the metaphysical conception should be precise enough to vouchsafe the standard (possibly incomplete) theories that we currently have about Ξs.

We shall see by the end of Part II that we shall have already secured this in the case of the natural numbers as our chosen species Ξ. We shall provide a constructive logicist account of zero, successor, natural number, and the abstraction operator 'number of', making some slight improvements over the treatment of the same in *AR&L*. (As already remarked, one can also extend this constructive logicist treatment to addition and multiplication of natural numbers; see [2009].) An appropriately deep logicist foundation has been laid, which accounts for what kind of things the natural numbers are, and thereby also enables one rigorously (and constructively, and relevantly) to derive as theorems the postulates of 'pure' Dedekind–Peano arithmetic, which the pure mathematician takes as first principles for the pure theory of the natural numbers. The aim in Parts III and IV is to achieve something analogous in the cases where the Ξs in question are the rational and the real numbers, respectively.

The 'genesis' part of 'logico-genesis' adverts to genesis within our system of thought and knowledge, rather than in the world itself. The logico-genetic theorizer is in no way committed to any form of social or intellectual constructivism, according to which mathematical objects are actually brought into existence by our first clear thoughts about them.[3] Rather, the logico-genetic theorizer can be a Platonist, for whom mathematical objects exist as a matter of necessity, wholly independently of any rational beings' thinking about them. So, when we speak subsequently of our mathematical ontology, we shall mean that part of Plato's heaven that has thus far been illuminated by our own intellectual searchlights.

Indeed, if Kronecker was right about the naturals being a divine gift (see the famous quote on p. vii), one could think of the natural logicist's investigations as switching on those searchlights to reveal what timelessly and necessarily exists. We would suggest the label *Kroneckerian Platonism* for the view (stripped of any theological commitments) that the natural numbers are platonic objects *sui*

[2]In *AR&L*, Chapter 20, we spoke of the philosophical or conceptual strand to the notion of number, as contrasted with the mathematical or structural strand (pp. 226–7). These would be characterized by what Wright calls, respectively, the metaphysical and epistemological 'projects' to be undertaken when providing a fully satisfactory account of numbers.

[3]See, for example, the Practice-Dependent Realism of Julian Cole (in Cole [2008], [2009]).

generis, intellectually accessible to the natural logicist, but without any further commitment to the existence of a completed infinite totality of the same. Certainly, every natural number exists, necessarily; but does $\mathbb{N}$ (or ω) itself? The Kroneckerian Platonist, who is also a constructivist, says No; and we are inclined to agree. The challenge, then, will be to explain how one can come to be apprised of the existence of real numbers, and of the fact that there are uncountably infinitely many of them, without any intellectual resort to so much as a completed, countably infinite totality. In Part IV we shall see that one can establish that there are uncountably infinitely many real numbers without postulating the existence of the set of natural numbers as a completed totality.

It should be pointed out just as quickly, however, that the logico-genetic theorizer can be a nominalist—at least, if s/he can rise to Philip Kitcher's challenge of indicating

> how we can interpret the ... language in which the classical problem of the continuum is solved without committing ourselves to the existence of abstract objects.[4]

The 'logico' part of 'logico-genesis' indicates that we must strive to ensure that the reasoning that brings about the genesis of Ξs in our grasp of mathematical ontology is, as far as is possible, logical in nature. Three qualifications ought to be entered at this stage, concerning how, exactly, one should construe the professed limitation to logical reasoning in a logico-genetic account.

First, the limitation does not entail that we cannot appeal at all to a non-logical source of intuition in fashioning a logico-genetic account. On the contrary: there may well be a non-logical source of intuition that yields certain axiomatic principles (though not necessarily about Ξs as such) from which the mathematical theory of Ξs will ultimately flow, in a suitably logical fashion. A good example of such a non-logical source is our intuitive understanding of the continuity of a geometric line (which we shall be concerned to explicate below). *Cf.* Shapiro [2000a], at p. 281:

> It might be more natural for our subject to conceive of the real number structure (or a possible system exemplifying it) by contemplating actual or possible physical *or geometric* magnitudes. (Emphasis added.)

It should be stressed here, however, that our concern in Part IV will be not so much to attain a conception of the structure that consists of the real numbers, but rather a conception of what exactly a real number is, and how, in virtue of what they are, real numbers can be involved in the usual operations and relations. We also want the correct conception of real number to explain how real numbers are applicable in the measurement of continuous magnitudes.

[4]Kitcher [1983], at p. 126.

Second, the limitation to logical reasoning does not entail that we cannot appeal to any principles normally regarded as mathematical. On the contrary, the Dedekind–Peano postulates for the natural numbers will be available both for the formulation, and for the derivation, of further principles governing other mathematical objects—in particular, the real numbers. A good example of such a principle presupposing the natural numbers is the Archimedean 'axiom' that governs the ordering of the reals. Although often referred to as Archimedes' *axiom*, it will actually be *derived* below (see Theorem 3, p. 280) from a particular limit axiom that will be stated and explained in due course. In Frege [1903; reprinted 1962], §§199–214, Frege did something similar, deriving Archimedes' axiom from a rather unusual form of continuity principle that Frege formulated (informally at §175, formally at §193). Interestingly, Frege's continuity principle is exactly Bolzano's theorem in §12 of Bolzano [1817] (which we shall discuss in Chapter 18), even though Frege does not mention Bolzano in this connection. We, however, shall have derived the Dedekind–Peano postulates by appealing to deeper, logical rules of inference governing the notions of *zero*, *successor*, and *natural number*. So, our own subsequent applications of the Dedekind–Peano postulates in our logico-genetic reasoning will count as suitably logical—even though most mathematicians regard the natural numbers as mathematical objects, rather than logical objects, and regard the Dedekind–Peano postulates as strictly mathematical statements rather than as inherently logical ones. Most mathematicians remain unaware of how the Dedekind–Peano postulates can be derived as theorems on a deeper, logicist account of the natural numbers. Indeed, Harvey Friedman has predicted that practicing mathematicians would simply regard the contemporary logicist's claim as 'quaint'.[5] Very well then; let us continue to engage in some Laura Ashley philosophy of mathematics.

A third and final point is that the limitation to logical reasoning makes one crucially aware of whatever explicit first principles (in the form of axioms or rules) one must acknowledge as the ultimate source for one's derived results. In the case of the reals, in Part IV, the challenge will be—if indeed recourse must be had to geometric intuition—to articulate as minimal a set as possible of first principles of a geometric nature. (See Chapter 18 for a discussion of the historical controversy over the legitimacy of geometrical considerations in the foundations of real analysis.) It is an extremely interesting inquiry: how little of our geometric understanding can we draw upon, in order to derive, logically, all of our conventional understanding of the real number system?

Even the mere posing of this question goes against what some may regard as received wisdom among contemporary foundationalists. Here, for example, is an opening passage from Feferman [2009], at p. 169:

> On the face of it, there are several distinct forms of the continuum as a mathematical concept: in geometry, as a straight line, in analysis as the real number system (characterized in one of several ways),

[5] Personal communication.

> and in set theory as the power set of the natural numbers and, alternatively, as the set of all infinite sequences of zeros and ones. Since it is common to refer to *the* continuum, in what sense are these all instances of the same concept? When one speaks of the continuum in current set-theoretical terms it is implicitly understood that one is paying attention only to the cardinal number that these sets have in common. Besides ignoring the differences in structure involved, *that requires, to begin with, recasting geometry in analytic terms.* [Emphasis added.]

The present work will, in effect, establish that this last italicized conclusion is mistakenly drawn. One does not have to recast geometry in analytic terms in order to establish an isomorphism between, say, the points on a (directed) line (with respect to a chosen segment as the unit) and all infinite sequences of zeros and ones. Rather, one can take the points on the line as primitive objects, *sui generis*, and show how to determine, for each one of them, a unique 'bicimal expansion' consisting of zeros and ones; and conversely, one can take the set of all bicimal expansions, and determine, for each of them, a unique corresponding point on a given (directed) line (relative to the chosen unit segment.) All this could have been done by Archimedes, well before Descartes invented real-analytic coordination for points in space.

By our 'conventional understanding' of the real number system, we mean the axiomatic presentation of the theory of the reals as forming a complete ordered field. Once the geometric primitives and axioms for this task have been selected, and shown to suffice, it will then be an interesting foundational task to determine where in the hierarchy of consistency strengths this geometric theory lies. One would expect it to be that of full second-order arithmetic (Z_2), the usual axiomatic system in the Friedman–Simpson program of reverse mathematics that is identified as 'the' system for analysis.[6]

Our neo-logicism concerning the natural numbers might have been expected to result in an attempt to furnish a fully logicist logico-genetic account of the real numbers. That, after all, was the aim of Frege, the first great logicist. For Frege, both the arithmetic of natural numbers and the theory of real analysis were to be revealed as bodies of inherently logical truths. He sought so to define the main mathematical concepts involved that the axioms of those two branches of mathematics would be derivable as theorems of his general logic. The arduous task of so deriving the mathematical axioms in question would reveal—*pace* Kant—that they were analytic. By contrast, for Frege, the axioms of Euclidean geometry were still synthetic—as Kant had maintained.

The logico-genetic account of the reals on offer in Part IV departs importantly from the methodological path that Frege had intended to follow. To be sure, we share Frege's logicist aspiration to establish at least the natural numbers as logical

[6] See Simpson [1999] for further details. See also p. 48 for Z_2's position in the hierarchy of consistency strengths.

objects, and to derive the Dedekind–Peano postulates that govern them from a deeper, purely logical foundation. Moreover, we claim to have succeeded where Frege himself had failed, for want of a consistent foundational logical theory. The natural numbers, though *sui generis*, are logical objects. They are recognizable and identifiable as such because of the role they play in our thoughts about objects that fall under sortal concepts. Our logico-genetic path to the natural numbers has proved to be fully logicist. And it does not take Hume's Principle as its point of departure.

The role of the natural numbers in our thoughts about other kinds of things is very fundamental. When we understand it properly, we are in a position to explain how and why the natural numbers are applicable (in the counting of any finite collection, or predicate-extension). That one should be able, in general, to explain the applicability of our mathematical thought about Ξs is another very important Fregean desideratum, as we have taken pains to explain above. It should be regarded as a prime condition of adequacy on any foundational account of our mathematical thought about Ξs.

In Part II we shall see that that condition of adequacy can be met, as far as the natural numbers are concerned. We are able to derive, for each natural number n, every instance of

$$\text{Schema N}: \qquad \#xFx = \underline{n} \;\leftrightarrow\; \exists_n xFx\,,$$

where the 'numerically exact' quantification $\exists_n xFx$ (there are exactly n objects x such that Fx) is of course definable in terms of the logical predicate of identity and the usual logical operators. The placeholder '$\underline{n}$' is to be replaced by the numeral, in successor-zero notation, for the natural number n.

In Part III we shall meet a similar condition of adequacy in our theorizing about the rationals. The rationals, like the naturals before them, will be shown to be logical objects, grasped by a method of abstraction that serves also to explain their applicability in our wider thought and talk (about fractional shares of things, for example). We shall be able to derive, for every rational number $p : q$ (where p is a natural number, and q is a non-zero natural number), every instance of

$$\text{Schema Q} \qquad \mathfrak{F}x(t, x \cong_\Phi \textbf{whole } \Phi) = p:q \quad \dashv\vdash \quad q \odot t \;\cong_D\; p \odot \textbf{whole } \Phi\,,$$

whose unfamiliar expressions will be explained when the rationals are upon us. Satisfaction of the adequacy condition employing Schema Q is what clinches our treatment of the rationals as fully logicist.

As far as the real numbers are concerned, however, we part company with Frege. In our considered view, there is no (extant) logico-genetic path to, or account of, the real numbers that both warrants our regarding them as purely logical objects and meets all of the following four conditions of adequacy, which we take to be philosophically paramount.

1. The account should intrinsically reveal or internally explain the applicability of real numbers in our thoughts about other kinds of things.

2. The account should identify the natural numbers with the naturals-among-the-reals; and it should identify the rational numbers with the rationals-among-the-reals.

3. The account should reveal enough of the metaphysical nature of the reals to allow one to derive the basic laws about the real numbers.

4. The account should reveal that there are uncountably many real numbers.

By laying down these explicit adequacy conditions on any logico-genetic theory of the reals, we venture into foundational terrain that has not yet been properly mapped, and is enormously interesting. Our tentative conclusion is that the logicist has to join forces with the Euclidean and the Archimedean, and concede a vital role to geometric intuition, in order to attain to an adequate conception of the reals. Trying to get the reals 'fully logicistically' will—or at least, so it appears to the present author—always involve violating one of the adequacy constraints.

So the following questions need to be addressed: What kind of objects are the real numbers, if they are not purely logical objects? What entitles us to think of them as existing? And how best do we understand their applicability in our thoughts about other kinds of things?

Mathematical theories are learned, developed, and communicated 'natively'. Each theory has its own special stock of concepts; and is 'about' its own special kinds of mathematical objects. The early proofs by great expositors of these theories treat their objects as *sui generis*, without presenting them as complicated sets drawn from the cumulative hierarchy of pure sets. The 'Bourbakization' of mathematics—the re-definition of all the concepts of different branches of mathematics in terms of sets alone—makes it harder for a beginner to understand what any particular mathematical theory is about. It makes mathematics, which is already abstract enough, seem utterly abstract, to the point of enjoying no enlivening or illuminating connection whatsoever with any other area of human thought—be it physics, computer science, or economics.

The more searingly abstract a presentation one provides for a mathematical theory, the more difficult it becomes to explain how it is in the very nature of the mathematical objects concerned that one's theory about them can be applied in reasoning about real-world phenomena and the regularities that underlie them. Ironically, it was Frege who made the most of the requirement that such applicability be explained—and who then did the most damage to that very prospect.

The reader will see that in Parts II, III, and IV of this work, particular attention is paid to satisfying, on the natural logicist approach, the four highly intuitive conditions of adequacy listed above. We shall briefly comment on conditions (3) and (4), and then devote the rest of this chapter to further comments on conditions (1) and (2).

Ad (3). Here again we part company with Wright [2000] at p. 320, who does not impose this (very) Fregean constraint on a neo-Fregean construction of analysis.

Ad (4). One might call this the 'Cantorian requirement': that one be able to show that the continuum of reals, on whatever construal one provides of them, is uncountable. Note that this does not really require that one recognize the continuum as a completed totality. Indeed, it does not even require that one recognize the natural numbers as forming a completed totality. All it requires is demonstrating that for no set X is there a function mapping to each subset of X some member of X. Suppose thereafter that one can assign to each real number a unique set of naturals. One could then conclude that, if the naturals form a set, then there are strictly fewer of them than there are reals. In this way the Kroneckerian can grasp the uncountability of the reals, without being committed to the existence either of the totality of naturals or of the totality of reals. The diagonal method of proof can also be deployed with limpid clarity with respect to our own preferred representation of the reals as countable bicimal expansions. Details will emerge in Part IV.

Ad (1): Adequacy condition (1) is a methodological one. It is to be satisfied by ensuring the derivability of all instances of the aforementioned Schema N (for the naturals—see p. 95), Schema Q (for the rationals—see p. 191) and Schema R (for the reals—see p. 251).

These three Schemas are numerical analogues of Tarski's celebrated Schema T for the theory of truth.

Schema T: s is true if and only if p.

One obtains an instance of Schema T by replacing 's' with a structural-descriptive name (in the metalanguage) of a sentence in the object language, and by replacing 'p' with a translation of that sentence into the metalanguage. The material adequacy condition for a (meta)theory of truth is that one should be able to derive (in that metatheory) all instances of Schema T involving sentences of the object language.

It is a mark in favor of the natural logicist's account that its provision of rules of inference for primitive logico-mathematical expressions ensures the satisfaction of adequacy condition (1). In the case of the natural logicist's theory of the natural numbers, for example, it is Schema N whose instances need to be derivable (and they are):

Schema N: $\#x\Phi(x) = \underline{n}$ if and only if there are exactly n Φs.

There are infinitely many instances of Schema N—one for each natural number n. For any theory of the natural numbers, the derivability of every instance of Schema N is a basic requirement of adequacy.

'Intrinsic revelation' and 'internal explanation' are philosophical terms of art that might admit of further explication. On the other hand, they might have to remain mere terms of art in these discussions—one knows one when one sees one, to adapt the words of the good Justice Potter Stewart (*Jacobellis v. Ohio 378 U.S. 184* (1964)).

In the case of number theory, one of the central logicist aims is to characterize the inferential behavior of the 'number-abstraction' operator $\#x$. This can be applied to formulae containing extra-logical primitives that are not themselves mathematical (such as 'x is a horse drawing the Emperor's carriage'). The applicability of number-talk to states of affairs in the external world is thereby made obvious. Similar remarks will apply to our proposed treatments of rational-number abstraction, and of real-number abstraction. For the time being we shall pass, however, on the question whether one can explicate precisely and in full generality how it is that applicability can be 'intrinsically evident' in one's treatment of mathematical objects of other kinds in general. Such a treatment of set theory, at the very least, would have to admit of Urelements, and in a general enough fashion for physical objects to qualify as Urelements. The treatment would have to allow one to use the set-abstraction operator $\{x| \ldots x \ldots\}$ on formulae containing the predicate Ux (for 'x is an Urelement', and/or terms denoting Urelements.[7]

The stress on 'internal' explanation rules out any structuralist account such as Dedekind's, and those of his abstractionist heirs such as Shapiro [2000b] and Hale [2000], for all of whom the explanation of applicability would be 'tacked on to' their structuralist account as an afterthought. Explaining applicability internally we take to be non-negotiable. So here we part company also with Wright [2000] at pp. 328–329, who enters doubts as to whether one should impose this Fregean constraint on a neo-Fregean construction of real analysis. The (Fregean) stress on accounting for applicability turns out—for Wright—to be an obstacle (in the case of the real numbers) to revealing them as purportedly purely logical objects.

Ad (2): Adequacy condition (2) is an ontological one. It is justified by the strong intuition, never abandoned in pedagogy, that the naturals are at the same time both rationals and reals. The natural number 1, for example, *is* the rational number 1, and *is* the real number 1. It is no facetious pun here that we insist that these are numerical identities. It is extraordinary that the foundational tradition could have lost sight of—or simply ceased to respect—the power of this intellectual insight in general. It is a mark in favor of the natural logicist's account that the insight in question is thoroughly respected.

Structuralism's abandonment of the need to respect these numerical identities is of relatively recent provenance. The abandonment is already clear in Dedekind's type-raising treatment of the real numbers as 'cuts' of the rationals. But one of the major influences on Dedekind was Dirichlet. And in Dirichlet's aforementioned treatise *Vorlesungen über Zahlentheorie*, first published in 1863, it is manifestly clear that he regards each kind of individual number as 'itself again' as one considers ever more expansive *Körper* of numbers closed under the operations of addition, multiplication, subtraction, and division (with non-zero divisors). Integers are 'themselves again' among the rationals. Rationals

[7]Thanks are owed to Damon Stanley for eliciting these remarks on 'intrinsic revelation' of applicability.

are 'themselves again' among the reals. And reals (amongst them, of course, the rationals), are 'themselves again' among the complex numbers. From Dirichlet again, in §159, at p. 435 (author's translation):[8]

> We turn now to consider that *Körper* J, which consists of all complex numbers of the form
> $$x + yi$$
> where x and y stand for arbitrary *rational* numbers ... This *Körper* J ... obviously contains also all rational numbers ...

Later, in §160, at p. 453, Dirchlet reprises this ontological point (author's translation):[9]

> Obviously the system R of all *rational* numbers forms a *Körper*, and this is the simplest or, as one can also say, the *smallest Körper*, because it is completely contained in every other *Körper* A. In fact, if one chooses from A an arbitrary number a distinct from zero, then the quotient of this number a with itself, i.e., the number 1, is, according to the definition [of a *Körper*—NT] also contained in A, and because from this number there arise through repeated addition and subtraction all integral rational numbers, and from these through division all rational numbers, R is completely contained in A.

One need only note that the *Körper* A can be the field of the real numbers, and it can also be the field of the complex numbers. It is absolutely clear that Dedekind has the 'ontologically reprising' conception of containment that we are arguing for here. The main way in which his conception differs from that of the natural logicist is in showing no interest at all in characterizing numbers (of any kind) in a way that would explain their applicability. His concerns are entirely 'pure mathematical';

[8] The original German is as follows (with word order changed because of the indicated omissions):

> Wir wenden uns nun ... zu der Betrachtung desjenigen Körpers J, welcher aus allen complexen Zahlen ... von der Form
> $$x + yi$$
> besteht, wo x und y willkürliche *rationale* Zahlen bedeuten ... . Dieser Körper J ... [enthält offenbar auch alle rationalen Zahlen] ...

[9] The original German is as follows:

> Offenbar bildet das System R aller *rationalen* Zahlen einen Körper, und dies ist der einfachste oder, wie man auch sagen kann, der *kleinste* Körper, weil er in jedem anderen Körper A vollständig enthalten ist. In der That, wählt man aus A nach Belieben eine von Null verschiedene Zahl a aus, so ist der Quotient dieser Zahl a in sich selbst, d. h. die Zahl 1, zufolge der Definition ebenfalls in A enthalten, und da aus dieser Zahl durch wiederholte Addition und Subtraction alle ganzen rationalen Zahlen, und hieraus durch Division alle rationalen Zahlen entstehen, so ist R gänzlich in A enthalten. [Emphasis in original.]

we note with interest his stress on how, possessed only of 0 and 1, we can generate (*reproducieren*) each of the rational numbers by (finitely many) iterations of the operations of addition, subtraction, multiplication, and division. For Dirichlet, the genesis of the rationals would therefore be operational; whereas for the natural logicist (see Part III), their genesis will turn out to be abstractive, and intimately tied to their applicability, and indeed will eschew algebraic operations altogether.

The earlier systems are contained (*enthalten*) in the later ones, as subsystems of them. In Dirichlet's treatment of these matters, there is no need to embark on the mental gymnastics of regarding the earlier systems as somehow injectable into the later ones, by 'structure-preserving' but identity-destroying mappings. That structuralist stratagem is utterly foreign to his elegant and powerful treatment of these fields.

The notion of identifying the natural (resp., rational) numbers with the naturals-(resp., rationals-)among-the-reals will be amplified in due course (pp. 243 ff.). It is a very natural but, surprisingly, *un*Fregean requirement. Yet it is a self-imposed condition of adequacy on this neo-Fregean project that we meet it. This particular pendulum must be swung back, in this author's humble opinion, in the general direction of Dirichlet. And in doing so it must dodge any further Dedekindian disturbance.

Our commitment to numerical identities under system-expansion also puts us in direct disagreement with Russell, who was not at all concerned to identify the natural numbers with the naturals-among-the-reals. Indeed, he was at pains to distinguish the two, but without providing any argument that this would be an intuitively desirable feature of a foundational account. In Russell [1919], at p. 64, we read:

> ... the fraction $m/1$ ... is by no means capable of being identified with the inductive cardinal number m ...

where by 'inductive cardinal' Russell means 'natural number'. His approach was the same concerning the rationals among the reals. On p. 72 we read:

> We have to define a new kind of numbers called "real numbers", of which some will be rational and some irrational. Those that are rational "correspond" to ratios, in the same kind of way in which the ratio $n/1$ corresponds to the integer n; but they are not the same as ratios.

So much for Russell. Let us return to Frege. Like any other 'type raiser' in pursuit of the reals, Frege thinks that the reals are entities (in his case: special kinds of classes) of a completely different kind than (say) the naturals. Thus his symbols for the naturals zero and one have slashes through them, in order to distinguish them from the reals 0 and 1. The present account disagrees strongly with Frege on this score. For the natural logicist, the natural zero *is* the real zero; the natural zero does not just have the real zero as some sort of Doppelgänger under an injection of the naturals into the reals. So, one's account of the reals must reveal the 'naturals' among them (the positive integral multiples of the unit) to be the familiar naturals.

The present author agrees with Frege, however, concerning the constraint that one's account of the nature of the various kinds of number must explain their applicability in our thought about other kinds of things. Our account disagrees with Frege (and with his logicizing and arithmetizing predecessor Dedekind) on the extent to which the logicist must make do without geometric intuition.

The reader will probably expect further elucidation of this apparently unschooled and unsophisticated intuition—which, one must note, was the intuition of a mathematical master such as Dedekind—in order to save it from the latter-day objections to be expected from contemporary structuralists (who now must be supposed to be more sophisticated than a Dedekind in their havoc-wreaking ontological intuitions).[10] These objections (the very raising of which should be seen as self-defeating) are based on the fact that the structuralist's way of getting the rationals from the naturals, and the reals from the rationals, are typically type-raising, and hence destructive of numerical identity. For example, a typical structuralist conception of the (non-negative) rationals is that they are equivalence classes of ordered pairs $\langle m, n \rangle$ of naturals (where $n \neq 0$). The favored representative of the equivalence class will be the ordered pair whose first and second members are, respectively, least within that equivalence class.[11] Once the rationals are in the picture, the reals can be obtained by (to choose the structuralist Dedekind's favored approach) taking ordered pairs of the form of $\langle L, R \rangle$, where L and R form a partition of the rationals, with every member of L being less than every member of R.

On these structuralist 'recipes', the natural number 1, for example, 'is not itself' when 'it' occurs as a rational. Rather, it 'is' the set $\{\langle n, n \rangle | 0 \neq n \in \mathbb{N}\}$. Moreover, neither the natural 1 nor the rational 1 *is* the real 1 when the latter is construed as the appropriate Dedekind cut of the form $\langle L, R \rangle$. (We prescind from specifying more precisely what these particular sets L and R would be, for 1.) It should be clear by now that anyone committed to such type-raising structuralist ploys to 'obtain' the rationals from the naturals and then the reals from the rationals, will be discombobulated by, and prone to object to, the (allegedly) 'naive' intuition of the natural logicist to the effect that every natural number is just itself again when occurring as a rational and when occurring as a real.

How is this intuition to be defended? Well, how about appealing to experts as authorities within the continuing tradition (and there are many of them, like-minded with Dirichlet), when, in philosophically honest moments, they explain to beginners how the rationals and the reals 'get into the picture'? The natural logicist's intuition is a guiding intuition, to which appeals are unapologetically

[10]Thanks are owed to Erich Jones for eliciting further such elucidation.

[11]It will follow from this that those first and second members are relatively prime. But formulating the condition for canonical representation does not need to invoke this algebraic fact; one can get by with reference only to the ordering of the naturals.

made by university teachers of advanced mathematics, when they are concerned to lay out the natural evolutionary progression in our thinking about numbers. First come the naturals, which are used for comparing the sizes of various finite collections. They are depicted with the conventional left-to-right progression that begins with zero, and extends 'infinitely far to the right', by making successive discrete jumps:

$$\begin{array}{cccc} 0 & 1 & 2 & \\ \cdot & \cdot & \cdot & \ldots \end{array}$$

At the very next stage, the university or high-school teacher might introduce the negative integers, by reflecting this picture to the left around 0, and mentioning debit and credit balances in bank accounts as a prime area of application. For present purposes, however, we can omit this foray into the negatives. Let us focus here on how the positive rationals come into the picture, among the whole numbers. And let us expand the picture somewhat, so as to attend for the time being to what happens just between 0 and 1. (What happens 'beyond 1', to the right in this picture, will emerge in due course.) The numbers m, k, p, q in what follows are of course natural numbers, which the natural logicist will already have furnished on purely logical grounds.

For each prime k, and each $m < k$, one can insert at the appropriate place in this interval the rational number $\frac{m}{k}$. Here is what happens as a result, on dealing with the primes 2 and 3:

$$\begin{array}{cccccc} 0 & \frac{1}{3} & \frac{1}{2} & \frac{2}{3} & 1 & \\ \cdot & \cdot & \cdot & \cdot & \cdot & \ldots \end{array}$$

Then, for each prime k, and each positive $m < k^2$ not a multiple of k, one can insert at the appropriate place in this interval the new rational number $\frac{m}{k^2}$. Here is what happens as a result, again dealing only with the primes 2 and 3:

$$\begin{array}{cccccccccccccc} 0 & \frac{1}{9} & \frac{2}{9} & \frac{1}{4} & \frac{1}{3} & \frac{4}{9} & \frac{1}{2} & \frac{5}{9} & \frac{2}{3} & \frac{3}{4} & \frac{7}{9} & \frac{8}{9} & 1 & \\ \cdot & \cdot & \cdot & \cdot & \cdot & \cdot & \cdot & \cdot & \cdot & \cdot & \cdot & \cdot & \cdot & \ldots \end{array}$$

One can see how this 'sprinkling in' of rationals between 0 and 1 progresses. For each prime k, and each positive $m < k^3$ not a multiple of k, one can insert at the appropriate place in this interval the new rational number $\frac{m}{k^3}$ ... and so on. The latter 'and so on' is captured by saying:

> For each non-zero natural number n, for each prime k, and each positive $m < k^n$ not a multiple of k, one can insert at the appropriate place in this interval the new rational number $\frac{m}{k^n}$.

This fills in not all, but (of course, countably) infinitely many of the rationals between 0 and 1. To extend the fillings-in beyond 1, in the same non-exhaustive manner, one simply drops the requirement that m be less than k^n, and accordingly says:

> For each non-zero natural number n, for each prime k, and each m not a multiple of k, one can insert at the appropriate place amongst its rational bed-fellows the new rational number $\frac{m}{k^n}$.

There will still, of course, be infinitely many rationals missing. We shall leave to the reader the task of working out that the most general (and at the same time most economical) recipe by means of which all the (positive) rationals that are not naturals will be brought into the picture, is to 'get in' (by a suitable generalization of the procedure partially illustrated above) all rationals of the form

$$\frac{p_1 \times \ldots \times p_k}{q_1 \times \ldots \times q_m}$$

where $p_1, \ldots, p_k$ and $q_1, \ldots q_m$ are sequences of primes, with none of the p_i identical to any of the q_j. Rationals in this form have relatively prime numerators and denominators. Positive rationals that are not naturals can also be written in the ultimately canonical form

$$\frac{p_1^{n_1} \times \ldots \times p_k^{n_k}}{q_1^{r_1} \times \ldots \times q_m^{r_m}}$$

where $p_1, \ldots, p_k$ and $q_1, \ldots q_m$ are now strictly increasing sequences of primes, with none of the p_i identical to any of the q_j; and where all the indicated exponents are non-zero naturals.

In this account of how the rationals come to be sprinkled amongst the naturals, we are of course assuming familiarity with the concept of primality, hence also with the binary operation of multiplication, in terms of which primality is defined. We must emphasize at this stage, however, that the account of the rationals that we shall be furnishing will not presuppose any knowledge of the familiar operations of addition and multiplication on the naturals. All we are doing here, with our remarks about the usual method of teaching beginners about fractions is that the algebraic manipulations are undertaken with an eye to 'preserving the naturals as themselves' amongst the rationals that are densely introduced among them.

To complete our remarks *ad (2)* above, one need only tell the story about the member of the school of Pythagoras who discovered the algebraic proof that no square of a natural can be twice any other such square. This resulted in the realization that the diagonal of the unit square cannot (by Pythagoras's own famous theorem about right-angled triangles) be assigned a rational measure of length in terms of the unit in question. So the magnitude $\sqrt{2}$ (which is needed for mensuration of a line-segment's length in terms of a given unit of length) is not a rational. One then proceeds to give some explanatory story about how to 'fill in' among the rationals all such irrational numbers—not only the (countably) infinitely many algebraic numbers, such as $\sqrt{2}$, but also the uncountably many non-algebraic (i.e., transcendental) reals, such as π, the circumference of a circle with unit diameter. Whatever story is told, it is narrated in such a way as to leave the abiding impression that one is 'homing in on' these irrational reals and inserting them among the rationals in the linear ordering in which the latter already sit, and whose field is going to be extended so as to accommodate the new real arrivals as welcome guests among the rationals, with whom they reside on an ontological par. That is to say, the rationals remain who or what they are or were, before they were so generous as to 'make space for' the overwhelming flood of reals as ontological immigrants and fellow-citizens of the real continuum $\mathbb{R}$. All the details of how this 'comes to be' will emerge in Part IV.

This promissory note completes our elucidation of condition of adequacy (2) above. Note that we have expounded just one explanation (among a few possible) of how commonly presented pedagogical expositions support the intuition that the naturals 'remain themselves' when the rationals are introduced. The foregoing explanation availed itself of some acquaintance with algebraic laws governing multiplication, division, and exponentiation. In Part III, however, our natural logicist explanation of the provenance of the rationals will be given without presupposing any acquaintance with those algebraic laws. Yet the method by which the rationals are introduced will nevertheless reveal, intrinsically, how they are applicable in our wider thought and talk about the world—over and above the counting of finite collections, for which, of course, the naturals themselves suffice.

The accounts of the rationals and of the reals on offer in this study (in Parts III and IV) are confined to the non-negative numbers. No special attempt is made to treat the negative integers at a separate stage—say, between the naturals and the rationals, which, as already remarked, is a frequently adopted approach. We would choose the option of 'reflecting' to the negatives only at the final stage, once the non-negative reals are in the picture.

Part II

Natural Logicism and the Naturals

Chapter 6

Introduction, with Some Historical Background

Abstract

The importance of constructive reasoning for logicism is emphasized. The aim is to furnish constructive derivations of the Dedekind–Peano postulates for arithmetic from the more basic rules of Natural Logicism for the natural numbers. Derivations of all instances of Schema N will likewise be constructive, in meeting the adequacy condition that one's account of the naturals should explain their applicability in our wider thought and talk about the world. A summary is provided of the main historical developments in logicist and neo-logicist theorizing about the natural numbers, from Frege through to Wright. The latter's 'HP-based' neo-logicism is criticized for its important shortcomings. The contrasting virtues of the alternative treatment that was called Constructive Logicism in *Anti-Realism and Logic* are described; and a few matters of priority are clarified.

The main figures associated with logicism—Dedekind, Frege, and Russell and Whitehead—were all committed to Classical Logic. The main figures associated with the rejection of strictly classical inferences—Brouwer the intuitionist, Weyl the predicativist, and Markov and Bishop the constructivists—definitely did not hold logicist views about fundamental mathematical theories (such as the theories of the natural, the rational, and the real numbers). Given this backdrop, it needs to be stressed that

Logicism is not the exclusive preserve of the classicist.

By a 'classicist', we mean one who insists that Classical Logic is the correct logic, and that mathematicians are entitled to use any of the strictly classical laws or rules of inference. By a 'constructivist', we mean one who insists that only the constructive part of Classical Logic is correct. The constructivist refuses to make unrestricted application of the strictly classical Law of Excluded Middle, or any of its constructive equivalents—any one of the strictly classical rules known as Double Negation Elimination, Classical Reductio, or Dilemma. The only exceptions would be in those circumstances where a convincing case can be made that the 'litmus sentence' that is being treated classically (i.e., as bivalent) is effectively

The Logic of Number. Neil Tennant, Oxford University Press.
DOI: 10.1093/oso/9780192846679.003.0006

decidable. (This might be done, for example, in connection with empirical testing of scientific theories. One could treat observation statements as effectively decidable, in principle.) We can set aside here the question how, once one has constructivized one's logic, one proceeds further along possibly different routes in 'constructivizing' or 'intuitionizing' one's conceptions of the various mathematical entities involved (to start with: the naturals, the rationals, and the reals).

The debate between constructivism and classicism is conventionally confined to the language of first-order logic with identity. But the debate can be extended into more interesting conceptual territory. In particular, participants in this debate, whether or not they are logicists, could pay attention to logicist attempts to show that at least certain branches of mathematics—or even certain central or important parts of them—are, fundamentally, part of logic. That would then enable both parties to the debate (constructivist and classicist) to characterize their constructivism or classicism, respectively, in the way they have already done. They could hew to their way of 'self-identifying' as constructivist and classicist, by adverting to their eschewal or adoption of certain logical rules that had initially characterized their respective positions.

To this end one would need to introduce new primitive expressions into the 'logical' vocabulary, for the primitive concepts of the branch of mathematics in question; and one would need to furnish those expressions with 'logical-looking' rules of inference. One would then need to examine whether such rules might suffice for a logical derivation of the 'first principles' that mathematicians adopt for the branch of mathematics in question. The aim, of course, would be to lay down such compellingly analytic rules that one could remove the scare quotes that we have employed in this paragraph.

It would be in such an examination that the debate between the constructivist and the logicist could be rejoined. Do these logicist derivations of first principles proceed in a clearly constructive vein? Or does one need recourse to strictly classical deductive moves, thereby revealing that the constructivist's repertoire is too meager to achieve the sought logicist reduction of the branch of mathematics in question?

Foremost among these branches of mathematics would be the theory of the natural (or so-called 'counting') numbers. Were those numbers (and our grasp of fundamental truths about them) simply 'given' to us by God (as Kronecker maintained)?;[1] or does that theory, in Kantian terms (but not, of course, as part of Kantian doctrine), arise solely from our grasp of concepts, and the operation of our understanding? Are its fundamental principles analytic? One who proposes to answer these questions in the affirmative is obliged to vindicate those answers in connection with the theory of the natural numbers. For this is ground zero of the still-ongoing debate about logicism. Such a vindication is the purpose of this Part of the current work.

We shall, however, go two steps further. We shall provide, first, a construct-

[1] Again, see the quote on p. vii.

ive logicist theory. This theory derives the mathematicians' traditional axioms for arithmetic in logicist fashion and indeed by means of constructive (and relevant) logic alone. The derivations will be given in Core Logic. It follows that the constructivist can rejoin the debate just mentioned, and prevail against the classicist. We shall also provide, second, a logicist foundation for arithmetic that reveals how the natural numbers can be applied in our wider thought and talk about the world. This was a significant desideratum for Frege; and we believe the current account achieves it. Moreover, it does so within the strict confines of Core Logic. See Chapter 9 for further details.

Note that it will suffice, for the natural logicist to be able to claim substantial success in this project, to recover the axioms of Dedekind–Peano arithmetic. Indeed, if the natural logicist manages to succeed only on Dedekind–Peano arithmetic, this might offer the explanation sought by Isaacson [1987] of why it is that the axioms of Dedekind–Peano arithmetic are so very 'natural'. As Isaacson puts it,

> ... Peano Arithmetic occupies an intrinsic, conceptually well-defined region of arithmetical truth. ... it consists of those truths which can be perceived directly from the purely arithmetical content of a categorical conceptual analysis of the notion of natural number.

We have already acknowledged Gödelian incompleteness in arithmetic, and we fully recognize the logical and epistemological challenge posed by it. We must set aside at this juncture, however, further investigations into the possibility that there are arguably logicist ways—such as, for example, adopting certain reflection principles[2]—of correctly extending incomplete arithmetical theories. If all possible future extensions of our axiomatized arithmetical theorizing can be made to fall within the scope of logicist method, this would constitute a full vindication of logicism's claim (at least, about the arithmetic of natural numbers). For the claim is really about what mathematicians can in principle prove. To frame logicism of any kind as a doctrine concerning provability-transcendent mathematical truth is to deprive logicism, in advance, and merely on the basis of question-begging realist dogma, of any prospect of substantial programmatic achievements.

At this point it will be useful to give the reader a brief summary of the main historical developments in logicist and neo-logicist theorizing about the natural numbers.

1884. Frege, in his epoch-making *Grundlagen der Arithmetik*, a work regarded by many as the founding document of analytic philosophy, argued that assigning a number to the Φs is to attribute a higher-level concept to the first-order sortal concept 'x is a Φ'. He also motivated a formalization of numerical referring terms in abstractive form: 'the number of Φs' was to be formalized (in more contemporary notation) as $\#x\Phi x$. Here, the operator # is a variable-binding term-forming

[2] See, for example, [2002b].

operator. It turns any first-order, one-place sortal predicate into a singular term.

1888. Dedekind, in *Was sind und was sollen die Zahlen?*,[3] gave a structuralist account of (systems isomorphic to) the sequence of natural numbers, in which 1 and s ('the successor of ...') were the distinguished notions. His key points were that 1 is initial, and that the mapping s is both total and one-one. Hence there are (countably) infinitely many natural numbers. That Dedekind chose 1 rather than 0 as his initial element is neither here nor there when one's concern is only to characterize the order type of the naturals. But of course it would be important if one were to proceed to develop the additive and multiplicative algebra of the natural numbers.

1889. Peano, in *Arithmetices principia, nova methodo exposita*,[4] presented the axioms for s and $+$, but (following Dedekind) for the series of natural numbers whose initial element is 1. It was only later (Peano [1898]) that Peano included 0 in place of 1 as the initial element, and gave his now famous 'recursion equations' for the arithmetical operations of addition and multiplication. Dedekind, *op. cit.*, had already derived these equations as theorems in his own treatment. Peano did not state the recursion equations for multiplication as axioms; instead, he derived them from a rather non-formal definition of $a \times b$ as $0[(+a)b]$—which he explains as what one obtains by performing on 0 the operation $+a$, exactly b times.

1893. Frege, in Volume 1 of his *Grundgesetze der Arithmetik*, gave his axioms for class theory, and derived *Hume's Principle*. This is a double-barreled abstraction principle of the kind explained on p. 13. It involves two occurrences of the abstraction operator in the identity statement on its left-hand side:

$$\text{HP} \qquad \#x\Phi x = \#x\Psi x \;\leftrightarrow\; \exists R\; Rxy[\Phi x \text{ 1-1 } \Psi y]\,.$$

In words: the number of Φs is identical to the number of Ψs if and only if there is a one-one relation between the Φs and the Ψs.

From HP, Frege then derived (with complete formal rigor, but using an *un*free logic) the Dedekind–Peano axioms for $(0,s)$-arithmetic. He did not remark explicitly on the fact that HP sufficed to this end. The main problem for Frege's would-be logicist approach to arithmetic, as is well known, is that his Basic Law V was shown by Russell (in 1903) to be inconsistent.

Another serious problem, however, lurks in the logical undergirding. This is that the identity relation is a one-one mapping of any domain onto itself. So, taking Φ for Ψ, the right-hand side of the resulting instance of HP is a logical theorem. Detaching leftwards, we find that HP entails the existence of $\#x\Phi x$, no

[3]The usual translation of this title into English is *The Nature and Meaning of Numbers*. But it would be better captured either by *What are the Numbers, and what Ought they to be?* or by *What are the Numbers, and what are they Supposed to be?*.

[4]Peano [1889].

matter what the predicate Φ may be. This problem will be inherited by anyone who subscribes to HP in its usual formulation, even if they use a free logic.

1965. Parsons, in his paper 'Frege's Theory of Number' (Parsons [1965]), observed that the Dedekind–Peano axioms (PA) had been derived by Frege from Hume's Principle alone.

1983. Wright, in his monograph *Frege's Conception of Numbers as Objects*, gave a proof-sketch for $HP \vdash PA$, in a classical, unfree logic. There are the following two problems with Wright's account, which we shall call 'HP-based neo-logicism'.

First, the HP-based neo-logicist account does not handle the usual canonical numerals for referring to numbers—neither those of Dedekind–Peano, which are of the form $s \ldots s0$, nor those of any place-notational system employing a base greater than 1, such as our familiar decimal system (employing base 10) or the bicimal system (employing base 2). This drawback is relatively minor, though, compared to the next one.

Second, HP-based neo-logicism still commits one, as Frege's account did, to the existence of $\#x\Phi x$ for any predicate or sortal concept Φ. Here is proof that this is so:

$$\dfrac{\dfrac{\overset{\text{2nd-order logical theorem:}}{x = y : \Phi x \overset{\text{1-1}}{\underset{\text{onto}}{\mapsto}} \Phi y}}{\exists R\, Rxy : \Phi x \overset{\text{1-1}}{\underset{\text{onto}}{\mapsto}} \Phi y} \qquad \overset{\text{Special instance of HP:}}{\#x\Phi x = \#x\Phi x \;\leftrightarrow\; \exists R\, Rxy : \Phi x \overset{\text{1-1}}{\underset{\text{onto}}{\mapsto}} \Phi y}}{\dfrac{\#x\Phi x = \#x\Phi x}{\exists! \#x\Phi x}}\ .$$

So Wright is committed to the existence of $\#x\, x = x$, the number of things *tout court*. Wright dubbed this 'anti-zero'. Anti-zero, if it existed, would be the cardinality of the whole universe—including that of set theory, if the thinker were committed to it. Yet, as Boolos [1997] (at p. 260) has pointed out, ZF does not have a cardinal number for the whole set-theoretical universe. If anti-zero existed, it would be at least as great as the cardinal number for the whole set-theoretical universe; and one would be at a loss to explain how the latter cardinal number could be absent, while anti-zero could be present. HP, after all, is supposed to hold across all discourses and their associated ontologies. This extraordinary commitment on the part of HP hardly recommends its version of neo-logicism to any thinker of more (ontologically) constructivist bent.

As stressed on p. 29, the regimenting logician needs to use a free logic in order to do justice to expert mathematical practice. Wright's ontological excesses are completely unnecessary when the aim is just to vouchsafe the existence of the natural numbers as logical objects, and the laws that govern them. The neo-logicist should be able to draw a line at 'Kroneckerian Platonism', committed to the existence of each natural number, but by no means committed to the existence of their totality.

1987. *AR&L* provided a Constructive Logicist account of arithmetic. Its most significant features worth stressing in the current context were the following.

1. *AR&L* raised the second objection above (to HP-based neo-logicism), which was later to become known as the 'Bad Company' objection.
2. *AR&L* proposed an adequacy condition on any logicist theory of number, employing what the author called Schema N, which says, informally, that the number of Φs is identical to $\underline{n}$ just in case there are exactly n Φs (here, $\underline{n}$ is the theorist's canonical numeral for the number n).
3. *AR&L* emphasized the need to separate 'numerosity' from 'number'.
4. *AR&L* placed emphasis likewise on the two main ways of referring to numbers —using numerals and using numerical abstraction terms—which could then be organically connected via Schema N.
5. *AR&L* argued that one could be innocent of the concept of number until one had numerical terms in one's language and would be willing to assert all instances of Schema N.
6. *AR&L* provided a natural-deduction formulation of primitive rules of inference for the new logico-mathematical expressions 0, s, and #, with single-barreled introduction and elimination rules for the abstraction operator #.
7. *AR&L* gave completely formal derivations of the Dedekind–Peano postulates for 0 and s, constructed in accordance with the new rules of inference, in a constructive, relevant, free logic.
8. *AR&L* explicitly avoided commitment to any cardinal numbers other than the natural numbers.

Features (1), (2), (7), and (8) deserve further comment in light of the subsequent literature.

Ad (1). As Linnebo [2009] puts it:

> The bad company problem is one of the most serious problems facing one of the most exciting philosophical approaches to mathematics. The approach in question is neo-Fregean logicism, broadly construed as the project of basing mathematics on abstraction principles, that is, on principles of the form
>
> $$(*)\ \S(\alpha) = \S(\beta) \leftrightarrow \alpha \sim \beta$$

> where the variables α and β range over entities of some sort, and where $\sim$ is an equivalence relation on this sort of entity. The problem is that not every abstraction principle is acceptable: some are downright inconsistent, while others are unacceptable for more subtle reasons.

It is no accident that Linnebo presents the problem of Bad Company as arising for double-barreled abstractionism. Single-barreled abstractionism is free of it.

Ad (2). The author's first published statement of Schema N was in 1984, as minuted at the University of Cambridge Moral Sciences Club on October 23rd of that year.[5] It was repeated in a presentation to the Scots Philosophical Club's annual meeting in November 1984. In June 1987, it was published again in *AR&L*.

The fact that Constructive Logicism afforded derivations of the Dedekind–Peano postulates and also submitted itself to the formal adequacy condition involving Schema N may be belated news for the reader. If so, she is probably in good company. Burgess [2005] (at p. 149) remarked, in a brief survey of the recent history of neo-logicism, that

> a fully rigorous deduction of the Peano postulates in Frege arithmetic was published by Tennant on his own, though unfortunately in a locus, Tennant (1987), where it escaped the attention of most philosophers and logicians who might have been interested.

It is curious how the account of the natural numbers given in *AR&L* could have escaped the attention of any reader of that work. Chapter 20 bore the title 'Constructive Logicism: An Adequate Theory of Number'; and Chapter 25 the title 'On Deriving the Basic Laws of Arithmetic: or, how to Frege–Wright a Dedekind–Peano'. Yet Hart [1989], even though writing for logicians and logically-minded philosophers, in the premier venue for reviews of work in logic and foundations, managed to omit mention altogether of the aims and achievements of those two chapters.

While the eventual publication of the adequacy condition with its Schema N in *AR&L* seems to have escaped attention, the publication six months later of the 'equivalence' N^q in Hale [1987] did not. Hale's N^q (*ibid.*, p. 223), on the construal that has since attracted it attention, is none other than our Schema N.

Ad (7). *On the logic as constructive:* this feature of *AR&L*'s derivations of the Dedekind–Peano postulates was noted by Burgess (*op. cit.*, at pp. 147 and 149). The author is grateful for that acknowledgment.

Hale and Wright were in error to claim (Hale and Wright [2001], p. 433) that the first derivation of the Peano axioms without reliance on excluded middle was Bell [1999]. Bell was unaware of *AR&L* when he wrote his paper (personal

[5] See [1984b]. Thanks are owed to Timothy Smiley for tracking this reference down.

communication). *AR&L*'s treatment of the natural numbers was constructive in the logical sense favored by the anti-realist, who avoids any logical commitment to excluded middle (and its strictly classical equivalents).

On the logic as free: Rumfitt [2003] at p. 209 stressed the importance of *AR&L*'s use of a free logic in avoiding the problem, for Wright's account, of commitment to 'Universal Countability'—that is, to the theorem that every concept has a cardinality.

In the critique of neo-logicism's possible use of a free logic provided by Shapiro and Weir [2000], their final conclusion is invalidly drawn, because of their confined focus on HP-based neo-logicism, and their apparent innocence of the use of free logic in the very different neo-logicist account furnished in *AR&L*.

Ad (8). Heck [1993] on so-called finite Frege arithmetic was there concerned, as *AR&L* had been, to derive the basic laws of arithmetic while incurring ontological commitment only to the natural numbers. To this end he restricted Hume's Principle to predicates with finite extensions. His treatment, however, is still classical. It is therefore natural to conjecture that the system provided in *AR&L* is simply the intuitionistic fragment of Heck's finite Frege arithmetic. Heck was unaware of *AR&L* when he wrote his paper (personal communication).

Rumfitt (*loc. cit.*, pp. 215–216) also recognized that *AR&L* gave an ontologically constructive treatment of numerical commitment:

> ... Tennant has proposed two principles of numerical existence:
>
> 1. there is a number of non-self-identical things (i.e., that zero exists)
>   and
> 2. if the number of Xs exists, and if there is one more Y than there are Xs, then the number of [Y]s exists too (he calls this the Ratchet principle).
>
> He shows how these principles entail the Peano postulates, even though they involve no commitment to the existence of any transfinite cardinal.

In this Part we revisit all the above features of Constructive Logicism in much greater detail. We provide proofs that are as succinct as possible, while still fully formalized. We also prove all instances of Schema N with complete rigor. This was work left to the reader in *AR&L*; but it is worth undertaking here in the necessary formal detail. This will provide full and final vindication of the overall merits of the Constructive Logicist account of arithmetic, compared with its neo-logicist competitors.

Chapter 7

Denoting Numbers

Abstract

Three main systems of notation for canonical numerals are examined: the Dedekind–Peano system based on s and 0; k-place-notational systems (for $k > 1$); and the system of Fregean numerals. The lengths of these numerals are, respectively, linear, logarithmic, and exponential in the size of the numbers they denote. It is stressed that numerals in a place notation can be decidably well-ordered without resorting to a grasp of addition, multiplication, or exponentiation. The Constructive Logicist avoids all the definitional prolixity of the Fregean and gives the pure Peanoan mathematician her due, by taking on her primitive symbols 0 and s as primitives of his own, and laying down rules governing them.

Let us read '$\#x\Phi x$' as 'the number of Φs'. The hash-symbol #—which, as mentioned on p. 32, Boolos called 'octothorpe'—is, as we have already remarked, what logicians call a *variable-binding term-forming operator*.

Consider an identity statement of the form

$$\#x\Phi x = ss \ldots s0 .$$

(In logician's English: 'The number of Φs is identical to the successor of the successor of ...the successor of zero.') Abstractive terms of the form $\#x\Phi x$ can be used in order to apply the natural numbers (also known as 'whole numbers', or 'counting numbers'), in counting the (finite) extension of any sortal, predicative expression Φ whatsoever. This ensures the universal applicability of natural-number talk. The sortal Φ can apply either to concrete or to abstract objects. Examples:

$\#x$(x is a person in this room);
$\#x$(x is a prime number between 2 and 20).

Pure number-theorists, however, talk only about numbers, and very often only about the structure they form, without using them to count any particular finite

The Logic of Number. Neil Tennant, Oxford University Press.
DOI: 10.1093/oso/9780192846679.003.0007

collections. Pure mathematicians can make do with just the so-called Dedekind–Peano numerals

$$0,\ s0,\ ss0,\ sss0, \ldots$$

as the canonical denoting terms in their language. Hence we have the usual choice of notational primitives—0 and s—by means of which one can form these canonical numerals within Dedekind–Peano arithmetic. By $\underline{n}$ we shall mean, as usual, the Dedekind–Peano numeral

$$\underbrace{s \ldots s}_{n \text{ occurrences of } s} 0$$

for the natural number n. Context will determine whether $\underline{n}$ is on occasion taken to be a numeral of another kind, such as one from a system of place notation.

Recall Quine's famous maxim *No entity without identity*. It invites the companion maxim *With identity comes entity*. Consider once again identity statements of the form

$$\#x\Phi x = ss \ldots s0 .$$

On the left we have a numerical abstractive term. On the right we have a numeral. If thinkers can be led to grasp such identity statements, and make judgments with them, then they must, surely, be committed to numbers as existents. Indeed, there is a line of argument along which they can be led, to the realization that numbers are necessary existents.[1]

The line of exposition and argument to be developed here can take in its stride any alternative system of canonical notation for natural numbers. We shall examine the three main alternatives: place notation (to some base greater than 1); Fregean numerals; and the Dedekind–Peano numerals. In discussing these notational systems, we shall be making points about the lengths of their numerals, as a function of the numbers they denote. The length of any symbolic expression such as a formula or a numeral is defined to be the number of primitive symbol occurrences that it contains.

Any system of place notation is based on two or more recognizably distinct ciphers. The binary place notation ('to base 2') uses only two ciphers—conventionally, 0 and 1. The decimal place notation ('to base 10') uses only our familiar ten Arabic ciphers. (Ciphers are often called *digits*.)

In principle, one could exploit a k-based place notation system, for any finite $k > 1$. The system would make use of k distinct ciphers

$$c_1, \ldots, c_k .$$

These would denote, respectively, the members of the initial segment

$$0, \ldots, k-1$$

[1] See [1997a].

of the natural numbers. The latter are what we shall call the sub-base numbers. In such a notation 'to base k', a place-notational sequence of ciphers

$$\gamma_n\gamma_{n-1}\cdots\gamma_0$$

(where γ_n is not the 'zero-cipher' c_1) denotes the number

$$\gamma_n k^n + \gamma_{n-1}k^{n-1} + \ldots + \gamma_1 k + \gamma_0 .$$

This affords a very economical (hyperlogarithmic) reduction in the length of the canonical numeral that stands for the number in question.

It might appear to the reader that any use of these more economical place-notation methods presupposes a grasp of addition, multiplication, and exponentiation. Indeed, we seemed to be relying on such a grasp when we explained what number would be denoted by the k-based place-notational sequence of ciphers $\gamma_n\gamma_{n-1}\cdots\gamma_0$. That number was represented as the foregoing complex sum of products of sub-base numbers γ_i with the result of raising the base k to the appropriate exponent i:

$$\sum_{i=0}^{n} \gamma_i k^i = \gamma_n k^n + \gamma_{n-1}k^{n-1} + \ldots + \gamma_1 k + \gamma_0 .$$

But this appearance is deceptive. The complex sum of products just displayed is really only offered as an algebraic afterthought. It is not essential to conceive of any canonical k-based numeral $\gamma_n\gamma_{n-1}\cdots\gamma_0$ in this way, in order to be able to use such numerals to count collections of things, and to compare the results of different counts. The latter tasks or applications can be carried out perfectly well just on the basis of a grasp of the decidable linear well-ordering of the numerals at one's disposal. Here, the numerals in question are finite sequences of the ciphers $c_1, \ldots, c_k$, subject to the condition that their first members are not the 'zero-cipher' c_1. There is an easy decision method to determine, of any two such sequences, whether one of them precedes the other in the linear well-ordering in question. Here is an informal description of the method:

> Shorter such sequences precede longer ones. If two such sequences are of the same length, then one makes use of the lexicographic ordering $c_1 \prec \ldots \prec c_k$ as follows. One inspects the two sequences from left to right, until one finds the first place at which they have distinct ciphers. Precedence is then given to the sequence whose cipher at that place $\prec$-precedes the cipher at that place in the other sequence.

Finally, in order to count using one's canonical k-based numerals, one needs only an effective (indeed: feasible) method for producing, after each numeral one has produced, the very next numeral in the decidable linear well-ordering at our disposal. That is, for any canonical numeral $\underline{n}$ in hand, one needs to be able, in reasonably short order, to determine the canonical numeral for the successor of n.

With a place-notation (to base k), that is easy to do. Here is an informal description of the algorithm:

> If the canonical k-based numeral for n ends with a cipher other than the 'final' one c_k (like '9' in decimal notation), simply replace that cipher at that occurrence with the one that it immediately $\prec$-precedes in our lexicographic ordering of the ciphers; and be done.
>
> But if that ending cipher (call it γ) *is* an occurrence of the 'final' one c_k (like '9' in the decimal system), then:
>
> > (i) one replaces γ with the 'zero-cipher' c_1;
> > (ii) one takes the sequence σ of ciphers up to but not including the ending cipher γ;
> > (iii) one treats σ as a new numeral (now: one cipher shorter than the numeral $\underline{n}$ with which one began) on which to effect this procedure of 'upping by one'.
>
> If and when one reaches the empty sequence upon repeating this procedure sufficiently many times, and the first cipher in the numeral $\underline{n}$ has been replaced by c_1, put an occurrence of c_2 immediately in front of the result thus far produced; and be done.

This algorithm generalizes to base k the familiar procedure we have of 'counting to base 10'.

That is the full extent of the 'arithmetical ability' that the user of our numerical notation system needs to possess. In particular, no mastery of addition or multiplication, let alone exponentiation, is called for.

With k-based place notation, however, one does have to sacrifice the universal simplicity of

$$\underline{sn} = s\underline{n}\,.$$

We make this sacrifice with our decimal system, so obviously the cost is not all that great. More prized, by far, by those who use decimal numerals is the logarithmic reduction in the length of those numerals as a function of the numbers that they denote. When we approach the foundational issues confronting a logicist account of arithmetic, however, the simplicity of the identity just displayed pays handsome dividends. It simplifies the statement of primitive rules of inference, as well as the construction of proofs that use them.

The Fregean regards the symbol 0 as a definitional abbreviation of the canonical #-term

$$\#x\neg x{=}x\,;$$

and regards $s0$ as a definitional abbreviation, in turn, of $\#x(x = 0)$, i.e.,

$$\#x\, x = \#x\neg x{=}x$$

(yes, it is well-formed). On this definitional route the very next Fregean numeral (for 2) would be $\#x(x = 0 \vee x = 1)$, i.e.,

$$\#x(x = \#x\neg x{=}x \vee x = \#x\, x = \#x\neg x{=}x)$$

(once again: yes, it is well-formed).

The Fregean route indicated here incurs the very opposite of logarithmic reduction—the length of the Fregean canonical numerals grows exponentially as a function of their denotations.

The s-0 notation is actually rather prolix, compared with canonical numerals in systems of place notation. The length of the Dedekind–Peano canonical numeral $\underline{n}$ is $n+1$. Nevertheless, the Dedekind–Peano numerals afford great theoretical simplicity, not least because of a rather subtle fact, remarked on above, and which we expressed metalinguistically as follows:

$$\underline{sn} = s\underline{n}\,.$$

This says that the numeral for the successor of n is obtained by prefixing an occurrence of the successor function symbol s to the numeral $\underline{n}$.

The Constructive Logicist wisely avoids the Fregean's definitional prolixity. In the pure-mathematical fragment of $(0, s)$-arithmetic, from which the binary functions of addition, multiplication, and exponentiation are absent, the only available canonical numerals are 'repeated successors of 0', i.e., terms of the form $s \ldots s0$. So the Constructive Logicist gives the pure Peanoan mathematician her due, by taking on her primitive symbols 0 and s as primitives of his own, and laying down rules governing them. The Constructive Logicist's canonical numerals

$$0, s0, ss0, \ldots ,$$

do not require any exponentially exploding definitional unfolding.

In this regard the Constructive Logicist is quite unlike the Fregean logicist, who is committed to the much more cumbrous definitional route just indicated, in order to generate his 'canonical numerals' for the objects that pure mathematicians talk about when they do pure arithmetic. And the Constructive Logicist acknowledges that of course the length of his canonical numeral $\underline{n}$ is $n+1$. He would remind any k-placer critic, however, that his (the Constructive Logicist's) account will go through with any k-based place notation (as an alternative to the Dedekind–Peano notation), provided only that it furnishes an effective (and feasible) method for determining the canonical k-based numeral for the successor of n from the canonical k-based numeral for n. And this, as made clear by the second algorithm described above, is indeed the case.

We shall have occasion to talk about intratheoretic interdeducibilities establishing the equivalence, according to some theory Θ, of two sentences φ and ψ. Instead of writing both

$$\Theta, \varphi \vdash \psi$$

and

$$\Theta, \psi \vdash \varphi$$

for this purpose, we shall write, more compactly,

$$\varphi \dashv_{\Theta} \vdash \psi \, ;$$

and when the theory Θ is understood from the context we shall simply write

$$\varphi \dashv\vdash \psi \, .$$

Often, of course, Θ will be the null theory, and we will accordingly be dealing with straightforwardly logical interdeducibilities.

We shall be investigating certain such interdeducibilities in a formal first-order language with identity, in which one has (as usual) a countably infinite supply of variables, conventionally listed as $x_0, x_1, x_2, \ldots$. The use here of numerical subscripts is for our metalinguistic convenience only. If we were to stick to $x, y, z, \ldots$, we would soon run out of distinguishable symbols. By using variables of the form x_k in formal sentences of the object language, we are not imputing to the users of the object language any necessary grasp (on account of the subscripts) of the ω-progression $0, 1, 2, \ldots$. We are, however, concerned to work out what expressive resources the object language would need to contain, and what inferential norms would have to govern their use, in order to credit the users with a grasp of the natural numbers.

Chapter 8

Exact Numerosity

Abstract

Numerosity statements are statements of the form 'There are exactly n Φs', where the number-word in place of n is understood adjectivally in English. A numerosity statement of this form does not commit one to the existence of the natural number n, or of any numbers at all. The question is how best to regiment these numerosity statements in first-order logical notation. Four different methods for doing so are presented. Each method involves so defining a regimenting formal sentence that, given any natural number n, one can effectively determine which formal sentence at first order regiments the numerosity statement, in English, that there are exactly n Φs. The four different regimentations, which are abbreviated as $\nabla_n x\Phi(x)$, $\Diamond_n x\Phi(x)$, $\mho_n x\Phi(x)$, and $\heartsuit_n x\Phi(x)$, are interdeducible.

We cease now to consider any use (by speakers of the language under study) of the Peano primitive expressions (0 and s). We imagine them deprived also of the variable-binding term-forming operator #. They cannot speak of the number of Φs. What is more, they have no digits either; so they have no place-notation for numbers. They have no numerals at all—no singular terms, simple or complex, whose referents would be numbers. We shall confine ourselves to consideration of a first-order language with identity, devoid of any expressions that are intended to be used in connection with numbers. Its speakers can be assumed to be innocent of any such (abstract) objects as numbers. They need not, however, be innocent of the *numerosities* of any of the various primitive or complex predicates in their language, should these predicates happen to be satisfied by at most finitely many objects.[1] This is because they have the identity predicate $=$, and the usual logical operators $\neg$, $\wedge$, $\vee$, $\rightarrow$, $\exists$, and $\forall$. And we shall see how these logical resources suffice for the formulation of statements of numerosity, even in the absence of any means for referring to numbers.

[1]The numerosities of which we speak here are the straightforward conventional ones, giving the sizes of finite collections. We are not using 'numerosity' in the recent and different technical sense introduced by Benci and Di Nasso [2003].

The Logic of Number. Neil Tennant, Oxford University Press. © Neil Tennant 2022.
DOI: 10.1093/oso/9780192846679.003.0008

We set out to explain here how in a 'number-innocent' first-order language with identity one can capture, formally, the informal thoughts (expressed in 'logician's English')

> There are no Φs.
>
> There is exactly one Φ.
>
> There are exactly two Φs.
>
> There are exactly three Φs.
>
> ⋮
>
> There are exactly n Φs.
>
> ⋮

Let us consider a useful analogy with the theory of computable functions. The notion of computable function, or algorithm, is one of which we have a firm pre-theoretical grasp. The challenge several decades ago was to explicate this notion by means of a suitably precise formal definition of a class of functions taking natural numbers as inputs, and producing natural numbers as outputs. We are now well aware of the various different explications or formal definitions that were offered during the 1930s by illustrious foundationalists such as Turing, Gödel, Kleene, Church, Post and others. Details need not detain us. The point is: their various definitions provably define the same class of functions. This is taken as strong evidence for the robust and stable character of the informal notion of computable function. It lends great plausibility to what is now known as the Turing–Church Thesis: that the computable functions on the natural numbers are exactly those defined in any of these various provably equivalent ways.

Taking a leaf out of that historical chapter, let us turn now to the notion of (finite) numerosity. This will be our analog of computable function—the informal, pre-theoretical notion standing in need of precise explication. And let us now address the question

> How is one to capture, formally, the informal thoughts (expressed in 'logician's English') of the form 'There are exactly n Φs'?

The natural answer will be to employ formal resources that are no stronger than what is needed for the job, and which will make absolutely precise the various thoughts just expressed. We submit that these formal resources are no more and no less than the language of first-order logic with identity as a logical primitive (and what it takes to express Φ itself).

It is well known that even in this austere language, logical equivalence classes of formal sentences can consist of infinitely many members. So it is fully to be expected that if we identify one way—a symbolic definiens $\exists_n x\Phi x$—to capture the thought that there are exactly n Φs, there will be potentially infinitely many other distinct formal sentences that are logically equivalent to it. It is reasonable to assume, however, that the infinitude of these alternative means of formal expression (capturing the same truth-conditions of the numerosity thought involved) will be owed to there being no upper limit (as a function of n) to the length of whatever formal sentence is being proposed as capturing the thought that there are exactly n Φs. Indeed, one optimistic response to this 'problem of plethora' would be to suggest that there might be canonically self-indicating *definientia* (in the formal language) for the *definiendum*-thought in question. Perhaps—so this optimist would suggest—there are a privileged few ways of formalizing the English sentence-form 'There are exactly n Φs', whose credentials will be impeccable.

The analogy with computable functions, of course, can be adduced once again to support this optimistic line of thinking. Compared with the in-principle infinitude of formal definitions of classes of functions coinciding with the class of computable functions, the privileged few are the famous ones due to Turing (i.e., Turing-machine computable functions), Gödel (general recursive functions), Kleene (functions stipulated by his finite equational systems), Church (functions defined in his λ-calculus), and Post (functions defined by his production systems). They are canonically self-indicating; their credentials are impeccable.

Heartened by the plausibility of the foregoing analogy, we turn now to the task of formally defining certain infinite sequences of sentence-forms

$$\phi_0 \, , \, \phi_1 \, , \, \phi_2 \, , \, \ldots \, , \, \phi_n \, , \, \ldots$$

in the formal first-order object language with identity plus whatever extra-logical expressions are involved in the formula that regiments '... is a Φ', that are intended to capture, respectively, the truth-conditions of the thoughts

There are no Φs.

There is exactly one Φ.

There are exactly two Φs.

There are exactly three Φs.

⋮

There are exactly n Φs.

⋮

We say 'infinite sequences' in the plural, since we do not wish to give the impression that there is any one particular form of definition specifying a unique infinite sequence of sentences of the object language that distinguishes itself from all competitors by 'getting the respective numerosities right'. The various numerosities can be 'got right' in several different ways—just as the computable functions can be captured by means of several different formal representations (Turing machines, general recursive functions, etc.).

Here we shall consider, altogether, four different ways of capturing the thought that there are exactly n Φs. They will be distinguished by the four special symbols

∇, $\Diamond$, $\heartsuit$, and $\mho$, with subscript n attached. Their definitions follow. These definitions enable one effectively to determine, given any number n, what the actual sentences are that are respectively abbreviated as $\nabla_n x\Phi x$, $\Diamond_n x\Phi x$, $\heartsuit_n x\Phi x$, and $\mho_n x\Phi x$.

Definition 4 ($\nabla_n x\Phi x$).
Basis clause:

$$\nabla_0 x\Phi x \ \equiv_{df} \ \neg\exists x\Phi x\,.$$

Inductive clause:

$$\nabla_{sn} x\Phi x \ \equiv_{df} \ \exists x_{sn}(\Phi x_{sn} \wedge \underline{\nabla_n x(\Phi x \wedge x \neq x_{sn})})\,.$$

The formal sentence $\nabla_n x\Phi x$ says 'There are exactly n Φs'.[2]

Definition 5 ($\Diamond_n x\Phi x$).
Basis clause:

$$\Diamond_0 x\Phi x \ \equiv_{df} \ \forall x\neg\Phi x\,.$$

Inductive clause:

$$\Diamond_{sn} x\Phi x \ \equiv_{df} \ \neg\forall x\neg\Phi x \wedge \forall x_{sn}(\Phi x_{sn} \rightarrow \underline{\Diamond_n x(\Phi x \wedge x \neq x_{sn})})\,.$$

Comment. Having the prefix '$\neg\forall x\neg\Phi x \wedge \ldots$' in the definiens might be seen as a fly in the ointment. But we are forced to include it; for otherwise we would be defining $\Diamond_{sn} x\Phi x$ as

$$\forall x_{sn}(\Phi x_{sn} \rightarrow \Diamond_n x(\Phi x \wedge x \neq x_{sn}))\,.$$

Unfortunately this displayed sentence—but not the definiendum $\Diamond_{sn} x\Phi x$, on its intended construal—is true if there are no Φs.

The next definition deals with the author's chosen style of numerosity statements in *AR&L*.

Definition 6 ($\heartsuit_n x\Phi x$).
Basis clause:

$$\heartsuit_0 x\Phi x \ \equiv_{df} \ \neg\exists x\Phi x\,.$$

Inductive clause:

For $k > 0$, we shall use the abbreviation $\heartsuit_k x\Phi x$ for the sentence

$$\exists x_1 \ldots \exists x_k \left(\bigwedge_{1 \le i < j \le k} x_i \neq x_j \ \wedge \forall x \left(\Phi x \leftrightarrow \bigvee_{1 \le i \le k} x = x_i \right) \right)\,.$$

[2] This definition is due to Quine [1972], §39. It is also used by Parsons [1965].

Comment. This is not an inductive definition. One would employ the method of inductive definition, however, to pin down exactly what the more deeply embedded multiple conjunctions and disjunctions are. Here we rely on their being 'obvious' to the reader.

Our fourth and final form of definition is of the $\mho$-sequence of numerosity statements in the object language. It is given in Bigelow [1988], where it is attributed on p. 49 to David Lewis. The guiding idea is simple:

'There are exactly 0 Φs' is once again regimented as $\neg\exists y\Phi y$.

'There is exactly 1 Φ' is regimented as $\exists x\forall y(y{=}x \leftrightarrow \Phi y)$.

To say 'There are exactly n Φs' (for $n{\geq}2$) is to say that there are at least n Φs and that it is not the case that there are at least sn Φs.

The clever part comes in saying what it is for there to be at least n Φs:

$$\forall x_1 \ldots \forall x_{n-1}\exists y\left(\bigwedge_{i=1}^{n-1} y{\neq}x_i \wedge \Phi y\right).$$

So, finally, we have

Definition 7 ($\mho_n x\Phi x$).
$\mho_0 xFx$ is defined to be the sentence $\neg\exists y\Phi y$.
$\mho_1 xFx$ is defined to be the sentence $\exists x\forall y(y{=}x \leftrightarrow \Phi y)$.
For $n \geq 2$, $\mho_n xFx$ is defined to be the sentence

$$\forall x_1 \ldots \forall x_{n-1}\exists y\left(\bigwedge_{i=1}^{n-1} y{\neq}x_i \wedge \Phi y\right) \wedge \neg\forall x_1 \ldots \forall x_n\exists y\left(\bigwedge_{i=1}^{n} y{\neq}x_i \wedge \Phi y\right).$$

For pleasant diversion, consider how to spell out that there are exactly twenty turtles[3] in this box, using $\heartsuit_{20}x\Phi x$ as one's chosen formalization. Here we go:

[3] We mean the special confection of caramel and pecans inside a chocolate coating, not the leatherback or any similar species.

$$\exists x_1 \exists x_2 \exists x_3 \exists x_4 \exists x_5 \exists x_6 \exists x_7 \exists x_8 \exists x_9 \exists x_{10} \exists x_{11} \exists x_{12} \exists x_{13} \exists x_{14} \exists x_{15} \exists x_{16} \exists x_{17} \exists x_{18} \exists x_{19} \exists x_{20}$$

$$((x_1 \neq x_2 \wedge x_1 \neq x_3 \wedge x_1 \neq x_4 \wedge x_1 \neq x_5 \wedge x_1 \neq x_6 \wedge x_1 \neq x_7 \wedge x_1 \neq x_8 \wedge x_1 \neq x_9 \wedge x_1 \neq x_{10} \wedge x_1 \neq x_{11}$$

$$\wedge x_1 \neq x_{12} \wedge x_1 \neq x_{13} \wedge x_1 \neq x_{14} \wedge x_1 \neq x_{15} \wedge x_1 \neq x_{16} \wedge x_1 \neq x_{17} \wedge x_1 \neq x_{18} \wedge x_1 \neq x_{19} \wedge x_1 \neq x_{20} \wedge$$

$$\wedge x_2 \neq x_3 \wedge x_2 \neq x_4 \wedge x_2 \neq x_5 \wedge x_2 \neq x_6 \wedge x_2 \neq x_7 \wedge x_2 \neq x_8 \wedge x_2 \neq x_9 \wedge x_2 \neq x_{10} \wedge x_2 \neq x_{11}$$

$$\wedge x_2 \neq x_{12} \wedge x_2 \neq x_{13} \wedge x_2 \neq x_{14} \wedge x_2 \neq x_{15} \wedge x_2 \neq x_{16} \wedge x_2 \neq x_{17} \wedge x_2 \neq x_{18} \wedge x_2 \neq x_{19} \wedge x_2 \neq x_{20} \wedge$$

$$x_3 \neq x_4 \wedge x_3 \neq x_5 \wedge x_3 \neq x_6 \wedge x_3 \neq x_7 \wedge x_3 \neq x_8 \wedge x_3 \neq x_9 \wedge x_3 \neq x_{10} \wedge x_3 \neq x_{11}$$

$$\wedge x_3 \neq x_{12} \wedge x_3 \neq x_{13} \wedge x_3 \neq x_{14} \wedge x_3 \neq x_{15} \wedge x_3 \neq x_{16} \wedge x_3 \neq x_{17} \wedge x_3 \neq x_{18} \wedge x_3 \neq x_{19} \wedge x_3 \neq x_{20} \wedge$$

$$x_4 \neq x_5 \wedge x_4 \neq x_6 \wedge x_4 \neq x_7 \wedge x_4 \neq x_8 \wedge x_4 \neq x_9 \wedge x_4 \neq x_{10} \wedge x_4 \neq x_{11}$$

$$\wedge x_4 \neq x_{12} \wedge x_4 \neq x_{13} \wedge x_4 \neq x_{14} \wedge x_4 \neq x_{15} \wedge x_4 \neq x_{16} \wedge x_4 \neq x_{17} \wedge x_4 \neq x_{18} \wedge x_4 \neq x_{19} \wedge x_4 \neq x_{20} \wedge$$

$$x_5 \neq x_6 \wedge x_5 \neq x_7 \wedge x_5 \neq x_8 \wedge x_5 \neq x_9 \wedge x_5 \neq x_{10} \wedge x_5 \neq x_{11}$$

$$\wedge x_5 \neq x_{12} \wedge x_5 \neq x_{13} \wedge x_5 \neq x_{14} \wedge x_5 \neq x_{15} \wedge x_5 \neq x_{16} \wedge x_5 \neq x_{17} \wedge x_5 \neq x_{18} \wedge x_5 \neq x_{19} \wedge x_5 \neq x_{20} \wedge$$

$$x_6 \neq x_7 \wedge x_6 \neq x_8 \wedge x_6 \neq x_9 \wedge x_6 \neq x_{10} \wedge x_6 \neq x_{11}$$

$$\wedge x_6 \neq x_{12} \wedge x_6 \neq x_{13} \wedge x_6 \neq x_{14} \wedge x_6 \neq x_{15} \wedge x_6 \neq x_{16} \wedge x_6 \neq x_{17} \wedge x_6 \neq x_{18} \wedge x_6 \neq x_{19} \wedge x_6 \neq x_{20} \wedge$$

$$x_7 \neq x_8 \wedge x_7 \neq x_9 \wedge x_7 \neq x_{10} \wedge x_7 \neq x_{11}$$

$$\wedge x_7 \neq x_{12} \wedge x_7 \neq x_{13} \wedge x_7 \neq x_{14} \wedge x_7 \neq x_{15} \wedge x_7 \neq x_{16} \wedge x_7 \neq x_{17} \wedge x_7 \neq x_{18} \wedge x_7 \neq x_{19} \wedge x_7 \neq x_{20} \wedge$$

$$x_8 \neq x_9 \wedge x_8 \neq x_{10} \wedge x_8 \neq x_{11}$$

$$\wedge x_8 \neq x_{12} \wedge x_8 \neq x_{13} \wedge x_8 \neq x_{14} \wedge x_8 \neq x_{15} \wedge x_8 \neq x_{16} \wedge x_8 \neq x_{17} \wedge x_8 \neq x_{18} \wedge x_8 \neq x_{19} \wedge x_8 \neq x_{20} \wedge$$

$$x_9 \neq x_{10} \wedge x_9 \neq x_{11}$$

$$\wedge x_9 \neq x_{12} \wedge x_9 \neq x_{13} \wedge x_9 \neq x_{14} \wedge x_9 \neq x_{15} \wedge x_9 \neq x_{16} \wedge x_9 \neq x_{17} \wedge x_9 \neq x_{18} \wedge x_9 \neq x_{19} \wedge x_9 \neq x_{20} \wedge$$

$$x_{10} \neq x_{11}$$

$$\wedge x_{10} \neq x_{12} \wedge x_{10} \neq x_{13} \wedge x_{10} \neq x_{14} \wedge x_{10} \neq x_{15} \wedge x_{10} \neq x_{16} \wedge x_{10} \neq x_{17} \wedge x_{10} \neq x_{18} \wedge x_{10} \neq x_{19} \wedge x_{10} \neq x_{20} \wedge$$

$$x_{11} \neq x_{12} \wedge x_{11} \neq x_{13} \wedge x_{11} \neq x_{14} \wedge x_{11} \neq x_{15} \wedge x_{11} \neq x_{16} \wedge x_{11} \neq x_{17} \wedge x_{11} \neq x_{18} \wedge x_{11} \neq x_{19} \wedge x_{11} \neq x_{20} \wedge$$

$$x_{12} \neq x_{13} \wedge x_{12} \neq x_{14} \wedge x_{12} \neq x_{15} \wedge x_{12} \neq x_{16} \wedge x_{12} \neq x_{17} \wedge x_{12} \neq x_{18} \wedge x_{12} \neq x_{19} \wedge x_{12} \neq x_{20} \wedge$$

$$x_{13} \neq x_{14} \wedge x_{13} \neq x_{15} \wedge x_{13} \neq x_{16} \wedge x_{13} \neq x_{17} \wedge x_{13} \neq x_{18} \wedge x_{13} \neq x_{19} \wedge x_{13} \neq x_{20} \wedge$$

$$x_{14} \neq x_{15} \wedge x_{14} \neq x_{16} \wedge x_{14} \neq x_{17} \wedge x_{14} \neq x_{18} \wedge x_{14} \neq x_{19} \wedge x_{14} \neq x_{20} \wedge$$

$$x_{15} \neq x_{16} \wedge x_{15} \neq x_{17} \wedge x_{15} \neq x_{18} \wedge x_{15} \neq x_{19} \wedge x_{15} \neq x_{20} \wedge$$

$$x_{16} \neq x_{17} \wedge x_{16} \neq x_{18} \wedge x_{16} \neq x_{19} \wedge x_{16} \neq x_{20} \wedge$$

$$x_{17} \neq x_{18} \wedge x_{17} \neq x_{19} \wedge x_{17} \neq x_{20} \wedge$$

$$x_{18} \neq x_{19} \wedge x_{18} \neq x_{20} \wedge$$

$$x_{19} \neq x_{20}) \wedge$$

$$\forall y(y \text{ is a turtle in this box}$$

$$\leftrightarrow$$

$$(y = x_1 \vee y = x_2 \vee y = x_3 \vee y = x_4 \vee y = x_5 \vee y = x_6 \vee y = x_7 \vee y = x_8 \vee y = x_9 \vee y = x_{10} \vee$$

$$y = x_{11} \vee y = x_{12} \vee y = x_{13} \vee y = x_{14} \vee y = x_{15} \vee y = x_{16} \vee y = x_{17} \vee y = x_{18} \vee y = x_{19} \vee y = x_{20})))$$

—or, for those who have been enlightened by Schema N (*q.v.*):

$$\#x(x \text{ is a turtle in this box}) = ssssssssssssssssssss0\,.$$

The reader is reminded that the numerical subscripts on the variables do not refer to numbers, in this 'number innocent' language. Had we wished, we could have used the first twenty letters of the alphabet in place of $x_1, \ldots, x_{20}$ respectively; or we could have used prime marks, as in

$$x', x'', x''', \ldots, x''''''''''''''''''''\,.$$

It is no wonder that natural languages have evolved with numerical expressions ('number words', such as *twenty*) in adjectival position, corresponding to the subscripted 'n's in our abbreviated forms for these otherwise unmanageably long sentences (such as $\nabla_n x\Phi x$, $\Diamond_n x\Phi x$, $\heartsuit_n x\Phi x$, and $\mho_n x\Phi x$) in a 'number innocent' language.

A formal abbreviation like $\nabla_k x\Phi x$ is of a longer formal sentence regimenting 'There are exactly k Φs'. The reader is reminded that the (formal) object language, at this stage, has no numerical expressions such as 0 and s, and certainly does not have the numerical abstraction operator #. These expressions will enter the object language only later, as we advance, on behalf of its speakers, to the formulation of Schema N. So the *ur*-object language with which we are currently dealing is based on the standard logical operators $\neg, \wedge, \vee, \rightarrow, \exists, \forall$ and $=$, plus primitive names, function signs and predicates for mundane discourse about medium-sized dry goods. Apples and baskets, say, and the relation of *being in*.

The various 'numerically exact quantifiers' ∇_k are not primitive logical operators in the object language. They are instead contextually defined. It is the standard existential quantifier that is doing the donkey-work in the definition of numerosity statements in the ∇-sequence.

With the definition of the $\Diamond$-sequence, a major part of that burden was shifted to the universal quantifier. A useful feature of the definitions of both the ∇-sequence and the $\Diamond$-sequence is that they are given inductively, calling for the embedding of a ∇_k- [resp., $\Diamond_k$-]sentence within the succeeding ∇_{sk}- [resp., $\Diamond_{sk}$-]sentence.

The object-linguistic sentence whose abbreviation is $\nabla_k x\Phi x$ is, to be sure, to capture the thought that there are exactly k Φs. But we stress again: the presumption that we grasp the natural numbers is confined to the metalevel. It does not (yet) amount to an imputation of such grasp to any speaker of the object language, even if that speaker is a 'logical saint' as far as knowledge of deducibility in the object language is concerned. The speaker of the object language will simply be able to use, and logically manipulate, those sentences of his language whose abbreviations we denote as $\nabla_k x\Phi x$, for various natural numbers k—numbers to which *we* have intellectual access, but which we are refraining (for the time being) from regarding as intellectually accessible by the speaker of the object language. Put bluntly: that speaker can understand that there are exactly seventeen apples in the basket, without yet being intellectually acquainted with the number 17.

Since we users of the *meta*language grasp the natural numbers, we were able to provide the foregoing inductive definitions of the ∇- and $\Diamond$-progressions of numerically exact quantifications in the object language. All we had to do was provide a basis clause for the zero-th case of each, and then give an inductive clause for the sn-th case, on the inductive assumption that we already have a definition of the n-th case. Of course, in furnishing such an inductive definition on the natural numbers, *we* have to grasp the natural numbers; but we are speakers of the *meta*language, so this much is dialectically safe.

The inductive clause for the ∇-sequence tells us that there are exactly sn Φs just in case some Φ is such that there are exactly n Φs distinct from it. Of course, if this existential claim is true, then there will be sn distinct witnesses to its truth. And this consideration iterates. So one attains the important insight that the order in which one might choose among available witnesses for the ever-deeply nested existentials within it is absolutely immaterial to the truth of the claim $\nabla_{sn}x\Phi x$. It follows that if that truth is eventually to be represented by reference to some abstract object determined by the Φs, then that object cannot be sensitive to any ordering of the Φs. Getting ahead of ourselves: we shall (eventually) be concerned only with cardinal numbers, not with ordinals.

Note that the thrust of this insight is orthogonal to any contrast (such as has been stressed by the likes of Benacerraf [1965], Lucas [2000], and Hale [2016]) between 'transitive' and 'intransitive' counting. This orthogonality is underscored even further when we examine the inductive definition of the $\diamondsuit$-sequence

$$\diamondsuit_0 x\Phi x\,,\ \diamondsuit_1 x\Phi x\,,\ \diamondsuit_2 x\Phi x\,,\ \ldots,\diamondsuit_k x\Phi x\,,\ \ldots\ .$$

In the definition of the various $\diamondsuit_k$, it is the universal quantifier that plays the important 'prefixing' role called for in the inductive clause that was played by the existential quantifier in the case of the various ∇_k. The ∇_k and $\diamondsuit_k$ forms will be shown[4] to be logically equivalent in the object language—a status that can be appreciated by the object-linguistic logical saint who is as yet unapprised of the concept of number. Indeed, the more conventional definition of 'There are exactly k Φs' given by the $\heartsuit$-sequence, and a much less conventional one given by the ℧-sequence complete a 'square circle' of equivalent definitions of exact numerosity. (See p. 90.) All these equivalences are accessible to the (number-innocent) logical saint just mentioned.

The formal sentence $\heartsuit_k x\Phi x$ can be read along these lines: 'there are things $x_1, \ldots, x_k$ that are pairwise distinct and are exactly the Φs'. In order to learn (from the formal statement alone) how many Φs there are (on this account) one would, in effect, have to count the purposely distinct variables $x_1, \ldots, x_k$. Remember that the last variable's having the subscript k is not a quick and easy method available to the user of the object language. For she could just as well have been provided (for the case $k = 3$, say) with the formal sentence

$$\exists y\exists z\exists w(y\neq z \wedge y\neq w \wedge z\neq w\ \wedge \forall x(\Phi x \leftrightarrow (x=y \wedge x=z \wedge x=w)))\,.$$

Since y, z and w have no numerical subscripts, and in particular since w does not have the telltale subscript 3, merely looking at the last of these three variables (namely, w) will not be enough to work out how many distinct Φs this sentence says there are. Instead, the user of the object language will now have to count the variables y, z and w and arrive at the tally of 3.

[4]See Metatheorem 4 on p. 150 in Chapter 13, which the reader can treat as a formal appendix to this Part, and skip without philosophical loss, if the technical work that it contains is not their cup of tea.

Alternatively, she could resort to a different strategy: she could say something like 'there are variables α_1, α_2 and α_3, all pairwise distinct, that are bound by initial existential quantifiers in a true sentence of the object language of such-and-such form …'. She would recover her numerical subscripts alright; but would still be vulnerable to the objection that what she has just said is equivalent to 'there are variables α, β and γ, all pairwise distinct, that are bound by initial existential quantifiers in a true sentence of the object language of such-and-such form …'. If she then tried to repeat the contemplated alternative strategy on this last circumlocution, she would be launched on a vicious regress.

There is a philosophically pleasing aspect, by contrast, to our first (and preferred) way of regimenting 'There are exactly k Φs', i.e., as $\nabla_k x\Phi x$. The inductive clause for the ∇-sequence captures an essential insight, to wit: there are exactly sn Φs just in case there is a Φ (it does not matter which one is picked—call it x) such that there are exactly n Φs other than x. Defining the numerosity quantifiers inductively in this way enables one to give the most elegant and canonical proofs possible of each instance of Schema N, as we shall presently see. Moreover, since the ∇-sequence was also the one chosen in Wright [1999], we have a fair standard against which to judge the difference between Constructive Logicism and HP-based neo-logicism in this regard.

We have at least four different ways to state exact numerosity:

$$\nabla_0\,,\ \nabla_1\,,\ \nabla_2\,,\ \ldots\ ,\ \nabla_n\,,\ \ldots$$

$$\Diamond_0\,,\ \Diamond_1\,,\ \Diamond_2\,,\ \ldots\ ,\ \Diamond_n\,,\ \ldots$$

$$\mho_0\,,\ \mho_1\,,\ \mho_2\,,\ \ldots\ ,\ \mho_n\,,\ \ldots$$

$$\heartsuit_0\,,\ \heartsuit_1\,,\ \heartsuit_2\,,\ \ldots\ ,\ \heartsuit_n\,,\ \ldots$$

Here, by way of illustration, are the respective four different ways to regiment

'There are exactly two Φs':

$$\begin{array}{ll}
\nabla_2 x\Phi x & \exists z(\Phi z\wedge\exists y((\Phi y\wedge y\neq z)\wedge\neg\exists x((\Phi x\wedge x\neq z)\wedge x\neq y))\,; \\
\Diamond_2 x\Phi x & \neg\forall x\neg x\Phi x\wedge\forall z(\Phi z\rightarrow(\neg\forall w\neg(\Phi w\wedge w\neq z)\wedge\forall y((\Phi y\wedge y\neq z)\rightarrow \\
 & \qquad\qquad \forall x\neg((\Phi x\wedge x\neq z)\wedge x\neq y))))\,; \\
\mho_2 x\Phi x & \forall y\exists x(x\neq y\wedge\Phi x)\wedge\neg\forall y\forall z\exists x((x\neq y\wedge x\neq z)\wedge\Phi x)\,; \\
\heartsuit_2 x\Phi x & \exists y\exists z(y\neq z\wedge\forall x(\Phi x\leftrightarrow(x=y\vee x=z)))\,.
\end{array}$$

These exact numerosity statements (for the case $n = 2$) are logically equivalent. Indeed, for every n, the four statements (of types ∇, $\Diamond$, $\heartsuit$, $\mho$) of n-foldness are logically equivalent. The arrows here represent logical implications:

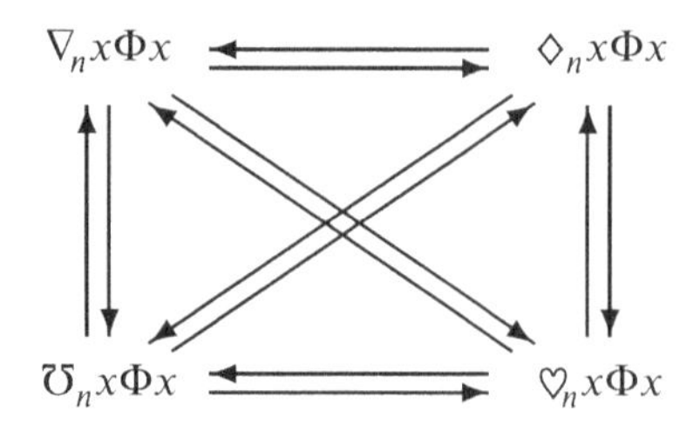

Moreover, there is an effective method for finding, given any two of them, the requisite proofs in each direction. This is because we are dealing with monadic first-order logic with identity and a single extralogical 'predicate' Φ. So, even if we restrict ourselves to (classical) core proofs, we have an effective method for finding the needed proofs to establish equivalence.[5] This means that the logical abilities needed are those of the 'logical paragon' rather than the 'logical saint'. See [2012b] for further explanation of the notion of logical *paragon*, which was summarized as an "ideally rational agent who never breaks the rules, and always 'gets its computations right'." Logical saints can do more than paragons, because they 'get right' the answers to non-effectively decidable problems, and the values of non-computable functions.

Metatheorem 2. *For all n, the statements $\nabla_n xFx$, $\Diamond_n xFx$, $\heartsuit_n xFx$ and $\mho_n xFx$ are interdeducible in the object language.*

Proof. Excessively tedious. See Metatheorem 4 on p. 150 for proof of the equivalence of $\nabla_n xFx$ with $\Diamond_n xFx$. □

Remember, the proof of this metatheorem is to be given in the *meta*language, and is 'general over *n*'. So it needs to use mathematical induction at the metalevel. And one is working in a metalinguistic fragment that is not monadic, hence is undecidable.

But (as already observed) for any particular value (say, *k*) of *n*, the speaker of the object language who is completely innocent of any notion of number can establish the logical equivalence of $\nabla_k xFx$, $\Diamond_k xFx$, $\heartsuit_k xFx$ and $\mho_k xFx$; and indeed can do so by applying an effective method to find the required proofs!—because the speaker is working in the monadic fragment of first-order logic with identity, which is decidable.

[5] It is well known that Intuitionistic Logic with just two monadic predicates is undecidable. But, with only one monadic predicate, it is decidable. So too, as a consequence, is Core Logic with just one monadic predicate. Cautionary note: the author has not yet established whether any of the proofs in question here requires the use of a strictly classical negation rule.

We, using the metalanguage, have certainly needed to grasp the natural numbers in order to understand the definitions of the various sequences of exact numerosity statements in the object language; but ...

> *nothing in a numerosity claim commits one to the existence of any natural numbers*

—unless it is about how many numbers of a certain kind there are. An example of this would be 'there are exactly two odd prime numbers less than 7'.

Recall that the definiendum

$$\nabla_1 xFx$$

turned out to have the definiens

$$\exists x_1(Fx_1 \wedge \neg\exists x(Fx \wedge x \neq x_1)).$$

This definiens, to be sure, contains a variable that we happen to have written as x_1. We reiterate an important point: that use of the numeral '1' as a subscript to a variable does not in any way imply that the speaker of the object language, in using the latter definiens as a sentence of his language, enjoys any conceptual or theoretical grasp of the natural numbers, or of the number 1 in particular. For the definiens could just as well have been written as

$$\exists y(Fy \wedge \neg\exists x(Fx \wedge x \neq y)).$$

The thought expressed by these two sentences is invariant under this relabeling of bound variables. The thought in question is that some F is such that no other thing is F. There is no reference here to the natural number 1. Nor is it 'quantified over'.[6]

The natural number 1 *is*, however, lurking in the shadows of Plato's cave. It will be drawn into the intellectual spotlight if and when (but only if and when) the thinker using the object language embraces the following interdeducibility (within the logic governing an appropriate extension of his language by means of the new primitive symbols 0, s and # appearing in the identity statement on the left):

$$\#x\Phi x = s0 \dashv\vdash \exists y(\Phi y \wedge \neg\exists x(\Phi x \wedge x \neq y)).$$

In English: the number of Φs is the successor of 0 (i.e., 1) if and only if some Φ is such that no Φ is distinct from it—i.e., if and only if there is exactly one Φ.

It is here that we see what further expressive resources speakers of the (first-order) object langage would need to possess in order to demonstrate an adequate grasp of number—either of particular numbers such as 1, or of numbers in general. (We are talking here, of course, about natural numbers—cardinalities of finite

[6] Unless, of course, F itself involves such quantification. But that is not generally the case; and that is what is important for the point being made here.

collections.) They would need to be able to use the variable-binding number-abstraction operator #, operating on open formulae Φx with x free, to produce singular terms $\#x\Phi x$ denoting numbers. Since any sortal predicate can take the place of Φ, this reveals the absolutely unlimited applicability of the notion of natural number: numbering can involve sortal predicates that hold of abstract objects, just as well as ones that hold of concrete objects.

The numbers would moreover also need to be identifiable in the way that pure mathematicians identify them when they are talking only about the numbers—that is, as n-fold successors of the special number 0. For pure mathematicians take themselves to be giving us the 'pure' truths about number. To that end, they use the primitive extralogical expressions 0 and s (in Dedekind–Peano arithmetic, for example).[7]

[7] Well, at any rate, mathematical logicians since Dedekind and Peano have used 0 and s as their primitives for the formation of canonical designations (numerals) denoting natural numbers. Ordinary mathematicians, of course, have simply helped themselves to the sophisticated tradition, established several centuries ago, of decimal place-notation. On these notational matters, see the discussion in Chapter 7.

Chapter 9

The Adequacy Condition Involving Schema N

Abstract

Schema N states that the two main ways of answering the question 'How many Φs are there?' (when there are only finitely many of them) are equivalent. Any account of the natural numbers needs to establish this equivalence. One way to answer the 'how many?' question is to say that there are exactly n Φs. That is, one makes a numerosity statement, or, formally, asserts one of its regimentations, of the kind explained in Chapter 8. The other way of answering the question is to say that the number of Φs is identical to the number n. Here, 'the number n' will be replaced by a numeral in whatever system of canonical notation one has chosen; and the singular term 'the number of Φs' will be regimented as the number-abstractive term $\#x\Phi(x)$. Suppose one has chosen the ∇-sequence of (regimentations of) numerosity statements. Suppose further that one has chosen the Dedekind–Peano system of canonical numerals. (In this system the numeral $\underline{n}$ that denotes n is a string of n occurrences of s followed by an occurrence of 0.) Then the instance for n of Schema N will be

$$\#x\Phi x = \underline{n} \dashv\vdash \nabla_n x\Phi x\,.$$

This chapter provides a detailed discussion of Schema N and its role in meeting the Adequacy Condition on any theory of natural numbers that it explain their applicability.

Pure mathematicians can set about proving their theorems without ever using the abstraction operator #. It simply does not feature in the language of Peano arithmetic.

The 'applied' truths, however, are every bit as important as the 'pure' ones. Schema N elevates the most important of them—biconditionals of the form

$$\#x\Phi x = \underline{n} \leftrightarrow \nabla_n x\Phi x,$$

or their corresponding interdeducibilities

$$\#x\Phi x = \underline{n} \dashv\vdash \nabla_n x\Phi x$$

—to comprise the essential core of the wider theory of natural numbers, both pure and applied.

The Logic of Number. Neil Tennant, Oxford University Press. © Neil Tennant 2022.
DOI: 10.1093/oso/9780192846679.003.0009

The way Schema N is to be framed below involves choosing the ∇-sequence of numerosity statements for use on its right-hand sides. That decision, as already stressed, is a conventional one. One could instead employ, say, the $\heartsuit$-sequence. The (right- and) left-hand sides of these biconditionals or interdeducibilities are formulable in a suitable extension of the *ur*-object language, but they are still at the object-linguistic level. This extension of the language is required in order to serve up the two kinds of terms that flank the identity sign on the left-hand sides.[1] The first kind of term is abstractive—$\#x\Phi x$, meaning 'the number of Φs'. The second kind of term is pure mathematical—numerals of the canonical form $s \dots s0$. The Schema N biconditionals form a core that must be recovered by any philosophically and mathematically adequate account of number.

Indeed, instances of Schema N (whether rendered as theorems of the foregoing biconditional form, or as the corresponding interdeducibilities) give our talk about numbers its very point. Constructive Logicism builds all these philosophical insights from Frege into the very foundations of number theory, allowing one to comprehend the resulting pure mathematical theory of the natural numbers—i.e., Dedekind–Peano successor-arithmetic—as an analytic or deductive spin-off confined to the pure-mathematical fragment of the language (0 and s), courtesy of the more expressive language that also involves # as a number-abstraction operator (in logicians' terms: a variable-binding term-forming operator).

For any natural number n, let $\underline{n}$ be the Dedekind–Peano numeral denoting n, that is, the term $s \dots s0$, containing n occurrences of s. We have already seen (in Chapter 8) that the statement

there are exactly n Φs

can be analyzed in the notation of first-order logic with identity in such a way as to involve no quantification over the natural numbers themselves, provided only that the sorts of things to which the predicate Φ could intelligibly apply do not include natural numbers. Thus, for example, the statement

there are exactly two apples

can be analyzed as follows:

$$\exists x \exists y(\neg x = y \wedge Ax \wedge Ay \wedge \forall z(Az \rightarrow (z = x \vee z = y)))\,.$$

And similarly for any adjectival numerical designation in place of 'two'. Here, there is no reference to, or quantification over, natural numbers themselves, unless —which is not the rule—the predicate Φ happens to be a number-theoretic one, intelligibly applying to natural numbers.

[1] It is purely conventional that we speak here of 'the' left-hand sides. Given that both $\leftrightarrow$ and $\dashv\vdash$ are commutative, the symmetry has to be broken somehow, and arbitrarily. We have chosen to break it by having the numerical identity always on the left.

At the risk of being repetitious: it is only we reflective users of the metalanguage who discern in the numerical subscripts of the inductively defined numerosity quantifiers 'there are exactly n things x such that ...' any hint of number. Indeed, without a prior grasp of the natural numbers it is questionable whether we could so much as understand how to apply Definition (4) (p. 84) in order to determine, for any given n, exactly which sentence of the object language the definiendum $\nabla_n x \Phi x$ actually is. (The same point would apply, of course to any alternative inductive definition of 'exact numerosity' statements, such as the ones in the $\Diamond$-sequence.) So it is very doubtful that we could demand of the users of the *un*extended object language (without the variable-binding term-forming operator #) that they be able to grasp Definition (4) and be able to apply it in order to generate the sentences

$$\nabla_0 x\Phi x\,,\ \nabla_1 x\Phi x\,,\ \nabla_2 x\Phi x\,,\ \ldots$$

even though these all count as well-formed within that unextended language.

Moreover, *we* need to have a prior grasp of number in order to so much as understand the import of the following material adequacy condition on the theory of number, and to understand why it is licitly imposed as an adequacy condition on any theory of natural number finding expression in the object language.

ADEQUACY CONDITION ON ANY THEORY OF NATURAL NUMBERS

One's theory of natural numbers (call it Θ) should deliver every instance of the following schema of interdeducibilities:

Schema N $\quad \#x\Phi x = \underline{n} \dashv_{\Theta} \vdash \nabla_n x\Phi x$

The theory Θ will consist of rules governing the primitive expressions 0 (zero), s (the successor of ...) and # (the number of ...). It will (so the logicist claims) furnish no more than the logic of the expressions 0, s and #.

Regarding our proposed Adequacy Condition, compare the well-known analog from Tarski:[2]

ADEQUACY CONDITION ON ANY THEORY OF TRUTH

One's theory of truth (call it Θ) should deliver every instance of the following schema of interdeducibilities:

Schema T $\quad T(s) \dashv_{\Theta} \vdash p$

where 's' is a structural-descriptive name, in the metalanguage, of a sentence of the object language, and 'p' is its translation into the metalanguage.

[2]See Tarski [1933 in Polish].

The analogy, which was pointed out in *AR&L*, is striking; and the authority of Tarski should lend our Adequacy Condition on any Theory of Number a measure of legitimacy.

Exploring the analogy a little further: note that in furnishing derivations of all instances of Schema T, one makes use of all the inferential rules of truth that make up one's theory of truth.[3] It would appear that there are no alternatives to the extant canonical derivations that could achieve the same end (establishing all instances of Schema T) while yet collectively eschewing any of the (metalinguistic) rules of inference governing the truth predicate. The rules in question capture the Tarskian satisfaction conditions for formulae with the various logical operators dominant in them.

If we now apply this observation by way of analogy to the case of Schema N, we would expect something similar: in order to furnish the derivations of all instances of Schema N, one should need to make use of all the inferential rules that make up one's theory of number. For, by satisfying the adequacy condition involving Schema N, there really ought not to be anything else one needs to do, in order to pin down exactly both what the natural numbers are, and how they are involved in counting the extensions of predicates in general. (In saying this, one is prescinding, of course, from matters of addition and multiplication.) So there ought not to be any theoretical slack (or shortfall) that can be taken up (or made good) only by postulating further such rules as do not find application in any proofs of instances of Schema N. Particular interest will attach, therefore, to the questions: 'Which rules of the theory of number suffice for the derivations of all instances of Schema N? Are there any primitive rules that have been proposed in the past, but which happen not to be needed for these derivations?' The answers will turn out to be both surprising and instructive.

Contrary to the impression that might be occasioned by a casual reading of p. 134 of Demopoulos and Clark [2005], Schema N was not propounded or formulated by Frege. In an unbroken paragraph that appears to be an expository account of what Frege did, Demopoulos and Clark write that in effect by following Frege's definitions of the terms involved,

> it is possible to prove in second-order logic that $\exists^n xFx \equiv n = NxFx$.

This is a notational variant of Schema N. Its instances are obtained by taking $n = 0, 1, 2, \ldots$.

But Frege did not ever state or prove Schema N. He contented himself, even as late as the *Grundgesetze*, with just the two instances 0 and 1 of the Schema.

1. The first paragraph of §75 of the *Grundlagen* gives the instance of Schema N for $n = 0$. In §96 and §98 of the *Grundgesetze I*, the formal proofs for this instance are given.

[3] This was evident from the treatment of the inferential theory of truth that was provided in *AR&L*, pp. 72–73.

2. In §78 of the *Grundlagen*, Frege's statements (2), (3) and (4) taken together give us the instance of Schema N where $n = 1$. In §§103–104 and §§106–107 of the *Grundgesetze I*, the formal proofs for this instance are given.

3. Frege did not, however, deal with any higher values of n, let alone with n universally quantified, anywhere in the *Grundlagen* or in the *Grundgesetze*.

We have seen that the right-hand sides of instances of Schema N do not commit one to the existence of natural numbers as abstract objects. The left-hand sides, however, do just that. The natural number n is denoted both by the abstractive term $\#x\Phi(x)$ and by the 'pure numerical' term $\underline{n}$. It might be thought that the particular sortal or 'count' predicates that we choose to put in place of Φ (predicates such as *x is a dollar coin, x is an atom, x is an apple; x is a dog; x is a human being; x is a natural number; x is a planet; x is a moon of Jupiter; x is a horse drawing the Emperor's carriage* ...) could somehow impart a 'sortal flavor' or 'dimensionality' to the natural numbers themselves. But that is not the case at all. It is the same natural number 3, or $sss0$, that is involved when we make such statements as

> the number of men in the triumvirate = $sss0$;
>
> the number of coins in my pocket = $sss0$;
>
> the number of primes strictly between 5 and 15 = = $sss0$; ...

The same point has been made by the analytical metaphysicist (van Inwagen [2009], at p. 53):

> ... number-words like "zero" or "three" or "seven" (and the word 'number' itself) do not change their meanings when they are applied to things in different logical or ontological categories. If I say that four is the number of the Stuart kings of England, the canonical Gospels, *and* the cardinal points of the compass, that's not a syllepsis like "Aunt Maude went home in a short while, a flood of tears, and a Buick." ... [N]umber-words are univocal in all their applications.

The numerical abstraction indicated by the operator # is what ensures the 'dimensionless' character of the natural numbers n that are designated by their numerals $\underline{n}$. The particular predicates Φ involved in the abstractive term $\#x\Phi(x)$ simply supply the respective 'criteria of counting'. The counting processes will terminate in the very same natural number 3, regardless of whether one is counting the men in the triumvirate, or the number of coins in my pocket, or the number of primes strictly between 5 and 15. This is because there is (so we shall assume, for the purposes of illustration) a one-one correspondence between the men in the triumvirate and the coins in my pocket; and between the coins in my pocket and the primes between 5 and 15. Also—and perhaps more importantly—there is a one-one correspondence between each of the predicate-extensions just mentioned, and the extension $\{0, 1, 2\}$ of the predicate '... is a natural number preceding 3'. Those one-one correspondences guarantee the dimensionless character of the numbers—in this example, of the number 3—as termini of the respective counts. Note that this point is unaffected by the different modal statuses of the statements in our example. It is mathematically necessary that the number of primes strictly between 5 and 15 be 3. But it is contingent that the number of coins in my pocket is 3. And some might wish to argue that it is analytic that the number of men in the triumvirate, should it exist, is 3. (That there is a triumvirate at all, however, is a contingent matter.)

Because of the great linguistic variety of potential substituends for Φ—predicates lexically simple or grammatically complex, predicates applying to concrete or to abstract objects—we realize immediately that the notion of number is universally applicable. All that matters is that any substituend for Φ should be a sortal predicate—one that 'divides its reference', and that provides a criterion of identity that enables the thinker to recognize one and the same Φ as the same again, and therefore be able to count the (finitely many) Φs that are in question.

The formal equivalence above for the case $n = 1$ can be expressed more succinctly by using our definiendum on its right-hand side rather than its definiens:

$$\#x\Phi x = s0 \dashv\vdash \nabla_1 x\Phi x\,.$$

This last is of course the second in an instructive series of interdeducibilities recognition of the need for which is essential for a grasp of the natural numbers (on the part of the speaker of the extended object language that now contains 0, s and #). The first interdeducibility of the series deals with the special number 0:

$$\#x\Phi x = 0 \dashv\vdash \nabla_0 x\Phi x$$

i.e.,

$$\#x\Phi x = 0 \dashv\vdash \neg\exists x\Phi x\,.$$

The number 0 is special, of course, because it is initial. The second interdeducibility of the series deals with the special number 1, or $s0$:

$$\#x\Phi x = s0 \dashv\vdash \nabla_{s0} x\Phi x$$

i.e.,

$$\#x\Phi x = s0 \dashv\vdash \exists y(\Phi y \wedge \neg\exists x(\Phi x \wedge x \neq y))\,.$$

Remember the tacit subscript Θ for the background theory within which these interdeducibilities are able to be established:

$$\#x\Phi x = s0 \dashv_{\Theta}\vdash \nabla_{s0} x\Phi x\,;$$

$$\#x\Phi x = s0 \dashv_{\Theta}\vdash \exists y(\Phi y \wedge \neg\exists x(\Phi x \wedge x \neq y))\,.$$

The theory Θ will consist of rules governing 0, s and #. It will not be the null theory; but (so the logicist claims) it will furnish no more than the logic of the expressions 0, s and #.

So far all our logical considerations have been confined to the formal first-order object language with identity. We have looked at various ways of stating numerosities in that language, but without referring to, or abstracting, or generalizing about numbers.

At this point we finally advance to a grasp of number on the part of the speaker of the object language (which language, at long last, is about to be extended so as to enable talk about numbers).

As we remarked earlier, Frege contented himself, even as late as the *Grundgesetze*, with just the two cases 0 and 1 of Schema N. He never did make the explicit and completely general point about natural numbers n that is made by the adequacy condition involving Schema N.

Chapter 10

The Rules of Constructive Logicism

Abstract

This chapter states and explains all the formal rules of inference that are involved in the Constructive Logicist account of the natural numbers. Natural-deduction rules of introduction and elimination govern the primitives 0, s, and #, as well as various pasigraphs (such as Nx, for 'x is a natural number') that are inferentially definable in terms of the primitives. We set out important inferences about 1–1 mappings, and define ancestrals of one-place functions by means of special introduction and elimination rules. The ancestral of the successor function affords a definition of Nx. All the reasoning involving these notions, by means of these rules, will be both constructive and relevant.

We proceed now to state the further (new) rules that the Constructive Logicist will employ in order to deal with the logico-arithmetical expressions 0 (zero), $s(\ldots)$ (the successor of ...), and $\#xF(x)$ (the number of Fs).

#-Introduction $$\frac{\#xFx = t \quad Rxy[Fx \text{ 1–1 } Gy]}{\#xGx = t}$$

'If the number of Fs is t and there are exactly as many Fs as Gs, then the number of Gs is t.'

#-Elimination (serial form) $$\frac{\#xFx = t \quad Rxy[Fx \text{ 1–1 } Gy]}{\#xGx = t}$$

'If the number of Fs is t and there are exactly as many Fs as Gs, then the number of Gs is t.'

The Logic of Number. Neil Tennant, Oxford University Press. © Neil Tennant 2022.
DOI: 10.1093/oso/9780192846679.003.0010

It will not have escaped the reader that this serial form of #-E is identical to the rule #-I just given. This oddity can be avoided by 'parallelizing' the elimination rule as follows:

#-Elimination (parallelized form)

$$\dfrac{\#xFx = t \qquad Rxy[Fx \text{ 1–1 } Gy] \qquad \begin{array}{c} \overline{\#xGx = t}^{(i)} \\ \vdots \\ \theta \end{array}}{\theta}{}^{(i)}$$

'If the number of Fs is t and there are exactly as many Fs as Gs, then whatever follows from the number of Gs being t follows.'

#-Elimination

$$\dfrac{\#xGx = t \qquad \begin{array}{c} \underbrace{{}^{(i)}\overline{\#x\mathcal{F}x = t} \;,\; \overline{\mathcal{R}xy[\mathcal{F}x \text{ 1–1 } Gy]}^{(i)}} \\ \vdots\ \mathcal{F}, \mathcal{R} \text{ parametric} \\ B \end{array}}{B}{}^{(i)}$$

The requirement that $\mathcal{F}$ and $\mathcal{R}$ be parametric in the subordinate proof of B is that they should occur only where indicated—that is, in the two assumptions that may be discharged. They may not occur in the conclusion B itself, nor in any other side-assumptions of that subordinate proof. The rule of #-Elimination says, 'If the number of Gs is t, then for some F the number of Fs is t and there are exactly as many Fs as there are Gs.'

0-Introduction

$$\dfrac{\begin{array}{c} \underbrace{{}^{(i)}\overline{F(a)} \;,\; \overline{\exists! a}^{(i)}} \\ \vdots \\ \bot \end{array}}{0 = \#xF(x)}{}^{(i)}$$

where the parameter a occurs only where indicated

0-Introduction is a rule of outright existence. The Constructive Logicist incurs commitment to the existence of 0 as a necessary existent, by taking for Fx the instance $\neg x = x$.

0-Elimination

$$\dfrac{0 = \#xF(x) \quad \exists! t \quad F(t)}{\bot}$$

---

s-Introduction
$$\frac{u = \#xFx \quad Rxy[Fx \text{ 1–1 } Gy, r]}{\#xGx = su}$$

'If u is the number of Fs and there is one more G (namely, r) than there are Fs, then the number of Gs is the successor of u.'

---

s-Elimination
$$\frac{\#xGx = su \qquad \begin{array}{c} \underbrace{\overline{u = \#x\mathcal{F}x}^{(i)} \;,\; \overline{\mathcal{R}xy[\mathcal{F}x \text{ 1–1 } Gy, a]}^{(i)}} \\ \vdots \;\; a, \mathcal{F}, \mathcal{R} \text{ parametric} \\ B \end{array}}{B}{\scriptstyle (i)}$$

'Whatever follows from u numbering one fewer thing than there are Gs follows from the statement that the number of Gs is the successor of u.'

Our present Introduction and Elimination rules for s allow, respectively, only for conclusions and major premises of the 'canonical identity' form

$$\#xGx = su\,.$$

To be sure, a successor-term is involved in such a canonical identity; but the other term is an abstractive one. This means that successors are countenanced as existing only by dint of being numbers of certain predicate extensions. This reflection justifies the following extra rule.

s-Elimination
$$\frac{u = st \qquad \begin{array}{c} \overline{u = \#x\mathcal{H}x}^{(i)} \\ \vdots \;\; \mathcal{H} \text{ parametric} \\ B \end{array}}{B}{\scriptstyle (i)}$$

Mapping 1-1, onto, except for one

A statement of the abbreviated form $Rxy[Fx \text{ 1-1 } Gy, r]$ means 'the relation R maps the Fs one-one onto all the Gs except for r (which is a G)', and registers a situation like the following:

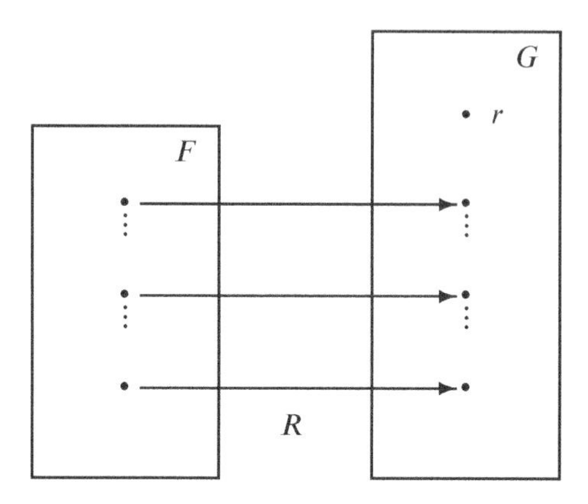

An important composition of 1-1 mappings

Suppose $Rxy[Fx \text{ 1-1 } Hy, a]$ and $Sxy[Kx \text{ 1-1 } Hy, b]$.
Let $(R, S, a, b)xy$ abbreviate $\exists z(Rxz \wedge Syz) \vee (Rxb \wedge Sya)$.
It represents the obvious 1-1 mapping from F onto K—
that is, we have $(R, S, a, b)xy[Fx \text{ 1–1 } Ky]$:

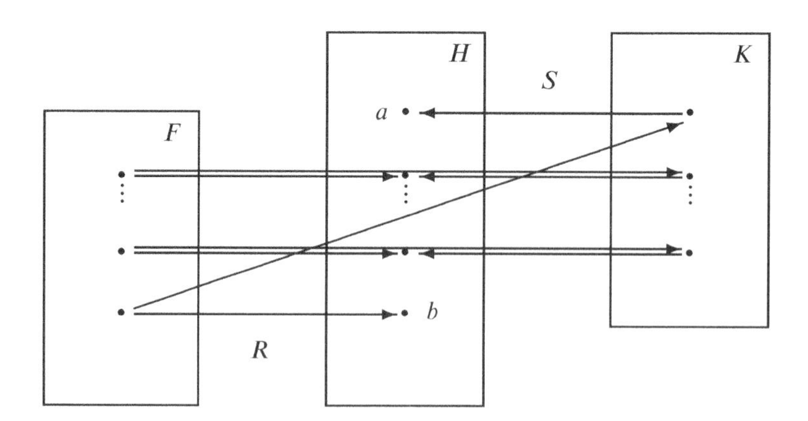

Ancestrals

Let f be a one-place function. We shall provide rules of inference to fix the meaning of any sentence of the form

$$r[\leq f]t,$$

in which the pasigraph $[\leq f]$ is to be treated as an atomic binary predicate (here, infixed between its two arguments r and t).[1] We allow these rules to discharge not only sentential assumptions but also applications of rules. (See Schroeder-Heister [1984].)

Frege's own explicit second-order definition of $r[\leq f]t$ would have been as an abbreviation for the following sentence (had he been sensitive to the requirements of working in a free logic):

$$\exists!r \wedge \exists!t \wedge \forall\Phi((\Phi r \wedge \forall x((\Phi x \wedge \exists!fx) \rightarrow \Phi fx)) \rightarrow \Phi t).$$

Ancestrals inferentially defined

$[\leq f]$-Introduction

$$\dfrac{\begin{array}{c} \underbrace{\dfrac{}{Fr}{\scriptstyle(i)} \quad , \quad \dfrac{Fu \quad \exists!fu}{Ffu}{\scriptstyle(i)}} \\ \vdots \; {\scriptstyle F \text{ parametric}} \\ Ft \end{array} \qquad \exists!r \qquad \exists!t}{r[\leq f]t}{\scriptstyle(i)}$$

The discharge indicated on the right is of any and all inferences of the form

$$\frac{Fu \quad \exists!fu}{Ffu},$$

for whatever choice of terms might be substituted for the placeholder u (parameters included). Each such inference corresponds to an appeal to the embedded formula $\forall x((\Phi x \wedge \exists!fx) \rightarrow \Phi fx))$ in the foregoing Fregean definition of the ancestral.

'Every F that transmits under existent f-images transmits from r to t'; that is, 't is only finitely many steps of f away from r'.

---

[1] If we were being completely scrupulous as neo-Fregeans (in regarding function signs as incomplete symbols), we would render this composite pasigraph $[\leq f]$ as involving a binding of the variable x in the functional expression $f(x)$: either $[\leq_x f(x)]$ or $[\leq_{\lambda x f(x)}]$. But in avoiding the extra clutter that would be thus involved here, we are following the normal definitional practice in mathematics.

$[\leq f]$-Elimination

$$\frac{r[\leq f]t}{\exists! r} \qquad \frac{r[\leq f]t}{\exists! t} \qquad \frac{r[\leq f]t \qquad Fr \qquad \begin{array}{c} \overset{(i)}{\overline{Fa}}, \overline{\exists! fa}^{(i)} \\ \underbrace{\qquad\qquad} \\ \vdots \;\; a \text{ parametric} \\ Ffa \end{array}}{Ft}\,(i)$$

(Here F is a placeholder for formulae.)

'Suppose $r[\leq f]t$. Then both r and t exist; and if F transmits under existent f-images, then Fr only if Ft.'

$<_f$ inferentially defined

We introduce the following introduction and elimination rules for the binary predicate $<_f$.

$<_f$-Introduction

$$\frac{t[\leq f]u \qquad \begin{array}{c} \overline{t=u}^{(1)} \\ \vdots \\ \bot \end{array}}{t <_f u}\,(1)$$

$<_f$-Elimination

$$\frac{t <_f u}{t[\leq f]u} \qquad \frac{t <_f u \qquad t=u}{\bot}$$

Ancestrals, special case: being a natural

Definition 8.

$$Nt \;\equiv_{df}\; 0[\leq s]t$$

't is a natural if and only if t is at most finitely many steps of successor away from zero.'

Note that an abbreviatory definition like this one can be stated as a simple inferential one for a new pasigraph (here, N):

N-Intro $\dfrac{0[\leq s]t}{Nt}$

N-Elim $\dfrac{Nt}{0[\leq s]t}$ (serial form) $\qquad \dfrac{Nt \qquad \begin{matrix} \overline{0[\leq s]t}^{\,(i)} \\ \vdots \\ \psi \end{matrix}}{\psi}\,(i)$ (parallelized form)

Ancestrals, special case:
$r = 0$, f is s; and $0[\leq s]t$ is abbreviated as Nt

N-Introduction

$$\dfrac{\begin{matrix} \underbrace{{}^{(i)}\overline{F0}\;,\quad {}^{(i)}\dfrac{Fu \quad \exists!su}{Fsu}} \\ \vdots\; F \text{ parametric} \\ Ft \end{matrix} \qquad \exists!0 \qquad \exists!t}{Nt}\,(i)$$

'Every F that transmits under existent s-images transmits from 0 to t'; or, put another way: 't is only finitely many steps of s away from 0'. That is, t is a natural number.

N-Elimination

$$\dfrac{Nt}{\exists!0} \qquad \dfrac{Nt}{\exists!t} \qquad \dfrac{Nt \qquad F0 \qquad \begin{matrix} \underbrace{{}^{(i)}\overline{Fa}\;,\; \overline{\exists!sa}^{\,(i)}} \\ \vdots\; a \text{ parametric} \\ Fsa \end{matrix}}{Ft}\,(i)$$

(This is the Peano postulate known as Mathematical Induction.)

(Here F is a placeholder for formulae.)

'Suppose Nt. Then both 0 and t exist; and if F transmits under existent s-images, then $F0$ only if Ft.'

In all the reasoning involved in our constructive logicist derivation of results in arithmetic, we shall make use only of introduction and elimination rules; so the reasoning will be both constructive and relevant.

Chapter 11

Formal Results of Constructive Logicism

Abstract

We prove in the metalanguage, by induction on natural numbers n, that derivations can be given in free Core Logic of all instances of Schema N ($\#x\Phi x = \underline{n} \dashv\vdash \nabla_n x\Phi x$). We also prove all of the Dedekind–Peano postulates for successor arithmetic, including the Principle of Mathematical Induction. To this end one needs only the rules of free Core Logic itself, the rules for 0, s and # set out in Chapter 10, and certain logical rules about one-one mappings that are clearly stated. Among the lemmas proved along the way to the Dedekind–Peano postulates is the result known as 'Frege's trick': any natural number is the number of naturals preceding it. All derivations are given with complete formal rigor, but with additional commentary in 'logician's English' to convey the gist of the formal work.

Simple inferences about 1-1 mappings

The following inferences are pretty immediate. They are formally secured by easy applications of the introduction and elimination rules for various mapping notions in *AR&L*, Ch. 25:

$$(\alpha) \qquad \frac{Rxy[Fx \text{ 1-1 } Gy, r]}{\exists! r}$$

$$(\beta) \qquad \frac{Rxy[Fx \text{ 1-1 } Gy, r]}{Gr}$$

$$(\gamma) \qquad \frac{Rxy[Fx \text{ 1-1 } Gy, r]}{Rxy[Fx \text{ 1-1}(y \neq r \wedge Gy)]}$$

$$(\eta) \qquad \frac{Gr \qquad\qquad \exists! r}{x = y[(x \neq r \wedge Gx) \text{ 1-1 } Gy, r]}$$

The Logic of Number. Neil Tennant, Oxford University Press. © Neil Tennant 2022.
DOI: 10.1093/oso/9780192846679.003.0011

These are the only special logical inferences concerning 1-1 mappings that are used when proving Metatheorem 3 (concerning the derivability of all instances of Schema N). The inferences (γ) and (η) are used only for that purpose; whereas (α) and (β) are used also in proofs of certain lemmas that follow, as are the following four rules.

$$(\nu)\qquad \frac{Fd \qquad\qquad\qquad\qquad \exists!d}{(Fx\wedge x\neq d\wedge Fy\wedge x=y)[Fx\wedge x\neq d \text{ 1-1 }, d]}$$

$$(\zeta)\qquad \frac{Rxy[Fx \text{ 1-1 } Hy, a] \qquad Sxy[Kx \text{ 1-1 } Hy, b]}{(R, S, a, b)xy[Fx \text{ 1-1 } Ky]}$$

$$(\xi)\qquad \frac{\exists!r}{\neg x=x\wedge y=r[\neg x=x \text{ 1-1 } y=r, r]}$$

$$(\omega)\qquad \frac{\exists!t \qquad\qquad \neg Gt \qquad\qquad Ft}{x=y[Fx\wedge Gx \text{ 1-1 } Fy\wedge(Gy\vee y=t), t]}$$

whence

$$\frac{\exists!t \qquad\qquad \neg t<t \qquad\qquad Nt}{x=y[Nx\wedge x<t \text{ 1-1 } Ny\wedge(y<t\vee y=t), t]}$$

Metatheorem 3. *Every instance of Schema N is derivable in the Constructive Logicist's Theory of Number, using only Core Logic* $\mathbb{C}$.

Proof. By induction, appealing to the inductive definition of $\nabla_n x\Phi x$ and the basic rules of inference governing 0, s, and #.

Basis step

The following two proofs show that

$$\#xFx = 0 \dashv\vdash \nabla_0 xFx \quad :$$

$$\dfrac{\dfrac{\nabla_0 xFx\text{, i.e., } \neg\exists xFx \qquad \dfrac{\overset{(1)}{\overline{Fa}} \quad \overset{(1)}{\overline{\exists!a}}}{\exists xFx}}{\bot}}{\#xFx=0}\,{\scriptstyle (1)\,(0\mathrm{I})}
\qquad\qquad
\dfrac{\dfrac{\overset{(2)}{\overline{\exists xFx}} \qquad \dfrac{\#xFx=0 \quad \overset{(1)}{\overline{Fa}} \quad \overset{(1)}{\overline{\exists!a}}}{\bot}\,{\scriptstyle (0\mathrm{E})}}{\bot}\,{\scriptstyle (1)}}{\neg\exists xFx}\,{\scriptstyle (2)}$$

i.e., $\nabla_0 xFx$

Inductive step

The following two proofs show that

$$\#xFx = \underline{sn} \dashv\vdash \nabla_{sn}xFx$$

appealing to the Inductive Hypothesis (IH) that

$$\#xFx = \underline{n} \dashv\vdash \nabla_{n}xFx\,.$$

Note that $\underline{sn} = s\underline{n}$.

First we show $\#xFx = \underline{sn} \vdash \nabla_{sn}xFx$:

$$
\dfrac{\#xFx=\underline{sn} \qquad \dfrac{\dfrac{\begin{array}{c}\dfrac{\overset{(1)}{\overline{\#xHx=\underline{n}}} \quad \dfrac{\overline{Rxy[Hx\text{ 1-1 }Fy,a]}^{(1)}}{Rxy[Hx\text{ 1-1 }y\neq a\wedge Fy]}{\scriptstyle(\gamma)}}{\#w(w\neq a\wedge Fw)=\underline{n}}{\scriptstyle(\#I)} \\ \vdots\ \text{by IH} \\ \nabla_{n}y(y\neq a\wedge Fy)\end{array} \quad \dfrac{\overline{Rxy[Hx\text{ 1-1 }Fy,a]}^{(1)}}{Fa}{\scriptstyle(\beta)}}{\nabla_{n}y(y\neq a\wedge Fy)\wedge Fa} \quad \dfrac{\overline{Rxy[Hx\text{ 1-1 }Fy,a]}^{(1)}}{\exists!a}{\scriptstyle(\alpha)}}{\exists x(\nabla_{n}y(y\neq x\wedge Fy)\wedge Fx)}}{\begin{array}{c}\exists x(\nabla_{n}y(y\neq x\wedge Fy)\wedge Fx)\\ \text{i.e., } \nabla_{sn}xFx\end{array}}{\scriptstyle(1)\ (sE)\ (H,R,a\text{ parametric})}
$$

Second, we show the converse, i.e., $\nabla_{sn}xFx \vdash \#xFx = \underline{sn}$:

$$
\dfrac{\begin{array}{c}\nabla_{sn}xFx,\ \text{i.e.,}\\ \exists x(\nabla_{n}y(y\neq x\wedge Fy)\wedge Fx)\end{array} \qquad \dfrac{\begin{array}{c}\dfrac{\overline{\nabla_{n}y(y\neq a\wedge Fy)\wedge Fa}^{(1)}}{\nabla_{n}y(y\neq a\wedge Fy)} \\ \vdots\ \text{by IH} \\ \#y(y\neq a\wedge Fy)=\underline{n}\end{array} \quad \dfrac{\dfrac{\overline{\nabla_{n}y(y\neq a\wedge Fy)\wedge Fa}^{(1)}}{Fa} \quad \overline{\exists!a}^{(1)}}{y=z[y\neq a\wedge Fy\text{ 1-1 }Fz,a]}{\scriptstyle(\eta)}}{\#xFx=\underline{sn}}{\scriptstyle(sI)}}{\#xFx=\underline{sn}}{\scriptstyle(1)}
$$

Note that the term $s\underline{n}$ *is* the term $\underline{sn}$. □

We provide now a constructive logicist derivation of the Dedekind–Peano Postulates for (0,s)-arithmetic, including the principle of mathematical induction, using only the formal rules that we have stated above. Lemmas 1–3 are not used for the derivation of later lemmas. Lemmas 12–30 are arranged according to their increasing logical depth: those whose proofs do not rely on earlier lemmas among those about to be proved are of logical depth 0; and each subsequent lemma is assigned logical depth $n + 1$ just in case n is the maximum logical depth of any lemma on which its proof relies. Lemma 30 is of logical depth 9; its proof relies on all preceding lemmas. This is quite arresting, given that it says that successor transmits naturalness.

LOGICAL DEPTH 0

None of the lemmas at this level relies on any preceding lemma.

Successor is one-one. (This is a Peano postulate.)

Lemma 1. $\dfrac{st=su}{t=u}$

Proof.
$$\begin{array}{c} st=su \\ \Pi_1 \quad : \\ t=u \end{array}$$

$$\dfrac{st=su \qquad \dfrac{\dfrac{st=su \quad \overline{su=\#x\mathcal{H}x}^{(1)}}{st=\#x\mathcal{H}x} \qquad \dfrac{\overline{su=\#x\mathcal{H}x}^{(1)} \qquad \dfrac{\overline{t=\#x\mathcal{G}x}^{(2)} \qquad \dfrac{\overline{u=\#x\mathcal{F}x}^{(3)} \qquad \dfrac{\overline{\mathcal{R}xy[\mathcal{F}x1\text{-}1\mathcal{H}y,a]}^{(3)} \quad \overline{\mathcal{S}xy[\mathcal{G}x1\text{-}1\mathcal{H}y,b]}^{(2)}}{(\mathcal{R},\mathcal{S},a,b)xy[\mathcal{F}x\ 1\text{-}1\ \mathcal{G}y]}{\scriptstyle(\zeta)}}{u=\#x\mathcal{G}x}{\scriptstyle(\#I)}}{t=u}{\scriptstyle(\text{Sub.=})}}{t=u}{\scriptstyle(3)\ (s\text{E})}}{t=u}{\scriptstyle(2)\ (s\text{E})}}{t=u}{\scriptstyle(1)\ (s\text{E}),\ \text{extra part}}$$

□

Note how the final step is an application of the ‘extra part’ of the Elimination rule for s that we justified earlier.

Π_1 will not be invoked in any subsequent proof in this series of lemmas.

Every natural exists

Lemma 2. $\dfrac{Nt}{\exists!t}$

Proof.
$$\begin{array}{c} Nt \\ \Pi_2 \quad : \\ \exists!t \end{array}$$

$$\text{i.e.,}\ \dfrac{\dfrac{Nt}{0[\leq_s]t}}{\exists!t}{\scriptstyle(\leq_s\text{E})}$$

□

So N is an existentially committal sortal predicate. Interesting and welcome though this result is, we shall not actually make any use of it in what follows.

Lemma 3. $$\frac{\exists! ft}{t[\leq f]ft}$$

Proof.

$$\begin{array}{c}\exists! ft \\ \Pi_3 \\ t[\leq f]ft\end{array} \quad : \quad \dfrac{\dfrac{\exists! ft}{\exists! t} \qquad \dfrac{\overline{Ft}^{(1)} \qquad \exists! ft}{Fft}{\scriptstyle (1)} \qquad \exists! ft}{t[\leq f]ft}{\scriptstyle (1)\,(\leq_f \mathrm{I})}$$

□

Special case: $\dfrac{\exists! ft}{t[\leq f]ft} \rightsquigarrow \dfrac{\exists! s0}{0[\leq s]s0} \rightsquigarrow \dfrac{\exists! s0}{N s0}$

'If the successor of zero exists, then it's a natural.'

---

0 is the number of non-self-identical things

Lemma 4. $0 = \#x(\neg x = x)$

Proof.

$$\begin{array}{c}\Pi_4 \\ 0 = \#x(\neg x = x)\end{array} \quad : \quad \dfrac{\dfrac{\dfrac{\overline{\exists! a}^{(1)}}{a = a} \qquad \overline{\neg a = a}^{(1)}}{\bot}}{0 = \#x(\neg x = x)}{\scriptstyle (1)\ 0\text{-Intro}}$$

□

---

0 cannot number a non-empty concept

Lemma 5. $$\frac{\exists H(\exists x Hx \wedge 0 = \#x Hx)}{\bot}$$

Proof. $\begin{array}{c}\exists H(\exists xHx \wedge 0=\#xHx)\\ \Pi_5\\ \bot\end{array}$:

$$\dfrac{\exists H(\exists xHx \wedge 0=\#xHx) \qquad \dfrac{\dfrac{\dfrac{}{\exists xFx \wedge 0=\#xFx}{\scriptstyle(2)}}{\exists xFx} \qquad \dfrac{\dfrac{\dfrac{}{\exists xFx \wedge 0=\#xFx}{\scriptstyle(2)}}{0=\#xFx} \quad \dfrac{}{Fb}{\scriptstyle(1)} \quad \dfrac{}{\exists!b}{\scriptstyle(1)}}{\bot}{\scriptstyle(0E)}}{\bot}{\scriptstyle(1)}}{\bot}{\scriptstyle(2)}$$

□

Lemma 6. $\dfrac{st = \#xHx}{\exists xHx}$

Proof. $\begin{array}{c}st = \#xHx\\ \Pi_6\\ \exists xHx\end{array}$:

$$\dfrac{st = \#xHx \qquad \dfrac{\dfrac{\dfrac{}{Rxy[Fx \text{ 1-1 } Hy, a]}{\scriptstyle(1)}}{\exists!a} \qquad \dfrac{\dfrac{}{Rxy[Fx \text{ 1-1 } Hy, a]}{\scriptstyle(1)}}{Ha}}{\exists xHx}}{\exists xHx}{\scriptstyle(1)\, sE}$$

□

Lemma 7. $\dfrac{\exists!t}{t[\leq f]t}$

Proof.

$\begin{array}{c}\exists!t\\ \Pi_7\\ t[\leq f]t\end{array}$:

$$\dfrac{\exists!t \qquad \dfrac{}{Ft}{\scriptstyle(1)} \qquad \exists!t}{t[\leq f]t}{\scriptstyle(1)(\leq_f \text{I})}$$

□

Special case: $\dfrac{\exists!t}{t[\leq f]t} \rightsquigarrow \dfrac{\exists!0}{0[\leq s]0} \rightsquigarrow \dfrac{\exists!0}{N0}$

'If zero exists, then it's a natural.'

Lemma 8. $\dfrac{t[\leq f]r \quad \exists! f r}{t[\leq f] f r}$

Proof.

$$\underbrace{t[\leq f]r,\ \exists! f r}_{\substack{\Pi_8 \\ t[\leq f] f r}} \quad : \quad \dfrac{\dfrac{t[\leq f]r}{\exists! t} \quad \exists! f r \quad \dfrac{\dfrac{t[\leq f]r \quad \dfrac{}{Ft}{\scriptstyle (2)} \quad \dfrac{\dfrac{}{Fa}{\scriptstyle (1)} \quad \dfrac{}{\exists! f a}{\scriptstyle (1)}}{F f a}{\scriptstyle (2)}}{Fr}{\scriptstyle (1)\,(\leq_f \mathrm{E})} \quad \exists! f r}{F f r}{\scriptstyle (2)}}{t[\leq f] f r}{\scriptstyle (2)\,(\leq_f \mathrm{I})}$$

□

Special case: $\dfrac{t[\leq f]r \quad \exists! f r}{t[\leq f] f r} \rightsquigarrow \dfrac{0[\leq s]r \quad \exists! s r}{0[\leq s] s r} \rightsquigarrow \dfrac{Nr \quad \exists! s r}{N s r}$

'Naturalness transmits under existent successors.'

Lemma 9. $\dfrac{f t[\leq f]u}{t[\leq f]u}$

Proof. $\begin{matrix} f t[\leq f]u \\ \Pi_9 \\ t[\leq f]u \end{matrix} \quad :$

$$\dfrac{\dfrac{\dfrac{f t[\leq f]u}{\exists! f t}}{\exists! t} \quad \dfrac{f t[\leq f]u}{\exists! u} \quad \dfrac{f t[\leq f]u \quad \dfrac{\dfrac{}{Ft}{\scriptstyle (2)} \quad \dfrac{f t[\leq f]u}{\exists! f t}}{F f t}{\scriptstyle (2)} \quad \dfrac{\dfrac{}{Fa}{\scriptstyle (1)} \quad \dfrac{}{\exists! f a}{\scriptstyle (1)}}{F f a}{\scriptstyle (2)}}{Fu}{\scriptstyle (1)\,(\leq_f \mathrm{E})}}{t[\leq f]u}{\scriptstyle (2)\,(\leq_f \mathrm{I})}$$

□

Lemma 10. $\dfrac{Fd \quad \exists!d \quad b=\#x(Fx\wedge\neg x=d)}{\#xFx=sb}$

Proof. $\begin{array}{c}\underbrace{Fd, \exists!d, b=\#x(Fx\wedge\neg x=d)} \\ \Pi_{10} \\ \#xFx=sb\end{array}$:

$$\dfrac{b=\#x(Fx\wedge\neg x=d) \qquad \dfrac{Fd \qquad\qquad \exists!d}{(Fx\wedge x\neq d\wedge Fy\wedge x=y)[Fx\wedge x\neq d \text{ 1-1}, d]}(v)}{\#xFx=sb}(sI)$$

□

Lemma 11. $\dfrac{t <_f t}{\perp}$

Proof. $\begin{array}{c} t <_f t \\ \Pi_{11} \\ \perp \end{array}$:

$$\dfrac{t <_f t \qquad \dfrac{\dfrac{\dfrac{t <_f t}{t[\leq f]t}(<_f\mathrm{E})}{\exists!t}}{t=t}}{\perp}(<_f\mathrm{E})$$

□

LOGICAL DEPTH 1

These lemmas rely on lemmas of Logical Depth 0.

Lemmas of logical depth $n+1$ rely on lemmas of logical depth n.

The successor of zero is the number of things identical to zero

Lemma 12. $s0 = \#x(x = 0)$

Proof. $\begin{array}{c}\Pi_{12} \\ s0 = \#x(x=0)\end{array}$:

$$\dfrac{\begin{matrix}\Pi_4\\ 0=\#x(\neg x=x)\end{matrix} \qquad \dfrac{\dfrac{\begin{matrix}\Pi_4\\ 0=\#x(\neg x=x)\end{matrix}}{\exists!0}}{\neg x=x \vee y=0[\neg x=x \text{ 1-1 } y=0,0]}(\xi)}{s0=\#x(x=0)}(sI)$$

□

---

0 is not a successor. (This is a Peano postulate.)

Lemma 13. $\dfrac{0=st}{\perp}$

Proof. $\begin{matrix}0=st\\ \Pi_{13}\\ \perp\end{matrix}$:

$$\dfrac{\dfrac{\begin{matrix}\Pi_4\\ 0=\#x(\neg x=x)\end{matrix} \quad 0=st}{\#x(\neg x=x)=st} \qquad \dfrac{\dfrac{\dfrac{}{Rxy[Fx \text{ 1-1 } \neg y=y,a]}(1)}{\neg a=a}(\beta) \qquad \dfrac{\dfrac{\dfrac{}{Rxy[Fx \text{ 1-1 } \neg y=y,a]}(1)}{\exists!a}(\alpha)}{a=a}}{\perp}}{\perp}(1)\,(sE)$$

□

Lemma 14. $\dfrac{\exists!sa}{\exists H(\exists xHx \wedge sa=\#xHx)}$

Proof. $\begin{matrix}\exists!sa\\ \Pi_{14}\\ \exists H(\exists xHx \wedge sa=\#xHx)\end{matrix}$:

$$\dfrac{\begin{matrix}\exists!sa\\ \text{i.e., } \exists x\, x=sa\end{matrix} \qquad \dfrac{\dfrac{}{c=sa}(2) \qquad \dfrac{\dfrac{\begin{matrix}\dfrac{\dfrac{}{c=sa}(2) \quad \dfrac{}{c=\#x\mathcal{G}x}(1)}{sa=\#x\mathcal{G}x}\\ \Pi_6\\ \exists x\mathcal{G}x\end{matrix} \qquad \dfrac{\dfrac{}{c=sa}(2) \quad \dfrac{}{c=\#x\mathcal{G}x}(1)}{sa=\#x\mathcal{G}x}}{\exists x\mathcal{G}x \wedge sa=\#x\mathcal{G}x}}{\exists H(\exists xHx \wedge sa=\#xHx)}}{\exists H(\exists xHx \wedge sa=\#xHx)}(1)\ sE\text{, extra part}}{\exists H(\exists xHx \wedge sa=\#xHx)}(2)$$

□

---

0 is a natural. (This is a Peano postulate.)

Lemma 15. $N0$

Proof. $\begin{matrix}\Pi_{15}\\ N0\end{matrix}$:

$$\dfrac{\begin{matrix}\Pi_4\\ 0 = \#x(\neg x = x)\end{matrix}}{\exists!0}$$
$$\Pi_7$$
$$N0$$

□

Lemma 16. *The property* $x = t \vee \exists y(t[\leq f]y \wedge x = fy)$ *transmits under existent* f*-images.*

Proof. $\begin{matrix}\underbrace{a = t \vee \exists y(t[\leq f]y \wedge a = fy),\ \exists! fa}\\ \Pi_{16}\\ fa = t \vee \exists y(t[\leq f]y \wedge fa = fy)\end{matrix}$:

$$\dfrac{}{t[\leq f]b \wedge a = fb}(1)$$
$$(1)\dfrac{}{t[\leq f]b \wedge a = fb} \qquad \dfrac{t[\leq f]b \wedge a = fb}{a = fb}$$
$$\dfrac{t[\leq f]b \wedge a = fb}{t[\leq f]b} \qquad \dfrac{a = fb}{\exists! fb}$$
$$\underbrace{\qquad\qquad\qquad\qquad}$$
$$(2)\dfrac{}{a = t} \qquad \Pi_8 \qquad \dfrac{}{t[\leq f]b \wedge a = fb}(1)$$
$$\dfrac{a = t}{\exists! t} \quad \dfrac{\exists! fa}{fa = fa} \quad \dfrac{}{a = t}(2) \qquad t[\leq f]fb \qquad \dfrac{t[\leq f]b \wedge a = fb}{a = fb} \quad \dfrac{\exists! fa}{fa = fa}$$
$$\Pi_7 \quad \dfrac{fa = fa \quad a = t}{fa = ft} \qquad \dfrac{t[\leq f]fb \quad a = fb}{t[\leq f]a} \quad \exists! fa$$
$$\dfrac{t[\leq f]t \quad fa = ft}{t[\leq f]t \wedge fa = ft} \quad \dfrac{\dfrac{}{a = t}(2)}{\exists! t} \qquad \dfrac{t[\leq f]a \quad fa = fa}{t[\leq f]a \wedge fa = fa} \quad \dfrac{\exists! fa}{\exists! a}$$
$$\dfrac{t[\leq f]t \wedge fa = ft \quad \exists! t}{\exists y(t[\leq f]y \wedge fa = fy)} \qquad \dfrac{(2)\dfrac{}{\exists y(t[\leq f]y \wedge a = fy)} \quad \dfrac{t[\leq f]a \wedge fa = fa \quad \exists! a}{\exists y(t[\leq f]y \wedge fa = fy)}}{\exists y(t[\leq f]y \wedge fa = fy)}(1)$$
$$\dfrac{a = t \vee \exists y(t[\leq f]y \wedge a = fy) \quad \exists y(t[\leq f]y \wedge fa = fy) \quad \exists y(t[\leq f]y \wedge fa = fy)}{\exists y(t[\leq f]y \wedge fa = fy)}(2)$$
$$\dfrac{\exists y(t[\leq f]y \wedge fa = fy)}{fa = t \vee \exists y(t[\leq f]y \wedge fa = fy)}$$

□

Lemma 17. $\dfrac{Nd \qquad b = \#x(Nx \wedge x < d)}{\#x(Nx \wedge x \leq d) = sb}$

Proof.

$$\begin{array}{c}\underbrace{Nd, b=\#x(Nx \wedge x<d)}\\ \Pi_{17}\\ \#x(Nx \wedge x \leq d)=sb\end{array} \quad :$$

$$\begin{array}{c}\underbrace{\dfrac{Nd \qquad \dfrac{\dfrac{\dfrac{Nd}{\exists! d}}{d=d}}{d \leq d}}{Nd \wedge d \leq d} \quad , \quad \dfrac{Nd}{\exists! d} \quad , \quad \begin{array}{c} b=\#x(Nx \wedge x<d)\\ \text{i.e., } b=\#x(Nx \wedge x \leq d \wedge x \neq d)\end{array}}\\ \Pi_{10[Fx/(Nx \wedge x \leq d)]}\\ \#x(Nx \wedge x \leq d)=sb\end{array}$$

□

Special case:

$$\begin{array}{c}\underbrace{Nb, b=\#x(Nx \wedge x<b)}\\ \Pi_{17}[d/b]\\ \#x(Nx \wedge x \leq b)=sb\end{array}$$

LOGICAL DEPTH 2

Lemma 18.

$$\frac{s0 \leq 0}{\exists H(\exists x Hx \wedge 0=\#xHx)}$$

Proof.

$$\begin{array}{c} s0 \leq 0\\ \Pi_{18}\\ \exists H(\exists x Hx \wedge 0=\#xHx)\end{array} \quad :$$

$$\dfrac{s0 \leq 0 \qquad \dfrac{\dfrac{\dfrac{\begin{array}{c}\Pi_4\\ 0=\#x(\neg x=x)\end{array}}{\exists x(x=0)} \qquad \begin{array}{c}\Pi_{12}\\ s0=\#x(x=0)\end{array}}{\exists x(x=0) \wedge s0=\#x(x=0)}}{\exists H(\exists x Hx \wedge s0=\#xHx)} \qquad \begin{array}{c}\overline{\exists! sa}^{(1)}\\ \Pi_{14}\\ \exists H(\exists x Hx \wedge sa=\#xHx)\end{array}}{\exists H(\exists x Hx \wedge 0=\#xHx)}\,{\scriptstyle (1)\,(\leq_s \mathrm{E})}$$

□

Lemma 19.

$$\frac{t[\leq f]u \qquad \neg t=u}{\exists y(t[\leq f]y \wedge u=fy)}$$

Proof.

$$\begin{array}{c}\underbrace{t[\leq f]u\,,\ \neg t=u}\\ \Pi_{19}\\ \exists y(t[\leq f]y \wedge u=fy)\end{array} :$$

$$\dfrac{\dfrac{t[\leq f]u \quad \dfrac{\dfrac{\dfrac{t[\leq f]u}{\exists!t}}{t=t}}{t=t \vee \exists y(t[\leq f]y \wedge t=fy)} \quad \begin{array}{c}\underbrace{\overline{a=t \vee \exists y(t[\leq f]y \wedge a=fy)}^{(1)},\ \overline{\exists!fa}^{(1)}}\\ \Pi_{16}\\ fa=t \vee \exists y(t[\leq f]y \wedge fa=fy)\end{array}}{u=t \vee \exists y(t[\leq f]y \wedge u=fy)}{\scriptstyle (1)(\leq_f E)} \quad \dfrac{\neg t=u \quad \overline{u=t}^{(2)}}{\bot} \quad \overline{\exists y(t[\leq f]y \wedge u=fy)}^{(2)}}{\exists y(t[\leq f]y \wedge u=fy)}{\scriptstyle (2)}$$

□

LOGICAL DEPTH 3

Lemma 20. $\neg s0 \leq 0$

Proof.

$$\begin{array}{c}\Pi_{20}\\ \neg s0 \leq 0\end{array} :$$

$$\dfrac{\begin{array}{c}\overline{s0 \leq 0}^{(1)}\\ \Pi_{18}\\ \exists H(\exists xHx \wedge 0=\#xHx)\\ \Pi_5\\ \bot\end{array}}{\neg s0 \leq 0}{\scriptstyle (1)}$$

□

Lemma 21. *If f obeys* $\dfrac{ft=fu}{t=u}$ *then f obeys* $\dfrac{a <_f fb}{a[\leq f]b}$

Proof.

$$\begin{array}{c}a <_f fb\\ \Pi_{21}\\ a[\leq f]b\end{array} :$$

$$\dfrac{\underbrace{\dfrac{a <_f fb}{a[\leq_f]fb}(<_f\mathrm{E}) \quad \dfrac{a <_f fb}{\neg a = fb}(<_f\mathrm{E})}_{\substack{\Pi_{19}[u/fb] \\ \exists y(a[\leq f]y \wedge fb = fy)}} \qquad \dfrac{\dfrac{\dfrac{\dfrac{}{a[\leq f]c \wedge fb = fc}(1)}{fb = fc}}{b = c} \quad \dfrac{\dfrac{}{a[\leq f]c \wedge fb = fc}(1)}{a[\leq f]c}}{a[\leq f]b}}{a[\leq f]b}(1)$$

□

Lemma 22. *If f obeys* $\dfrac{ft = fu}{t = u}$ *then f obeys* $\dfrac{ft[\leq f]fu \quad \neg t[\leq f]u}{t[\leq f]u}$

Proof. $\underbrace{ft[\leq f]fu,\ \neg t[\leq f]u}_{\substack{\Pi_{22} \\ t[\leq f]u}}$:

$$\dfrac{\underbrace{ft[\leq f]fu\ ,\ \dfrac{\dfrac{\dfrac{\dfrac{\dfrac{}{ft = fu}(1)}{t = u}}{t[\leq f]u \quad \neg t[\leq f]u}}{\bot}}{\neg ft = fu}(1)}_{\substack{\Pi_{19} \\ \exists y(ft[\leq f]y \wedge fu = fy)}} \qquad \dfrac{\dfrac{\dfrac{\dfrac{}{ft[\leq f]a \wedge fu = fa}(2)}{fu = fa}}{u = a} \quad \dfrac{\dfrac{}{ft[\leq f]a \wedge fu = fa}(2)}{ft[\leq f]a}}{ft[\leq f]u}}{\substack{ft[\leq f]u \\ \Pi_9 \\ t[\leq f]u}}(2)$$

□

No natural is less than 0

Lemma 23. $\dfrac{Nt \quad t < 0}{\bot}$

Proof.

$$\underbrace{Nt,\ t<0}_{\textstyle\substack{\Pi_{23}\\ \bot}} \quad :$$

$$\dfrac{\underbrace{\substack{Nt\\ \text{i.e., } 0[\le_s]t}\ ,\ \dfrac{t<0}{\neg 0=t}{\scriptstyle <_s\text{-E}}}_{\textstyle\substack{\Pi_{19}\\ \exists y(0[\le_s]y \wedge 0=sy)}} \qquad \dfrac{\dfrac{}{0[\le_s]a \wedge 0=sa}{\scriptstyle(1)}}{\substack{0=sa\\ \Pi_{13}\\ \bot}}}{\bot}{\scriptstyle(1)}$$

□

LOGICAL DEPTH 4

Lemma 24. *If f obeys* $\dfrac{ft=fu}{t=u}$ *then f obeys* $\dfrac{\neg t[\le f]u}{\neg ft[\le f]fu}$

Proof.

$$\begin{array}{c}\neg t[\le f]u\\ \Pi_{24}\\ \neg ft[\le f]fu\end{array} \quad :$$

$$\dfrac{\dfrac{\neg t[\le f]u \qquad \underbrace{{\scriptstyle(1)}\dfrac{}{ft[\le f]fu}\ ,\ \neg t[\le f]u}_{\textstyle\substack{\Pi_{22}\\ t[\le f]u}}}{\bot}}{\neg ft[\le f]fu}{\scriptstyle(1)} \qquad \text{Special case:} \quad \begin{array}{c}\neg t\le u\\ \Pi_{24}\\ \neg st\le su\end{array}$$

□

---

0 is a natural and numbers its natural predecessors (the basis for the inductive proof of Frege's trick)

Lemma 25. $N0 \wedge \#x(Nx \wedge x<0)=0$

Proof. $\dfrac{\Pi_{25}}{N0 \wedge \#x(Nx \wedge x<0)=0}$:

$$\dfrac{\begin{matrix}\Pi_{15} \\ N0\end{matrix} \qquad \dfrac{\dfrac{\overline{Na \wedge a<0}^{(2)} \qquad \begin{matrix}\underbrace{\overline{Na}^{(1)} \;,\; \overline{a<0}^{(1)}} \\ \Pi_{23} \\ \bot\end{matrix}}{\bot}(1)}{\#x(Nx \wedge x<0)=0}(2)\,(0\mathrm{I})}{N0 \wedge \#x(Nx \wedge x<0)=0}$$

□

LOGICAL DEPTH 5

Lemma 26. $\dfrac{Nt}{\neg st \leq t}$

Proof. $\begin{matrix} Nt \\ \Pi_{26} \\ \neg st \leq t \end{matrix}$:

$$\dfrac{Nt \qquad \begin{matrix}\Pi_{20} \\ \neg s0 \leq 0\end{matrix} \qquad \begin{matrix}\overline{\neg sa \leq a}^{(1)} \\ \Pi_{24} \\ \neg ssa \leq sa\end{matrix}}{\neg st \leq t}(1)\,(\leq_s \mathrm{E})$$

□

LOGICAL DEPTH 6

Lemma 27. $\dfrac{\#x(Nx \wedge x \leq b)=sb \qquad Nb}{\#x(Nx \wedge x<sb)=sb}$

Proof.

$$\begin{array}{c}\underbrace{\#x(N x\wedge x\leq b)=sb,\ Nb}\\ \Pi_{27}\\ \#x(N x\wedge x<sb)=sb\end{array}\ :$$

$$\dfrac{\#x(Nx\wedge x\leq b)=sb \qquad \dfrac{\dfrac{\dfrac{\dfrac{\overline{Na\wedge a\leq b}^{(2)}}{Na} \qquad \dfrac{\begin{array}{c}\underbrace{\dfrac{\overline{Na\wedge a\leq b}^{(2)}}{a\leq b} \quad \dfrac{\#x(Nx\wedge x\leq b)=sb}{\exists! sb}}\\ \Pi_8\\ a\leq sb\end{array} \qquad \dfrac{\dfrac{\overline{a=sb}^{(1)} \quad \dfrac{\overline{Na\wedge a\leq b}^{(2)}}{a\leq b}}{sb\leq b} \quad \begin{array}{c}Nb\\ \Pi_{26}\\ \neg sb\leq b\end{array}}{\bot}}{a<sb}(1)}{Na\wedge a<sb} \qquad \dfrac{\dfrac{\overline{Na\wedge a<sb}^{(2)}}{Na} \quad \begin{array}{c}\dfrac{\overline{Na\wedge a<sb}^{(2)}}{a<sb}\\ \Pi_{21}\\ a\leq b\end{array}}{Na\wedge a\leq b}}{x=y[(Nx\wedge x<sb)1\text{-}1(Ny\wedge y\leq b)]}(2)}{\#x(Nx\wedge x<sb)=sb}(\#1)$$

□

LOGICAL DEPTH 7

The inductive step for Frege's trick

Lemma 28. $\dfrac{Nb\wedge \#x(Nx\wedge x<b)=b \qquad \exists! sb}{Nsb\wedge \#x(Nx\wedge x<sb)=sb}$

Proof.

$$\begin{array}{c}\underbrace{Nb\wedge \#x(Nx\wedge x<b)=b,\ \exists! sb}\\ \Pi_{28}\\ Nsb\wedge \#x(Nx\wedge x<sb)=sb\end{array}\ :$$

$$\dfrac{Nb\wedge \#x(Nx\wedge x<b)=b \qquad \dfrac{\begin{array}{c}\underbrace{\overline{Nb}^{(1)}\ ,\ \exists! sb}\\ \Pi_8\left[\begin{smallmatrix}t/0\\ f/s\\ r/b\end{smallmatrix}\right]\\ Nsb\end{array} \qquad \begin{array}{c}\underbrace{\begin{array}{c}\underbrace{\overline{Nb}^{(1)},\ \overline{b=\#x(Nx\wedge x<b)}^{(1)}}\\ \Pi_{17}[d/b]\\ \#x(Nx\wedge x\leq b)=sb\end{array},\ \overline{Nb}^{(1)}}\\ \Pi_{27}\\ \#x(Nx\wedge x<sb)=sb\end{array}}{Nsb\wedge \#x(Nx\wedge x<sb)=sb}}{Nsb\wedge \#x(Nx\wedge x<sb)=sb}(1)$$

□

LOGICAL DEPTH 8

Frege's trick: every natural number numbers its natural predecessors

Lemma 29. $\dfrac{Nt}{t = \#x(Nx \wedge x < t)}$

Proof.

$$\begin{array}{c} Nt \\ \Pi_{29} \\ t = \#x(Nx \wedge x < t) \end{array} :$$

$$\dfrac{\dfrac{Nt \qquad \begin{array}{c}\Pi_{25}\\ N0 \wedge \#x(Nx \wedge x<0)=0\end{array} \qquad \begin{array}{c}\overbrace{\overline{Nb \wedge \#x(Nx \wedge x<b)=b}^{\,(1)} \;,\; \overline{\exists!sb}^{\,(1)}}\\ \Pi_{28}\\ Nsb \wedge \#x(Nx \wedge x<sb)=sb\end{array}}{Nt \wedge t = \#x(Nx \wedge x < t)}{\scriptstyle (1)}}{t = \#x(Nx \wedge x < t)}$$

□

LOGICAL DEPTH 9

Successor transmits naturalness. (This is a Peano postulate.)

Lemma 30. $\dfrac{Nt}{Nst}$

Proof.

$$\begin{array}{c} Nt \\ \Pi_{30} \\ Nst \end{array} :$$

$$\begin{array}{c}\underbrace{Nt \qquad \dfrac{\dfrac{\begin{array}{c}Nt\\ \Pi_{29}\\ t = \#x(Nx\wedge x<t)\end{array} \qquad \dfrac{\dfrac{Nt}{\exists!t} \qquad Nt \qquad \begin{array}{c}\Pi_{11}\\ \neg t<t\end{array}}{x=y[Nx\wedge x<t \text{ 1-1 } Ny\wedge(y<t\vee y=t),t]}{\scriptstyle (\omega)} \qquad \dfrac{Nt}{\exists!t}}{\#x(Nx\wedge(x<t\vee x=t))=st}}{\exists!st}}\\ \Pi_8\\ Nst\end{array}$$

□

We have the following summary of the most important results of Constructive Logicism.

1. $N0$ (Lemma 15)

2. $\dfrac{Nt}{Nst}$ (Lemma 30)

3. $\dfrac{0=st}{\bot}$ (Lemma 13)

4. $\dfrac{st=su}{t=u}$ (Lemma 1)

5. $$\dfrac{Nt \quad F0 \quad \begin{matrix} \overbrace{\overline{Fa}^{(i)}, \overline{\exists!sa}^{(i)}} \\ \vdots \; a \text{ parametric} \\ Fsa \end{matrix}}{Ft}(i)$$ (N-Elim, i.e., Mathematical Induction)[1]

Frege's trick: $\dfrac{Nt}{t = \#x(Nx \wedge x < t)}$ (Lemma 29)

All instances of Schema N:

$$\frac{\#xFx = \underline{n}}{\nabla_n xFx} \quad \frac{\nabla_n xFx}{\#xFx = \underline{n}}$$ (Metatheorem 3)

Constructive Logicism's proofs of instances of Schema N are direct, fully formalized, canonical, and elegant. The interested reader might wish to compare them with the informal but still lengthier deductions in Wright [1998]. Constructive Logicism's use of introduction and elimination rules (rather than HP) and of Dedekind–Peano numerals (rather than canonical Fregean numerals) is what gives it the edge in this regard. It should be stressed that this comparison is based on our use of the same definition of numerosity statements as the one used by Wright. These are the numerosity statements in the ∇-sequence.

Our proof that every instance of Schema N is derivable was by induction in the metalanguage. In the basis we used the introduction and elimination rules for 0.

---

[1]We hope this might allay the worry that 'Writers on the foundations of arithmetic have found it difficult to state in a convincing way why the principle of mathematical induction is evident.' (Parsons [2008] at p. 264.) Surely a very feasibly inspectable, fully formalized proof in accordance with primitives rules of inference is evidence enough?

In the inductive step, in the direction from numerical identity to numerosity, we used the introduction rule for # and the elimination rule for s; while in the direction from numerosity to numerical identity we used the introduction rule for s.

The disquotational theorist about truth maintains that all one needs to know about truth are the biconditional instances of Tarski's Schema T. This is not a tall order, since all that is required is the ability to tell whether a given sentence in the metalanguage is an instance of Schema T. There is an effective method for doing so. By analogy, the 'disnumerical' theorist about number could maintain that all one needs to know about number are the instances of Schema N. It is not surprising that all the rules that the Constructive Logicist provides find application in the derivations of those instances.

It also provides us with the motivation to identify the Introduction and Elimination rules for #.

Schema N comes in as many flavors as there are definitions of ω-sequences of exact numerosity statements. *AR&L* gestured at the ♡-sequence as an appropriate choice, since it would in all likelihood have been the form of numerosity statement most familiar to the average philosophical reader with a basic training in formal logic. But any of the four logically equivalent forms already described here would do. The following diagram highlights with boxes two flavors of Schema N from among the four available—the one gestured at in *AR&L* (using ♡) and the one that we have studied more closely here (using ∇). Each spoke consisting of two-way arrows and extending from the hub of the numerical identity statement is a version of Schema N.

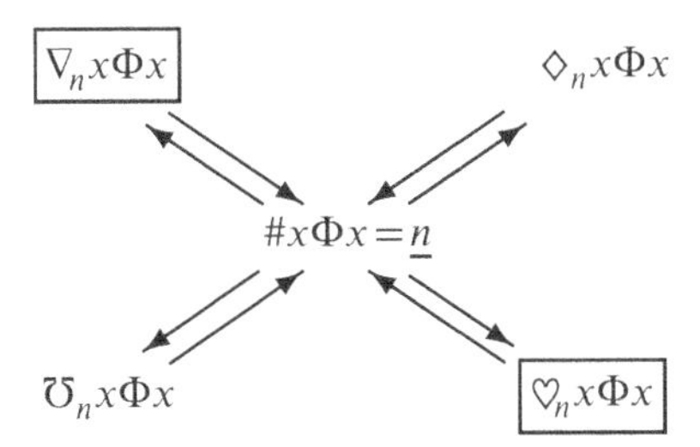

An interesting question, which the author has not yet investigated, is whether any of the 'side' or 'diagonal' equivalences among forms of numerosity statements would enjoy shorter proofs were they to proceed via the identity statement now placed at the hub of the diagram. Thus, for example, would the formal-logical journey

$\nabla_n x\Phi x$ ⇄ $\diamond_n x\Phi x$

$\#x\Phi x = \underline{n}$

$\mho_n x\Phi x$ $\heartsuit_n x\Phi x$

be any shorter for taking the spoked route?

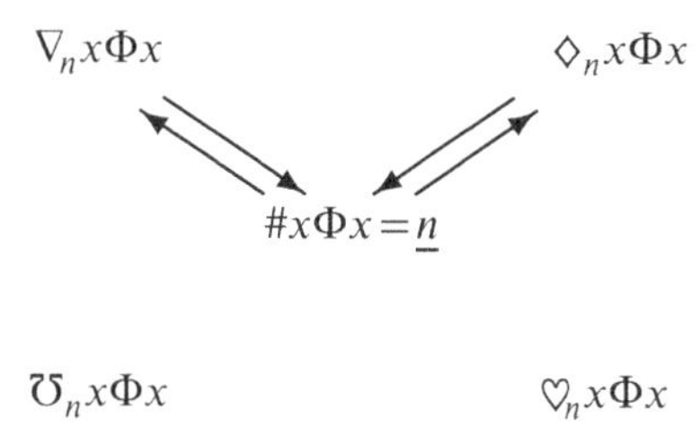

If the answers to this question and to the five other obvious ones like it turn out to be affirmative, that would underscore just how useful it is, logically, to hypostasize the natural numbers, and to adopt language that enables one to refer to them and make statements of identity about them.

Chapter 12

Reflections on Counting

Abstract

This chapter is devoted to motivating, and answering, the question 'When we count a finite collection of objects, why do we always recite our numerals, as we "flip through" the objects one by one, in their *standard ordering*?' Canonical numerals are standardly recited in their intrinsic ordering of increasing size of numbers thereby denoted. We should be aware of how the length of any numeral of a certain kind depends on the size of the number it is to denote. With Dedekind–Peano numerals (of the form $s \ldots s0$), and with Dedekind–Peano–Frege numerals (of the form $\#x(Nx \wedge x \leq s \ldots s0)$) the length of the numerals is a linear function of the number denoted. But in any place notation, from binary onward (including, in particular, our standard decimal notation) that function is logarithmic. (Starkly at odds with these tractable cases is the numeral system of the Fregean, for which, as we saw in Chapter 7, the length of a numeral is exponential in the number denoted.) But even with the linearly and logarithmically increasing numerals here mentioned, the question addressed in this chapter, about reciting numerals in their standard ordering, calls for careful consideration of the reasons why.

We can take as the paradigm #-term to be shown to denote the successor of n the 'Frege–Dedekind–Peano' numeral' $\#x(Nx \wedge x \leq \underline{n})$, which denotes the number of numbers less than or equal to n. This requires, of course, that we define both N and $\leq$, as has been done above. Every number then turns out to be the denotation of a (canonical) #-term.

This approach enables us to pare down our rules to just those needed for proofs of instances of Schema N. Ironically, it thereby establishes applicability in general by securing, first, the necessary existence of the natural numbers construed both as the denotations of numerals and as the denotations of canonical number-abstraction terms involving only a predicate of numbers. So this is a sort of logical confirmation that we determine the numerosity of concrete predicate-extensions by counting them, i.e., by putting them into one-one, onto correlations with the extension of the appropriate canonical predicate of the form 'x is a natural number preceding n'. Such is the role in our mental lives of reciting canonical well-orderings of number-expressions ('one, two, three, ...') as we check off *seriatim* all the (finitely many) objects falling under the predicate in question. (It also calls

The Logic of Number. Neil Tennant, Oxford University Press. © Neil Tennant 2022.
DOI: 10.1093/oso/9780192846679.003.0012

into question the distinction between intransitive and transitive counting.)

When we count *seriatim* (as opposed to subitizing),[1] we standardly recite our canonical numerals in their intrinsic ordering of increasing size of numbers thereby denoted. We shall therefore speak of the standard sequence (or standard ordering) of either numbers denoted, or numerals used to denote them. With the Dedekind–Peano canonical numerals $\underline{n}$, this intrinsic ordering of increasing size of numbers thereby denoted happily coincides with the intrinsic ordering of increasing size (i.e., length) of the canonical numerals themselves:[2]

$$\begin{array}{l} 0 \\ s0 \\ ss0 \\ sss0 \\ \vdots \end{array}$$

This is also true of the sequence of canonical 'Frege–Dedekind–Peano' terms

$$\begin{array}{l} \#x(Nx \wedge x \leq 0) \\ \#x(Nx \wedge x \leq s0) \\ \#x(Nx \wedge x \leq ss0) \\ \#x(Nx \wedge x \leq sss0) \\ \vdots \end{array}$$

This sequence also has the conventional feature that it begins with (what counts as) $\underline{1}$.[3] It is not true, however, of any sequence of canonical numerals in place notation. For example, the sequence of canonical numerals in binary place notation runs

$$\begin{array}{l} 0 \\ 1 \\ 10 \\ 11 \\ \vdots \end{array}$$

and we see already in this initial segment two equal-length pairs of numerals. In the more familiar decimal place notation the initial segment consisting of the first ten canonical numerals (from 0 through 9, inclusive) are all of length 1. And in any place-notation, whatever its base (two or ten, in these last two examples), one encounters increasing lengths of segments of same-length numerals.

[1] Subitizing is the cognitive phenomenon of being able to 'tell in an instant', by looking at a small collection of medium-sized objects, how many of them there are. Only very small collections can be subitized by the average human agent.

[2] We set aside as superfluous the point that almost everyone starts counting a non-empty collection with 1 rather than with 0. We can accommodate this with a trivial adjustment.

[3] Note how these 'Frege–Dedekind–Peano' abstractive terms contain Dedekind–Peano numerals after the less-than-or-equal-to sign.

That, however, is a consequence of the main virtue of these place-notations; they afford logarithmic reduction in the length of numerals required canonically to denote ever-larger numbers.

That is also why we have to internalize algorithms to decide, of any two given canonical numerals, which precedes the other in the standard sequence. Such is the role of rote childhood chanting of the ‘1, 2, 3 …’ variety. Every such algorithm is grounded in the brute fact of transitive closure of the relation of immediate succession of the k single digits for the k-based place notation in question. Thus, for our familiar decimal notation (where $k = 10$) we have the sequence of immediate successions

$$0 < 1 < 2 < 3 < 4 < 5 < 6 < 7 < 8 < 9$$

and the transitive closure $<^*$ of the relation of immediate succession thus exhibited therefore coincides with the relation ‘…is to the left of __’ in the foregoing display. The fundamental point is that for any two distinct single digits k_1, k_2, we can effectively decide which one of ‘$k_1 <^* k_2$’ or ‘$k_2 <^* k_1$’ is true (for the chosen place notation). Exactly one of these will be true. On that basis it is then easy to extend $<^*$ to the relation $<^{**}$ (the standard ordering) of numerals consisting of more than one digit. One can effectively decide of any two given finite sequences $\underline{n}, \underline{m}$ of such digits (each beginning with a digit other than 0) which one of them precedes the other in the standard sequence (i.e., in said extension of $<^{**}$). Again, there will be a uniquely correct, effectively determinable answer.[4] Such sequences make up the (infinitely many) remaining canonical numerals in the place notation in question.

So we do see a useful role for the rote learning of the standard ordering $<^{**}$ of all our canonical numerals. It increases in its sophistication from reciting the single digits in their standard ordering, to learning how to count (‘intransitively’) using canonical place-notational numerals consisting of more than one digit, again in the standard ordering $<^{**}$ that extends the standard ordering $<^*$ of the single digits themselves. This part of the decision-method for precedence—involving canonical numerals consisting of more than one digit—is invariant over all place notations. All that distinguishes these place notations from one another is the ‘look-up table’ for their single digits. And they must all have a ‘zero’. Thereafter, the method for determining precedence among multi-digit numerals is the same, regardless of how many distinct single digits the notation employs.

A subtle question now arises, which might perplex even a sophisticated and numerate thinker:

[4] This is why Benacerraf was careful to speak of *recursive* ω-progressions. (See, however, our remarks in Chapter 2, footnote 20, about the recantation in Benacerraf [1996] of the recursiveness requirement in his famous 1965 paper ‘What Numbers Could Not Be’.) The present author is not persuaded by Benacerraf’s Byzantine thought-experiment in support of his recantation, but for reasons that would take us too far astray to set out conclusively here. The presumption here continues to be that the relation ‘x precedes y’ needs to be effectively decidable. We described the algorithm for determining precedence on p. 77.

> When we count a finite collection of objects, why do we always recite our numerals, as we 'flip through' the objects one by one, in their standard ordering?

To the reader who might be perplexed by this question, let us point out a perverse possibility that could arise. To make matters easier, let us consider a smallish collection of objects of kind Φ—say, a collection of seven Φs—and assume that the agent counting this collection does not 'subitize' it. That is, the counter actually needs to count the Φs in order to determine the correct canonical answer (in the form of a canonical numeral) to the question 'How many of these objects (Φs) are there?'.

In whatever system S of canonical numerals one employs, let the numeral denoting the number n be called n_S. Our question is provoked by the following possibility. The counter who uses system S has 7! (7-factorial) ways to establish a one-one mapping, onto the seven Φs, of the numerals standardly preceding n_S—and thereby of the numbers preceding 7 that these numerals denote.

Suppose the counter is using our familiar decimal place notation. Our question arises, however, regardless of the choice of kind of canonical numerals. It arises for any place notation, binary or beyond, as well as for the Dedekind–Peano (0, s)-numerals, and for the canonical 'Frege–Dedekind–Peano' terms of the form $\#x(Nx \wedge x < \underline{n})$.[5] This is because counting is done in time. Counting is a linear process. When we envisage a one-one mapping R of the numerals or numbers preceding 7 onto the Φs:

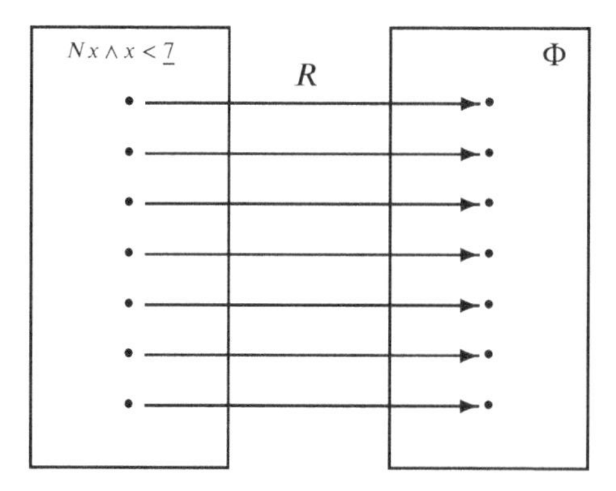

what we have just depicted is all there is to there being 7 Φs (i.e., to the number of Φs being 7).

The diagram shows precisely that

$$\#x\Phi x = \#x(Nx \wedge x < \underline{7}).$$

[5]Note than in these 'Frege–Dedekind–Peano' terms of the form $\#x(Nx \wedge x < \underline{n})$, the embedded numeral $\underline{n}$ is of the Dedekind–Peano kind!

Appealing then to the theorem

$$\underline{n} = \#x(Nx \wedge x < \underline{n})$$

we can conclude that

$$\#x\Phi x = \underline{7}.$$

The dots in the left rectangle represent the numbers in the extension of the predicate $(Nx \wedge x < \underline{7})$ in their sevenfoldness; but note that those dots have not been labeled with numerals! Now of course if the counting takes place in the standard way (i.e., using the numerals in their standard succession, through time) and the counting takes place from top to bottom, then the correct labeling of the dots on the left would be as follows:

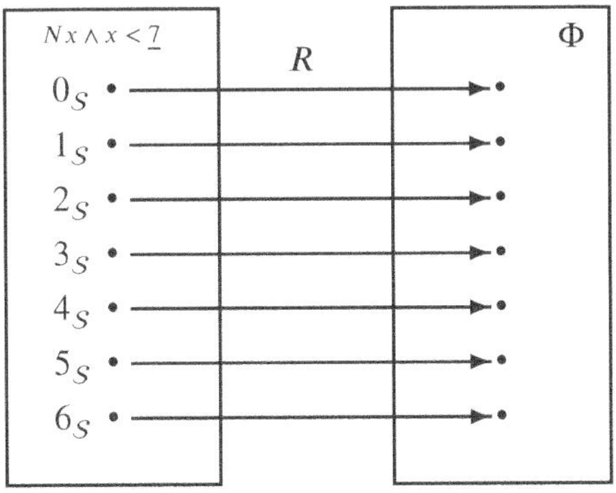

$Nx \wedge x < \underline{7}$

R

Φ

0_S
1_S
2_S
3_S
4_S
5_S
6_S

But suppose the counter has instead established (through time, from top to bottom) the following deviant one-one onto correlation of the S-numerals preceding 7_S onto the Φs:

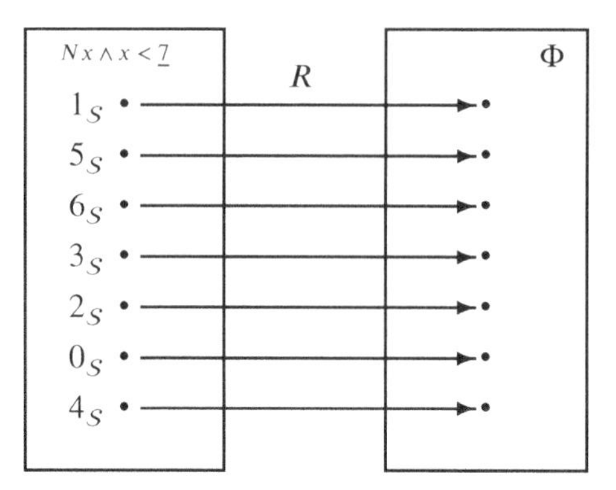

Suppose, that is, that the counter actually recited '1, 5, 6, 3, 2, 0, 4', in that order, in order to complete his count of the seven Φs. This deviant act of counting still establishes the truth of

$$\#x\Phi x = \#x(Nx \wedge x < \underline{7})\ ![6]$$

And there are

$$7! - 2 \ = \ 5038$$

yet further deviant ways that one could label the dots on the left, from top to bottom, with the S-numerals preceding 7_S in the standard ordering.

Our subtle and perplexing question that we said earlier had to be answered can now be expressed in this way:

> Why is it that we always choose the standard ordering when determining cardinalities of finite collections, when it would appear that with any n-membered collection there would be $(n! - 1)$ alternative orderings-in-recitation of the numerals preceding n_S, any of which orderings would actually suffice to establish the sought fact that
>
> $$\#x\Phi x = \#x(Nx \wedge x < \underline{n})\ ?$$

The answer to this question has to invoke pragmatic considerations.

Consider first how in our thought-experiment involving but seven Φs to be counted, the deviant correlations-through-time that were inviting consideration actually involved the first seven numerals in the standard ordering. With larger numbers than 7, this sort of thing would be a fluke.

If, on the one hand, too many numerals were to be taken ('guessed') from the intial segment of the standard ordering, and the counter were to set about

[6] This is an exclamation mark, not the symbol for the factorial function.

correlating them one-one with Φs, she would not use up all her chosen ('guessed') numerals by the time she had used up all the Φs themselves. So the 'count' would fail, since it would not do what it is required to do, namely: establish (for the right n) a one-one, onto correlation of the first n numerals (in the standard ordering) with the Φs that are to be counted. There would be 'gaps' in the sequence of numerals actually used up. The largest among them would, if misconstrued as an answer to the question 'How many Φs are there?', be crashingly incorrect.

If, on the other hand, too few numerals were to be 'guessed' at the outset as exactly the ones necessary and sufficient for a successful count, the counter would be thwarted by incompletion. Of course she may seek to resume or continue the count, by selecting more numerals (hopefully an initial segment in the standard ordering of the as yet unused ones); but in order to know 'where in the sequence' of numerals to choose the new least one, she would not be able, in general, to take the very next one after the last one she had used before running out of her initially chosen numerals. Rather, she would have to go back over the numerals she had used, in order to locate the largest one; and only then proceed with a new selection (for the as yet uncounted Φs) to finish off the task of counting. Locating the largest numeral used, if those used were used in other than their standard ordering, would be unnecessarily time-consuming.

And this now affords a segue into the most compelling of pragmatic considerations (apart from the danger, just described, of getting a plainly wrong answer!). We have already stressed that counting takes place in time; it is a time-consuming process. And any time-consuming cognitive task places a premium on the time used. It will always be to one's advantage to take as little time as possible in the execution of any such task. And one of the things one has to guard against is interruptions or distractions that might result in a costly waste of whatever effort one has expended thus far in the partial execution of a task. (Think, for example, of one of our ancestors trying hastily to determine how many pebbles he has left for his sling, or arrows for his bow, in the face of looming dangers requiring an appropriate strategic response.) That is why, when we count, we always recite the numerals *seriatim*, in their standard ordering. For, by the simple stratagem of 'setting to one side', or 'ticking off', the objects counted thus far, leaving to the other side, or 'unticked', those that have yet to be counted, we can withstand the otherwise costly ravages of interruptions and distractions. All one has to recall is the very last numeral one had recited before the interruption or distraction occurred. Then one could resume one's task of counting where one had left off. The only time lost would be no more than that consumed by the interruption or distraction itself. One could, moreover, share the task with other counters who might take over for one after such an interruption or distraction. All one would have to do is indicate to them which of the Φs had already been counted, and what numeral one had reached before one's own (partial) count ended.

Minimizing one's vulnerability to interruptions or distractions is a consideration that is fine-grained. It applies at every stage one might reach. That is, at every point in a process of counting, one would want to be able to say, with minimal further computational effort, exactly how many objects one had counted by that stage. That is, we have to minimize demands on memory and time. The only way to do this is to make it always be the case that the most recent numeral reached—which is the one most easily recalled, and by-itself-sufficient—is the controlling one. The standard succession of canonical S-numerals (in any notation-system S) emerges as the unique solution to this stage-by-stage optimization problem. Every sub-count must count as a count. It follows that in order to count with cardinal numbers, we have to use them in their ordinal sequence.

These considerations by themselves would impose significant selective pressures for the adoption, by the community, of a standard ordering of their numerals, an ordering to be respected throughout every act of counting, individual or collective. It would also prepare the cognitive ground for a grasp of addition—the union of two disjoint collections of cardinalities n and m would have $(n + m)$ members. The canonical numeral corresponding to $(\underline{n} + \underline{m})$, i.e., to $\underline{m + n}$, would be reached most efficiently by beginning with the count of the larger of the two collections—say, the first one (assuming $n > m$)—by pronouncing '$\underline{n - 1}$' at the outset and then continuing the count, using succeeding numerals in their standard ordering, until one had finished thus 'shift-counting' the objects in the second collection. One would thereby obtain the correct canonical answer to the 'How many?' question regarding the union of the two collections.

Chapter 13

Formal Results about the Inductively Defined Numerically Exact Quantifiers

Abstract

This chapter is devoted to the excruciating drudgery of a logical monk actually doing the work that a logical saint would find unnecessary, to establish the metatheorem which states that for all n, and for all substituends for Φ, one has

$$\nabla_n x \Phi x \dashv\vdash \Diamond_n x \Phi x\,.$$

Note that although for any particular n one can effectively find the requisite proofs in monadic first-order logic, the proof of the metatheorem itself, because of its general form, does not proceed within monadic first-order logic. An important philosophical corollary of this metatheorem is that no ordering of the Φs—be it one intrinsic to them, or imposed upon them arbitrarily in the act of counting—can possibly figure into the truth-conditions of numerosity statements to the effect that 'there are exactly this-many Φs'.

In this chapter, less technically oriented readers may omit reading the technical details of proofs of results, and take those results on trust. They are invited to skip ahead to the paragraph of prose on p. 150 immediately preceding the statement of Metatheorem 4.

Recall that $\exists!t$ means that t exists. It is short for $\exists x\, x=t$.

Lemma 31. *For all n, for all k, for all m > k, for all substituends for* Φ*, we have*

$$\left.\begin{array}{r} \exists!a_1,\ldots,\exists!a_k \\ \exists!b_1,\ldots,\exists!b_m \\ \Phi a_1,\ldots,\Phi a_k \\ \Phi b_1,\ldots,\Phi b_m \\ a_i \neq a_j\ (1\leq i<j\leq k) \\ b_i \neq b_j\ (1\leq i<j\leq m) \\ \nabla_n x(\Phi x \wedge \bigwedge_{1\leq i\leq k} x\neq a_i) \\ \nabla_n x(\Phi x \wedge \bigwedge_{1\leq i\leq m} x\neq b_i) \end{array}\right\} \vdash \bot$$

The Logic of Number. Neil Tennant, Oxford University Press. © Neil Tennant 2022.
DOI: 10.1093/oso/9780192846679.003.0013

Proof. By induction on n. *Warning to the unsuspecting reader*: the basis step to follow is surprisingly long.

For the basis, where $n=0$, we need to show that for all k, for all $m > k$, for all substituends for Φ, we have

$$\left.\begin{array}{r} \exists!a_1,\ldots,\exists!a_k \\ \exists!b_1,\ldots,\exists!b_m \\ \Phi a_1,\ldots,\Phi a_k \\ \Phi b_1,\ldots,\Phi b_m \\ a_i \neq a_j\ (1 \leq i < j \leq k) \\ b_i \neq b_j\ (1 \leq i < j \leq m) \\ \nabla_0 x(\Phi x \wedge \bigwedge_{1\leq i\leq k} x \neq a_i) \\ \nabla_0 x(\Phi x \wedge \bigwedge_{1\leq i\leq m} x \neq b_i) \end{array}\right\} \vdash \bot$$

i.e., by the basis clause of Definition (4)

$$\left.\begin{array}{r} \exists!a_1,\ldots,\exists!a_k \\ \exists!b_1,\ldots,\exists!b_m \\ \Phi a_1,\ldots,\Phi a_k \\ \Phi b_1,\ldots,\Phi b_m \\ a_i \neq a_j\ (1 \leq i < j \leq k) \\ b_i \neq b_j\ (1 \leq i < j \leq m) \\ \neg\exists x(\Phi x \wedge \bigwedge_{1\leq i\leq k} x \neq a_i) \\ \neg\exists x(\Phi x \wedge \bigwedge_{1\leq i\leq m} x \neq b_i) \end{array}\right\} \vdash \bot$$

We remind the reader that this basis-clause statement is to be established for all k and for all $m > k$. So the smallest possible values would be $k = 0$ and $m = 1$. In this case, the mention of the a_i disappears; and the deducibility claim to be established is therefore

$$\left.\begin{array}{r} \exists!b_1 \\ \Phi b_1 \\ \neg\exists x\Phi x \\ \neg\exists x(\Phi x \wedge x \neq b_1) \end{array}\right\} \vdash \bot$$

Indeed, we have the even stronger deducibility

$$\left.\begin{array}{r} \exists!b_1 \\ \Phi b_1 \\ \neg\exists x\Phi x \end{array}\right\} \vdash \bot$$

But this localized observation does not dispose of the general case (arbitrary $k < m$); it deals only with the case where $k = 0$ and $m = 1$. And even though one can see easily how to generalize it to arbitrary m while keeping $k = 0$, there is still the need to deal differently and more resourcefully with the truly general case of arbitrary $0<k<m$.

So suppose now that $0<k<m$. We need to consider every possible combination of identity and distinctness assumptions of the forms $t=u$ or $t\neq u$ (only one of such a pair being chosen), where t and u are distinct parameters chosen from the combined list $a_1, \ldots, a_k, b_1 \ldots, b_m$. These assumptions will give rise to (core) *reductio* proofs of the forms

$$\begin{array}{cc} \underbrace{\Delta_1\,,\ t=u} & \underbrace{\Delta_2\,,\ t\neq u} \\ \Pi_1 & \Pi_2 \\ \bot & \bot \end{array}$$

where Δ_1 and Δ_2 are sets of permitted premises from the list given above, with each of Δ_1 and Δ_2 containing neither $t=u$ nor $t\neq u$. From any two such *reductio* proofs it is easy to determine a (core) proof of $\bot$ from $\Delta_1 \cup \Delta_2$.

All such assumptions of the form $a_i = a_j$ and of the form $b_i = b_j$ will of course deductively imply $\bot$, since we already have premises to the effect that the $a_1, \ldots, a_k$ are pairwise distinct, and the $b_1, \ldots, b_m$ likewise. So the remaining 'identities' to contemplate are those of the form $a_i = b_j$. For any distinct i, i' we have the simple proofs

$$\dfrac{a_i\neq a_{i'} \qquad \dfrac{a_i=b_j \quad a_{i'}=b_j}{a_i=a_{i'}}}{\bot} \qquad\qquad \dfrac{b_i\neq b_{i'} \qquad \dfrac{a_j=b_i \quad a_j=b_{i'}}{b_i=b_{i'}}}{\bot}$$

to establish the sought inconsistency. In each case the topmost pair of premises tells us that the relation of 'setting equal to' is (respectively) being assumed to be many-one or one-many. That immediately falls foul of the assumed pairwise distinctness of $a_1, \ldots, a_k$ and of $b_1, \ldots, b_m$.

The only remaining way (which will nevertheless prove to be futile!) to try to escape such rapid and trivial *reductio ad absurdum* of identity assumptions is to entertain ones of the form $a_i = b_j$ that collectively make for a one-one injection of the list of parameters $a_1, \ldots, a_k$ into (but not onto) the list of parameters $b_1 \ldots, b_m$. That this injection will not be onto is guaranteed by the assumption that $k < m$. In these circumstances there will be at least one parameter (call it b) among $b_1 \ldots, b_m$ that is not involved in any identity of the form $a_i = b$, and indeed is being assumed to be distinct from each of $a_1, \ldots, a_k$. We will then have

$$\left.\begin{array}{r} \exists! b \\ \Phi b \\ b\neq a_i\ (1 \leq i \leq k) \end{array}\right\} \vdash \exists x(\Phi x \wedge \bigwedge_{1\leq i\leq k} x\neq a_i)\ ;$$

whence obviously we find

$$\left.\begin{array}{r} \exists!b \\ \Phi b \\ b \neq a_i \ (1 \leq i \leq k) \\ \neg\exists x(\Phi x \wedge \bigwedge_{1\leq i\leq k} x \neq a_i) \end{array}\right\} \vdash \bot .$$

So the last imagined escape route is well and truly blocked.

Usually the basis step for an inductive proof is quite easy—or, at least, short. But for the lemma at hand it has been unusually roundabout. That inconvenience is about to be offset, however, by the logically simple progression of the inductive step.

Inductive Hypothesis: For all k, for all $m > k$, for all substituends for Φ, we have

$$\left.\begin{array}{r} \exists!a_1, \ldots, \exists!a_k \\ \exists!b_1, \ldots, \exists!b_m \\ \Phi a_1, \ldots, \Phi a_k \\ \Phi b_1, \ldots, \Phi b_m \\ a_i \neq a_j \ (1 \leq i < j \leq k) \\ b_i \neq b_j \ (1 \leq i < j \leq m) \\ \nabla_n x(\Phi x \wedge \bigwedge_{1\leq i\leq k} x \neq a_i) \\ \nabla_n x(\Phi x \wedge \bigwedge_{1\leq i\leq m} x \neq b_i) \end{array}\right\} \vdash \bot$$

Inductive Step: Show that for all k, for all $m > k$, for all substituends for Φ, we have

$$\left.\begin{array}{r} \exists!a_1, \ldots, \exists!a_k \\ \exists!b_1, \ldots, \exists!b_m \\ \Phi a_1, \ldots, \Phi a_k \\ \Phi b_1, \ldots, \Phi b_m \\ a_i \neq a_j \ (1 \leq i < j \leq k) \\ b_i \neq b_j \ (1 \leq i < j \leq m) \\ \nabla_{sn} x(\Phi x \wedge \bigwedge_{1\leq i\leq k} x \neq a_i) \\ \nabla_n sx(\Phi x \wedge \bigwedge_{1\leq i\leq m} x \neq b_i) \end{array}\right\} \vdash \bot$$

By the inductive clause of Definition (4) the inconsistency to be proved is

$$\left.\begin{array}{r} \exists!a_1, \ldots, \exists!a_k \\ \exists!b_1, \ldots, \exists!b_m \\ \Phi a_1, \ldots, \Phi a_k \\ \Phi b_1, \ldots, \Phi b_m \\ a_i \neq a_j \ (1 \leq i < j \leq k) \\ b_i \neq b_j \ (1 \leq i < j \leq m) \\ \exists y((\Phi y \wedge \bigwedge_{1\leq i\leq k} y \neq a_i) \wedge \nabla_n x((\Phi x \wedge \bigwedge_{1\leq i\leq k} x \neq a_i) \wedge x \neq y) \\ \exists y((\Phi y \wedge \bigwedge_{1\leq i\leq m} y \neq b_i) \wedge \nabla_n x((\Phi x \wedge \bigwedge_{1\leq i\leq m} x \neq b_i) \wedge x \neq y) \end{array}\right\} \vdash \bot$$

This holds if and only if, for parameters c and d chosen for elimination of the respective existentials displayed, we have

$$\left.\begin{array}{r} \exists!a_1,\ldots,\exists!a_k,\ \exists!c \\ \exists!b_1,\ldots,\exists!b_m,\ \exists!d \\ \Phi a_1,\ldots,\Phi a_k \\ \Phi b_1,\ldots,\Phi b_m \\ a_i \neq a_j\ (1 \leq i < j \leq k) \\ b_i \neq b_j\ (1 \leq i < j \leq m) \\ (\Phi c \wedge \bigwedge_{1\leq i\leq k} c \neq a_i) \wedge \nabla_n x((\Phi x \wedge \bigwedge_{1\leq i\leq k} x \neq a_i) \wedge x \neq c) \\ (\Phi d \wedge \bigwedge_{1\leq i\leq m} d \neq b_i) \wedge \nabla_n x((\Phi x \wedge \bigwedge_{1\leq i\leq m} x \neq b_i) \wedge x \neq d) \end{array}\right\} \vdash \bot$$

This in turn holds just in case

$$\left.\begin{array}{r} \exists!a_1,\ldots,\exists!a_k,\ \exists!c \\ \exists!b_1,\ldots,\exists!b_m,\ \exists!d \\ \Phi a_1,\ldots,\Phi a_k,\ \Phi c \\ \Phi b_1,\ldots,\Phi b_m,\ \Phi d \\ a_i \neq a_j\ (1 \leq i < j \leq k) \\ b_i \neq b_j\ (1 \leq i < j \leq m) \\ \bigwedge_{1\leq i\leq k} a_i \neq c \\ \nabla_n x((\Phi x \wedge \bigwedge_{1\leq i\leq k} x \neq a_i) \wedge x \neq c) \\ \bigwedge_{1\leq i\leq m} b_i \neq d \\ \nabla_n x((\Phi x \wedge \bigwedge_{1\leq i\leq m} x \neq b_i) \wedge x \neq d) \end{array}\right\} \vdash \bot$$

Now treat c as a_{k+1}, and treat d as b_{m+1}:

$$\left.\begin{array}{r} \exists!a_1,\ldots,\exists!a_k,\ \exists!a_{k+1} \\ \exists!b_1,\ldots,\exists!b_m,\ \exists!b_{m+1} \\ \Phi a_1,\ldots,\Phi a_k,\ \Phi a_{k+1} \\ \Phi b_1,\ldots,\Phi b_m,\ \Phi b_{m+1} \\ a_i \neq a_j\ (1 \leq i < j \leq k) \\ b_i \neq b_j\ (1 \leq i < j \leq m) \\ \bigwedge_{1\leq i\leq k} a_i \neq a_{k+1} \\ \nabla_n x((\Phi x \wedge \bigwedge_{1\leq i\leq k} x \neq a_i) \wedge x \neq a_{k+1}) \\ \bigwedge_{1\leq i\leq m} b_i \neq b_{m+1} \\ \nabla_n x((\Phi x \wedge \bigwedge_{1\leq i\leq m} x \neq b_i) \wedge x \neq b_{m+1}) \end{array}\right\} \vdash \bot$$

and rearrange:

$$\left.\begin{array}{r} \exists!a_1,\ldots,\exists!a_k,\ \exists!a_{k+1} \\ \exists!b_1,\ldots,\exists!b_m,\ \exists!b_{m+1} \\ \Phi a_1,\ldots,\Phi a_k,\ \Phi a_{k+1} \\ \Phi b_1,\ldots,\Phi b_m,\ \Phi b_{m+1} \\ a_i \neq a_j\ (1 \leq i < j \leq k+1) \\ b_i \neq b_j\ (1 \leq i < j \leq m+1) \\ \bigwedge_{1\leq i\leq k+1} a_i \neq a_j \\ \nabla_n x(\Phi x \wedge \bigwedge_{1\leq i\leq k+1} x \neq a_i) \\ \bigwedge_{1\leq i\leq m+1} b_i \neq b_j \\ \nabla_n x(\Phi x \wedge \bigwedge_{1\leq i\leq m+1} x \neq b_i) \end{array}\right\} \vdash \bot$$

It is easy to see that this is vouchsafed by the Inductive Hypothesis.

□

Lemma 32. *For all n, for all substituends for Ψ,*

$$\exists!a,\ \Psi a,\ \nabla_n x\Psi x,\ \nabla_n x(\Psi x \wedge x \neq a) \ \vdash \ \bot$$

Proof. By induction on n. For the basis (where $n = 0$) we need to show that for all substituends for Ψ we have

$$\exists!a,\ \Psi a,\ \nabla_0 x\Psi x,\ \nabla_0 x(\Psi x \wedge x \neq a) \ \vdash \ \bot$$

In fact, we can show something even stronger: for all substituends for Ψ we have

$$\exists!a,\ \Psi a,\ \nabla_0 x\Psi x \ \vdash \ \bot$$

Here is the proof:

$$\dfrac{\begin{array}{l}\nabla_0 x\Psi x, \text{ i.e.:} \\ \neg\exists x\Psi x\end{array} \qquad \dfrac{\Psi a \quad \exists!a}{\exists x\Psi x}}{\bot}$$

Inductive Hypothesis: Suppose the result holds for $m > 0$: for all substituends for Ψ, we have

$$\exists!a,\ \Psi a,\ \nabla_m x\Psi x,\ \nabla_m x(\Psi x \wedge x \neq a) \ \vdash \ \bot,$$

Inductive Step: Using the Inductive Hypothesis, show that the result holds for sm: for all substituends for Ψ, we have

$$\exists!a,\ \Psi a,\ \nabla_{sm} x\Psi x,\ \nabla_{sm} x(\Psi x \wedge x \neq a) \ \vdash \ \bot$$

i.e.,

$$\exists!a,\ \Psi a,\ \exists y(\Psi y \wedge \nabla_m x(\Psi x \wedge x \neq y)),\ \exists y((\Psi y \wedge y \neq a) \wedge \nabla_m x((\Psi x \wedge x \neq a) \wedge x \neq y)) \ \vdash \ \bot.$$

This deducibility holds just in case the following one holds, where we use the independent parameters b and c to instantiate the first and second existentially quantified premises respectively:

$$\exists! a,\ \Psi a,\ \exists! b,\ \Psi b,\ \nabla_m x(\Psi x \wedge x \neq b),\ \exists! c,\ \Psi c,\ c \neq a,\ \nabla_m x((\Psi x \wedge x \neq a) \wedge x \neq c)\ \vdash\ \bot.$$

This is a special case of Lemma 31.

□

Lemma 33. *For all k, for all substituends for Φ,*

$$\nabla_k x(\Phi x \wedge x \neq a)\,,\ \exists! a\,,\ \Phi a\,,\ \exists! b\,,\ \Phi b\ \vdash\ \nabla_k x(\Phi x \wedge x \neq b)$$

Proof. By induction on k. For the basis (where $k=0$) we need to show that for all substituends Φ we have

$$\nabla_0 x(\Phi x \wedge x \neq a)\,,\ \exists! a\,,\ \Phi a\,,\ \exists! b\,,\ \Phi b\ \vdash\ \nabla_0 x(\Phi x \wedge x \neq b)$$

In fact, we can show something even stronger: for all substituends Φ we have

$$\nabla_k x(\Phi x \wedge x \neq a)\,,\ \exists! b\,,\ \Phi b\ \vdash\ \bot$$

Here is the proof:

$$\dfrac{\dfrac{\nabla_0 x(\Phi x \wedge x \neq a) \quad \overline{b=a}^{\,(1)}}{\nabla_0 x(\Phi x \wedge x \neq b)} \qquad \dfrac{\begin{array}{c}\nabla_0 x(\Phi x \wedge x \neq a),\ \text{i.e.:}\\ \neg\exists x(\Phi x \wedge x \neq a)\end{array} \quad \dfrac{\dfrac{\Phi b \quad \overline{b \neq a}^{\,(1)}}{\Phi b \wedge b \neq a} \quad \exists! b}{\exists x(\Phi x \wedge x \neq a)}}{\bot}}{\nabla_0 x(\Phi x \wedge x \neq b)}\,{}^{(1)}$$

Note how the negative horn of the Dilemma marked (1) has conclusion ⊥— something that is permitted in Classical Core Logic. This application of Dilemma is constructively accessible, since its litmus sentence is the identity $b=a$; and the identity relation among things being counted is decidable.

Inductive Hypothesis: Suppose the result holds for $n>0$: for all substituends Φ, we have

$$\nabla_n x(\Phi x \wedge x \neq a)\,,\ \exists! a\,,\ \Phi a\,,\ \exists! b\,,\ \Phi b\ \vdash\ \nabla_n x(\Phi x \wedge x \neq b),$$

i.e.,

$$\exists y((\Phi y \wedge y \neq a) \wedge \nabla_{n-1} x((\Phi x \wedge x \neq a) \wedge x \neq y))\,,\ \exists! a\,,\ \Phi a\,,\ \exists! b\,,\ \Phi b\ \vdash$$

$$\exists y((\Phi y \wedge y \neq b) \wedge \nabla_{n-1} x((\Phi x \wedge x \neq b) \wedge x \neq y)).$$

Inductive Step: Using the Inductive Hypothesis, show that the result holds for sn: for all substituends Φ, we have

$$\nabla_{sn}x(\Phi x \wedge x \neq a)\,,\ \exists!a\,,\ \Phi a\,,\ \exists!b\,,\ \Phi b \ \vdash\ \nabla_{sn}x(\Phi x \wedge x \neq b),$$

i.e.,

$$\exists y((\Phi y \wedge y \neq a) \wedge \nabla_{n} x((\Phi x \wedge x \neq a) \wedge x \neq y))\,,\ \exists!a\,,\ \Phi a\,,\ \exists!b\,,\ \Phi b \ \vdash$$

$$\exists y((\Phi y \wedge y \neq b) \wedge \nabla_{n} x((\Phi x \wedge x \neq b) \wedge x \neq y)).$$

We face the challenge here of some rather long formal sentences that have to be fitted into the horizontal space begrudged them both by natural deduction and by the dimensions of this page. So we shall resort to describing the overall formal proof in stages, rather than trying to squeeze it onto the page all in one go. The formal proof of the last deducibility claim proceeds by Dilemma at its final step. The positive horn is $a = b$; the negative horn, accordingly, is $a \neq b$. In the positive horn, it is clear that a single application of substitutivity of identicals secures the sought result; while for the negative horn, there is further work to do (constructing the embedded subproof Π):

$$\dfrac{\dfrac{\nabla_{sn}x(\Phi x \wedge x \neq a) \quad \overline{a = b}^{\,(1)}}{\nabla_{sn}x(\Phi x \wedge x \neq b)} \qquad \begin{array}{c} \underbrace{\nabla_{sn}x(\Phi x \wedge x \neq a),\ \exists!a,\ \Phi a,\ \exists!b,\ \Phi b,\ \overline{a \neq b}^{\,(1)}} \\ \Pi \\ \nabla_{sn}x(\Phi x \wedge x \neq b) \end{array}}{\nabla_{sn}x(\Phi x \wedge x \neq b)}{\scriptstyle (1)}$$

It remains, then, to construct Π, which takes the more detailed form

$$\begin{array}{c} \underbrace{\exists y((\Phi y \wedge y \neq a) \wedge \nabla_{n} x((\Phi x \wedge x \neq a) \wedge x \neq y)),\ \exists!a,\ \Phi a,\ \exists!b,\ \Phi b,\ a \neq b} \\ \Pi \\ \exists y((\Phi y \wedge y \neq b) \wedge \nabla_{n} x((\Phi x \wedge x \neq b) \wedge x \neq y)) \end{array}$$

The last step of Π will be $\exists$-Elimination, involving the parameter c; for this step we therefore seek a parametric subproof of the form

$$\begin{array}{c} \underbrace{\exists!c,\ (\Phi c \wedge c \neq a) \wedge \nabla_{n} x((\Phi x \wedge x \neq a) \wedge x \neq c),\ \exists!a,\ \Phi a,\ \exists!b,\ \Phi b,\ a \neq b} \\ \Pi' \\ \exists y((\Phi y \wedge y \neq b) \wedge \nabla_{n} x((\Phi x \wedge x \neq b) \wedge x \neq y)) \end{array}$$

This reduces straightforwardly (here foreshadowing some obvious $\wedge$-Eliminations) to finding a proof of the form

$$\underbrace{\exists!c,\ \Phi c,\ c\neq a,\ \nabla_n x((\Phi x \wedge x\neq a)\wedge x\neq c),\ \exists!a,\ \Phi a,\ \exists!b,\ \Phi b,\ a\neq b}_{\Pi''}$$
$$\exists y((\Phi y \wedge y\neq b)\wedge \nabla_n x((\Phi x \wedge x\neq b)\wedge x\neq y))$$

We shall construct Π'' as follows. Note that the deductive passages indicated by vertical dots could be accomplished by using any of the extra premises just stated for Π''; but such appeal to these extra premises will need to be made only with the passage that invokes the Inductive Hypothesis.

The embedded proof Σ below will take shape in due course.

Let Λ abbreviate the set

$$\{\exists!c, \Phi c, c\neq a, \nabla_n x((\Phi x \wedge x\neq a)\wedge x\neq c), \exists!a, \Phi a, \exists!b, \Phi b, a\neq b\}$$

$$\dfrac{\exists!c \qquad \dfrac{\dfrac{\Phi c \qquad \dfrac{\underbrace{\Lambda,\ \overline{c=b}^{(2)}}_{\Sigma} \atop \bot}{c\neq b}{(2)}}{\Phi c \wedge c\neq b} \qquad \begin{matrix}\nabla_n x((\Phi x \wedge x\neq a)\wedge x\neq c)\\ \vdots \text{ by equivalence of matrices}\\ \nabla_n x((\Phi x \wedge x\neq c)\wedge x\neq a)\\ \vdots \text{ by IH with } (\Phi x \wedge x\neq c) \text{ as substituend}\\ \nabla_n x((\Phi x \wedge x\neq c)\wedge x\neq b)\\ \vdots \text{ by equivalence of matrices}\\ \nabla_n x((\Phi x \wedge x\neq b)\wedge x\neq c)\end{matrix}}{(\Phi c \wedge c\neq b)\wedge \nabla_n x((\Phi x \wedge x\neq b)\wedge x\neq c)}}{\exists y((\Phi y \wedge y\neq b)\wedge \nabla_n x((\Phi x \wedge x\neq b)\wedge x\neq y))}$$

Let us call Ξ the subproof that we already have above of

$$\nabla_n x((\Phi x \wedge x\neq b)\wedge x\neq c);$$

and let us now have a closer look at how Σ is put together.

The embedded diproof Ω below will take shape in due course.

Here now is the (dis)proof Σ:

$$\underbrace{\exists!a, \exists!b, \Phi a, \Phi b, a\neq b,\ \begin{matrix}\dfrac{\overset{\Xi}{\nabla_n x((\Phi x \wedge x\neq b)\wedge x\neq c)} \quad c=b}{\nabla_n x((\Phi x \wedge x\neq b)\wedge x\neq b)}\\ \vdots \text{ by equivalence of matrices}\\ \nabla_n x(\Phi x \wedge x\neq b),\end{matrix} \qquad \begin{matrix}\dfrac{\nabla_n x((\Phi x \wedge x\neq a)\wedge x\neq c) \quad c=b}{\nabla_n x((\Phi x \wedge x\neq a)\wedge x\neq b)}\\ \vdots \text{ by equivalence of matrices}\\ \nabla_n x((\Phi x \wedge x\neq b)\wedge x\neq a)\end{matrix}}_{\Omega}$$
$$\bot$$

All eyes can now be on the disproof Ω. Setting Ψx to be $(\Phi x \wedge x \neq b)$, in anticipation of an application of Quine's maxim of shallow analysis, we note that the outstanding problem of finding a proof of the form

$$\underbrace{\exists!a\,,\ \exists!b\,,\ \Phi a\,,\ \Phi b\,,\ a\neq b\,,\ \nabla_n x(\Phi x \wedge x\neq b)\,,\ \nabla_n x((\Phi x \wedge x\neq b)\wedge x\neq a)}_{\substack{\Omega \\ \bot}}$$

can be reduced to that of finding one of the form

$$\underbrace{\exists!a\,,\ \Psi a\,,\ \nabla_n x\Psi x\,,\ \nabla_n x(\Psi x \wedge x\neq a)}_{\substack{\Omega' \\ \bot}}$$

And such a disproof Ω' exists, courtesy of Lemma 32. □

The following core-logical deducibilities are obvious:

$$\forall x(Fx \to \Phi x),\ \exists xFx \vdash_{\mathbb{C}} \exists x(Fx \wedge \Phi x)$$

$$\exists x(Fx \wedge \Phi x) \vdash_{\mathbb{C}} \exists xFx$$

The following sequent is not generally valid:

$$\exists x(Fx \wedge \Phi x) : \forall x(Fx \to \Phi x)$$

It is valid, however, for certain choices of Φ, such as are involved in the present study, having to do with numbering. We shall show that the following core-logical deducibility holds for all natural numbers n:

$$\exists x(Fx \wedge \nabla_n y(Fy \wedge y \neq x)) \vdash_{\mathbb{C}} \forall x(Fx \to \nabla_n y(Fy \wedge y \neq x))$$

The general deducibility

$$\forall x(Fx \to \Phi x),\ \exists xFx \vdash_{\mathbb{C}} \exists x(Fx \wedge \Phi x)$$

has, of course, the substitution instance

$$\forall x(Fx \to \nabla_n y(Fy \wedge y\neq x)),\ \exists xFx \vdash_{\mathbb{C}} \exists x(Fx \wedge \nabla_n y(Fy \wedge y\neq x))$$

So it can be called upon whenever it is needed.

Lemma 34. *For all natural numbers n, and for all predicates F,*

$$\exists x(Fx \wedge \nabla_n y(Fy \wedge y \neq x)) \vdash_{\mathbb{C}} \forall x(Fx \to \nabla_n y(Fy \wedge y \neq x))$$

Proof. By induction on n, exploiting Definition (4) of the numerically exact quantifiers ∇_n.

The basis step, for $n=0$, requires us to prove, for any predicate F, the sequent

$$\exists x(Fx \wedge \nabla_0 y(Fy \wedge y \neq x)) \ : \ \forall x(Fx \rightarrow \nabla_0 y(Fy \wedge y \neq x))$$

By Definition (4), this is the sequent

$$\exists x(Fx \wedge \neg\exists y(Fy \wedge y \neq x)) \ : \ \forall x(Fx \rightarrow \neg\exists y(Fy \wedge y \neq x))$$

Its core-logical proof is as follows.

$$\begin{array}{c}
\overline{Fc\wedge c\neq a}^{(5)} \quad \overline{c=b}^{(7)} \quad \overline{a=b}^{(6)} \\
\hline
c\neq a \qquad\qquad c=a \\
\hline
\dfrac{\qquad\bot\qquad}{}{}^{(6)} \\
\overline{Fa}^{(2)} \quad a\neq b \\
\hline
Fa\wedge a\neq b \quad \overline{\exists!a}^{(1)} \quad \overline{Fb\wedge\neg\exists y(Fy\wedge y\neq b)}^{(4)} \\
\hline
\exists y(Fy\wedge y\neq b) \qquad \neg\exists y(Fy\wedge y\neq b) \\
\hline
\overline{Fc\wedge c\neq a}^{(5)} \qquad\qquad \bot \\
\hline
Fc \qquad\qquad c\neq b \ {}^{(7)} \\
\hline
Fc\wedge c\neq b \quad \overline{\exists!c}^{(5)} \quad \overline{Fb\wedge\neg\exists y(Fy\wedge y\neq b)}^{(4)} \\
\hline
\exists y(Fy\wedge y\neq b) \qquad \neg\exists y(Fy\wedge y\neq b) \\
\hline
\overline{\exists y(Fy\wedge y\neq a)}^{(3)} \qquad\qquad \bot \\
\hline
\exists x(Fx\wedge\neg\exists y(Fy\wedge y\neq x)) \qquad\qquad \bot \ {}^{(5)} \\
\hline
\bot \ {}^{(4)} \\
\hline
\neg\exists y(Fy\wedge y\neq a) \ {}^{(3)} \\
\hline
Fa\rightarrow\neg\exists y(Fy\wedge y\neq a) \ {}^{(2)} \\
\hline
\forall x(Fx\rightarrow\neg\exists y(Fy\wedge y\neq x)) \ {}^{(1)}
\end{array}$$

Inductive Hypothesis: There is a core proof, for any predicate F, of the sequent

$$\exists x(Fx \wedge \nabla_k y(Fy \wedge y \neq x)) \ : \ \forall x(Fx \rightarrow \nabla_k y(Fy \wedge y \neq x))$$

Inductive Step: Using the Inductive Hypothesis (if necessary), show that there is a core proof, for any predicate F, of the sequent (or argument)

$$\frac{\exists x(Fx \wedge \nabla_{sk} y(Fy \wedge y \neq x))}{\forall x(Fx \rightarrow \nabla_{sk} y(Fy \wedge y \neq x))}$$

The inductive clause of Definition (4), relabeling variables to suit our present purposes, is

$$\nabla_{sk} y\Phi y \ \equiv_{df} \ \exists z(\Phi z \wedge \nabla_k w(\Phi w \wedge w \neq z))$$

In the problem sequent at hand, the subformula $Fy \wedge y \neq x$ is playing the role of Φy. So we need to make the following substitutions:

for Φw substitute $Fw \wedge w \neq x$;
for Φy substitute $Fy \wedge y \neq x$;
for Φz substitute $Fz \wedge z \neq x$.

Upon doing so, the inductive clause of Definition (4) becomes

$$\nabla_{sk}y(Fy \wedge y \neq x) \equiv_{df} \exists z((Fz \wedge z \neq x) \wedge \nabla_k w((Fw \wedge w \neq x) \wedge w \neq z))$$

Our sequent to be proved then becomes the argument

$$\frac{\exists x(Fx \wedge \exists z((Fz \wedge z \neq x) \wedge \nabla_k w((Fw \wedge w \neq x) \wedge w \neq z)))}{\forall x(Fx \rightarrow \exists z((Fz \wedge z \neq x) \wedge \nabla_k w((Fw \wedge w \neq x) \wedge w \neq z)))}$$

in which we now have only the numerically exact quantifier ∇_k appearing, rather than ∇_{sk}. We can now set about constructing a proof of this last inference.

We can construct one by taking a terminal step of $\exists$-Elimination provided only that we can find a parametric subproof

$$\underbrace{\exists!a_1\,,\ Fa_1\,,\ \exists z((Fz \wedge z \neq a_1) \wedge \nabla_k w((Fw \wedge w \neq a_1) \wedge w \neq z))}_{\substack{\Pi_1\\ \forall x(Fx \rightarrow \exists z((Fz \wedge z \neq x) \wedge \nabla_k w((Fw \wedge w \neq x) \wedge w \neq z)))}}$$

We shall find this, in turn, provided only that we can find a parametric subproof

$$\underbrace{\exists!a_1\,,\ Fa_1\,,\ \exists!a_2\,,\ (Fa_2 \wedge a_2 \neq a_1) \wedge \nabla_k w((Fw \wedge w \neq a_1) \wedge w \neq a_2)}_{\substack{\Pi_2\\ \forall x(Fx \rightarrow \exists z((Fz \wedge z \neq x) \wedge \nabla_k w((Fw \wedge w \neq x) \wedge w \neq z)))}}$$

This we can obtain by easy $\wedge$-Eliminations, provided only that we can find a proof of the form

$$\underbrace{\exists!a_1\,,\ Fa_1\,,\ \exists!a_2\,,\ Fa_2\,,\ a_1 \neq a_2\,,\ \nabla_k w((Fw \wedge w \neq a_1) \wedge w \neq a_2)}_{\substack{\Pi_3\\ \forall x(Fx \rightarrow \exists z((Fz \wedge z \neq x) \wedge \nabla_k w((Fw \wedge w \neq x) \wedge w \neq z)))}}$$

Such a proof Π_3 will be constructed by taking a terminal step of $\forall$-Introduction applied to the parametric subproof

$$\underbrace{\exists!a_1\,,\ Fa_1\,,\ \exists!a_2\,,\ \exists!b_1\,,\ Fa_2\,,\ a_1 \neq a_2\,,\ \nabla_k w((Fw \wedge w \neq a_1) \wedge w \neq a_2)}_{\substack{\Pi_4\\ Fb_1 \rightarrow \exists z((Fz \wedge z \neq b_1) \wedge \nabla_k w((Fw \wedge w \neq b_1) \wedge w \neq z))}}$$

The proof Π_4 can end with a step of $\rightarrow$-Introduction applied to the subproof

$$\underbrace{\exists!a_1\,,\ Fa_1\,,\ \exists!a_2\,,\ \exists!b_1\,,\ Fa_2\,,\ a_1 \neq a_2\,,\ Fb_1\,,\ \nabla_k w((Fw \wedge w \neq a_1) \wedge w \neq a_2)}_{\substack{\Pi_5\\ \exists z((Fz \wedge z \neq b_1) \wedge \nabla_k w((Fw \wedge w \neq b_1) \wedge w \neq z))}}$$

Let ψ be the conclusion of Π_5, i.e.,

$$\psi =_{df} \exists z((Fz \wedge z \neq b_1) \wedge \nabla_k w((Fw \wedge w \neq b_1) \wedge w \neq z)).$$

The proof Π_5 will be constructed by two applications of Dilemmas, applied to subproofs Σ_1, Σ_2 and Σ_3 as follows, whose respective premise-sets Δ_1, Δ_2 and Δ_3 contain only premises that we have already indicated as permitted for Π_5:

$$\dfrac{\begin{array}{c}\underbrace{\Delta_1\ ,\ \overline{b_1=a_1}^{(1)}}\\ \Sigma_1\\ \psi\end{array} \qquad \dfrac{\begin{array}{c}\underbrace{\Delta_2\ ,\ \overline{b_1=a_2}^{(2)}}\\ \Sigma_2\\ \psi\end{array} \qquad \begin{array}{c}\underbrace{\Delta_3\ ,\ \overline{b_1\neq a_1}^{(1)}\ ,\ \overline{b_1\neq a_2}^{(2)}}\\ \Sigma_3\\ \psi\end{array}}{\psi}\,(2)}{\begin{array}{c}\psi,\ \text{i.e.,}\\ \exists z((Fz\wedge z\neq b_1)\wedge\nabla_k w((Fw\wedge w\neq b_1)\wedge w\neq z))\end{array}}\,(1)$$

It remains now to display Σ_1, Σ_2 and Σ_3.

$$\Sigma_1 = \dfrac{\exists! a_2 \qquad \dfrac{\dfrac{Fa_2 \qquad \dfrac{a_1\neq a_2 \quad b_1=a_1}{a_2\neq b_1}}{Fa_2\wedge a_2\neq b_1} \qquad \dfrac{\nabla_k w((Fw\wedge w\neq a_1)\wedge w\neq a_2) \quad b_1=a_1}{\nabla_k w((Fw\wedge w\neq b_1)\wedge w\neq a_2)}}{(Fa_2\wedge a_2\neq b_1)\wedge\nabla_k w((Fw\wedge w\neq b_1)\wedge w\neq a_2)}}{\exists z((Fz\wedge z\neq b_1)\wedge\nabla_k w((Fw\wedge w\neq b_1)\wedge w\neq z))}$$

$$\Sigma_2 = \dfrac{\exists! a_1 \qquad \dfrac{\dfrac{Fa_1 \qquad \dfrac{a_1\neq a_2 \quad b_1=a_2}{a_1\neq b_1}}{Fa_1\wedge a_1\neq b_1} \qquad \dfrac{\begin{array}{c}\nabla_k w((Fw\wedge w\neq a_1)\wedge w\neq a_2)\\ \vdots\ \text{by logical equivalence of matrices}\\ \nabla_k w((Fw\wedge w\neq a_2)\wedge w\neq a_1)\end{array} \quad b_1=a_2}{\nabla_k w((Fw\wedge w\neq b_1)\wedge w\neq a_1)}}{(Fa_1\wedge a_1\neq b_1)\wedge\nabla_k w((Fw\wedge w\neq b_1)\wedge w\neq a_1)}}{\exists z((Fz\wedge z\neq b_1)\wedge\nabla_k w((Fw\wedge w\neq b_1)\wedge w\neq z))}$$

$$\Sigma_3 = \dfrac{\exists! a_1 \qquad \dfrac{\dfrac{Fa_1 \quad a_1\neq b_1}{Fa_1\wedge a_1\neq b_1} \qquad \begin{array}{c}\underbrace{\nabla_k w((Fw\wedge w\neq a_1)\wedge w\neq a_2),\ \exists! a_2\ ,\ Fa_2\ ,\ \exists! b_1\ ,\ Fb_1}\\ \vdots\ \text{by Lemma 33}\\ \nabla_k w((Fw\wedge w\neq a_1)\wedge w\neq b_1)\\ \vdots\ \text{by logical equivalence of matrices}\\ \nabla_k w((Fw\wedge w\neq b_1)\wedge w\neq a_1)\end{array}}{(Fa_1\wedge a_1\neq b_1)\wedge\nabla_k w((Fw\wedge w\neq b_1)\wedge w\neq a_1)}}{\exists z((Fz\wedge z\neq b_1)\wedge\nabla_k w((Fw\wedge w\neq b_1)\wedge w\neq z))}$$

Note that we have not had to appeal to the Inductive Hypothesis. □

We make a prosaic pause here to stress a simple point: Lemmas 31–34 are in (or about) a monadic first-order logic with identity. The object language is not yet being taken to contain mathematical expressions such as 0 and s, or the number-abstraction operator #. We have simply been investigating some of the logical powers of a logical saint who speaks a very simple monadic first-order object language with identity, and who, for the time being, is utterly innocent of any knowledge of number. The knowledge that if $k < m$ then there is no one-one mapping from k Φs onto m Ψs is knowledge that *we* have exploited, at the *meta*level, in order to prove some general results about what the logical saint, operating at the object level while ignorant of numbers, can nevertheless (even if only very arduously) prove.

Metatheorem 4. *For all n, and for all substituends for Φ, we have*

$$\nabla_n x\Phi x \dashv\vdash \Diamond_n x\Phi x$$

Proof. By complete induction on n.
Basis. It is trivial that (for all substituends for Φ) we have

$$\nabla_0 x\Phi x \dashv\vdash \Diamond_0 x\Phi x$$

—for this simply says, by the basis clauses of Definitions (4) and (5), that

$$\neg\exists x\Phi x \dashv\vdash \forall x\neg\Phi x$$

Inductive Hypothesis (for $k \geq 0$): For all substituends for Φ and for all $m \leq k$ we have

$$\nabla_m x\Phi x \dashv\vdash \Diamond_m x\Phi x$$

Inductive Step: Since $sk > 0$, it suffices to use the Inductive Hypothesis to show that for all substituends for Φ we have

$$\nabla_{sk} x\Phi x \dashv\vdash \Diamond_{sk} x\Phi x$$

So by the inductive clauses of Definitions (4) and (5) we need to show:

$$\exists x_{sk}(\Phi x_{sk} \wedge \nabla_k x(\Phi x \wedge x \neq x_{sk})) \dashv\vdash \exists x\Phi x \wedge \forall x_{sk}(\Phi x_{sk} \rightarrow \Diamond_k x(\Phi x \wedge x \neq x_{sk}))$$

We can make a convenient alphabetical change of bound variable to simplify what we have to show, which is:

$$\exists y(\Phi y \wedge \nabla_k x(\Phi x \wedge x \neq y)) \dashv\vdash \exists x\Phi x \wedge \forall y(\Phi y \rightarrow \Diamond_k x(\Phi x \wedge x \neq y)) \ldots \ (*)$$

We shall first address (*) from the left to the right. If we can supply the embedded subproof Π accomplishing the deductive transition indicated below, we shall be done.

$$
\dfrac{\exists y(\Phi y \wedge \nabla_k x(\Phi x\wedge x\neq y)) \qquad \dfrac{\dfrac{\overset{(4)}{\overline{\exists! a}} \quad \overset{(3)}{\overline{\Phi a}}}{\exists x\Phi x} \qquad \dfrac{\overset{(4)}{\overline{\Phi a\wedge \nabla_k x(\Phi x\wedge x\neq a)}} \quad \dfrac{\dfrac{\begin{array}{c}\underbrace{\overset{(4)}{\overline{\exists! a}}\,,\ \overset{(3)}{\overline{\Phi a}}\,,\ \overset{(3)}{\overline{\nabla_k x(\Phi x\wedge x\neq a)}}\,,\ \overset{(2)}{\overline{\exists! b}}\,,\ \overset{(1)}{\overline{\Phi b}}} \\ \Pi \\ \Diamond_k x(\Phi x\wedge x\neq b)\end{array}}{\Phi b\rightarrow \Diamond_k x(\Phi x\wedge x\neq b)}{\scriptstyle (1)}}{\forall y(\Phi y\rightarrow \Diamond_k x(\Phi x\wedge x\neq y))}{\scriptstyle (2)}}{\forall y(\Phi y\rightarrow \Diamond_k x(\Phi x\wedge x\neq y))}{\scriptstyle (3)}}{\exists x\Phi x\wedge \forall y(\Phi y\rightarrow \Diamond_k x(\Phi x\wedge x\neq y))}}{\exists x\Phi x\wedge \forall y(\Phi y\rightarrow \Diamond_k x(\Phi x\wedge x\neq y))}{\scriptstyle (4)}
$$

The subproof Π can be constructed using Dilemma, with horn assumptions $a=b$ and $a\neq b$, and by appeal to the Inductive Hypothesis, provided only that we can furnish the embedded subproof Π':

$$
\Pi \;=\; \begin{array}{c}\dfrac{\dfrac{\nabla_k x(\Phi x\wedge x\neq a) \quad \overset{(1)}{\overline{a=b}}}{\nabla_k x(\Phi x\wedge x\neq b)} \qquad \begin{array}{c}\underbrace{\exists! a\,,\ \Phi a\,,\ \nabla_k x(\Phi x\wedge x\neq a)\,,\ \exists! b\,,\ \Phi b\,,\ \overset{(1)}{\overline{a\neq b}}} \\ \Pi' \\ \nabla_k x(\Phi x\wedge x\neq b)\end{array}}{\nabla_k x(\Phi x\wedge x\neq b)}{\scriptstyle (1)} \\ \vdots \ \text{by IH} \\ \Diamond_k x(\Phi x\wedge x\neq b)\end{array}
$$

And we have Π' courtesy of Lemma 33.

It remains to address the deducibility (*) from the right to the left. So we seek to show

$$\exists x\Phi x \wedge \forall y(\Phi y \rightarrow \Diamond_k x(\Phi x\wedge x\neq y)) \ \vdash\ \exists y(\Phi y \wedge \nabla_k x(\Phi x\wedge x\neq y))$$

By $\wedge$-Elimination, it will suffice to show

$$\exists x\Phi x\,,\ \forall y(\Phi y \rightarrow \Diamond_k x(\Phi x\wedge x\neq y)) \ \vdash\ \exists y(\Phi y \wedge \nabla_k x(\Phi x\wedge x\neq y))\ ;$$

for which, by $\exists$-Elimination, it will suffice to show

$$\exists! a\,,\ \Phi a\,,\ \forall y(\Phi y \rightarrow \Diamond_k x(\Phi a\wedge x\neq y)) \ \vdash\ \exists y(\Phi y \wedge \nabla_k x(\Phi x\wedge x\neq y))\ ;$$

The proof of the latter is as follows:

$$
\dfrac{\forall y(\Phi y\rightarrow \Diamond_k x(\Phi x\wedge x\neq y) \qquad \dfrac{\exists! a \qquad \dfrac{\Phi a \qquad \dfrac{\overset{(2)}{\overline{\Phi a\rightarrow \Diamond_k x(\Phi x\wedge x\neq a)}} \quad \Phi a \quad \begin{array}{c}\overset{(1)}{\overline{\Diamond_k x(\Phi x\wedge x\neq a)}} \\ \vdots \ \text{by IH} \\ \nabla_k x(\Phi x\wedge x\neq a)\end{array}}{\nabla_k x(\Phi x\wedge x\neq a)}{\scriptstyle (1)}}{\Phi a\wedge \nabla_k x(\Phi x\wedge x\neq a)}}{\exists y(\Phi y\wedge \nabla_k x(\Phi x\wedge x\neq y))}}{\exists y(\Phi y\wedge \nabla_k x(\Phi x\wedge x\neq y))}{\scriptstyle (2)}
$$

□

Metatheorem 4 shows that for the logical saint using the object language, it would not matter which form of definition one were to adopt for the formal numerosity statements that need to appear on the right-hand sides of instances of Schema N. In this regard, $\nabla_n x\Phi x$ and $\Diamond_n x\Phi x$ are interchangeable in Schema N. We shall leave as an exercise for the reader the detailed proofs that would be required in order to complete the 'square circle' of equivalencies involving our four different forms of numerosity statement:

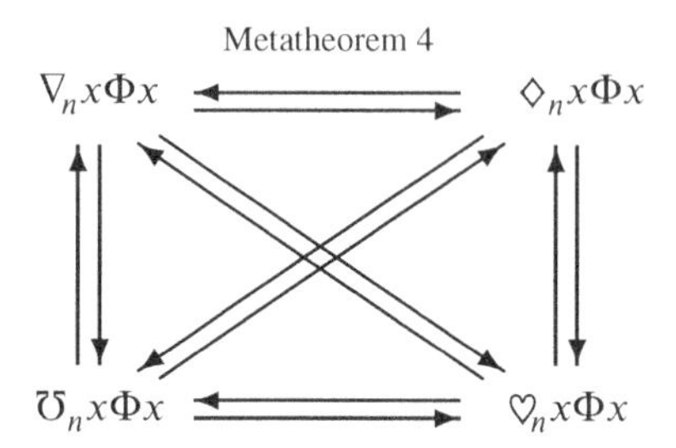

With Metatheorem 4 we have provided only the first such equivalence. But that particular equivalence is enough to enable us to make an important philosophical point, to wit: no ordering of the Φs—be it one intrinsic to them, or imposed upon them arbitrarily in the act of counting—can possibly figure into the truth-conditions of numerosity statements to the effect that 'there are exactly this-many Φs'. The equivalence of $\nabla_n x\Phi x$ with $\Diamond_n x\Phi x$ guarantees that. Clearly there are five equivalences still begging for direct two-way proof; but we shall spare that exercise for the interested reader.[1]

[1] We say *direct* because one could cheat by, say, directly proving any three sides of the rectangle, without proving the fourth side and without proving the diagonals. Or one could directly prove the two diagonals, and one of the four sides, neglecting the remaining three sides. Or one could directly prove any two parallel sides and one of the diagonals, neglecting the other pair of parallel sides and the other diagonal. Interestingly, it would be extremely difficult to prove a simple clockwise or anti-clockwise circuit; for it would appear that any inductive proof of any one arrow requires simultaneous proof of its reversal (i.e., of the converse implication).

Part III

Natural Logicism and the Rationals

Chapter 14

What Would a Gifted Child Need in Order to Grasp Fractions? The Case of Edwin

Abstract

After the austerely formal work that, one hopes, has been edifying thus far for readers who have reached the end of Part II, the author owes them some entertainment and levity. The reader is introduced to Edwin the Fractionator. Edwin is able to attain ontological commitment to rational numbers on the basis only of his grasp of the naturals. He does this without having learned anything about addition or multiplication or division on the naturals. Not only does he recognize the existence of fractions; he also understands their applicability in our thought and talk about the wider world. It is gratifying that his kindness and commitment to egalitarian sharing, in conjunction with his lessons as a Constructive Logicist, afford him this intellectual achievement.

We turn now to the (non-negative) rational numbers, or fractions as they are sometimes called. Almost everyone knows that a fraction is concocted somehow from two whole numbers (or naturals). The question is: how, exactly? What we contend is the right answer is, at the same time, both straightforward and subtle. It has also not been given before. The reader is asked to indulge the author in a flight of fictitious fancy to a deeper understanding of how accounting for the way rational numbers are applied reveals to us what they are; and reveals, also, that the natural numbers are among them.

Edwin is a very young but gifted little boy. He is a whiz with straight edge and compass. He can also count; but he cannot yet add whole numbers. He cannot multiply them either—let alone deal with subtraction and division. Edwin is just a budding constructive logicist who has attained, thus far, a grasp of only 'zero', 'the successor of ...', and '... is a whole number'. (He has, as it happens, been taken only as far in matters arithmetical as the reader of this book. He would not have understood, though, the material about polynomials in our discussion of systems of place notation, in Chapter 7.) Edwin has managed to prove that the number of Fs is $\underline{n}$ if and only if there are exactly n Fs; and that n is the number

The Logic of Number. Neil Tennant, Oxford University Press. © Neil Tennant 2022.
DOI: 10.1093/oso/9780192846679.003.0014

of whole numbers preceding n.[1] This he proved by mathematical induction, a method which, as we have seen, is available to the Constructive Logicist even in advance of adopting any mathematical operations like addition and subtraction.

This story about Edwin will no doubt strike any reader who knows a little about our culturally evolved arithmetical pedagogy as extremely far-fetched. And so it is. The point is only that Edwin's intellectual capacities are plausibly possible for a maturing rational agent. He does not even have to be an arithmetical or logical 'saint'. He just needs to be gifted in hitherto unusual ways. And what is possible for Edwin is possible for any thinker who can 'go along with our story' about his intellectual capacities. We are relying on the time-honored distinction between order of discovery (which often evolves, with recapitulation, into a rather arbitrary order of pedagogical presentation), and order of (foundational) justification. For Edwin, these happen to coincide. For the rest of us, it has taken millenia to prise these orders apart, in order to arrive at a proper philosophical understanding of the role of numbers in our intellectual lives.

Edwin's parents have raised him to be an absolutely fair and even-handed little fellow, always ready to share. His egalitarian inclinations have matured to the point where he always seeks to share things in equal measures—ensuring that each person's portion is 'the same'.

For example, when five identical[2] pizzas were delivered for his birthday party, with seven other playmates invited, Edwin immediately divvied up the five pizzas so as to be able to give each of the eight persons present the same amount of pizza. He counted those present: 1, 2, 3, 4, 5, 6, 7, 8; whereupon he took out his straight edge and compass, and his pizza wheel. Each pizza he halved. Then he halved the half-pieces. Then he halved the resulting quarter-pieces. Having thus cut up a whole pizza, he checked his handiwork by counting the pieces he had created, nodding with satisfaction as his count ended with eight. He did all this with each pizza in turn. When he had finished cutting up the fifth pizza, he reminded himself of how many pizzas had now been cut up: he confirmed he had five piles of same-sized pizza pieces, with each pile consisting of eight pieces.

He counted five of the resulting pieces (which of course were eighth-pieces) into a little pile. Then he counted another five of them into a second pile. Continuing in this way, he counted the final five pieces into a pile, making eight piles in all. Beaming, he offered each of his seven guests their own pile, and took the remaining one for himself.

---

[1]Our meta-notation '$\underline{n}$' refers to the canonical numeral that Edwin uses to denote the natural number n. His father, who is a computer scientist, explained to Edwin that there are both length-reducing numerals in systems of place notation, as well as 'length-respecting' ones such as the Peano numerals $s \ldots s0$, with n occurrences of s. Our story can proceed without even revealing what choice of canonical numerals Edwin eventually chose. As we saw in Chapter 7, he would be able to count (with, say, our standard numerals in decimal notation) without needing any grasp of the usual algebraic operations on the natural numbers.

[2]Here we use the word 'identical' from common parlance, and not in the logician's or metaphysician's exigent sense. What we mean is that the pizzas were the same in all important respects—diameter and thickness of crust, diameter and thickness of topping, etc.

Edwin had divided each pizza into a number of equal pieces, that number (8) being the number of people involved; and each of them had received the same number of pieces, namely the number (5) of pizzas involved. Because the pizzas were all 'the same', Edwin could distribute the pizza pieces in any order he wished. But, if one of the pizzas had been thicker (say) than all the others, or made with a very different topping, then he would have given each person an eighth piece of that one, and only thereafter not worried about the order in which the pieces of the four remaining pizzas were distributed.

A few months later, Edwin's brother had a party, and invited ten guests. With the two brothers, that made twelve in all. Their mother upped the pizza order: seven of them (all identical) were delivered. Edwin didn't skip a beat. He first inscribed a hexagon within each pizza perimeter, cut along the three diagonals and then bisected each of the six resulting pieces. That gave him twelve identical pizza pieces.

Edwin had not multiplied 6 by 2 to get 12; nor had he added 6 and 6 to get 12. He had simply seen a paper-and-pencil version of this construction by someone on YouTube, to obtain a regular dodecagon. He recalled the operation of marking out radii around the circumference of the circle (as it happens, and necessarily so, six times); then the operation of bisecting each of the six central angles thus created.

Edwin repeated the process with each of the other six pizzas. Now he had seven piles, each containing twelve pizza pieces. As he had done on the previous occasion, he apportioned seven pieces to his first chosen guest; then seven more to the next; and so on. Once again, he did not need to do this in any particular order. As before, each pizza had been divided into a number of equal pieces, that number (12) being the number of people involved; and each of them received the same number of pieces, namely the number (7) of pizzas involved.

Edwin's consummate achievement came just a few weeks later: this time, seventeen people were to be served, and an as yet unknown number of pizzas were to be delivered. As each pizza came in, Edwin pulled off a virtuoso geometrical feat, owed to Gauss: he managed (with straight edge and compass) to mark the vertices of a regular 17-gon on the perimeter of each pizza, and then cut from each such vertex to the center. He had seen the animated diagram on *Wikipedia* showing how to do this. By the time the final pizza had been delivered, he had lost count of how many times he had carried out this elaborate construction. So he counted the resulting piles of seventeen equal pizza pieces; and the result was eleven. Without hesitation, he then placed on each person's plate eleven pizza pieces. As before, each pizza had been divided into a number of equal pieces, that number (17) being the number of people involved; and each of them received the same number of pieces, namely the number (11) of pizzas involved.

It would be fair to say, on the basis of all this behavior, that Edwin could fractionate, at least with things like pizzas, whose convenient radial and rotational symmetry made it easy to divide them into any required number of equal parts.

(He refused to let his parents order rectangular pizzas for his parties. The corner pieces had crusts at two edges, the other border pieces had crusts at one edge, and the pieces in the middle were completely covered with toppings. He had no way of dividing rectangular pizzas equally, except into halves or quarters.)

The family could provide seating for at most 25 people at a pizza party, and, as it happened, they never had a party with exactly 7, 9, 11, 13, 14, 18, 19, 21, 22, or 23 people to be served. Unknown to his parents or to Edwin, he would not have been able to use straight edge and compass, with his pizza cutter, to cut up a (circular) pizza into n equal pieces where n is any of the aforementioned numbers. For the Gauss–Wantzel theorem states that a necessary and sufficient condition for straight-edge-and-compass constructibility of a regular n-gon is that n be the product of a power of 2 and any non-negative number of distinct Fermat primes, i.e., primes of the form

$$2^{(2^i)} + 1.$$

(Gauss established the sufficiency of the latter condition in 1796; Wantzell established its necessity in 1837.)

Was Edwin's grasp of fractions limited to this special case of circular pizzas, and to those whose 'denominators' (as *we* would call them) are of the form

$$2^k p_1 p_2 \dots p_m$$

where k and m are non-negative integers, and the p_is (when $m > 0$) are distinct Fermat primes?

Certainly, Edwin's pizza-cutting prowess was so limited; but, arguably, not his intellectual grasp of fractions. For he knew what would be required of him to cut up a pizza into (say) eleven equal portions; it's just that he knew of no method so to do, using only straight edge and compass. Indeed, no one could know of such a method; for none exists.

Edwin's inability to manifest in pizza-cutting actions his fully verbalizable knowledge would count as at most a temporary setback. For unwittingly his parents decided on a new choice of foodstuff, one that happened to allow for full manifestation of his grasp of fractions. They switched from pizzas (thought to be a little too fattening) to Slim Jim pepperoni sticks.[3] Here Edwin's Euclidean chops were up to the task of division into any number of equal portions. The following diagram is a Euclidean reminder.[4]

[3]For the European reader: these are long, thin, absolutely straight identical right-cylinders of processed meat. If you want to avoid nitrates and go organic with grass-fed beef, you could try Nick's Sticks instead. You can get these at Lucky's on High Street, across from the Giant Eagle north of the Ohio State campus.

[4]We use 11 here where Euclid used 3—see his *Elements*, Book 6, Proposition 9.

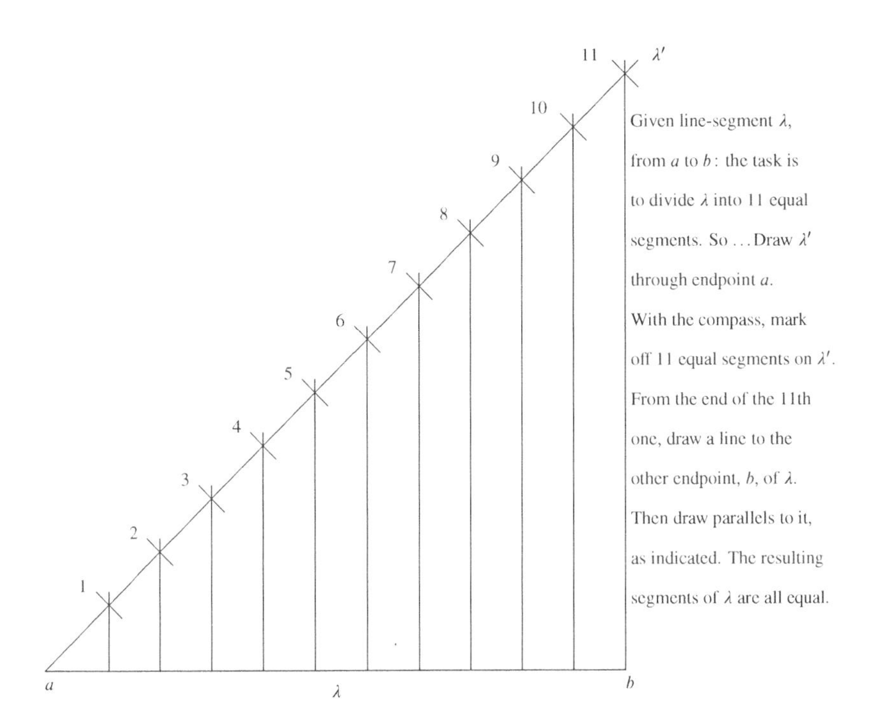

Without loss of generality, one can limit this construction to the case where the vertical lines are perpendicular to λ, as indeed they are in our diagram. One can do that by erecting the rightmost perpendicular through b, and then rotating around a (clockwise or anti-clockwise, as required) our 11-segmented line λ' until its 11th mark lies on that perpendicular through b. Then all the other perpendiculars to λ can be dropped from the remaining equally spaced marks on λ' labeled 1 through 10.

We can see now what Edwin would do with any pepperoni stick λ needing to be cut up into any given number n of equal segments. There is no need to labor the point with any further detailed examples.

Inspired by the foregoing diagram for the case $n = 11$, Edwin had a bright idea for a solution to the pizza-cutting case involving 11 shares. He took for λ a thin taut inelastic string that he had cut to size after winding it end-to-end around a pizza. So the piece of string was exactly as long as the circumference of the pizza. Then he used the method illustrated in the diagram to mark off 11 equal segments on the string. Then he wound it back around the pizza, with the points marked 0 and 11 coinciding. Edwin used the marks on the string to notch the pizza crust eleven times. He thereby ensured the equality of the eleven pieces 'as near as dammit', as his father would say. 'To within the tiny epsilon of the pizza-cutting crumbs.' (It goes without saying that Edwin already knew how to determine the *center* of any circular pizza, toward which he would have to guide his pizza-cutter from the notches around its edge.) And Edwin could pull this trick for any value of n when divvying up a circular pizza. No longer was he subject to the constraints imposed by the Gauss–Wantzel theorem. He could now cope with pizza parties of 7, 9, 11, 13, 14, 18, 19, 21, 22, or 23 people.

When assessing whether Edwin's grasp of fractions is purely conceptual—a matter of Kantian understanding; or whether it depends essentially on the exercise of Kantian 'pure intuition' (here, of space) because of resources brought to bear on the 'cutting problem'—it is important to realize that Edwin's recourse to any Euclidean or Gaussian geometric methods for the task of cutting is his way of making it the case that the shares thus created are all dimensionally equal. His grasp of *fractionating* can prescind entirely from the question of exactly how one might create a certain number of equal shares out of the things that one is given. The exercise of geometric intuition is confined to equal-share *creation*. But the issue of whether Edwin's grasp of fractions is conceptual or intuitive (in the relevant Kantian senses) can be decided by attending to the following more limited question:

> Does Edwin understand how to ensure equal sharing of p pizzas (say) among q people on the happy assumption that the work of dividing any pizza into q equal parts can be accomplished by someone on Edwin's behalf, and on his instruction, so that he can in due course be presented with the result of that outsourced work, and thereafter take it upon himself to see to only the *distribution* of (equal) shares?

When the answer to *this* question (more limited in scope, even if necessarily rather prolix) is affirmative, it is reasonable to say that Edwin's grasp of fractions is a purely conceptual achievement. It resides in the Kantian understanding. It is independent of any exercise of geometric intuition that might be involved in *creating* a certain number of dimensionally equal pieces.

At this stage in our exposition, it is worth pointing out also that when it is impossible to share p objects of a certain kind equally among q people, while keeping those objects intact, this impossibility is a *logical* one. It does not need any *mathematical* explanation involving the additive and/or multiplicative properties of the natural numbers. The impossibility can be expressed, roughly (that is, in English), as follows: this collection of p objects cannot be partitioned into q subcollections that are, pairwise, in one-one correspondence. (Note that the uses here of 'p' and 'q' are *adjectival*.) To be sure, once we have developed our theory of the natural numbers to a certain stage, we can give expression to this fact in a more 'ontologizing' way, by saying that the natural number p cannot be divided by the natural number q with remainder zero; or, equivalently, for no non-zero natural number k is it the case that $p = q \times k$. This, however, merely re-states the more fundamental 'logical' fact with some mathematical dressing.[5]

Let us return to Edwin's distribution of pizzas. A useful analogy here would be with the standard distinction made by the supporter of analyticity—the distinction between such sensory experience as may be required in order to acquire mastery of certain concepts (such as 'red' and 'green'); and whatever further sensory experience might be needed (here, in fact, none) in order, once one has mastered those concepts, to determine the truth value of a sentence such as 'Nothing can be both red and green simultaneously all over'. This sentence is analytically true; no sensory experience is needed in order to appreciate its truth. Likewise, Edwin's exercise of his concepts when fractionating is just that: a purely conceptual matter. It matters not that his exercise of those concepts might need to be preceded by the application of some geometric knowledge in bringing him to the point where he can then set about displaying his grasp of fractions by ensuring that each person now receives p q-ths of a pizza.

The foregoing considerations in support of the contention that Edwin's grasp of fractionating is (in Kantian terms) a conceptual matter will prevail through all further developments of our account of what it is to grasp the rationals.

So far we have been discussing Edwin's understanding of fractions in the context where there are more people to be victualed than pizzas to be shared: that is, where the number p of pizzas is less than the number q of people to share them. It is clear, however, that this is no great limitation on solving the problem of how to ensure equal shares within those settings where $p \geq q$.

When $p = q$, each person gets exactly one pizza.

When $p > q$, each person gets, at the first stage, a certain whole number n (say) of whole pizzas, until the stage is reached where there are fewer pizzas left for further sharing than there are people to provide for. This includes the case where no pizzas are left. But, if some pizza(s) is (are) left, that ushers in the second stage, which is of the kind already dealt with above—where $p < q$. It also spares Edwin much of the work of cutting that would otherwise be called for.

Edwin is a smart enough child to economize on that work. He therefore welcomes the use of the natural number n in question as part of the final 'count'—the number of uncut ones—of pizzas constituting an equal share. He knows, though, that he must now undertake some cutting in order to ensure q equal shares of the remaining, as-yet-unshared pizzas. The number k of those pizzas is now exceeded by q. So in this second stage Edwin is back in the problem-setting with which we began, that of sub-unity shares. He has to ensure q equal shares of the remaining k pizzas, knowing that $k < q$. Edwin can simply count the remaining pizzas in order to determine k. Of course we, on the sidelines, also know that $p = (n.q) + k$, and we can calculate k as $p - (n.q)$; but Edwin does not need to

[5]This observation creates difficulties for the classification, in Lange [2013], of the need for a 'distinctively mathematical' explanation of the impossibility of evenly distributing twenty-three strawberries among three children without cutting any of the strawberries. Note here our use of the adjectival expressions 'twenty-three' and 'three'. The impossibility in Lange's example, as we have just explained, is a *logical* one.

know this in order to proceed, and does not need so to calculate. He is on his way, however, to being able to report that the original p pizzas can be shared equally among q people (where $p \geq q$) by ensuring that each person receives n whole pizzas plus (if $p > q$) a fractional sub-unity share appropriate for dividing the remaining k pizzas among those q people. The operator 'plus' here, by the way, is that of fusion of things constituted wholly by pairwise disjoint whole pizzas and/or pizza parts. Edwin is not adding numbers. Yet.

Chapter 15

Past Accounts of the Rationals as Ratios

Abstract

Rational numbers are ratios $\frac{p}{q}$ of two natural numbers (with $q \neq 0$). Their ordering is dense. Rational numbers are also special cases of ratios of dimensional magnitudes—the latter, typically, being lengths of line segments. It is now known that collectively these dimensional magnitudes form the ordering of the reals. And this ordering is not just dense, but is also continuous. This chapter begins with a brief survey of how the rationals have figured, or been treated, from the time of Eudoxus through to present-day double-barreled abstractionism. Then it turns to a more detailed study of Euclid's account of ratios, and their method of abstraction. Euclid's method proves to be a precursor of double-barreled abstractionism. But this kind of abstractionism fails to ensure that any natural number is 'itself again', *qua* rational number. And the Euclidean method of abstraction has the drawback that it does not *create* (or explain our entitlement to be committed to the existence of) rational numbers on the basis of our prior grasp of natural numbers. The method employed in Natural Logicism that will 'get' the rationals from the naturals and recognize the naturals as themselves again *qua* rationals will be explained in Chapter 16.

Logicists have not paid much attention to the rational numbers as abstract Platonic entities to be created, or constructed, or recognized, by logical means. An interesting exception is Bostock [1979], of whom there will be some appropriately modulated echoes below.

Dedekind, in *Stetigkeit und irrationale Zahlen* (1872) took the rationals as already somehow given,[1] before proceeding to define real numbers as his famous cuts on the rationals. Later, in *Was sind und was sollen die Zahlen?* (published in 1888) he turned to the problem of constructing the natural numbers by logical means. He never did the same, however, for the rationals. So a worst-case logicist scenario is that those famous cuts of his might have been performed on entities of a kind we-know-not-exactly-what.

Frege [1884; reprinted 1961], the famous *Grundlagen der Arithmetik*, addressed the natural numbers, constructing them (albeit informally) by rather dif-

[1]The first sentence of §1 of Dedekind [1872] begins 'Die Entwickelung der Arithmetik der rationalen Zahlen wird hier zwar vorausgesetzt ...'. This is rendered, at p. 3 of the English translation Dedekind [1901], as 'The development of the arithmetic of rational numbers is here presupposed ... '.

The Logic of Number. Neil Tennant, Oxford University Press. © Neil Tennant 2022.
DOI: 10.1093/oso/9780192846679.003.0015

ferent logical means. A completely formal treatment was to follow in Frege [1893; reprinted 1962], the first volume of his *Grundgesetze der Arithmetik* (1893), in which he defined the (finite, of course) natural number n to be the—who knows *how* infinitely large—class of all (value-ranges of) functions that map n objects to the True.[2] Among these value-ranges would be the infinitely many concepts under which exactly n objects fall. In the second volume of the *Grundgesetze* (1903), he attempted a logicist treatment of the real numbers; but nowhere did he address the rationals as a separate kind of mathematical entity, to be constructed or recognized in their own special way. The rationals would simply drop out as special cases of reals (used for the measurement of continuous magnitudes), with no focused characterization of the rationals' own idiosyncratic or distinctive conditions of application, as fractions or ratios, in our wider thought about the world.[3] Such applications, as the tale about Edwin the Fractionator reveals, can properly and separately precede and prescind from any actual measurement of continuous magnitudes.

It is rather peculiar that the rationals have been left out in the logicist cold in this way. There has been but one recent neologicist attempt (at least, since the publication in 1983 of Wright's *Frege's Conception of Numbers as Objects*) to make good on this lacuna. Shapiro [2000a] gave a 'double-barreled' abstractionist principle for the rationals, constructing them out of naturals. His abstraction principle characterizes the 'quotient abstraction' operator, applied to pairs of naturals in a given order:

$$Q(m,n) = Q(p,q) \quad \leftrightarrow \quad (n = 0 \wedge q = 0) \vee (n \neq 0 \wedge q \neq 0 \wedge m.q = n.p)\,.$$

This particular abstraction principle is problematic, however, in that it requires us to acknowledge the existence of rationals of the form $\frac{k}{0}$ (all of them identical, by the way, no matter what the choice of k)[4]—or, in Shapiro's notation, of the form $Q(k,0)$. Here is proof that this is so:

$$\dfrac{\dfrac{\dfrac{0{=}0 \quad 0{=}0}{0{=}0 \wedge 0{=}0}}{(0{=}0 \wedge 0{=}0) \vee (0{\neq}0 \wedge 0{\neq}0 \wedge k.0{=}0.k)} \quad Q(k,0){=}Q(k,0) \leftrightarrow (0{=}0 \wedge 0{=}0) \vee (0{\neq}0 \wedge 0{\neq}0 \wedge k.0{=}0.k)}{\dfrac{Q(k,0){=}Q(k,0)}{\exists ! Q(k,0)}}$$

And this is something that practicing mathematicians say we should not do. For them, such 'ratios' (with denominator 0) 'do not exist', or are 'undefined'. The regimenting logician needs to respect this important feature of mathematical practice, and not force any abstraction principle into the Procrustean bed already occupied by other existentially over-committal double-barreled abstraction principles,

---

[2] Thanks are owed to a referee for this level of exegetical precision.

[3] This is a feature that has been stressed concerning Eudoxus's theory of proportions, as adopted by Euclid in Book V of his *Elements* (see §15).

[4] Thanks to Ethan Brauer for this observation.

such as (most notably) Hume's Principle, as in Wright [1983]:

$$\#x\Phi x = \#x\Psi x \quad \leftrightarrow \quad \exists R\ Rxy : \Phi x \underset{\text{onto}}{\overset{1\text{-}1}{\mapsto}} \Psi y\,.$$

Here, the abstraction operator # is supposed to yield cardinal numbers. And the over-commitment in this setting (as we have already seen) is to a cardinal number for every $\Phi(x)$, no matter what $\Phi(x)$ may be; in particular, $\Phi(x)$ may be $x = x$, resulting in commitment to there being such a cardinal number as that of all things *tout court*.

As we have just seen, Shapiro's abstraction principle for quotients is in a similar fashion existentially over-committal, regardless whether the underlying logic is free. So it incurs the same kind of objection as the one raised against Wright.

Another point that can be raised in objection to Shapiro's abstraction principle is that it requires (as one readily sees from its right-hand side) that one already have a grasp of addition and multiplication on the naturals. But, as we have seen with Edwin, one can be a fractionator without having mastered either of these two (admittedly rather basic) operations. It is enough to be able to count, in order then to be able to fractionate. And if one can pass from being a competent fractionator to a recognition of fractions themselves as abstract entities (which, as we shall in due course see, is eminently feasible), then one can attain to the rationals 'plus'-lessly and 'times'-lessly—surprising though this might seem to anyone taught first how to add and to multiply whole numbers before learning about fractions. We shall be clearing a way to more direct acquaintance with rational numbers than our conventional early schooling would lead one to expect.

A final shortfall of Shapiro's double-barreled abstractionist account is that it does not address at all the question of how the rational numbers are applicable in our thought and talk about the wider world. It simply generates a new structure (commonly called $\mathbb{Q}$) out of an old one (commonly called $\mathbb{N}$). Moreover, on this account $\mathbb{N}$ is not an actual substructure of $\mathbb{Q}$, embedded therein; rather, $\mathbb{N}$ turns out to be at best isomorphic to a substructure of $\mathbb{Q}$ consisting of counterparts to the naturals, but not consisting of the naturals themselves.

The reader might form the impression that perhaps we need to look back earlier—even way back, to the likes of Eudoxus and Euclid—for some suggestive ideas that might guide a modern logicist onto a more productive path leading toward the rationals as numbers *sui generis*. We shall indeed do so; but we shall find in these ancients' account shortfalls similar to those just remarked on. For the Eudoxan account, as found in Euclid, is, as we shall see below, best formalized as 'double-barreled' abstraction in the same vein as Shapiro's—though, to be sure, with interestingly different details of execution.

So let us take a closer look now at Euclid's definition of the notion of ratio. In Book V of his *Elements*, Definition 5 reads as follows, in Heath's translation:

> Magnitudes are said to **be in the same ratio**, the first to the second and the third to the fourth, when, if any equimultiples whatever be

> taken of the first and third, and any equimultiples whatever of the second and fourth, the former equimultiuples alike exceed, are alike equal to, or alike fall short of, the latter equimultiples respectively taken in corresponding order.

In order to see how this qualifies as a definition of ratios (or rational numbers) by abstraction, let us regiment it in first-order logical notation. We shall assume we have the natural numbers to quantify over (by means of the sortal variables k, n), and an operator $\odot$ to express whole-number multiples of a magnitude μ:[5]

$$n \odot \mu$$

A good example of such a magnitude μ would be the length of a line-segment:

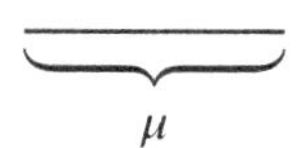

of which n layings-on-end in a straight line would have the length $n \odot \mu$:

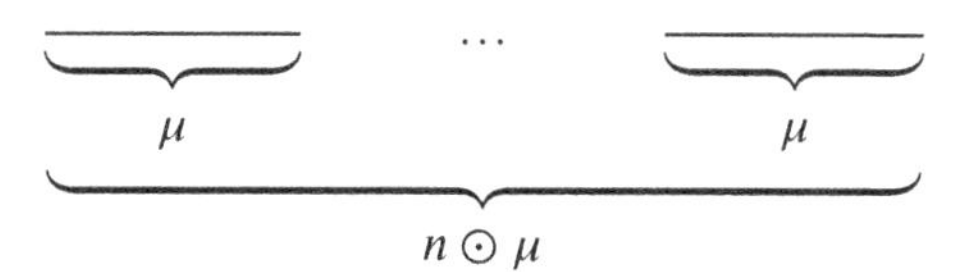

Let us now take a closer logical look at what Euclid's definition says. He speaks of four magnitudes. We shall call them μ_1, μ_2, μ_3, and μ_4. And he considers equimultiples of μ_1 and μ_3, along with possibly different equimultiples of μ_2 and μ_4. We shall call the equimultiples in question

$$k \odot \mu_1, \quad k \odot \mu_3, \quad n \odot \mu_2, \quad n \odot \mu_4 \, .$$

Note that multiples of magnitudes are themselves magnitudes, and accordingly fall within the range of the sortal variable μ and its ilk.

Concentrate now on the right-hand side of Euclid's definition, which is

> ... if any equimultiples whatever be taken of the first and third, and any equimultiples whatever of the second and fourth, the former equimultiuples alike exceed, are alike equal to, or alike fall short of, the latter equimultiples respectively taken in corresponding order.

This can be regimented as

$$\forall k \forall n \left(\begin{array}{c} k\odot\mu_1 > n\odot\mu_2 \ \wedge \ k\odot\mu_3 > n\odot\mu_4 \\ \vee \\ k\odot\mu_1 = n\odot\mu_2 \ \wedge \ k\odot\mu_3 = n\odot\mu_4 \\ \vee \\ k\odot\mu_1 < n\odot\mu_2 \ \wedge \ k\odot\mu_3 < n\odot\mu_4 \end{array} \right) \tag{15.1}$$

[5] We shall see in due course how the Constructive Logicist can define this notion, using also some basic mereological terms. See Definition 9 on p. 182.

The notions of exceeding, being equal to, and falling short of, as applied to magnitudes, have been rendered by the three distinct and familiar symbols $>$, $=$, and $<$. These, of course, are interrelated by well-understood constraints; they are not logically independent of each other. Right away we can observe that the following is always understood to hold:

$$\forall x \forall y (x < y \rightarrow \neg y > x)$$

This means that we can in effect do without $>$, say, and deal only with $<$. The following axioms are always taken to govern $<$ and $=$ (where the variables x, y, and z are taken to range over magnitudes of the kind in question):

$$\begin{array}{rl} \text{ASYMMETRY} & \forall x \forall y (x < y \rightarrow \neg y < x) \\ \text{TRICHOTOMY} & \forall x \forall y (x < y \vee x = y \vee y < x) \\ \text{TRANSITIVITY} & \forall x \forall y \forall z ((x < y \wedge y < z) \rightarrow x < z) \end{array}$$

Let the set of these axioms be called $\mathcal{O}$.

ASYMMETRY logically implies

$$\text{IRREFLEXIVITY} \quad \forall x \neg x < x$$

whence

$$\text{DISTINCTNESS} \quad \forall x \forall y (x < y \rightarrow \neg x = y)$$

Against the background of the axioms in $\mathcal{O}$, the right-hand side of Euclid's definition could also be regimented as follows:

$$\forall k \forall n \left(\begin{array}{ccc} k \odot \mu_1 > n \odot \mu_2 & \leftrightarrow & k \odot \mu_3 > n \odot \mu_4 \\ & \wedge & \\ k \odot \mu_1 = n \odot \mu_2 & \leftrightarrow & k \odot \mu_3 = n \odot \mu_4 \\ & \wedge & \\ k \odot \mu_1 < n \odot \mu_2 & \leftrightarrow & k \odot \mu_3 < n \odot \mu_4 \end{array} \right) \tag{15.2}$$

This is because from the axioms in $\mathcal{O}$ the equivalence of (15.2) and (15.1) follows.

Lemma 35.

$$\mathcal{O}, (15.2) \vdash (15.1)$$

Proof. Exercise. □

Lemma 36.

$$\mathcal{O}, (15.1) \vdash (15.2)$$

Proof. Exercise. □

It also follows from the axioms in $\mathcal{O}$ that the three disjuncts just displayed in (15.1) are mutually exclusive, if (15.1) holds.

Lemma 37.

$$\frac{\mathcal{O}\ ,\ \ (15.1),\ \text{i.e.,}\ \forall k\forall n\begin{pmatrix} k\odot\mu_1>n\odot\mu_2\ \wedge\ k\odot\mu_3>n\odot\mu_4 \\ \vee \\ k\odot\mu_1=n\odot\mu_2\ \wedge\ k\odot\mu_3=n\odot\mu_4 \\ \vee \\ k\odot\mu_1<n\odot\mu_2\ \wedge\ k\odot\mu_3<n\odot\mu_4 \end{pmatrix}}{\forall k\forall n\begin{pmatrix} \neg((k\odot\mu_1<n\odot\mu_2\ \wedge\ k\odot\mu_3<n\odot\mu_4)\wedge(k\odot\mu_1=n\odot\mu_2\ \wedge\ k\odot\mu_3=n\odot\mu_4)) \\ \wedge \\ \neg((k\odot\mu_1<n\odot\mu_2\ \wedge\ k\odot\mu_3<n\odot\mu_4)\wedge(k\odot\mu_1>n\odot\mu_2\ \wedge\ k\odot\mu_3>n\odot\mu_4)) \\ \wedge \\ \neg((k\odot\mu_1=n\odot\mu_2\ \wedge\ k\odot\mu_3=n\odot\mu_4)\wedge(k\odot\mu_1>n\odot\mu_2\ \wedge\ k\odot\mu_3>n\odot\mu_4)) \end{pmatrix}}$$

Proof. Exercise □

For the next stage of our discussion it will be useful to introduce the abbreviation

$$\forall k\forall n\, R(k, n, \mu_1, \mu_2, \mu_3, \mu_4)$$

for these two displayed sentences (15.1) and (15.2) that are equivalent *modulo* the foregoing axioms for linear ordering; and, indeed, to abbreviate it further to

$$\mathcal{R}(\mu_1, \mu_2, \mu_3, \mu_4)$$

—or, even more suggestively for the points about to be made, to

$$\mathcal{R}(\langle\mu_1, \mu_2\rangle, \langle\mu_3, \mu_4\rangle)\,.$$

The angle brackets $\langle\ ,\ \rangle$ here are not to be read in the usual way as representing the formation of an ordered pair. They simply afford a convenient way to group terms so that it is easy to see how they are being taken 'two at a time'. The aim is to reduce $\mathcal{R}$ from an apparently four-place to an apparently two-place relation—whereupon it becomes easier to grasp why Lemmas (38), (39), and (40) are called Reflexivity, Symmetry, and Transitivity respectively. Note that none of Lemmas (38), (39), and (40) relies for its proof on the axioms in $\mathcal{O}$.

Lemma 38 (Reflexivity)**.**
$\mathcal{R}(\langle\mu_1, \mu_2\rangle, \langle\mu_1, \mu_2\rangle)$

Proof. We are required to prove the following:

$$\forall k\forall n\begin{pmatrix} k\odot\mu_1 < n\odot\mu_2\ \leftrightarrow\ k\odot\mu_1 < n\odot\mu_2 \\ \wedge \\ k\odot\mu_1 = n\odot\mu_2\ \leftrightarrow\ k\odot\mu_1 = n\odot\mu_2 \\ \wedge \\ k\odot\mu_1 > n\odot\mu_2\ \leftrightarrow\ k\odot\mu_1 > n\odot\mu_2 \end{pmatrix}.$$

The proof is obvious. □

Lemma 39 (Symmetry).
$\mathcal{R}(\langle\mu_1,\mu_2\rangle,\langle\mu_3,\mu_4\rangle) \rightarrow \mathcal{R}(\langle\mu_3,\mu_4\rangle,\langle\mu_1,\mu_2\rangle)$

Proof. We are required to prove the following argument:

$$\frac{\forall k \forall n \left(\begin{array}{c} k\odot\mu_1 < n\odot\mu_2 \leftrightarrow k\odot\mu_3 < n\odot\mu_4 \\ \wedge \\ k\odot\mu_1 = n\odot\mu_2 \leftrightarrow k\odot\mu_3 = n\odot\mu_4 \\ \wedge \\ k\odot\mu_1 > n\odot\mu_2 \leftrightarrow k\odot\mu_3 > n\odot\mu_4 \end{array} \right)}{\forall k \forall n \left(\begin{array}{c} k\odot\mu_3 < n\odot\mu_4 \leftrightarrow k\odot\mu_1 < n\odot\mu_2 \\ \wedge \\ k\odot\mu_3 = n\odot\mu_4 \leftrightarrow k\odot\mu_1 = n\odot\mu_2 \\ \wedge \\ k\odot\mu_3 > n\odot\mu_4 \leftrightarrow k\odot\mu_1 > n\odot\mu_2 \end{array} \right)}.$$

The proof is obvious. □

Lemma 40 (Transitivity).
$(\mathcal{R}(\langle\mu_1,\mu_2\rangle,\langle\mu_3,\mu_4\rangle) \wedge \mathcal{R}(\langle\mu_3,\mu_4\rangle,\langle\mu_5,\mu_6\rangle)) \rightarrow \mathcal{R}(\langle\mu_1,\mu_2\rangle,\langle\mu_5,\mu_6\rangle)$

Proof. We are required to prove the following argument:

$$\frac{\forall k \forall n \left(\begin{array}{c} k\odot\mu_1 < n\odot\mu_2 \leftrightarrow k\odot\mu_3 < n\odot\mu_4 \\ \wedge \\ k\odot\mu_1 = n\odot\mu_2 \leftrightarrow k\odot\mu_3 = n\odot\mu_4 \\ \wedge \\ k\odot\mu_1 > n\odot\mu_2 \leftrightarrow k\odot\mu_3 > n\odot\mu_4 \end{array} \right) \quad \forall k \forall n \left(\begin{array}{c} k\odot\mu_3 < n\odot\mu_4 \leftrightarrow k\odot\mu_5 < n\odot\mu_6 \\ \wedge \\ k\odot\mu_3 = n\odot\mu_4 \leftrightarrow k\odot\mu_5 = n\odot\mu_6 \\ \wedge \\ k\odot\mu_3 > n\odot\mu_4 \leftrightarrow k\odot\mu_5 > n\odot\mu_6 \end{array} \right)}{\forall k \forall n \left(\begin{array}{c} k\odot\mu_1 < n\odot\mu_2 \leftrightarrow k\odot\mu_5 < n\odot\mu_6 \\ \wedge \\ k\odot\mu_1 = n\odot\mu_2 \leftrightarrow k\odot\mu_5 = n\odot\mu_6 \\ \wedge \\ k\odot\mu_1 > n\odot\mu_2 \leftrightarrow k\odot\mu_5 > n\odot\mu_6 \end{array} \right)}.$$

The proof is obvious. □

The right-hand side of Euclid's definition in effect says that a certain relation $\mathcal{R}$ obtains among the term-pairs as just clarified:

$$\forall k \forall n\, \mathcal{R}(k,n,\langle\mu_1,\mu_2\rangle,\langle\mu_3,\mu_4\rangle).$$

This relation $\mathcal{R}$, as we have just seen, is an equivalence relation. This means that we can now proceed to abstract from the members of each equivalence class, to attain to the abstract objects corresponding to those equivalence classes. These abstract objects, of course, are the ones we are supposed to think of as ratios.

To see this formally, we need to complete our regimentation of Euclid's definition:

$$\text{SameRatio}(\mu_1 : \mu_2\ ;\ \mu_3 : \mu_4) \;\leftrightarrow\; \forall k \forall n\, \mathcal{R}(k,n,\langle\mu_1,\mu_2\rangle,\langle\mu_3,\mu_4\rangle)$$

The crucial move of the Fregean 'double-barreled' abstractionist can now be made:

$$\mu_1 : \mu_2 = \mu_3 : \mu_4 \quad \leftrightarrow \quad \forall k \forall n \, R(k, n, \mu_1, \mu_2, \mu_3, \mu_4)$$

where both $\mu_1 : \mu_2$ and $\mu_3 : \mu_4$ are understood as objects whose condition for identity is spelled out on the right-hand side. Other well-known notational conventions (regarding the left-hand side of the biconditional) would render the abstraction principle for such objects as

$$\mu_1/\mu_2 = \mu_3/\mu_4 \quad \leftrightarrow \quad \forall k \forall n \, R(k, n, \langle \mu_1, \mu_2 \rangle, \langle \mu_3, \mu_4 \rangle)$$

or as

$$\frac{\mu_1}{\mu_2} = \frac{\mu_3}{\mu_4} \quad \leftrightarrow \quad \forall k \forall n \, R(k, n, \langle \mu_1, \mu_2 \rangle, \langle \mu_3, \mu_4 \rangle) \, .$$

This would be the way of the Fregean double-barreled abstractionists, appealing to the general form of their abstraction principle. What we have here is a Euclidean alternative to Shapiro's abstraction of quotients. But neither of these methods involves a variable-binding abstraction operator.

When variable-binding is not involved with the abstracts in question—as is the case here, with Euclid's ancient and Shapiro's recent abstraction of rationals; and as is the case with Frege's famous example of directions of lines—the Fregean double-barreled abstractionists' abstraction principle takes the simple form

$$\text{abstract}(t) = \text{abstract}(u) \quad \leftrightarrow \quad \text{FirstOrderEquivalenceRelation}(t, u).$$

But when variable-binding is involved for the abstracts in question, their abstraction principle takes the more complex form

$$\text{abstract}_x \Phi x = \text{abstract}_x \Psi x \quad \leftrightarrow \quad \text{HigherOrderEquivalenceRelation}(\Phi, \Psi).$$

What would ratios be, according to the Fregean double-barreled abstractionist who casts Euclid's definition into the foregoing form? Suppose you are given two magnitudes μ and ν of the same kind (lengths of line-segments, temporal durations, or whatever) and you proceed to 'abstract' to their ratio $\frac{\mu}{\nu}$. What sort of entity *is* this ratio, in general? We shall see that such ratios cannot (in general) be just the rational numbers.

The ratio $\frac{\mu}{\nu}$ cannot, in general, be a natural number, because, although $\frac{2}{1}$ might (indeed: should) be so taken, certainly $\frac{1}{2}$ cannot be. This latter point is hardly a surprise. Nor, however, can the ratio $\frac{\mu}{\nu}$ be, in general, a rational number. This came as a surprise to certain ancients, such as Pythagoras. Today, however, we are familiar with the celebrated counterexample that had found its way into Euclid:

$$\frac{\text{diagonal of square } \sigma}{\text{side of square } \sigma} \, .$$

An even more telling counterexample, not known until much later, would be

$$\frac{\text{circumference of circle } \sigma}{\text{diameter of circle } \sigma}.$$

For this ratio is not just irrational; it is transcendental (i.e., non-algebraic).[6]

So ... what is a ratio of magnitudes, in general? If it is not an entirely new kind of mathematical entity, the conservative best guess would be: it's a magnitude. But now, of course, there is a slight complication. A ratio of two lengths is not itself a length; a ratio of two temporal periods is not itself a temporal period; and so on. For any dimension $\mathcal{D}$, a ratio of two $\mathcal{D}$-magnitudes is not itself a $\mathcal{D}$-magnitude. Rather, it is a dimensionless magnitude—also known (in the most general case) as a real number.

Can our passage to the dimensionless reals really be that effortless? Can we simply help ourselves to but a single intellectually accessible, dimension-imbued, continuum of magnitudes, such as lengths of line-segments, and then abstract to the dimensionless reals by taking ratios?

If this is an acceptable methodology for the double-barreled abstractionists, they will have to temper their long-cherished conception of their method as one that brings new kinds of entities within our ken.[7] The way of attaining a conception of the dimensionless reals that is floated here (on behalf of the double-barreled abstractionist) is heavily freighted by its provenance in a pre-existing and firmly enjoyed conception of at least one dimension-imbued continuum of magnitudes (such as lengths of line-segments). The magnitudes have to be taken from a continuum in order to ensure that their ratios will in turn exhaust the continuum of the dimensionless reals. No new kind of structure of entities is being attained here; all that is happening is that dimensionality is being shed, and the entities within the continuum are being conceived as unfreighted by any dimension.

Euclid's method appears to take one straight to the reals, without tarrying at the rationals. Euclid does not even need (as Dedekind did) to presuppose the existence of the rationals. He works immediately with continuous magnitudes, takes ratios of them to de-dimensionalize, and *voilà*: one has the dimensionless reals. Among the latter, to be sure, are the rationals; but these form a special kind of reals whose own distinctive status has yet to be characterized. To follow Euclid's method is to take a low road, from the naturals to the reals. The high road would have wended its way from the naturals, via the rationals, and would have ended eventually with the reals. That is how our *Verstand* was supposed to work. One would fill in (densely) with rationals among the naturals; then one would fill in yet again (with irrationals, to ensure continuity) in order to attain the reals.

[6]The irrationality of π was established by Johann Heinrich Lambert [1768]; that π is moreover transcendental was established by Ferdinand von Lindemann [1882].

[7]Mancosu [2016] (at p. 24) calls this a *thick* way to define the concept of ratio, because 'the notion of ratio has no other definitional introduction than by means of the identity appearing in the left-hand side of the relevant abstraction principle'.

If one already has the rational numbers (by some logico-genetic method or other), then taking ratios will not take one beyond the rationals to any new sort of entity.[8]

But: if one begins, more modestly, with just the natural numbers (attained in some logico-genetic fashion), then, by taking ratios of them, one can and will attain, in general, to a new kind of entity—namely, the familiar (non-negative) rational numbers. This is the creative generation adverted to in the very label 'rational'. Shapiro's quotient-abstractionism gets the ontological target (almost) right; but, as we have argued, it does so at the misguided cost of allowing for the mathematically prohibited operation of division by zero, and at the methodological cost of presupposing more than is necessary in the way of conceptual basics. Any satisfactory alternative method of creatively abstracting the rationals when given only the naturals will therefore have to differ significantly from the methods of Euclid and of Shapiro.

Their two ways of generating the rationals (i.e., by taking ratios—by Euclid, of magnitudes, and by Shapiro, of naturals) share the distinct disadvantage that the natural numbers themselves have to be replaced by 'counterparts' that are ratios, not the actual natural numbers themselves. Euclid's abstractive method for ratios, applied as double-barreled abstraction, is type-raising. The natural number n has to be reconstrued as the 'natural-number'-ratio $\frac{n}{s0}$. What story can be spun to turn the latter object, the ratio $\frac{n}{s0}$, into the natural number n itself? How can the embeddability of the natural numbers themselves into the rationals be conceived so as to respect the very identity of the naturals *qua* (special instances of) rationals? How can we respect the profoundly motivating intuition that we attain to the (non-negative) rationals by taking the naturals, already given somehow, and interspersing among and between them all the non-whole-number fractions $\frac{p}{q}$ for which p is not a whole-number multiple of q? As already explained at some length in Chapter 4, we supply these extra rationals in thought so as to densely fill between the already existing natural numbers—among which we already have an ordering relation '$<$' that obeys the axioms $\mathcal{O}$. (This objection to Euclid's abstraction of those rationals that 'correspond' to the naturals is the same kind of objection that was raised earlier against Shapiro's double-barreled abstractionist principle that aimed to create the rationals from the naturals.)

It strikes this thinker that the double-barreled abstractionists cannot spin their story so as to avoid the forced structuralist recourse of seeing $\mathbb{N}$ as embeddable into $\mathbb{Q}_{\geq 0}$, and accordingly seeing each natural number n as having its corresponding, but metaphysically distinct, counterpart $\frac{n}{s0}$ within $\mathbb{Q}_{\geq 0}$.

The natural logicist needs a way to attain to the (non-negative) rationals—one that will preserve the metaphysical identity of the natural number n (acquired

[8] It is worth noting that nothing that Euclid says or proves about magnitudes in Book V requires one to consider the possibility of irrational magnitudes. It is only in Book X that one learns of incommensurable magnitudes, such as the length of the side of a square, and the length of its diagonal. Throughout Book V's theory of ratios, one would be free to regard the extension of the term 'magnitude' as consisting only of rational magnitudes. Arguably, Occam's Razor would so commend.

from its debut as described by Constructive Logicism) when it re-enters the abstractive stage in its new role as also a rational number. This (as explained on p. 14 and again on p. 32) the natural logicist will do by eschewing the double-barreled method of abstraction (which lays down a necessary and sufficient condition for the identity of two abstracta) and deploying instead the method of stipulating the assertability and commitment conditions (expressed by introduction and elimination rules, respectively) for canonical identity statements of the form

$$t = \alpha \ldots,$$

where α is the abstraction operator in question and t is a placeholder for any singular term whatsoever—not necessarily an abstractive term.

In assessing the ontological productivity of Euclid's definition of ratios, a great deal depends on what he might have meant by 'magnitude', when considering a ratio of any two of them. What is the most obvious interpretation that would occur to the mathematically sophisticated reader? Such a reader is aware that Euclid was primarily concerned with the study of geometric points, lines, and planes, as well as circles and other curves describable as loci of points 'moving' under certain constraints. The most obvious or canonical interpretation of 'magnitude' in this intellectual setting is 'measure of length of a line-segment'. For this purpose, a unit length needs to be settled upon (call it **m**, and think: *meter*), whereupon the length of any given line-segment λ can be measured in terms of **m**. The magnitude μ that results will be the dimensionalized measure of how many copies of length **m** are taken up in measuring the length of λ. Let the *How many?* question have the answer ℓ. We then have the following statements of identity of magnitudes:

$$\text{length}(\lambda) = \mu = \ell \odot \mathbf{m}$$

If, say, exactly three layings-on-end of (copies of) the unit length **m** account for λ, we shall have

$$\text{length}(\lambda) = \mu = 3 \odot \mathbf{m}$$

We would also have, in a suitably sophisticated extension of the basic ideas,

$$\text{length-of-circumference(circle of diameter } \mathbf{m}) = \pi \odot \mathbf{m}$$

In our imagined example of the line-segment λ, we need to distinguish between the dimensionless real number ℓ and the dimensionalized magnitude μ, or $\ell \odot \mathbf{m}$, which is imbued with the dimension in question, namely length, whose unit of measure is **m**. The magnitudes of which Euclid speaks are like μ—they are dimensionalized. We happen to have chosen the dimension of length by way of illustration. Remaining fully within the Euclidean context, we could also have chosen area, or volume. Venturing beyond that context, we could make the same points by reference to mass, or temporal duration. There are now many dimensions of scientific interest that are 'in principle' measurable by means of magnitudes forming (as is commonly supposed) a continuum (like lengths).

Suppose, however, that the magnitudes do not quite form a continuum, but rather form only a dense linear unbounded ordering. All that we have said thus far could be reconstrued so as to hold for this more impoverished setting. The diagonal of a square of side **m** would in principle escape exact measurement, as would the circumference of a circle of diameter **m**; but the more impoverished setting could still accommodate any actual outcome of attempted measurement, since these only ever involve 'approximating' magnitudes, for which the 'dimensionless' number ℓ is rational. And even in such cases, the approximation will be by some (decimal, say) expansion that might not actually 'nail' the number ℓ in question, even though it is rational. For example, the approximating decimal expansion to (say) ten decimal places for $\frac{1}{3}$ is 0.3333333333. Since the 3s go on *ad infinitum* in the decimal expansion for $\frac{1}{3}$, this ten-place approximation does not nail it. This phenomenon, by the way, is not peculiar to deci-mal expansion for rationals in the interval (0,1). It is manifest in any k-mal place notation, for finite $k \geq 2$, including bici-mals (for which $k=2$). For any k-mal place notation, there are always infinitely many rationals in the interval (0,1) whose k-mal expansions involve infinitely recurring finite sequences of digits, among which at least one digit is not the chosen one for zero.

We are now in a position to inquire what exactly Euclid's definition of ratios 'produces'. Does it produce anything new in our mathematical ontology, from 'more basic' or intellectually 'more accessible' entities (namely, the magnitudes of which he speaks)? We can answer as follows—systematically ignoring any negative numbers, which we do not need to take into consideration for any of our present purposes.

1. **If the dimensional magnitudes form a continuum,** then ratios turn out to be dimensionless reals; they form the system $\mathbb{R}$ of (non-negative) real numbers. So taking ratios only de-dimensionalizes. It does not produce anything 'structurally new'.

2. **If the dimensional magnitudes form only a dense linear unbounded ordering,** then ratios turn out to be dimensionless rationals; they form the system $\mathbb{Q}$ of (non-negative) rational numbers. So taking ratios only de-dimensionalizes. It does not produce anything 'structurally new'.

3. **If the 'dimensional' magnitudes form only an ω-progression,** (in effect, the system $\mathbb{N}$ of natural numbers), then ratios (with non-zero denominators) turn out to be (and to exhaust) the (non-negative) dimensionless rationals; they form $\mathbb{Q}$. So taking ratios both de-dimensionalizes (if dimensions are involved at all with the magnitudes whose ratios are being taken) and produces new entities (namely, those rationals that are not naturals).

But—with respect to (3)—how are the rationals that *are* the naturals to be seen to be such?

This last question is a challenging one. It demands an answer from the abstractionist who believes that abstraction merely *adds to* the furniture of the universe ('filling in gaps', as it were, among entities already attained), rather than replacing it wholesale with whole classes of more complicated new entities that displace the older, simpler ones that were perfectly adequate unto the intellectual tasks required of them.

Chapter 16

Mereology and Fraction Abstraction

Abstract

The chapter seeks to show how rational numbers—fractions—are entities to which rational thinkers are logically entitled. It begins by introducing mereology as part of our conceptual and methodological framework for eventually attaining a grasp of fractions. The basic concepts of mereology are laid out, with their formal notations. The treatment of identity is discussed. Mereology is the theory of the part-whole relation, and is of very low consistency strength; indeed, it is arguably analytically true. Mereological fusion is treated here as an abstraction operator, in this study's preferred single-barreled fashion, with introduction and elimination rules in free Core Logic. The notion of a dimensional magnitude (such as length) is introduced, along with the correlative notion of dimensional equality (such as line-segment congruence). One can define whole-number multiples of dimensional magnitudes (such as lengths of line segments; or 'identical' pizzas). This enables one to address the problem of characterizing what constitutes an equal share of p dimensionally equal items when these are to be divvied up into q dimensionally equal shares. An easy application of fractional abstraction then delivers the rational number $\frac{p}{q}$. The introduction and elimination rules for fractional abstraction furnish easy proof of all instances of Schema Q. One learns too why q cannot be 0, and why the rational number $\frac{n}{1}$ *is* the natural number n.

Let us consider now just how austere or modest an intellectual scaffolding is actually required, and suffices, for one to attain to the concept of a rational number (or, in more familiar parlance: fractions). The results of such an investigation might be surprising. It turns out that by bringing certain mereological concepts to bear,[1] we can greatly reduce the presupposed 'arithmetical load' on the naturals that needs to be borne *en route* to the rationals. By importing mereological considerations into our conceptual enterprise, we also lay the necessary groundwork for explaining the applicability of the rationals in our wider thought and talk about the world.

Mereology is the theory of the part-whole relation. It is also of extremely low

[1] The first source (as far as the present author is aware) to draw on resources in mereology in an attempt to logicize the rational numbers is Bostock [1979]. But we shall strike out in new directions in doing so.

The Logic of Number. Neil Tennant, Oxford University Press. © Neil Tennant 2022.
DOI: 10.1093/oso/9780192846679.003.0016

consistency strength—an important consideration for any logicist seeking a logical grounding of familiar mathematical objects and structures. Originally mereology was of a nominalistic bent. It concerned itself only with concrete individuals, and avoided talking about abstract entities, in particular entities of 'higher type', such as properties or sets. Mereology need not, however, be understood as hostile to the existence of abstract objects. As Achille Varzi writes (Varzi [2016], §1),

> ... there is no necessary link between the analysis of parthood relations and the philosophical position of nominalism. ... mereology is simply an attempt to lay down the general principles underlying the relationships between an entity and its constituent parts, whatever the nature of the entity, just as set theory is an attempt to lay down the principles underlying the relationships between a set and its members. Unlike set theory, mereology is not committed to the existence of abstracta: the whole can be as concrete as the parts. But mereology carries no nominalistic commitment to concreta either: the parts can be as abstract as the whole.

The source of many of our intuitions about the part-whole relation, however, is spatial, or spatio-temporal. Basic claims about mereological operations and relations are particularly easy to motivate in the context of, say, two-dimensional regions of the Euclidean plane. But, insofar as ordinary physical objects are space-occupying, one can also motivate mereological claims by thinking about extended bodies in three dimensions (or even by thinking about four-dimensional worms, their time-slices, and concoctions thereof). Mereology is a conceptual enterprise, and should not be hostage to empirical fortune in such matters as (i) whether there are any mereological atoms—that is, individuals that have no proper parts; or (ii) whether any natural kind has infinitely many members; or (iii) whether the best geometry for the description of space (or spacetime) is Euclidean or non-Euclidean. Our thinking about regions is really topological, not geometric.[2]

The most important mereological relations (whether taken as primitive or defined) are the following.[3]

$x \sqsubseteq y$	x is part of y
$x \sqsubset y$	x is a proper part of y
$x \circ y$	x overlaps y
$x \rceil y$	x is disjoint from y

By means of any one of the relations just listed, the other three relations can be defined as follows.

[2]For the early Carnap, it was the topological core of geometries, both Euclidean and non-Euclidean, that survived as synthetic *a priori* after the adoption of non-Euclidean geometry by relativity theorists. See Carnap [1922].

[3]Historically, there has been a notational farrago, with no canonical choice of notation having been settled upon. We do our best here to choose notations that will be reasonably perspicuous and easy to remember.

With $\sqsubseteq$ primitive:

$$\begin{array}{lll} x \sqsubset y & \equiv_{df} & x \sqsubseteq y \wedge \exists z(z \sqsubseteq y \wedge \neg(z \sqsubseteq x)) \\ x \circ y & \equiv_{df} & \exists z(z \sqsubseteq x \wedge z \sqsubseteq y) \\ x \mathrel{\rceil\!\lfloor} y & \equiv_{df} & \neg(x \circ y) \end{array}$$

With $\sqsubset$ primitive:

$$\begin{array}{lll} x \sqsubseteq y & \equiv_{df} & \forall z(z \sqsubset x \rightarrow z \sqsubset y) \\ x \circ y & \equiv_{df} & \exists z(z \sqsubseteq x \wedge z \sqsubseteq y) \\ x \mathrel{\rceil\!\lfloor} y & \equiv_{df} & \neg(x \circ y) \end{array}$$

With $\circ$ primitive:

$$\begin{array}{lll} x \sqsubseteq y & \equiv_{df} & \forall z(z \circ x \rightarrow z \circ y) \\ x \sqsubset y & \equiv_{df} & x \sqsubseteq y \wedge \exists z(z \circ y \wedge \neg(z \circ x)) \\ x \mathrel{\rceil\!\lfloor} y & \equiv_{df} & \neg(x \circ y) \end{array}$$

With $\mathrel{\rceil\!\lfloor}$ primitive:

$$\begin{array}{lll} x \sqsubseteq y & \equiv_{df} & \forall z(z \mathrel{\rceil\!\lfloor} y \rightarrow z \mathrel{\rceil\!\lfloor} x) \\ x \sqsubset y & \equiv_{df} & x \sqsubseteq y \wedge \exists z(z \sqsubseteq y \wedge z \mathrel{\rceil\!\lfloor} x) \\ x \circ y & \equiv_{df} & \neg(x \mathrel{\rceil\!\lfloor} y) \end{array}$$

These definitions have been stated in such a way that one does not need to avail oneself of identity as a primitive. The expectation is that extensionality will hold in the form of the following general equivalences:

$$\begin{array}{l} \forall x \forall y(x = y \leftrightarrow \forall z(z \sqsubseteq x \leftrightarrow z \sqsubseteq y)); \\ \forall x \forall y(x = y \leftrightarrow \forall z(z \sqsubset x \leftrightarrow z \sqsubset y)); \\ \forall x \forall y(x = y \leftrightarrow \forall z(z \circ x \leftrightarrow z \circ y)); \text{ and} \\ \forall x \forall y(x = y \leftrightarrow \forall z(z \mathrel{\rceil\!\lfloor} x \leftrightarrow z \mathrel{\rceil\!\lfloor} y)). \end{array}$$

Whichever mereological relation is taken as primitive, identity could be defined by means of the appropriate one of these general equivalences, thus:

$$\begin{array}{l} x = y \equiv_{df} \forall z(z \sqsubseteq x \leftrightarrow z \sqsubseteq y); \\ x = y \equiv_{df} \forall z(z \sqsubset x \leftrightarrow z \sqsubset y); \\ x = y \equiv_{df} \forall z(z \circ x \leftrightarrow z \circ y); \text{ and} \\ x = y \equiv_{df} \forall z(z \mathrel{\rceil\!\lfloor} x \leftrightarrow z \mathrel{\rceil\!\lfloor} y). \end{array}$$

Then, via one's definitions of the other mereological relations, one should be able to derive the other general equivalences in the list given above. In place of the first of these general equivalences, for the purpose of defining identity in terms of $\sqsubseteq$, one could take

$$\forall x \forall y(x = y \leftrightarrow (x \sqsubseteq y \wedge y \sqsubseteq x)).$$

Alternatively, one could take identity as primitive. Then one would need to be able to derive each of the general equivalences above by means of one's definitions and theoretical axioms and rules of inference. Moreover, if identity is taken as primitive, then some of the foregoing definitions of mereological relations can be simplified.

The most important mereological operations are the following.

$t \sqcup u$	the sum (fusion) of t and u
$t \sqcap u$	the product (nucleus; common part) of t and u

The taking of a sum or a product is here represented as a binary operation. But of course the operations in question can be applied more generally, to the members of any given family or class of individuals. In order, however, to avoid presupposing the language and theory of sets in our mereological theorizing about individuals and their sums and products, we can resort to the use of first-order schematic predicates Φ:

$\bigsqcup x\Phi(x)$	the sum (fusion) of all individuals x such that $\Phi(x)$
$\bigsqcap x\Phi(x)$	the product (nucleus) of all individuals x such that $\Phi(x)$

One's axioms and rules of inference for mereology would have to specify appropriate existence conditions for such sums and products. Because these conditions might in some cases not be met, and the complex singular term in question accordingly not denote, mereology should be based on a free logic.

Note that $\bigsqcap x\Phi(x)$ can be defined in terms of $\bigsqcup$—as the fusion of all individuals that are part of every Φ:

$$\bigsqcap x\Phi(x) \;=_{df}\; \bigsqcup x\forall y(\Phi y \rightarrow x \sqsubseteq y).$$

We shall therefore concentrate on providing rules only for $\bigsqcup$ as an abstraction operator. First we have its introduction rule.

$$(\bigsqcup\text{-I})\quad \dfrac{\begin{matrix}\underbrace{\overline{\Phi a}^{(i)}\ ,\ \overline{\exists!a}^{(i)}}\\ \vdots \\ a \sqsubseteq t\end{matrix} \qquad \exists z\Phi z \qquad \exists!t \qquad \begin{matrix}\overline{a \sqsubseteq t}^{(i)} \\ \vdots \\ \exists y(\Phi y \wedge a \circ y)\end{matrix}}{t = \bigsqcup x\Phi x}{\scriptstyle (i)}$$

In words: Suppose that one has shown that

(i) every Φ is part of t;

(ii) something is Φ;

(iii) t exists; and

(iv) every part of t overlaps some Φ.

Then one may infer that t is the fusion of (all) Φs.

Corresponding to the introduction rule for $\bigsqcup$ is the following four-part elimination rule. These four parts respectively express the inferential commitments corresponding to the four assertability conditions that are expressed by the corresponding sub-proof schemata or premises of the introduction rule.

$$(\bigsqcup\text{-E1})) \quad \frac{t = \bigsqcup x\Phi x \quad \Phi(u) \quad \exists! u}{u \sqsubseteq t} \qquad (\bigsqcup\text{-E2}) \quad \frac{t = \bigsqcup x\Phi x \quad \begin{matrix} \underbrace{\overset{(i)}{\overline{\Phi a}}\ ,\ \overset{(i)}{\overline{\exists! a}}} \\ \vdots \\ \psi \end{matrix}}{\psi}{\scriptstyle (i)}$$

$$(\bigsqcup\text{-E3}) \quad \frac{t = \bigsqcup x\Phi x}{\exists! t} \qquad (\bigsqcup\text{-E4}) \quad \frac{t = \bigsqcup x\Phi x \quad u \sqsubseteq t}{\exists y(\Phi y \wedge u \circ y)}$$

An important binary operation is subtraction:

$t - u$	the fusion of all parts of t that are not part of u i.e., $\bigsqcup x(x \sqsubseteq t \wedge \neg x \sqsubseteq u)$

We shall find it convenient to be able to talk also of the fusion of pairwise disjoint things:

$t \amalg u$	the sum (fusion) of the disjoint things t and u
$\amalg x\Phi(x)$	the sum (fusion) of all pairwise disjoint individuals x such that $\Phi(x)$

The notion of $\mathcal{D}$-fusion of $\mathcal{D}$-magnitudes depends very much on the dimension $\mathcal{D}$ concerned. In the case of the length of line-segments, a 'length'-fusion is (canonically) formed (from the various length-magnitudes that are being fused) by straight layings-on-end, so as to form a single line-segment out of them. In the different case where the dimension is that of the weight of a physical object, spatial re-arrangement of objects to be fused is not essential. If, however, the weight of their fusion is to be measured, they must all be put together, with no other objects, on an appropriately sized pan of a weighing scale. Whatever the context, common sense dictates what is to count as fusion.

Associated with any dimension $\mathcal{D}$ (such as length) is the fundamental dimensional-logical notion of $\mathcal{D}$-equality, symbolized by $\cong_{\mathcal{D}}$. With the dimension of length (call it $\mathcal{L}$) as the chosen example of $\mathcal{D}$, we have two line-segments μ and ν being $\mathcal{L}$-equal (i.e., equally long):

$$\mu \cong_{\mathcal{L}} \nu$$

just in case they are congruent in the sense of Euclidean geometry. The line-segments μ and ν could, for example, be opposite sides of a parallelogram; or adjacent sides of a square; or the diagonals of a rectangle. In general, though, they need not share any point, and (in the three-dimensional case) they need not lie in the same plane.

Just as common sense dictates what is to count as fusion, so too common sense dictates what is to count as a 'residue' resulting from the subtraction of a part from a whole. Such a residue need not be part of the whole in question. To illustrate: suppose the line-segment μ has the line-segment ν as a (proper) part. There are two cases to consider:

1. ν is an end-segment of μ. Then any line-segment $\mathcal{L}$-equal to $\mu - \nu$ counts as a residue resulting from the subtraction of ν from μ.

2. ν is not an end-segment of μ. Then $\mu - \nu$ consists of two disjoint line-segments, both of them parts of μ; and any line-segment $\mathcal{L}$-equal to the result of laying these two line-segments end-to-end counts as a residue resulting from the subtraction of ν from μ.

We shall abbreviate the notion 'ρ is a residue resulting from subtracting from μ a part ν' as $\mathcal{R}(\rho, \mu, \nu)$.

We now define whole-number multiples of a dimensionalized magnitude μ. Definition 9 is by mathematical induction, to which the Constructive Logicist is of course entitled, without yet having mastered either addition or multiplication on the naturals.

Note that Definition 9 is not a definition of what might be meant by an identity statement of the form '$t = n$ layings on end of μ'. (It would be a mistake to think that the latter quoted sentence-form gets the logical form of our definienda right.) Here we are not looking for introduction and elimination rules of the single-barreled kind, which is our usual goal in connection with genuine identities. This is because what we are setting out to define are not the inferential roles, or truth-conditions, of identities at all. Rather, the definienda of Definition 9 are ternary predications, involving a natural number and two magnitudes. We are seeking, with Definition 9, to confer a precise sense on statements of the form '(the magnitude) ν is $\mathcal{D}$-equal to (one could also say: is $\mathcal{D}$-congruent to) n layings-on-end of (the magnitude) μ'.[4]

Definition 9. *Suppose μ and ν are $\mathcal{D}$-magnitudes. Then (as basis)*

$$0 \odot \mu \cong_{\mathcal{D}} \mu - \mu\,;$$
$$s0 \odot \mu \cong_{\mathcal{D}} \mu\,;$$

and (as inductive clause)

[4]Thanks are owed to Damon Stanley for comments eliciting this clarification.

> *ν is $\mathcal{D}$-equal to $(sn) \odot \mu$*
> *if and only if*
> *any residue that results by subtracting from ν a part $\mathcal{D}$-equal to μ is $\mathcal{D}$-equal to $n \odot \mu$.*

Formally:

$$\nu \cong_D (sn) \odot \mu$$

$$\leftrightarrow$$

$$\forall \nu' [(\nu' \cong_D \mu \ \wedge \ \nu' \sqsubseteq \nu) \rightarrow \forall \rho (\mathcal{R}(\rho, \nu, \nu') \rightarrow \rho \cong_D n \odot \mu)] .$$

Definition 10. *Suppose μ and ν are $\mathcal{D}$-magnitudes, and that q is a nonzero natural number. Then we say that ν is $\mathcal{D}$-equal to a q-th part of μ—in symbols:*

$$\text{-}th(\nu, q, \mu)$$

—just in case

$$q \odot \nu \cong_D \mu .$$

Recall our discussion at the end of Chapter 14. It concerned the sharing of p pizzas among q people, in the supra-unity case where $p = (q.n) + k$ with $k < q$. Using the technical vocabulary now at our disposal, we can return to this discussion to observe that a single share will be the pizza-equivalent of the 'disjoint fusion'

$$t \amalg u$$

of two disjoint sub-shares t and u, where

$$t \cong_P n \odot \textbf{whole pizza}$$

and

$$q \odot u \cong_P k \odot \textbf{whole pizza}.$$

We consider first what should be called dimensionalized ratios. A side σ of a square is equal (in length) to one quarter (i.e., one 4-th) of its perimeter γ:

$$\text{-th}(\sigma, 4, \gamma)$$

Equivalently:

$$4 \odot \sigma \cong_D \gamma$$

Appealing to the basis clause in Definition 9, we can also write this as

$$4 \odot \sigma \cong_D 1 \odot \gamma$$

We understand the two sides of this last statement of $\mathcal{L}$-equality to be dimensionalized. We want now to be able to express the same thought by means of an $\mathcal{L}$-equality in which σ is isolated by itself on one side. Something along the following lines would do:

$$\sigma \cong_{\mathcal{L}} (1:4) \odot \gamma$$

Focusing now on the right-hand side $(1:4) \odot \gamma$, we realize that the dimensonalizing can be thought of as originating solely in its contained term γ; while the term $(1:4)$ need not be dimensionalized at all. What we are seeking is a treatment according to which this thought will be vindicated: the ratio $(1:4)$ will turn out to be a dimensionless entity, a so-called rational number. But we must not get ahead of ourselves here; we have to earn the right to use an equality statement like this last one.

We do not need to resort to such a rich setting of magnitudes as lengths (albeit only while considering whole-number multiples of a chosen unit) in order to attain to the rational numbers in this fashion. In fact, we can make very good sense of the rationals as acquiring a 'life of their own' (in our thought about the world) by hewing to sortal concepts and the whole numbers that we use to count the individuals forming their extensions. This is conceptual ground already tilled to fertile effect by the Fregean. And this is the route we take on behalf of Edwin the Fractionator. We shall follow him on his remarkable route to mastery of rationals as dimensionless abstract entities, even before he learns how to add and to multiply natural numbers.

Consider, then, the following sort of claim in an account of Edwin's intellectual maturation. He has in his hand a pile t of congruent pieces of pizza, this pile being a mereological fusion of five pairwise disjoint pizza-parts, each of them one-eighth of a whole pizza. The following is an expression of this fact, in the form to whose use we seek to earn the right:

$$t \cong_{\mathcal{P}} (5:8) \odot \textbf{whole pizza}.$$

The denotation of t here is 'dimensionalized' (or, rather, mereologically constituted) by the property $\mathcal{P}$ of being made up of pizza parts. The denotation of t is not a number of any kind; that denotation is constituted by pizza-parts. It is a pizza-equivalent of five-eighths of a whole pizza. Here, 'of a' is rendered as the binary function $\odot$.

That, at least, is how we would put matters, even if by so doing we are not, strictly, rendering Edwin's thoughts about the matter in a faithful way. For Edwin is himself apprised only of the natural numbers. He is in a situation where five pizzas are to be shared equally among eight people. And he knows how to ensure that each person receives a share that is the pizza-equivalent of a pile like t.

Besides the obvious

$$\text{WholePizza}(\textbf{whole pizza}),$$

Edwin's relevant pieces of knowledge are threefold:

$$8 = \#x\text{EqualShare}(x); \quad 5 = \#x\text{WholePizza}(x); \quad 8 \odot t \cong_D 5 \odot \textbf{whole pizza}.$$

Note that one can infer from these, using the free-logic rules

$$\frac{A(t)}{\exists! t} \qquad \frac{\exists! f(t)}{\exists! t}$$

only that the natural numbers 5 and 8 exist. Edwin is not (yet) in a position to infer from the foregoing three pieces of knowledge—using rules thus far available to him—that

$$\exists!(5:8).$$

He will be able to infer this numerical existence claim, however, as soon as he adopts the following instance of a rule whose general form will be stated soon:

$$\frac{8 \odot t \cong_P 5 \odot \textbf{whole pizza}}{t \cong_P (5:8) \odot \textbf{whole pizza}} \, .$$

For, he will be able to continue, as a free logician, as follows:

$$\cfrac{\cfrac{t \cong_P (5:8) \odot \textbf{whole pizza}}{\exists!\, (5:8) \odot \textbf{whole pizza}}}{\exists!\, (5:8)} \, .$$

The first step is an application of the Rule of Atomic Denotation, since $\cong_P$ is an atomic binary predicate; the second step is an application of the Rule of Functional Denotation, since $\odot$ is a binary function symbol. (The reader is reminded that these two rules were stated on p. 12.)

Edwin the Fractionator becomes Edwin the Committer-to-Fractions as soon as he infers from his aforementioned piece of knowledge

$$8 \odot t \cong_D 5 \odot \textbf{whole pizza}$$

a 'new way of expressing the matter', namely that an equal share t of five pieces among eight people is (the pizza-equivalent of) five-eighths of a whole pizza:

$$t \cong_P (5:8) \odot \textbf{whole pizza}.$$

Before, Edwin was master of expressions of the form

$$v \cong_D w \odot \mu$$

only for whole-number multiples w of the magnitude (or **whole**) μ. Now, possessed of a new rule, he is master of fractional multiples of such magnitudes; he has, in effect, extended the domain of the binary operation $\odot$ with respect to its first argument place (the one for dimensionless numbers).

If all this strikes the reader as a little too swift, let us reexamine the steps in more detail. When Edwin cuts a whole pizza into eight equal (and, obviously, pairwise disjoint) parts, he is apprised of, and recognizes as entities, the pizza-magnitude **whole pizza**, and (since he is a Constructive Logicist[5]) the natural number 8. Each of the eight equal pieces (or 'pizza magnitudes') that he has produced by cutting can be described by the following term denoting a pizza-magnitude:

result-of-cutting-(**whole pizza**)-into-equal-parts-numbering-(8)

What we have here is a denoting term constructed from the binary function-sign

result-of-cutting-( )-into-equal-parts-numbering-( )

applied to the arguments **whole pizza** and 8 in that order. And this term, to repeat, denotes a pizza-magnitude. As such, it is eligible to feature in place of the dots in our earlier inductively defined compound form of expression

$$n \odot (\ldots)$$

denoting whole-number multiples of given magnitudes.

In the Edwin example, n is 5. So Edwin can use the term

5 $\odot$ (result-of-cutting-(**whole pizza**)-into-equal-parts-numbering-(8))

to think about what he has done. And what he has done is this: he has produced eight equal shares of five pizzas. Each share consists of five of the pizza-pieces that resulted from cutting each of the five pizzas into eight equal parts. Let the pizza-magnitude to which such a share is equal be called t. Then Edwin is apprised of the fact that

$t \cong_{\mathcal{P}}$ 5 $\odot$ (result-of-cutting-(**whole pizza**)-into-equal-parts-numbering-(8))

Another way of expressing this, reversing the order of the two arguments (namely, the pizza-magnitude argument and the number-argument), would be by means of the pizza-equality

$t \cong_{\mathcal{P}}$ 5 $\odot$ (result-of-cutting-into-(8)-equal-parts (**whole pizza**)).

Programmers in Prolog have no trouble using functions and predicates in which words are interspersed with the arguments to which the predicate or function in

[5] As a Constructive Logicist, Edwin is able to derive the following instance of Schema N:

$$\#x(x \text{ is a piece of pizza}) = 8 \;\dashv\vdash\; \text{there are exactly eight pieces of pizza.}$$

question applies. But the logician usually prefers to have all the arguments lined up consecutively, separated only by commas. So, regimenting as logicians on Edwin's behalf (but not venturing out of his own thought-world), we can make so bold as to recast the expression

result-of-cutting-into-(8)-equal-parts (**whole pizza**)

as

result-of-cutting-into-equal-parts(8, **whole pizza**),

and accordingly recast the foregoing pizza-equality as

$$t \cong_p 5 \odot (\text{result-of-cutting-into-equal-parts}(8, \textbf{whole pizza})).$$

Now we can appeal to the '-th' suffix of English, to shorten this to

$$t \cong_p 5 \odot ((8)\text{-th of a } (\textbf{whole pizza})),$$

or even

$$t \cong_p 5 \odot ((8)\text{-ths of a } (\textbf{whole pizza})),$$

given that the plural is called for in connection with any number that, like 5, is greater than 1. Here we are once again indulging a Prolog-programmer's taste for interspersing words and function-arguments. If, however, we revert once again to the logician's style of regimenting, we can re-write the last equality (more mischievously) as

$$t \cong_p 5 \odot (\text{-th of}(8, \textbf{whole pizza}))$$

Now, Edwin is well aware that any natural number (such as 8) is dimensionless. That t is a pizza-magnitude arises solely from the presence, on the right-hand side of this last statement of equality of pizza-magnitudes, of the pizza-magnitude-denoting term **whole pizza**. So Edwin is entitled to re-group terms in such a way as to emphasize this insight. Accordingly, he thinks it is time to group the numerical terms together, but in such a way as to show, by notational asymmetry, that 5 is the number of pizzas and 8 is the number of equal shares. So he now writes (and thinks) more succinctly that

$$t \cong_p (5:8) \odot \textbf{whole pizza}$$

And Edwin has thereby created in thought (or recognized at last) the numerical fraction 5:8, and has extended the domain of the binary function $\odot$ so as to encompass such fractions in its first (dimensionless-numerical) argument place. He is now committed to the existence of the ratio—or rational number—5:8.

Let us now think of fractions in general as having the form $p : q$, where p and q are natural numbers. (We shall rule out later the possibility that q be 0.) Here is Edwin's general form of an existentially committal rule of Ratio-Introduction, telling us (courtesy of the background rules of free logic) that ratios do indeed exist, and play the role expected of them:

$$:\text{-I} \qquad \frac{q \odot t \ \cong_D \ p \odot \mathbf{whole}}{t \ \cong_D \ (p:q) \odot \mathbf{whole}} \ .$$

The general derivation of commitment to ratios as dimensionless entities is

$$\cfrac{\cfrac{t \cong_D (p:q) \odot \mathbf{whole}}{\exists!\ (p:q) \odot \mathbf{whole}}\ \text{Rule of Atomic Denotation}}{\exists!\ (p:q)}\ \text{Rule of Functional Denotation}$$

Edwin will come to realize, however, that the rule can be stated even more austerely. There is no need to fixate on any particular magnitude specified as **whole**. (It helps to do so with the pizza example, but any particular magnitude can have fractional parts.) Let us therefore replace **whole** in the statement of the foregoing rule with an arbitrary magnitude v (of the same dimension D as t):

$$:\text{-I} \qquad \frac{q \odot t \ \cong_D \ p \odot v}{t \ \cong_D \ (p:q) \odot v}$$

The rule is stated on the understanding that p and q are natural numbers. Moreover, the rule gives one intellectual access to the rationals (i.e., entities of the form $p:q$) even when the magnitude v is not necessarily one from a continuum, such as the length of a line-segment. The rule applies even when v takes only discrete 'dimensioned' values, such as **whole pizza**. So the rule could be modified even further, and still give one access to the rationals.

To see this, let Φ be a 'whole' thing in the extension of some sortal predicate, and suppose further that any two distinct whole (hence: disjoint) Φs (say, x and y) are 'dimensionally equal' *qua* Φs: $x \cong_\Phi y$. Good examples of such Φs would be: cricket balls; Edwin's pizzas (recall footnote 2); Slim Jims; sugar cubes; coins of any one denomination; A4 pages from a ream; eight-ounce blocks of a standard brand of sharp cheddar; etc. The relation $\cong_\Phi$ of Φ-equality can of course also hold between parts of whole Φs, and between fusions of such parts. It does not follow from the Φ-equality of z and w that both z and w are whole Φs. It only follows that they are fusions of parts of one or more whole Φs. Nor does it follow that they are disjoint.

With this clarification of what we might mean by $\cong_\Phi$, the :-Introduction rule can be stated for the following more limited range of potential applications:

$$:\text{-I} \qquad \frac{q \odot t \ \cong_\Phi \ p \odot \Phi}{t \ \cong_\Phi \ (p:q) \odot \Phi} \ .$$

Edwin's competence with fractionating shows that he knows what it is, in general, for the premise of this rule to be true. Then, when he consciously extends that competence by adopting this ratio-introducing rule, he finally gains intellectual access to the (positive) rational numbers, by virtue of the re-carving of content that produces the conclusion. The conclusion

$$t \cong_{\Phi} (p:q) \odot \Phi$$

of (:-I) can be read quite felicitously in logician's English as

t is (equal to) p q-ths of a Φ.

Edwin 'consciously extends [his] competence', of course, only courtesy of subscribing also to the two very important rules of free logic called the Rule of Atomic Predication and the Rule of Functional Denotation. This is an unusual insight afforded by the Constructive Logicist's approach. One has to have the whole arsenal of canons governing (constructive) logical reasoning for a first-order language containing singular terms that might (even, necessarily)[6] fail to denote.

Having introduced the :-Introduction rule above, we now address the question of a corresponding :-Elimination rule. This is particularly straightforward. It is simply the converse of the :-Introduction rule:

$$:\text{-E} \qquad \frac{t \cong_D (p:q) \odot \Phi}{q \odot t \cong_D p \odot \Phi} \,.$$

It is the premise of (:-E) that can be read as

t is (equal to) p q-ths of a Φ,

and we have argued above that anyone using a free logic is committed, upon holding this premise to be true, to the existence of an entity to be denoted as $p : q$. This entity is a special kind of number: a rational number. It is that fraction of a **whole** Φ that t constitutes. We can regiment this fractional expression as

$$\mathfrak{F}x(t, x \cong_{\Phi} \textbf{whole } \Phi).$$

Now we may consider a genuine identity statement (not just one of Φ-equality) of the form

$$\mathfrak{F}x(t, x \cong_{\Phi} \textbf{whole } \Phi) = p:q$$

What are its truth conditions? Answer: that t be p q-ths of a (whole) Φ. Our theory of rationals must vouchsafe this.

To see how our theory can be in a position to do so, let us work up to the rationals via the naturals as a special case, within the context where we are not counting the extension of a sortal predicate, but rather are deploying our mereological notion of dimensionally-equal magnitudes. Suppose t is a pile of pizzas,

[6] Examples: $\{x|\neg x \in x\}$; $\{x|x \text{ is an ordinal}\}$; $\frac{p}{0}$; 'the largest prime number'; $\sum_{x\geq 1} \frac{1}{n}$.

considered as their fusion. We would want to be able to secure, for any natural number n, the following interdeducibility:

$$\#x(t, x \cong_{\mathcal{P}} \textbf{whole } \mathcal{P}) = \underline{n} \quad \dashv\vdash \quad t \cong_{\mathcal{P}} \; n \odot \textbf{whole } \mathcal{P}.$$

That is, the number of whole-pizza equivalents constituting t is identical to $\underline{n}$ just in case t is $\mathcal{P}$-equal to n whole pizzas.

We want, however, to be able to encompass more than just whole numbers of whole-pizza equivalents; we want also to deal with fraction(al number)s of whole-pizza equivalents. That is, we want to graduate to

$$\mathfrak{F}x(t, x \cong_{\mathcal{P}} \textbf{whole } \mathcal{P}) = p : q \quad \dashv\vdash \quad t \cong_{\mathcal{P}} \; (p : q) \odot \textbf{whole } \mathcal{P}.$$

and, more generally, to

$$\mathfrak{F}x(t, x \cong_{\Phi} \textbf{whole } \Phi) = p : q \quad \dashv\vdash \quad t \cong_{\Phi} \; (p : q) \odot \textbf{whole } \Phi.$$

And both the easiest and most intellectually honest way to do this is to take each direction as inferentially primitive:

$$\mathfrak{F}\text{-I} \quad \frac{t \cong_{\Phi} \; (p : q) \odot \textbf{whole } \Phi}{\mathfrak{F}x(t, x \cong_{\Phi} \textbf{whole } \Phi) = p : q} \; ; \qquad \mathfrak{F}\text{-E} \quad \frac{\mathfrak{F}x(t, x \cong_{\Phi} \textbf{whole } \Phi) = p : q}{t \cong_{\Phi} \; (p : q) \odot \textbf{whole } \Phi} \; .$$

These inferences really do strike one as analytic. The formal sentence

$$t \cong_{\Phi} \; (p : q) \odot \textbf{whole } \Phi$$

says 't is equal to this fraction (i.e., $p : q$) of a (whole) Φ'; while the formal sentence

$$\mathfrak{F}x(t, x \cong_{\Phi} \textbf{whole } \Phi) = p : q$$

merely 'pulls the fraction out' to stand unadorned on the right-hand side of the identity: 'that fraction of a (whole) Φ constituted by t is (identical to) $p : q$'.

In our continuing example of Edwin's divvying of five pizzas among eight people, we are working with what we called earlier a 'sub-unity case': one where the fractional number $p : q$ has $p < q$. But we must be able to deal also with the 'supra-unity' cases: those where $p \geq q$. Thus, we must find a felicitous reading of the abstraction operator $\mathfrak{F}$ for 'fractional' numbers that will cover both cases. We must allow $\mathfrak{F}$-terms to denote not just sub-unity fractions, but also numbers that are the result of 'adding' (an operation yet to be defined) a sub-unity fraction to a natural number n. That 'addition' will be called for only when both the fusion of q equal shares consisting of that (natural) number n of whole Φs does not exhaust the fusion of the p available Φs, and the latter fusion would not exhaust any fusion of q equal shares consisting of $s(n)$ whole Φs.

Our theory must therefore enable us to derive every instance of the following interdeducibility schema, where t is any fusion of Φ-parts, and p and q are arbitrary natural numbers.[7] The right-hand side of Schema Q states the truth-conditions, in a way that is not rational-number committal, that have to be fulfilled in order for the left-hand side, which is rational-number committal, to hold. The left-hand side is an identity statement involving two different kinds of terms.

Schema Q $\mathfrak{F}x(t, x \cong_\Phi \textbf{whole } \Phi) = p : q \quad \dashv\vdash \quad q \odot t \cong_\Phi p \odot \textbf{whole } \Phi.$

Let us now discuss the two sides of the identity statement on the left-hand side.

First, there is the abstractive term

$$\mathfrak{F}x(t, x \cong_\Phi \textbf{whole } \Phi)$$

whose dominant operator is the variable-binding

$$\mathfrak{F}x(t, x \cong_{\mathcal{D}} \textbf{unit of } \mathcal{D})$$

which takes the term t and the unary predicate $x \cong_{\mathcal{D}}$ **unit of** $\mathcal{D}$ to form, in general, 'that fraction of a $\mathcal{D}$-unit constituted by t'—or, on the more general reading sought for $\mathfrak{F}$, 'that (potentially fractional) number of $\mathcal{D}$-units constituted by t'. This allows for natural numbers to be among the entities that can be denoted by $\mathfrak{F}$-terms.

It also allows for non-natural rationals greater than 1, as implicitly called for in our undertaking to elaborate the discussion so as to deal with fractions lying between any non-zero natural number and its successor. Recall that we were concerned with the sharing of p pizzas among q people, in the supra-unity case where

$$p = (q.n) + k \ (k < q).$$

We observed that a single share will be the pizza-equivalent of the 'disjoint fusion'

$$t \amalg u$$

of two disjoint sub-shares t and u, where

$$t \cong_{\mathcal{P}} n \odot \textbf{whole pizza}$$

and

$$q \odot u \cong_{\mathcal{P}} k \odot \textbf{whole pizza}.$$

We can now transform the latter characterization of u to

$$u \cong_{\mathcal{P}} (k : q) \odot \textbf{whole pizza}.$$

We shall clearly wish to be able to reason as follows, once we have introduced addition as an operation on the rational numbers themselves:

$$\frac{t \cong_{\mathcal{P}} n \odot \textbf{whole pizza} \qquad u \cong_{\mathcal{P}} (k : q) \odot \textbf{whole pizza}}{t \amalg u \cong_{\mathcal{P}} (n + (k : q)) \odot \textbf{whole pizza}}$$

[7] Well, not quite arbitrary; as promised, we shall be explaining why one has to rule out the possibility that q be 0.

A number-abstraction operator of the same Fregean logico-linguistic category as $\mathfrak{F}$ is also exactly what one needs in order to push this treatment further, so as to deal with the real numbers as dimensionless entities involved in the measurement of continuous (and not just: densely ordered) dimensional magnitudes.[8] And for that theory of the reals, there is a Schema R, appropriately analogous to Schema Q for the rationals. We shall be discussing Schema R in Part IV.

That ends our discussion of the first kind of numerical term in the identity statement on the left-hand side of Schema Q. It is the kind of term that enables us to understand how rational numbers come to be applied in our wider thought and talk about the world.

We turn now to the second kind of numerical term. This is the 'fractional' term $p : q$, now clearly seen to denote a dimensionless entity, namely a fraction, or rational number. This kind of 'strictly numerical' term is all that the pure mathematician needs in order to pursue her studies of the rationals. We have not yet said enough about how to take those studies much further, into the additive and multiplicative properties of the rationals; but we have said enough to pin down exactly what kind of things the rational numbers are. Moreover, it will follow from what we have said that

(i) the additive, multiplicative and ordering structure of the rationals as characterized thus far is the familiar one;

(ii) any rational $p : q$ is identical to a rational $p' : q'$ in canonical form—that is, where p' and q' have no prime factors in common; and

(iii) $p_1 : q_1 = p_2 : q_2 \dashv\vdash p_1 . q_2 = p_2 . q_1$.

All this remaining work can be deferred to a future study.

The Constructive Logicist has now extended to the rationals the same sort of treatment that he has already provided for the abstraction of the naturals:

$$\textbf{Schema N} \qquad \#x\Phi(x) = \underline{n} \;\dashv\vdash\; \exists_n x\Phi(x)\,.$$

Here, the right-hand side spells out the numerically non-committal truth conditions (that there be exactly n Φs) for the identity statement on the left-hand side. This identity involves the abstractive term $\#x\Phi(x)$ and the numerical (purely mathematical) term $\underline{n}$, which is the numeral that denotes the natural number n. Once again, it is the abstractive term that enables one to explain how the concept of number in question (here, natural number) is applicable in our wider thought and talk about things in general; while the numeral is all that the pure mathematician needs in order to pursue her studies as a number theorist.

Using appropriate introduction and elimination rules for 0, s and #, as we have seen in Part II, the Constructive Logicist can derive, in free Core Logic, all instances of Schema N. We noted how the right-hand sides of those instances are

[8] This treatment is furnished in [2010].

ontologically innocent of natural numbers (assuming natural numbers are neither referred to nor quantified over within the substituends Φ); while it is their left-hand sides that incur the ontological commitment to natural numbers that arises from the 'recarving of propositional content' afforded by Schema N.

Schema Q is directly analogous to Schema N in this regard, as far as rational numbers are concerned. And instances of Schema Q are readily forthcoming by easy application of the rules furnished above.

Metatheorem 5. *Every instance of Schema Q holds.*

Proof.

$$\dfrac{\dfrac{\mathfrak{F}x(t, x \cong_\Phi \textbf{whole } \Phi) = p : q}{t \cong_\Phi (p : q) \odot \textbf{whole } \Phi}\ \mathfrak{F}\text{-E}}{q \odot t \cong_\Phi p \odot \textbf{whole } \Phi}\ \text{:-E} \qquad \dfrac{\dfrac{q \odot t \cong_\Phi p \odot \textbf{whole } \Phi}{t \cong_\Phi (p : q) \odot \textbf{whole } \Phi}\ \text{:-I}}{\mathfrak{F}x(t, x \cong_\Phi \textbf{whole } \Phi) = p : q}\ \mathfrak{F}\text{-I}$$

□

Interestingly, the deductive work involved for Schema N, though reasonably straightforward, is not as simple as that for Schema Q. It is as though the Constructive Logicist has to make a more significant long-term investment of intellectual resources in order to attain to the naturals;[9] which, once he has them, then yield the rationals as a relatively easy dividend. Pythagoras would have been pleased—at least, until learning of the irrationality of $\sqrt{2}$![10]

The right-hand proof above can be extended with one application of the Rule of Atomic Denotation, thus:

$$\dfrac{\dfrac{\dfrac{q \odot t \cong_\Phi p \odot \textbf{whole } \Phi}{t \cong_\Phi (p : q) \odot \textbf{whole } \Phi}\ \text{:-I}}{\mathfrak{F}x(t, x \cong_\Phi \textbf{whole } \Phi) = p : q}\ \mathfrak{F}\text{-I}}{\exists!\, p : q}\ .$$

We also have the following slightly different route from the same rationally non-committal premise to the same rationally committal conclusion:

$$\dfrac{\dfrac{\dfrac{q \odot t \cong_\Phi p \odot \textbf{whole } \Phi}{t \cong_\Phi (p : q) \odot \textbf{whole } \Phi}\ \text{:-I}}{\exists!\, (p : q) \odot \textbf{whole } \Phi}}{\exists!\, p : q}\ .$$

This deducibility tells us only that in situations where q shares Φ-equal to t amount to p Φs, the theorist who has adopted the introduction and elimination rules for both ':' and $\mathfrak{F}$ can (indeed: must) acknowledge the existence of the rational number $p : q$. This same theorist is one who is already committed to the existence

[9] The Constructive Logicist is, after all, trying to recreate for himself what Kronecker thought had been God's gift to [hu]mankind!

[10] In this connection, the reader might be interested in [2016].

of each and every natural number. Thought-experimentally it is but a short step to recognizing the existence of any rational number $p : q$ where $p < q$. One has only to contemplate the possibility of arbitrarily increasing the number q of Φs to be shared among any smaller number of parties. This leads the natural logicist to adopt the simple rule

$$\frac{Np \quad Nq}{\exists!\, p : sq}\ .$$

We undertook at the outset the task of showing how it is that when we attain our grasp of the rationals (recognizing them as entities for the first time), we nevertheless recognize among them the natural numbers, whose provenance lies in the counting of finite collections (i.e., finite extensions of sortal predicates).

Let us revisit Edwin the Fractionator. For Edwin, the rational $(p : q)$ is the number of Φs in each of q equal shares of p Φs. In our original example, which involved sub-unity shares, the rational $(5 : 8)$ was the number of pizzas in each of 8 equal shares of 5 pizzas. (We have to think of all the Φs being 'the same', in whatever dimensional respect is involved for judgments of equality.) Edwin has been ensuring that the shares are equal, and that together they exhaust the available Φs. We shall make this tacit constraint explicit as the following fusion requirement. This requirement applies, of course, to supra-unity shares as well as to sub-unity ones.

Fusion Requirement:
The fusion of the shares must be the fusion of the Φs that are to be shared.

Let us now consider some special cases. What happens when $q = 1$ (that is, when only one person is present to consume the p pizzas)? That is, what number is $(p : 1)$? Well, the rational $(p : 1)$ is the 'fractional' number of Φs in a single share of p Φs. But that—given the Fusion Requirement—is none other than the natural number p itself! So our explanation of the applicability conditions for rational numbers produces the welcome result that the rational number $(p : 1)$ is, in general, simply the natural number p—'viewed in a fresh light', as it were.

And let us not neglect another special case—where $p = 0$. What is the rational number $(0 : q)$, where $q > 0$? Well, the rational $(0 : q)$ is the 'fractional' number of Φs in each of q equal shares of no Φs at all. This number—again, given the Fusion Requirement—is surely 0! So we have, in general, that $(0 : q) = 0$.

What about the other extreme case, where $q = 0$? Why should $(p : 0)$ be undefined, i.e., not exist? Well, the rational $(p : 0)$, if it did exist, would be the 'fractional' number of Φs in each of 0 equal shares of p Φs. That is, $(p : 0)$ would be the 'fractional' number of Φs in a non-existent share of p Φs. Now, that might strike one as the number 0—until one recalls the requirement that the fusion of the equal shares has to be equal to the fusion of the Φs themselves. And this is impossible when one has p Φs $(p > 0)$ and non-existent shares thereof. So $(p : 0)$ does not exist—as the mathematicians insist.

Chapter 17

Taking Stock and Glimpsing Beyond

Abstract

This abstract is not so much a summary of the big stones laid thus far, but rather some point-work in the cementing that holds them all together. It is one of the longest of the chapter abstracts, for this, the shortest of the chapters. A summary is given of what the Constructive Logicist has been able to attain by means of core reasoning in accordance with natural-deduction rules of introduction and elimination, especially for carefully designed abstraction operators. The naturals and the rationals are fully within Kroneckerian purview. But now one must prepare to engage with the reals. The hard deductive work was to obtain access to the naturals, and the Dedekind–Peano truths about them. Once entitled to the naturals, one's passage to the rationals is somewhat easier, courtesy of apt forms of expression afforded by mereology, and another pair of 'single-barreled' introduction and elimination rules, this time for fractional abstraction. Looking ahead to dealing with the reals, however, one has to be mindful of the complications involved in their inherently infinitary nature. One's '*ontological* entitlement' to them will not be as straightforward as it was in the case of the naturals and the rationals. But one now has a *methodological* bridgehead from the earlier treatment of the rationals: a way of producing a numerical representation for a 'sub-unit part'. This makes one's grasp of the reals closely cognate with one's grasp of the rationals (except for the matter of the reals' uncountability). This is reflected in the similarity of structure between Schema Q and Schema R.

We realize now that we have charted a path to grasp of the rationals (via the naturals) as abstract existents. And we have done so without yet relevantly drawing upon any considerations of Eudoxan or Euclidean ratios (of measurable magnitudes) and without even having attained to a grasp of addition and multiplication on the naturals.

With Edwin, we are now positioned to discover much more about the rationals. Their existence, and their essential nature, have been fixed by wholly *a priori* considerations summoning intellectual resources only from the logic of the naturals (expressed via 0, s, N and $\#$) and from mereology, the analytic study of parts and wholes (here, expressed via $\sqsubseteq$ and $\bigsqcup$).

Because of the way we have rooted our grasp of rationals as applicable to things in general, we can now excogitate yet further foundational facts about them.

The Logic of Number. Neil Tennant, Oxford University Press. © Neil Tennant 2022.
DOI: 10.1093/oso/9780192846679.003.0017

In particular, we have worked out that the naturals sit among the rationals, but with their own original and indigenous rights as denizens of Plato's heaven. They have not surrendered any of those rights to any one-for-one 'representatives' to the new assembly of rationals. The naturals re-appear as themselves, again, occupying positions of distinction within the wider polity of the rationals.

In similar fashion, we shall be able to work out, *a priori*—exercising only concepts of the understanding—that the Cancellation Law holds for rationals. Thus, each rational enjoys a canonical form $p : q$ with p and q having no prime factor in common. We shall also be able to work out (independently, without relying on the Cancellation Law) that the rationals form a dense linear ordering. Provided only that we can now furnish such an ordering, we would be in a position to offer Dedekind the ordered rationals that he presupposed, and which he needed, in order then to perform cuts on the same so as to attain to his (type-raised) conception of the reals.

But we know in advance that no rational number ρ can (metaphysically) be identified as one and the same entity as any ordered pair (L, R) of rationals to one of whose members ρ belongs.[1] So we decline to follow Dedekind in his generation of the reals, among which the rationals themselves must reappear; for we want to recognize the rationals as themselves again when they reappear as reals, densely embedded among them. And this is impossible with any type-raising method at all of 'generating' the reals from the rationals, such as Dedekind's method of taking cuts of the rationals. A similar objection would hold against Cauchy's method of identifying the reals with (certain equivalence classes of) convergent infinite sequences of rationals.

As it happens—in a further excursus into more challenging terrain—the Natural Logicist will attain to the reals by appealing, along the way, to the rationals, now that they are in hand. The Natural Logicist is called the Constructive Logicist when dealing with just the naturals and the rationals, because his account of these two kinds of number involves wielding only concepts of the understanding. But, when advancing to our treatment of the reals, the constructivist angle is harder to push for. Our treatment of the reals will, however, merit the phrase 'natural logicist'. This is because it will be furnished via new introduction and elimination rules in the tradition of 'natural deduction'. The adjective 'logicist' is still warranted because the knowledge of first principles will be derived strictly logically, by applying the new rules. And this is so even though the intellectual resources deployed in convincing oneself of the validity of the new rules involve more than mere conceptual grasp, by encompassing, as they do, synthetic (geometric) insight *a priori* as well.

The reals will be revealed as obeying their own Schema R, strikingly analogous to the above Schema Q for the rationals. The reals will also welcome in their collective midst both the naturals (denizens by logical birthright) and the rationals

[1] In order to see this, we do not even need to consider whether every member of L is less than every member of R.

(as special cases produced by our generative method for the reals in general, and recognizably themselves again). It will transpire that any real r will consist of a natural part (i.e., the greatest natural less than or equal to r) along with a sub-unit ratio-part, with the latter being a rational if and only if r itself is a rational.

This 'sub-unit ratio-part' of a real cannot in general correspond to, or be, a sub-unit rational of the kind Edwin could construct in Chapter 14. This has been known since Pythagoras. And, since then, we have also learned from Cantor's diagonal proof that there are uncountably infinitely many reals. (The Cantorian proof is intellectually accessible to the Constructive Logicist, even if only stated conditionally on the existence of certain totalities to which he does not wish to commit—see Chapter 24.) It follows that there are uncountably infinitely many 'sub-unit ratio-parts' of reals that are not sub-unit rationals of the kind Edwin could construct in Chapter 14.

Both Schema Q and Schema R enable us to conceive of the numbers in question (rational or real, respectively) as being composed of a natural part, and a sub-unit part. With both kinds of number, there is a dimension-laden notion of 'addition' (or aggregation, or fusion, or what-you-will) that is not the actual pure-mathematical operation of addition that will in due course be attained on the dimensionless entities of the two kinds in question (i.e., the rationals and the reals). At the methodological level, it turns out, there is greater kinship between our conception of the rationals and our conception of the reals than there is between either of them, on the one hand, and, on the other, our conception of the naturals. The methodological gulf that has been crossed in advancing from the naturals to the rationals appears to be wider than that which now remains to be crossed in advancing from the rationals to the reals.

But—here's the rub—our method of generating the reals, unlike our method of generating the rationals, will have to draw on *a priori* resources that are synthetic. We shall be arguing that recourse to synthetic *a priori* grasp of the continuity of lines in Euclidean space is at the very root of our conception of the (dimensionless) real numbers. We can only attain to them, however, by engaging with them first in their canonical dimensional setting, as numbers measuring the lengths of straight-line segments in terms of a unit length. The latter unit plays the same sort of role in generating the sub-unit reals as did a 'whole Φ' play in Edwin's generation of the sub-unit rationals.[2]

It emerges, then, that Kant was right about both the naturals and the rationals sharing the same kind of *a priori* status in our mathematical ontology, but which the irrational reals lacked. The problem, however, was that Kant could not even bring himself to acknowledge the irrational reals as genuine entities in their own right. As revealed in van Atten [2012], this was because Kant refused to accept the idea of a potentially, let alone completed, infinite sequence of already exist-

[2]This approach to the reals was fully set out in an unpublished work titled 'What are the reals, really?'. An earlier version of it was the unpublished typescript Tennant 2010, 'Why arithmetize the reals? why not geometrize them?', referred to in van Atten [2012], at p. 6, fn. 16. The current version is Part IV of this work.

ing (abstract) objects as itself a mathematical object.[3] Once we free ourselves from that crippling restriction on Kant's part, the path is clear to a generation of the irrational reals in a way that is ironically very much in keeping with Kant's overall philosophical temper. For Kant, our pure *a priori* geometric intuition is synthetic. And this is true, especially, of our intuition concerning the continuity of lines, which is all that we shall be drawing on when generating the reals. Kant regarded the reals (as Newton did) as providing, first and foremost, for the measurement of geometric magnitudes in terms of a unit magnitude. What Kant lacked, however, was the necessary openness to thinking of an infinite monotonic sequence of points on a line as a single self-subsistent abstract object, whether 'merely potential' or completed.

A question (raised by a referee), could arise here, on behalf of any constructivist who might balk at being asked to recognize self-subsisting infinite objects: *would this not just be Kant's balk?* The matter is delicate, but arguably resolvable by bringing in a carefully principled distinction between the respective conditions under which the worrisome and not-so-worrisome infinite objects are respectively and in general generated. Consider the thinker who 'makes a free choice', or even makes a law-governed choice, of yet another digit in, say, a decimal or bicimal expansion that is to represent (or *be*?) a real number in the unit interval. There is no possibility that this thinker could ever be done by fully generating the expansion. By contrast, the mensurator who is given a fixed line-segment that is shorter than the chosen unit-segment, in principle has his or her 'hands tied' in determining (by the method which we shall be expounding) what the successive digits should be, as he or she generates 'the number' (or the partial representation of that number) as the process of measurement proceeds. The thinker (i.e., the mensurator, in this context) is beholden to external facticity in making his or her choices of digits. Geometric reality can in principle dictate that the reals that are generable as measurements in terms of a unit enjoy a certain kind of determinacy that is not enjoyed by the sequences of digits produced by free choices, or would-be applications of rules, on the part of the thinker concerned.

[3]Thanks here to Mark van Atten for pointing out that Kant's position was so pessimistic as to warrant the words 'potentially, let alone'.

Part IV

Natural Logicism and the Reals

Chapter 18

The Trend toward Arithmetization

Abstract

The tension is explored between geometrizing approaches to the real numbers, and arithmetizing ones. After examining crucial statements by Newton, Gauss, and Frege, the conclusion emerges that the conception of real number as a ratio of magnitudes managed to survive the nineteenth-century shift from the geometrizing way to the arithmetizing way. Given these thinkers' respectively different foundational views, this testifies to the robustness of that conception of the reals. The question to address is whether any major foundationalist thinker has ever provided compelling reasons or argument for this emergent nineteenth-century tendency. Why should one eschew (let alone: reject) recourse to geometric concepts or intuitions or principles or understanding, in the attempt to provide a satisfactory foundation for real analysis? In trying to identify such a thinker, one must examine carefully the works of the two figures whose seminal writings are most frequently cited in this connection: Bolzano and Dedekind. But their arguments turn out to be unconvincing. It is hard to resist the conclusion that there emerged within the tradition a mere *preference* for algebraic as opposed to geometric modes of presentation and reasoning in differential and integral calculus. The chapter closes with an exploration of the role of what mathematicians themselves call intuition when selecting the 'first principles' from which they then deduce their theorems.

The so-called 'arithmetization of analysis' proceeds by taking natural numbers as basic, then defining the negative integers and the rational numbers in familiar ways. After that, real numbers are defined in terms of Cauchy sequences of rationals, or Dedekind cuts of the rationals, or in some other equivalent way.

It is argued here that the most illuminating definitional (or should one say: 'revelatory'?) route to the real numbers should not proceed via arithmetization. Instead, it should begin with certain geometric conceptions as basic, and define real numbers in terms of them. The best and simplest way to do this, moreover, has the result that the naturals and the rationals re-appear as themselves again, as reals.

The basic geometric conceptions (in addition to that of *point*) of which we shall avail ourselves are the simplest synthetic ones constructible, *à la* Euclid, by means of ruler and compass: (directed) *line* and *circle*. These two simple

The Logic of Number. Neil Tennant, Oxford University Press. © Neil Tennant 2022.
DOI: 10.1093/oso/9780192846679.003.0018

conceptions are to be distinguished from the post-Cartesian, analytic conceptions that one can attain by deploying coördinatization and complicated algebraic equations.[1] Such 'analytic geometric' conceptions incurred Newton's disdain. He was concerned to stress the great synthetic simplicity of lines and circles, and took Euclidean geometry to be the synthetic study of these. We shall follow Newton in this regard, and flesh out fully his conception of the reals—as the numbers that arise from using a unit magnitude (of a given continuously varying dimension) to measure any magnitudes of that dimension. For this pristine purpose, lines and circles will suffice.

We provide a rigorous definition of real numbers, and derive their basic properties, by considering them as measures of lengths of line-segments. We show how to generate the canonical bicimal representation of any point in the unit segment by means of essentially geometric, but absolutely *a priori* considerations. Finally, we show how to determine the canonical bicimal representation of the limit of an infinite progression of points in the open unit segment. (The choice of bicimals is in the interests of simplicity. The method can easily be generalized to any k-mal notation, with $k > 2$.)

The result is an exercise in logico-genetic theorizing in the foundations of mathematics. The inspiration is broadly logicist, but with due attention paid both to the intuitive sources of certain kinds of mathematical knowledge, and to the need to account for the applicability of mathematics in our thought about the world. The methodology just sketched is in keeping with the basic conception of the reals held by three of the greatest thinkers about these matters. The following three quotes, from Newton, Gauss, and Frege show that they were in fundamental agreement about the nature of real numbers. But Newton was a geometrically-minded thinker; Frege was an arithmetically-minded one; and Gauss was transitional in this regard.

That the conception of real number as a ratio of magnitudes has survived the shift from the geometrizing way to the arithmetizing way testifies to the robustness of that conception. What we intend to investigate, in this Part, is whether we might be able to return to the 'old' way, and prosecute it more successfully for being better equipped with logical methods and resources that were developed only after the turn was taken to the 'new' way.

Here, now, are the promised quotes.

> By *Number* we understand not so much a Multitude of Unities, as the abstracted *Ratio* of any Quantity, to another Quantity of the same kind, which we take for Unity. And this is threefold; integer, fracted, and surd: An *Integer* is what is measured by Unity, a *Fraction*, that

[1] Note that we are using here the contrasting terms 'analytic' and 'synthetic' as these are used by geometers, not by Kantian philosophers.

which a sub-multiple Part of Unity measures, and a *Surd*, to which Unity is incommensurable.

—**Isaac Newton**[2]

Now, mathematics really teaches general truths concerning the relations of quantities, and the goal is to represent [darzustellen] quantities which have known relations *to known quantities* or *to which known quantities* have known relations—i.e., to make possible an idea [Vorstellung] of this. But we can have an idea of a quantity in two ways, either by immediate intuition [unmittelbare Anschauung] (an immediate idea), or by comparison with other quantities given by immediate intuition (mediate idea). The duty of the mathematician is accordingly either actually to represent the sought-for quantity (geometric representation or construction), or to indicate the way and manner in which, from the idea of an immediately given quantity, one can achieve the idea of the sought quantity (arithmetical representation). This happens by means of *numbers*, which show how many times one must imagine the immediately given quantity reiterated[fn] if one is to obtain an idea of the sought quantity. One calls the former quantity the *unit*, and the procedure itself *measurement*.

—**Carl Friedrich Gauss**[3]

We have conceived of a real number as a ratio of quantities and thereby ruled out a formal[ist account of] arithmetic. ... In doing so we have directed attention to the quantities as the objects between which such a ratio obtains.

... The (cardinal) numbers answer to the question "How many objects of such-and-such a kind are there?" while the real numbers can be regarded as measurement-numbers, which tell one how large a given quantity is, compared with a unit-quantity.

—**Gottlob Frege**[4]

---

[2]Newton [1728] at p. 2. (The first sentence was quoted in Bigelow [1988] at p. 71.)

[3]Gauss [1996] at p. 294.

[4]Frege [1903; reprinted 1962], §157 at p. 155. Author's translation. The German is

> Wir haben die reelle Zahl als Grössenverhältnis aufgefasst und so die formale Arithmetik ... ausgeschlossen. Damit haben wir auf die Grössen hingewiesen als auf die Gegenstände, zwischen denen ein solches Verhältnis stattfindet.[fn] [fn: Hier befinden wir uns in Uebereinstimmung mit Newton.]

The rest of this chapter is a sustained historical investigation of some of the issues already raised, but in particular of the tension between geometrizing approaches to the reals, and arithmetizing ones.

The investigation seeks an answer to the following question, which has perplexed several leading historians and philosophers of mathematics to whom it has been posed:

> Who was the first major foundationalist thinker, on the basis of *reasons* or *argument* (however inconclusive), explicitly to reject recourse to geometric concepts or intuitions or principles or understanding, in the attempt to provide a satisfactory foundation for real analysis?

The recommendation (or statement of the methodological maxim) that one ought to avoid all matters geometric goes back at least to Dedekind's *Stetigkeit und Irrationale Zahlen*. This work was published late, in 1872. Its breakthrough idea had come fourteen years earlier, in 1858. At pp. 3–4 Dedekind writes in an engaging and revelatory way of his earlier struggle in the autumn of 1858 to furnish 'eine wirklich wissenschaftliche Begründung der Arithmetik' (a really scientific foundation for Arithmetic [i.e., real analysis]).[5] This passage is one of the most important 'position statements' ever written on foundational matters, and will be quoted in full. It contains many points that merit careful reflection and critical analysis:

> In discussing the concept of the approach of a variable magnitude to a fixed limiting value—in particular, in proving the theorem that every magnitude which grows continually, but not beyond all limits, must certainly approach a limiting value—I took refuge in geometrical evidence. Even now I regard such invocation of geometric intuition [Anschauung] in a first presentation of the differential calculus as exceedingly useful from a pedagogic standpoint, and indeed it is indispensable, if one does not wish to lose too much time. But no one will deny that this form of introduction into the differential calculus can make no claim to being scientific. For myself this feeling of dissatisfaction was so overpowering that I resolved to meditate on the question until I should find a purely arithmetical and perfectly rigorous foundation [Begründung] for the principles of infinitesimal analysis. The statement is frequently made that the differential calcu-

> … Die Anzahlen antworten auf die Frage: „wieviele Gegenstände einer gewissen Art giebt es?“ während die reellen Zahlen als Maasszahlen betrachtet werden können, die angeben, wie gross eine Grösse verglichen mit einer Einheitsgrösse ist.

Frege does not source his reference to Newton, but we can safely assume that Newton [1728] would have served this purpose well.

[5]The date of 1853 in the English translation Dedekind [1996b], at p. 793, of the preface to the first edition of Dedekind's later work *Was sind und was sollen die Zahlen?* is in error. The German original (Dedekind [1932], at p. 339) has 1858.

> lus deals with continuous quantities, yet an explanation of this continuity is nowhere given; even the most rigorous expositions of the differential calculus do not base their proofs upon continuity but they either appeal more or less consciously to geometric representations or to representations suggested by geometry, or they depend upon theorems which are never established in a purely arithmetical manner. Among these, for example, belongs the above-mentioned theorem, and a more careful investigation convinced me that this theorem, or any one equivalent to it, can be regarded as a more or less sufficient foundation for infinitesimal analysis. It only remained to discover its true origin in the elements of arithemtic [*sic*], and thereby to secure a real definition of the essence of continuity. I succeeded on November 24, 1858 ...[6]

What Dedekind arrived at was his ground-breaking concept of a *cut*. Its significance is deservedly widely recognized, despite the amusing detraction one reads in the following 1930 review by E. T. Bell (Bell [1930]), the distinguished historian of mathematics:

> ... it would be difficult to find anywhere a more superb illustration of the usual idiotic logic of history than in the rise of Dedekind's popular scientific reputation. For one mathematician who knows his way about in the Dedekind theory of ideals, there are probably hundreds who have been familiar with the Dedekind cut from their youth up. The thing is notorious; every tyro is indoctrinated with it in his advanced calculus. And now, according to the customary irony of time, this cut, for which Dedekind is hundreds-to-one more famous than for his work in algebraic numbers, seems to be turning into something like a very bad pun, for it is a schism in the official faiths of analysis and a prolific source of interminable polemics. Dedekind himself is said to have hesitated nearly two years before committing it to print.

Rather than side with Bell, one can grant Dedekind his due, and seek to detract from it only with more sober argument about the methodological issues involved.

It is clear that Dedekind is writing on the presumption—assumed to be so widespread as not to call for any justificatory argument—that one should have no recourse at all to geometric intuitions or first principles when founding the theory of the real numbers. This presumption, said Dedekind, 'no one will deny'. Colin McLarty (personal correspondence) demurs slightly here. According to McClarty, Dedekind does not really say he would reject any geometric approach. He just says no such foundation is known, and firmly declares he will look to arithmetic.

[6] This translation, due to W. W. Beman and extensively revised by William Ewald, is from Dedekind [1996a] at p. 767.

Dedekind indeed wanted[7] 'a *purely arithmetical* and perfectly rigorous foundation for the principles of infinitesimal analysis'. [Emphases added.] Given, however, the earlier widespread reliance on geometrical pictures and intuitions concerning continuity and convergence, it is difficult to regard Dedekind's insistence on an arithmetizing approach as not involving at the same time a rejection of any geometrizing approach.

The presumption receives further emphatic statement in Dedekind's later work (1888) *Was sind und was sollen die Zahlen?*, which, like the earlier work, was published much later than it could (or should) have been. In the preface to the first edition (pp. 790–791 in Dedekind [1996b]) Dedekind writes

> In speaking of arithmetic (algebra, analysis) as merely part of logic I mean to imply that I consider the number-concept *entirely independent of the notions or intuitions of space and time*—that I rather consider it an immediate product of the pure laws of thought. ... It is only through the purely logical process of building up the science of numbers and by thus acquiring the continuous number-domain that we are enabled accurately to investigate our notions of space and time by bringing them into relation with this number-domain created in our mind.[fn] [Emphasis added.]

Once again we see the presumption at work: in laying a foundation for the theory of real numbers, one must avoid any recourse to geometric intuition.

How did such a presumption become so widespread? In whose works did it originate? (Dedekind provides no references.) Has there ever been a cogent marshaling of reasons for ignoring our geometrical grasp when thinking foundationally about the reals? (Dedekind provides none.)

Interestingly, as Heath points out (Euclid [1956], p. 236) Dedekind himself states his cut principle in a thoroughly geometric setting, in §3 of *Stetigkeit und Irrationale Zahlen*:

> If all points of a straight line fall into two classes such that every point of the first class lies to the left of every point of the second class, there exists one and only one point which produces this division of all the points into two classes, this division of the straight line into two parts.[8]

---

[7]This English translation is from Dedekind [1996a], p. 767. The German original, in Dedekind [1872], at p. 4, is: 'eine rein arithmetische und völlig strenge Begründung der Prinzipien der Infinitesimalanalysis'.

[8]The translation of this passage in Dedekind [1996a] is as follows:

> If all points of *the* straight line fall into two classes such that every point of the first class lies to the left of every point of the second class, *then* there exists one and only one point which produces this division of *all points* into two classes, this *severing* of the straight line into two *portions*. [Contrastive emphases added.]

A careful reading of §3 of *Stetigkeit und Irrationale Zahlen*, far from uncovering a well-argued case for eschewing geometric intuition, can give rise to qualms as to whether Dedekind has not rather, contrary to his own best intentions, inadvertently revealed reasons for attending to such intuitions when theorizing about the reals.

Dedekind concedes that irrationals are usually introduced in a way that is 'based directly upon the conception of extensive magnitudes' [such as length—NT]. He complains the conception 'is nowhere carefully defined'—a potential objection to be borne in mind, and to be revisited and rebutted by the geometrizing logico-geneticist upon completion of his own account of the reals. For those employing the conception in question, 'number is explained as the result of measuring such a magnitude by another of the same kind' [the *unit*—NT]; so Dedekind here echoes the opening quotes we gave from Newton and Gauss—and was later to be echoed by Frege in turn, after his own careful reading of Dedekind.

Schirn [1996], at p. 19, attributes the following thesis to Frege:

> There is a remarkable difference between geometry and arithmetic in the way in which their fundamental principles are grounded.

Schirn sources this thesis to the first page of Frege's doctoral dissertation of 1873 (*Kleine Schriften*, at p. 1). On p. 21 Schirn writes:

> At the outset of his post-doctoral dissertation *Rechnungsmethoden, die sich auf eine Erweiterung des Größenbegriffes gründen* (1874), Frege aims at illustrating [the foregoing thesis] by investigating the notion of quantity. This notion is said to have gradually freed itself from intuition and made itself independent. Its range of application is indeed so comprehensive that *Frege is certainly right in denying that it derives from intuition*. [Emphasis added.]

Schirn then quotes from *Kleine Schriften* at p. 50: 'The elements of all geometrical constructions are intuitions, and geometry refers to intuition as the source of its axioms.'[9]

So on Schirn's account (which we have no reason to challenge), Frege acquiesces in the assumed success of 'de-intuitionizing' (hence also, in light of the last quote: de-geometrizing) the science of quantity (i.e., the theory of real numbers). Frege appears to make no more searching an attempt than Dedekind, to argue for or justify the emerging dogma that real analysis had to be emancipated from, or purged of, or made completely independent of, geometric intuition.

---

[9]The original German reads

> Die Elemente aller geometrischen Konstruktionen sind Anschauungen, und auf Anschauung verweist die Geometrie als Quelle ihrer Axiome. Da das Objekt der Arithmetik keine Anschaulichkeit hat, so können auch ihre Grundsätze aus der Anschauung nicht stammen.

Let us return to the point at which we left our exposition of Dedekind's views, at the echo of Newton and Gauss. Now comes Dedekind's rabbit out of the hat:

> *Instead of this I demand that arithmetic shall develop out of itself.* [Emphasis added.]

Just a few lines later Dedekind claims that when we compare the domain of rational numbers with a straight line, we find

> in the former a gappiness, incompleteness, discontinuity; but to the straight line we ascribe absence of gaps, completeness, continuity.

Quite so, one wishes to say; quite so. 'In what then does this continuity consist?' asks Dedekind.

> Everything must depend on the answer to this question, and only through it shall we obtain a scientific basis for the investigation of *all* continuous domains.

Indeed; but that aim can be attained by analyzing the essence of continuity, with the paradigm example of an idealized Euclidean straight line firmly in mind, and subsequently extrapolating to other continuous domains the essential features uncovered by such analysis. Moreover, Dedekind's motivation at the very outset of §3 was the received (intuitively and geometrically demonstrated!) wisdom that

> The straight line L is infinitely richer in point-individuals than the domain R of rational numbers in number-individuals.

That post-Pythagorean realization is what provokes the foundational mission to 'create' or 'discover' the irrational number(-individual)s that can correspond to those point-individuals on the line to which no rational number(-individual)s correspond.

> By vague remarks upon the unbroken connection in the smallest parts obviously nothing is gained ...

Dedekind continues:

> ... the problem is to indicate a precise characteristic of continuity that can serve as the basis for valid deductions.

A few lines later he propounds his principle of continuity in the form quoted above, concerning the straight line.

Now the logico-genetic theorizer of geometrical bent can agree with Dedekind that the last thing one wants is an unhelpfully murky, 'hand-waving' definition of linear continuity adverting to 'unbroken connection in the smallest parts' or the like. But this is to cheapen and underestimate the far more sophisticated, and perfectly rigorous, formulations that can be devised in geometric vocabulary of the sought principle of continuity. Dedekind's own is one such, and is stated in thoroughly geometric terms. There are equally good alternatives, however, employing only geometric vocabulary. Dedekind's definition of reals-as-cuts makes reference to two classes of points, both of which of course must have uncountably many members, since they form a cut-partition of all the points on a geometric line. But one can get by with the arguably simpler and more economical notion of a countably infinite sequence of points.

Thus far, §3 of *Stetigkeit und Irrationale Zahlen* fails to convince. And it ends on a weak consideration:

> If space has a real existence at all it is *not* necessary for it to be continuous; many of its properties would remain the same even if it were discontinuous. And if we knew for certain that space were discontinuous there would be nothing to prevent us, in case we so desired, from filling in its gaps in thought and thus making it continuous; this filling up would consist in a creation of new point-individuals and would have to be carried out in accordance with the above principle.

Russell later echoed this view (but without attributing it to Dedekind). In Russell [1919], at p. 140, he wrote

> We naturally regard space and time as continuous, or, at least, as compact; but this ... is mainly prejudice. ... A world in which all motion consisted of a series of small finite jerks would be empirically indistinguishable from one in which motion was continuous.

Russell does not explain, however, how he had come to change his mind on this score. In Russell [1897], when he was giving a transcendental argument for those *a priori* principles that he thought would have to govern space as a 'form of externality', he wrote, at p. 142,

> ... we cannot speak of change, whether continuous or discrete, without imagining time. Let us, therefore, allow time to be known, and discuss whether the temporal change, in any other form of externality, is necessarily continuous[fn]. We must reply, I think, that continuity is necessary. ... change must be continuous ...

We return now to consider the last quote from Dedekind. There appear to be two dialectical confusions here, if the intent was to give further reason for upholding the arithmetizing method. First, Dedekind is clearly referring to physical space in contemplating the possibility of discontinuity. But this is to fail to realize that the geometrizer who seeks to provide a foundation for real analysis will be having recourse to a logically refined conception of idealized Euclidean straight lines, which are themselves abstract objects, given in (pure) intuition. This recourse is not hostage to empirical fortune; it does not turn, for its validation, on physical space proving to be continuous rather than discontinuous. Second, extolling the human mind by saying that (if physical space were discontinuous) we would be able in thought to 'fill up its gaps' invites the *tu quoque* that Dedekind had just shown his reader how to do so using geometrical rather than arithmetical notions.

Our reading of Dedekind leaves us empty-handed, then, in our search for a principled rationale for eschewing geometric intuition. We can perhaps make some progress on the 'merely historical' question (as opposed to the justificatory one) by looking more closely at some of Dedekind's illustrious forebears.

The following quotes are taken from a study by Craig Fraser (see Fraser [2003]) of eighteenth-century mathematics, which traces the emergence and ascendance, mainly in the works of Euler and Lagrange, of a preference for algebraic as opposed to geometric modes of presentation and reasoning in differential and integral calculus. Nowhere, as far as the present author can tell, did either Euler or Lagrange present reasoned arguments for the methodological maxim that no recourse should ever be had to geometric intuition, when providing a foundation for real analysis. In these quotes, we have emphasized certain phrases in order to underscore the present author's contention that what we witness here is an account of a change in fashion, rather than a reasoned, prescriptive break with earlier foundational tradition.

> Although the theme of analysis was well established at the time [1736], there was in [Euler's] work something new: the beginning of an explicit awareness of the distinction between analytical and geometrical methods and an emphasis on the *desirability* of the former in proving theorems of the calculus. (p. 308)

> From the very beginning of his mathematical career in the 1730s, Euler *imparted a new direction* to the calculus by clearly emphasizing the importance of separating analysis from geometry. (pp. 309–310)

> Euler had succeeded in showing that the basic subject matter of the calculus—what in some ultimate sense the calculus is "about"—*could* be conceived independently of geometry in terms of abstract relations between continuously variable magnitudes. (p. 311)

> In his mid-century treatises Euler, as part of his program of separating analysis from geometry, made the algebraic conception of differentiation fundamental. In so doing he made the concept of the *algorithm* primary in his understanding of the foundations of the calculus. (p. 315)

> The algebraic calculus of Euler and Lagrange was rooted in the formal study of functional equations, algorithms, and operations on variables. The values that these variables received, their numerical or geometrical interpretation, was logically of secondary concern. Such

> a conception, strongly operational and instrumentalist in character, *should be contrasted with* the geometrical approach of the early calculus, which relied heavily on diagrammatic representations and intuitions of spatial continuity. The geometrical emphasis of the early calculus conditioned how the subject was understood, allowing it to be experienced intellectually as an interpreted, meaningful body of mathematics. (pp. 324–325)

What needs to be noted here is that the account is one of an emerging preference for the algebraic method of presenting and deriving results in the calculus, already in hand as a mature (or rapidly maturing) branch of mathematics. This does not, however, speak to the radical foundational problem posed at the outset:

> Show how we are entitled to our concept of Ξs, and to the underlying presumption that there are such things as Ξs, structured in the way they must be if our mathematical theory about Ξs is to be true.

The following situation is possible—and, we contend, realized in the history of our thinking about the real numbers. In the following schema, for Ξs read 'reals' and for Γ read 'geometric'. The schema could well have other instances in the history of mathematics.

> **Ξ-Γ Schema.** The only way to establish entitlement to our concepts of Ξs is to employ Γ-intuitions. But, once such entitlement has been established, and we have attained the sought first principles about Ξs, and the theory of Ξs undergoes further development, the theory of Ξs achieves a 'life of its own', and can be understood and manipulated without recourse to Γ-intuitions. Indeed, the further reaches of the theory of Ξs can outstrip any guidance that could be afforded by Γ-intuitions. For, the original Γ-intuitions were consulted only for the formulation of the simplest and most self-evident fundamental principles that were involved in subsequently attaining to the first principles about Ξs. Subsequent reasoning about Ξs can 'outrun' the reach of Γ-intuitions.

We can therefore take in our stride the examples noted by Felix Klein (see Klein [1996b], pp. 960–961), where analytic reasoning succeeds but 'the [geometric] imagination seems to fail utterly when we try to form a mental image of the result'.

Bolzano had also remarked earlier that

> In *stereometry* we are often concerned with such complex spatial objects that even the most lively imagination is not able to imagine them clearly any more; but we none the less continue to operate with our *concepts* and find truth. (Bolzano [1996b], end of §9)

Such cases are to be expected, even if the original recourse to geometric intuition proves to be essential for the delivery of the first principles of analysis, from which point onwards logical reasoning is our only reliable guide.

David McCarty (personal correspondence) has written

> Of great importance was the research by Gauss, Hamilton, the Grassmans and others into complex numbers, quaternions, and vectorial systems that are strictly algebraic or computational in initial conception. These mathematicians often struggled long and hard to give their systems some "geometric meaning," e.g., Argand diagrams in the case of complex numbers. But most of them realized that the "geometric meanings" were not, strictly speaking, required for the coherence of the underlying, non-intuitional mathematics.

This too is consistent with the picture on offer here. If recourse to geometric intuition is even so much as helpful (let alone: essential) in the grounding (and perhaps also in some of the initial development) of the theory of the reals, then one would expect there to be a kind of intellectual dependency, or hangover, of geometric thinking on the part of theorists struggling to understand wider systems (such as the complex number system) within which the reals are embedded. Old and previously helpful imaginative pictures and techniques die hard. They may not be appropriate guides in the new fields. Nevertheless, they could well have been essential—in the foundational, or justificatory sense—to our attaining to a proper conception of the reals themselves, as dimensionless numbers forming a complete ordered field.

Note that that is the conception we are striving to vouchsafe: a conception of the reals as dimensionless, *qua* numbers, and therefore not constitutively tied to any particular dimensionality of measurement, such as length or temporal duration or any other.

We saw in the opening quotes with which this study began that there is a continuous line of thought (no pun intended) from Newton through Gauss to Frege, according to which (real) numbers are dimensionless ratios of quantities. Immediately after the earlier quote from Gauss [1996] is the following passage:

> These different relations of quantities and the different means of representing quantities are the foundation of the two primary mathematical disciplines. Arithmetic considers quantities in arithmetical relations, and represents them arithmetically; geometry considers quantities in geometric relations, and represents them geometrically. To represent geometrically quantities that have arithmetical relations—as was so common among the ancients—is no longer so common today; otherwise one would have to regard this as a part of geometry. On the contrary, one *applies* the *arithmetical manner of representation* extremely frequently to quantities in geometric relation, for example in trigonometry, and also in the theory of bent lines, which

> one considers a geometric discipline. That the moderns *so strongly prefer* the arithmetical manner of representation to the geometric is not without a reason, especially since our method of counting (by tens) is so much easier than that of the ancients. [Emphases added.]

Once again, we note only an expression of a preference. This falls far short of a methodological argument to the effect that one ought to eschew geometric intuition altogether when founding the theory of reals. The explanation for the inclination to arithmetize rather than geometrize appeals to the modern availability of the convenient and flexible system of decimal place-notation for numbers. This is hardly a conceptual or justificatory argument that no logico-genetic path to the (dimensionless) real numbers may have its origin in fundamentally geometric intuition.

Michael Potter (personal correspondence) has pointed out that the well-known pathologies, such as Weierstraß's everywhere continuous but nowhere differentiable function[10]—the function in question is

$$\sum_{n=0}^{\infty} a^n \cos(b^n \pi x),$$

where $0 < a < 1$, b is an odd natural number, and $ab > 1 + \frac{3\pi}{2}$ —and Peano's space-filling curve[11] cannot have played a role in creating the climate of presumption we are challenging here, since Dedekind certainly would not have known about these pathologies back in the Autumn of 1858. Further to Potter's point, we draw the reader's attention to the fact that Bolzano's earlier discovery, in 1834, of the 'Weierstraßian' functions did not come to the attention of the mathematical community until after he (Bolzano) died. In his introduction to the reprinting Bolzano [1974] of Bolzano's *Beyträge* ... (Bolzano [1810], whose English translation is Bolzano [1996b]), Hans Wußing writes, at p. XIV,

> It was a real sensation in the history of mathematics, when in the 1920s it turned out, upon the opening up of the ›Functionenlehre‹ from Bolzano's posthumous papers, that Bolzano had given the very first example of a function continuous over a whole interval, but nowhere differentiable therein, 45 years before K. Weierstraß (1815–1897)! [12]

This historical surprise puts the matter of such functions into a wholly different perspective, from the point of view of our inquiry into the justificatory origin of

[10] See Weierstraß [1872].

[11] See Peano [1890].

[12] Author's translation. The German is

Es war eine echte mathematikhistorische Sensation, als sich in den 20er Jahren bei der Erschließung der ›Functionenlehre‹ ... aus Bolzanos Nachlaß ergab, daß Bolzano das allererste Beispiel einer in einem ganzen Intervall stetigen, aber dort nirgends differenzierbaren Funktion konstruiert hatte, 45 Jahre vor K. Weierstraß (1815–1897)!

the methodological eschewal of geometric intuition when providing a foundation for real analysis. Writing of the same surprise, William Ewald, in his introductory note to the English translation of Bolzano's *Rein analytischer Beweis*... (Bolzano [1817] in Bolzano [1996c], at p. 227), argues

> Bolzano's ambition was not so much to attain some superior brand of mathematical certainty as to reveal the objective reasons for the truth of the intermediate value theorem—to uncover its true logical foundations. And *a fortiori* Bolzano's quest for rigour in his [Bolzano [1817]] was not prompted by the 'challenge to geometric intuition' presented by the discovery of continuous nowhere-differentiable functions; on the contrary, it was Bolzano's rigour that made his subsequent discovery of such counter-intuitive phenomena possible. (The discovery is in [Bolzano [1930]], §75; the passage was written in 1834.)

So, the historical irony is that Bolzano, unfortunately, does not get credit for the discovery of how catastrophically the casually assumed link between continuity and differentiability can be severed, a discovery which is, even today, almost universally credited to Weierstraß; and that to suggest that it was such a discovery that led to the mistrust and eschewal of geometric intuition might be to put the cart before the horse. The casual assumption is that the continuity of a function at a point guarantees its differentiability at that point; whence also, its continuity at every point within an interval guarantees its differentiability at every point within that interval. To falsify this, all we need is a function which at some single point is continuous but not differentiable. What Bolzano (and, later, Weierstraß) gave was a function that was continuous at every point within a certain interval, but differentiable at no point within that interval. It is as powerful a counterexample as could possibly be asked for, given the logical structure of the assumption thereby counterexemplified.

In any case, the neglected Bolzano could not have influenced Dedekind at all. Dedekind himself says as much. In his preface to the second edition of *Was sind... ?*, Dedekind, anxious to establish priority for his definition of the infinite, writes of his

> wearisome labour, which in all its essentials I had completed several years before the appearance of Cantor's memoir [Cantor [1878]] and *at a time when the work of Bolzano was unknown to me, even by name.*[13] [Emphasis added.]

One has to imagine that Dedekind's ignorance of Bolzano's work in this particular regard would have to have been accompanied also by ignorance of Bolzano's

[13] See Dedekind [1996b], at p. 795. In this connection Dedekind had, just a few lines earlier, made reference only to Bolzano [1851], citing §20 of that work.

earlier work on continuity and limits, and of Bolzano's accompanying statements of foundational methodology.

So the opening question of this chapter:

> Who was the first major foundationalist thinker, on the basis of reasons or argument (however inconclusive), explicitly to reject recourse to geometric concepts or intuitions or principles or understanding, in the attempt to provide a satisfactory foundation for real analysis?

now reasserts itself; for we have two great figures—Bolzano and Dedekind—apparently working quite independently of each other, yet committed to a fully 'logicist' or 'arithmetizing' renunciation of recourse to geometric intuition, in their search for a proper foundation for real analysis.

Of the two, it was actually Bolzano who provided the better worked-out philosophical or methodological rationale for the way he chose to proceed. In this regard, both his *Beyträge*... (Bolzano [1810]) and his *Rein analytischer Beweis*... (Bolzano [1817]) are key.

Ewald writes, at p. 168 in Ewald [1996b], that

> Bolzano was the first mathematician *explicitly to reject* the traditional geometric and spatial approach to foundations, calling instead, on explicitly *logical* grounds, for a 'purely analytic' grounding of the calculus—that is, a grounding in *arithmetic*. [First emphasis added.]

Bolzano emphasized the importance of finding the ultimate justificatory basis [Grund] on which a judgment rests, even if the judgment in question 'strike[s] us as simple or indubitable' (p. 169). Ewald goes on (p. 170) to say that §11 of Bolzano [1810]

> argues that arithmetic (or, as he calls it, *general mathesis*) is logically antecedent to geometry. It was this step—in an essentially philosophical treatise—that led Bolzano to his 'purely analytic' investigations of the real continuum, to his rigorous definition of *limit*, and to his proofs of the intermediate value theorem and the Bolzano–Weierstraß theorem.

What Ewald does not remark upon are the historical (but challengeable) roots of Bolzano's insistence on the 'purity' of arithmetical method. As Michael Detlefsen observes (see Detlefsen [2008], at pp. 179–180) Aristotle's prohibition of *metabasis eis allo genos* or 'crossing from one genus to another in the course of a proof' was

> a prime motive of [Bolzano's] early attempts to 'arithmetize' analysis. This arithmetization, or, perhaps better, this *de-geometrization*, was wanted in order to combat what Bolzano saw as a pervasive type of circularity in proofs in analysis—a circularity borne of impurity.

> The impurity represented by the importation of geometric considerations into the proofs of genuinely algebraic or analytic theorems had serious consequences. In particular, it inverted the objective ordering of truths. In so doing, it introduced circularities of reasoning into analysis. (p. 182)

At p. 186 Detlefsen quotes the emphatic echo of Aristotle's dictum in Bolzano [1996a], at p. 173. We shall quote here more fully the Bolzano passage in question:

> ... I believed I could not be satisfied with a completely strict proof *if it were not even derived from concepts* which the thesis to be proved contained, but rather made use of some fortuitous alien, *intermediate concept* [*Mittelbegriff*], which is always an erroneous [metabasis eis allo genos].

Bolzano's de-geometrizing in analysis receives emphatic statement in the Preface of this work, with yet another echo of the Aristotelian dictum (Bolzano [1996c], §I, at p. 228):

> ... it is an intolerable offence against *correct method* to derive truths of *pure* (or general) mathematics (i.e., arithmetic, algebra, analysis) from considerations which belong to a merely *applied* (or special) part, namely *geometry*. Indeed, have we not felt and recognized for a long time the incongruity of such [metabasis eis allo genos]?

Thus far in our examination of Bolzano we have read only statements of methodological prescription. But we have not yet encountered any reasoned argument in support of it. The closest we come to this, in Bolzano, now follows (Bolzano [1996c], *loc. cit.*):

> ... if one considers that the proofs of the science should not merely be *confirmations* [*Gewissmachungen*], but rather *justifications* [*Begründungen*], i.e., presentations of the objective reason for the truth concerned, then it is self-evident that the strictly scientific proof, or the objective reason, of a truth which holds equally for *all* quantities, whether in space or not, cannot possibly lie in a truth which holds merely for quantities which are in *space*.

This is the only genuine attempt to ground the prohibition against recourse to geometric intuition, or against the employment of specifically geometric vocabulary or concepts, in the founding of real analysis.

Chapter 19

Resisting the Trend toward Arithmetization

Abstract

The investigations in Chapter 18 revealed that there is no dispositive argument against the exercise of geometric intuition in the logico-genesis of real analysis. This chapter sets about resisting that downgrading of geometric intuition. For it is crucially involved in one's attaining a grasp of the real numbers in a form that is enlightened enough to meet the four conditions of adequacy on which this work has laid such stress. The concern here is to identify exactly how much has to be vouchsafed by synthetic *a priori* intuition in order for logic to 'do the rest' in ensuring grasp of the reals. The view to be developed is that a very simple and elemental geometric intuition is all one needs. Moreover, it is one that is not shaken by the development of non-Euclidean geometries. The intuition is this. *Any sequence of points on a line that proceeds strictly left-to-right and all of whose points are to the left of some bound has a leftmost right bound.* This is an *a priori* intuitive conviction that finds no expression in Euclid. But it would be shared immediately by any Euclidean who is brought to understand the proposition involved. (It is implicit in Archimedes' famous method of exhaustion.) What the de-geometrizers failed to anticipate is how the logical tradition would at last deliver, in the form of Gentzen's system of natural deduction, a way of ensuring absolute formal rigor in one's deductive reasoning. The logico-geneticist can take the aforementioned continuity principle as axiomatic, and then proceed with purely logical reasoning. One will be able to see how and why one can generate infinite bicimals (say) as canonical representations of real numbers; and why it is that one talks, nowadays almost unwittingly, of the real *line*. The chapter closes by revisiting Bolzano and Dedekind, and examining the contributions of Cauchy and Weierstraß in laying a more rigorous foundation for real analysis. It is a belated irony that 'Weierstraß'sche Strenge' can be co-opted by the natural logicist so as to ensure the ultimate foundational rigor of an elemental intuition about the continuity of a line. For it was Weierstraß who ensured genuine rigor in defining central mathematical concepts by using iterated quantifiers. All one needs thereafter is Gentzenian rigor in unpacking them.

One can challenge Bolzano's bald assertion—conditional on the view (with which we concur) that a proof of a mathematical claim should present 'the objective reason for the truth concerned'—that it is

> *self-evident* that the strictly scientific proof, or the objective reason, of a truth which holds equally for *all* quantities, whether in space or

The Logic of Number. Neil Tennant, Oxford University Press. © Neil Tennant 2022.
DOI: 10.1093/oso/9780192846679.003.0019

> not, cannot possibly lie in a truth which holds merely for quantities which are in *space*.

A great deal turns on what he means by a truth holding 'merely' for spatial quantities. If Bolzano means that some of the reasons given in support of the truth in question are true only of spatial quantities—or at least are not true of every other kind of quantity that is measurable by reals—then of course reasons of that kind should not feature in the objective grounding of principles about dimensionless real numbers. For these principles must be applicable to any kind of real-measurable quantity. But it is difficult to cite any such reasons that are, so to speak, space-specific, and that do not likewise hold for dimensions other than the spatial, dimensions which are nevertheless susceptible to measurement by real numbers, in terms of an appropriate unit of measurement.

To any contemporary follower of Bolzano, the geometrizing logico-geneticist can point out that the appeal that he intends to make to geometric intuition has two important features, which immunize that appeal against Bolzano's misgivings or criticisms:

1. the logico-geneticist draws on such intuition in order to supply only the most basic and uncontroversial first principles, formulable by means of a very limited vocabulary of extra-logical primitives; and

2. the logico-geneticist is careful to ensure that the first principles thus adopted by recourse to geometric intuition are principles that one would require to be true upon reinterpretation of those primitives in any of the alternative dimensions (other than the geometric line) to which one intends to apply real numbers in measurement.

In this way, the logico-geneticist can have recourse to geometric intuition—intuition about a particular measurable dimension, namely that of spatial length—while at the same time guaranteeing its invariance, or universality, for all dimensions which, like spatial length, are to admit of real measurement in terms of some appropriate unit.

The important contribution, here, of a fully rigorous logical analysis both of the sentences involved, and of the proofs involving them, is twofold. First, rigor can be ensured for the foundational reasoning; and, second, 'dimension invariant' truth can be ensured for the first principles that one adopts. Spatial length serves as a kind of 'arbitrary representative paradigm' for all real-measurable dimensions. Whatever is presumed true of spatial length is equally true of any of those other dimensions, upon appropriate reinterpretation of primitive expressions such as 'above/coincident with/below', 'less than/equal to/greater than', and 'unit'.

Cauchy's *Cours d'Analyse* of 1821 is often credited with initiating the much-needed rigorization of the calculus. Still, the new rigor resided at an informal level, as is illustrated by Cauchy's definition of the continuity of a function, in Cauchy [2009], Ch. 2. At the outset (p. 21) he defines what he means by 'infinitely small' quantity:

> We say that a variable quantity becomes *infinitely small* when its numerical value decreases indefinitely in such a way as to converge towards the limit zero.

To speak of a variable quantity as decreasing toward the limit zero is to invite the modern reader to conceive of it as the value of a function $g(x)$ whose values tend to zero as its independent variable x tends either to a particular limit, or grows beyond any finite bound. But this is not how Cauchy would wish one to understand it; because that would be already to apply the concept of continuity of a function, which he has yet to define. Here is his definition of that notion (p. 26):

> Let $f(x)$ be a function of the variable x, and suppose that for each value of x between two given limits, the function always takes a unique finite value. If, beginning with a value of x contained between these limits, we add to the variable x an infinitely small increment a, the function itself is incremented by the difference[fn]
>
> $$f(x+a) - f(x),$$
>
> which depends both on the new variable a and on the value of x. Given this, the function $f(x)$ is a continuous function of x between the assigned limits if, for each value of x between these limits, the numerical value of the difference
>
> $$f(x+a) - f(x)$$
>
> decreases indefinitely with the numerical value of a. In other words, the function $f(x)$ is continuous with respect to x between the given limits if, between these limits, *an infinitely small increment in the variable always produces an infinitely small increment in the function itself*. [Emphasis added.]

One can see from the informality of this definition that Cauchy was really nowhere near nailing the notions involved with complete logical precision. It would be a tall order to expect a trained modern logician to produce a univocal regimentation, in first-order logical symbolism, of a definition framed in these terms. To claim otherwise would be to read back into Cauchy a logical precision that was really only provided later, by Weierstraß. The latter's great contribution—now fondly referred to as the 'epsilon–delta' method—was to get clear about the relative scopes of the universal and existential quantifiers involved in the definitions of a function's limit at a point, of its continuity at a point, of its continuity over an interval, and of its uniform continuity over an interval. The same method (of alternating quantifications over reals) was employed to make suitably rigorous and logically precise the definition of the derivative of a function at a point.

We saw earlier that Weierstraß's pathological function bears his name by dint of unhappy neglect of Bolzano; and that (according to Ewald) the direction of real influence (in Bolzano's case) was from his independently motivated, arithmetizing methodology to his discovery of such a function.

Weierstraß's name, however, might be invoked in a prima-facie more compelling connection, which is the invention of the above-mentioned 'epsilon-delta' method of rigorizing statements of limits and of continuity of functions. Klein (see Klein [1996a], at p. 966) writes approvingly of the 'Weierstraß'sche Strenge, as it is called'. Our opponent's suggestion would be that it was this signal contribution to arithmetization that finally gave the arithmetizers the ideological edge against any of their more geometrically-minded competitors (as far as laying the foundation of real-number theory was concerned). By quantifying over positive real numbers with appropriately nested existential and universal quantifiers, Weierstraß achieved an illumination of core concepts of the calculus that had escaped his more geometrically-minded predecessors, including the founders of the calculus, Newton and Leibniz. In this way, Weierstraß consummated a methodological trend initiated by Cauchy (see Cauchy [2009], first published in 1921). For, as Ivor Grattan-Guinness says in connection with Cauchy's notion of limit,

> An important application of limits was to replace geometrical intuition about continuity . . . . (Grattan-Guinness [1997], at p. 374)
>
> Weierstraß's inheritance of Cauchy's style meant not only improving rigour but also avoiding geometry. (*ibid.*, at p. 482)

By way of immediate rebuttal, two points should be noted.

1. By Dedekind's own admission he arrived at his conception of *cut* in the Autumn of 1858, and was already motivated then by his arithmetizing and degeometrizing methodological view. It is highly unlikely that Weierstraß's own considered ideas would have exerted much of a foundational influence on Dedekind by this time. For, as Grattan-Guinness observes (*ibid.*, at p. 481)

    > The career of Karl Weierstraß (1815–97) shows one massive discontinuity. In the mid-1850s he was lifted from obscurity as a schoolteacher to become professor at Berlin, and by the 1860s he was recognized as one of the finest mathematicians of his time. . . .
    >
    > The work on analysis . . . made Weierstraß the successor to Cauchy . . . Somewhat unusually, he prosecuted his views almost entirely through lectures rather than in publications, which came in quantity only when he began to prepare his own editions of his works in the mid-1890s, shortly before his death.

2. Our opponent's suggestion is that it was the 'epsilon-delta' method that finally gave the arithmetizers an ideological edge. But arguably (Cauchy's

> and) Weierstraß's contribution did nothing of the sort. To be sure, Weierstraß achieved some much-needed clarity of quantificational structure in statements of limits and continuity. But—and this is crucial—he achieved it to the lasting benefit of both sides of this particular foundational debate (geometrizers *v.* arithmetizers). For, the geometrically minded foundationalist can happily acquiesce in and appropriate the Weierstraßian quantificational analysis, and turn it to his own advantage in formulating—rigorously and precisely—a geometrical version of what is meant by the limit- and continuity-statements in question. By way of brief illustration of this point, compare the following geometrized definition of what it is for a sequence $\gamma_0, \gamma_1, \ldots$ of points on a Euclidean line to be a Cauchy sequence (the unfamiliar notations here are explained on pp. 263 ff.):
>
> $$\forall n\, \exists m \forall i > m \forall j > m \lfloor \gamma_i, \gamma_j \rfloor \lhd [0, \frac{1}{2^n}]$$
>
> with the usual expression of the Cauchy condition in number-theoretic terms:
>
> $$\forall \epsilon (0 < \epsilon \;\; \rightarrow \;\; \exists m\ \forall i > m\ \forall j > m \ \mid \gamma_i - \gamma_j \mid < \epsilon),$$
>
> with the points γ_i and γ_j already regarded as points on the real 'line', that is, as real numbers.

There is another interesting pathology that might have played a role. McCarty (personal correspondence) drew the present author's attention to Dedekind's claim that there is a model of Euclidean geometry in two dimensions that is a proper, discontinuous subset of the real plane. Dedekind describes how this is so in his Preface to the first edition of *Was sind und was sollen die Zahlen?*, in the remarks there on his earlier "Continuität" essay. Dedekind drew attention to the algebraic numbers that had been characterized in Dirichlet [1894], §160.[1] Dedekind's account is as follows.[2]

> If we select three non-collinear points A, B, C at pleasure, with the single limitation that the ratios of the distances AB, AC, BC are algebraic numbers[fn. reference to Dirichlet], and regard as existing in space only those points M, for which the ratios of AM, BM, CM to AB are likewise algebraic numbers, then [it is easy to see that the space made up of the points M is] everywhere discontinuous. But in spite of this discontinuity, and despite the existence of gaps in this space, all constructions that occur in Euclid's *Elements*, can, so far as I can see, be just as accurately effected here as in perfectly continuous space; the discontinuity of this space would thus not be noticed in

[1] The citation here is of the fourth, revised and expanded, edition. In the first edition, in 1863, it was §159. It was §159 in the second edition also. It was in the third edition that the material was to be found in §160.

[2] We use here, with two indicated improvements, the English translation provided by Wooster Woodruff Beman in Dedekind [1901], at pp. 37-38.

> Euclid's science, would not be felt at all. If anyone should say that we cannot conceive of space as anything else than continuous, I should venture to doubt it and to call attention to the fact that a far advanced, refined scientific training is demanded in order to perceive clearly the essence of continuity and to understand that besides rational quantitative relations, also irrational, and besides algebraic, also transcendental quantitative relations are conceivable. It appears to me all the more beautiful that, without any notion of measurable quantities and simply by a finite system of simple steps of thought, man can advance to the creation of the pure continuous number-domain; and only by this means [is it in my opinion] possible for him to render the notion of continuous space clear and definite.

The interpretability of Euclid's *Elements* in a domain of points in a plane with algebraic numbers as their coordinates does not in any way clinch the view that geometric intuition would be wanting in providing the means by which to understand the crucial feature of continuity of the reals. For there is nothing sacrosanct, and certainly nothing theoretically complete, about Euclid's choice of first principles. Indeed, Euclid has been faulted for not having properly come to grips with considerations of continuity. His being remiss in this way undermines the cogency of certain proofs of his—such as his very first proof, of Proposition I, in Book I of the *Elements*.[3] It was Hilbert's special contribution, in Hilbert [1903] (English translation Hilbert [1971]), to put Euclidean geometry on a properly rigorous footing, by supplying the missing first principles concerning continuity (in addition to regimenting more precisely Euclid's thoughts about the relation of *betweenness*). Hilbert's Axiom V, 2 (**Axiom of line completeness**), however, is not stated as a formal sentence, or schema, of the geometric object-language. Rather, it is formulated as a meta-statement, or model-theoretic claim, to the effect that no line satisfying the other axioms (among them, Archimedes' axiom) can be extended by the addition of more points and still satisfy those axioms. This is not our preferred way (see below) of explicating the concept of continuity. We shall be formulating a principle of continuity that is in an appropriate geometrical object-language, augmented only with enough expressive power to enable one to talk about infinite sequences of points on a line. Moreover, we shall be proving that our principle of continuity enables one to logically derive Archimedes' axiom from the remaining geometrical axioms that we use.

Still, the main point at issue is whether Dedekind's point about interpretation using only algebraic numbers somehow implies that geometrical resources will be inadequate to the task of laying a foundation for real analysis. We dispute this implication. One can formulate purely geometric axioms that are powerful enough, and in an object-language for geometry that is expressively rich enough, for one to be able to advance strictly beyond Euclid and furnish a logico-geometric

[3] See Heath's commentary on the needed principle of continuity, in Euclid [1956], at pp. 234–240. For a more recent discussion that surveys many writers' views on this topic, see Panza [2012].

foundation for the theory of reals. The resulting theory will *not* be subject to Dedekind's accommodation of the Euclidean plane via algebraic coordinatization. But it will be no less 'Euclidean' for that. The simple observation to be made here is that Euclid himself did not go far enough in articulating, axiomatically and in an appropriately expressive language, all that is implicit within his own (and our) Euclidean conception of ideal straight lines, and the plane, as continuous domains of points.

A simple Euclidean construction that allows of infinite iteration produces a limit point that cannot be accommodated in the Dedekindian interpretation that uses only algebraic numbers. There is no good reason why even an ancient Euclidean geometer (such as Archimedes) would not have been willing to postulate the existence of such a limit, had the question of its existence been posed. The limit in question is a point on the line, not an infinitary object concocted out of points—so one cannot adduce the usual reluctance to countenance completed as opposed to potential infinities as the reason for anti-geometric heel-dragging here. Indeed, the assumption of such a limit was at least implicit in Eudoxus's and Archimedes' so-called method of exhaustion. Here is the construction.

Take a circle of unit diameter. Draw two perpendicular diameters. Draw line-segments to connect their points of intersection with the circle, so as to form a square. This is a regular 4-gon, the first in a series of regular 2^n-gons (for $n > 1$) that we shall now describe. Given any 2^k-gon in the series, construct the succeeding 2^{k+1}-gon by bisecting the sides of the 2^k-gon, and then drawing line-segments to connect the perpendicular bisectors' points of intersection with the circle with the immediately neighboring vertices of the 2^k-gon. One thereby inscribes on each side of the 2^k-gon an isosceles triangle with that side as base, and with its opposite vertex on the circle. The two equal sides of the isosceles triangle, together, exceed the base of the triangle in length. Thus the perimeter of the 2^{k+1}-gon is longer than the perimeter of the 2^k-gon.

Now mark off a countably infinite sequence of points $\gamma_0, \gamma_1, \ldots$ on a directed line, with an origin O, and with the unit that defined our chosen circle, as follows. To mark off γ_n, lay end-to-end, beginning at the origin O and moving to the right, 2^{n+2} copies of a side of the 2^{n+2}-gon already constructed. γ_n will be the point reached by the right-hand end of the 2^{n+2}-th copy. Thus the segment $[0, \gamma_n]$ will be exactly as long as the perimeter of the 2^{n+2}-gon. Hence the sequence of points $\gamma_0, \gamma_1, \ldots$ is strictly increasing to the right. Moreover, every point in the sequence lies to the left of the point that is 4 units to the right of the origin O.

By the axiom called **Right limits ...** on p. 269, the sequence $\gamma_0, \gamma_1, \ldots$ has a leftmost right limit point. Call it γ. In terms of our chosen unit, the length of the segment $[O, \gamma]$ is the transcendental number π. Dedekind's point about the sufficiency of algebraic coordinates for the points in Euclidean space that are constructible by (ruler and) compass is therefore of very limited interest, and provides no rein at all on more carefully thought-out, rather than strictly *Elements*-based, Euclidean geometrizing when laying a foundation for the theory of reals.

Detlefsen (personal correspondence) disagrees with the suggestion that the results of non-Euclidean geometry (and other "monsters" of geometric intuition) were too new and too fresh in 1850 to be able to prompt Dedekind's confident rejection of geometric intuition as a foundational basis for analysis. Detlefsen claims that they were already well known in the 1820s. On the other hand, one reads in Torretti [2010] the claim that '*Lobachevskian* geometry received little attention before the late 1860s.' [Emphasis added.] One also reads in Kagan [1957], at pp. 71–72, that

> On February 24, 1856 Lobachevsky died. His ideas, incomprehensible during his lifetime, seemed to be quite forgotten. ... However, these remarkable ideas did not remain in oblivion for long. The world learnt about non-Euclidean geometry from Gauss's letter to Schumacher, published after the death of Gauss in 1865. ... Helmholtz was the first to attempt to acquaint wider groups of scientific workers with [Lobachevsky's ideas].

Helmholtz did this in his 1868 lecture in Göttingen, and his 1869 lecture at Heidel berg University, on which were based his essay 'On the Origin and Significance of Geometrical Axioms'.[4]

Now, although Lobachevsky was the first non-Euclidean geometer to publish his ideas (see Lobachevsky [1829]), there were others—such as Gauss and János Bolyai—who were developing similar ideas at around the same time. In Gauss's case, the ideas—never written up—went back to 1792.[5] In Bolyai's case, his breakthrough, independent of Lobachevsky's, came in the early 1830s. Moreover, Gauss drew attention to Lobachevsky's 1829 paper, in a letter that Gauss wrote to János Bolyai's father Farkas, only a few years after that paper's publication. (This point is owed to George Schumm.) Where, then, might the truth lie, in so far as the question concerns influences from this quarter on Dedekind's foundational thinking?

Apart from the secretive and non-publishing Gauss at Dedekind's own institution, which non-Euclidean geometer might have had his ideas reach and influence Dedekind, to the point where Dedekind felt obliged to exercise such anti-geometric methodological caution? As far as Lobachevsky [1829] is concerned, the Russian journal in this case (*Kazan Messenger*) was probably too obscure for Dedekind to have learned of Lobachevsky's ideas from it—unless his colleague Gauss drew his attention to it, as he (Gauss) had done for Farkas Bolyai in the early 1830s. The later publications Lobachevsky [1837] and Lobachevsky [1856] (both in French) and Lobachevsky [1840] (in German) are more likely to have filled that role.

George Schumm (personal correspondence) makes the point that the 1837 paper appeared in what was supposedly the leading mathematics journal of his

[4] See von Helmholtz [1971].

[5] See Ewald's introductory note to the selections titled 'Gauss on Non-Euclidean geometry', Ewald [1996a], at p. 297.

day (*Journal für die reine und angewandte Mathematik—a.k.a.* Crelle's Journal). If, however, publication in that venue might be expected to have had significant impact, it certainly did not register with Russell, who was an assiduous scholar of French and German contributions to geometric thought and philosophizing about geometry. In Russell [1897], at pp. 10–11, we read

> *Lobatchewsky*, a professor in the University of Kasan, first published his results, in their native Russian, in the proceedings of that learned body for the years 1829–1830. Owing to this double obscurity of language and place, they attracted little attention, until he translated them into French[fn: Crelle's Journal, 1837.] and German[fn:Theorie der Parallellinien, Berlin, 1840. Republished, Berlin, 1887. Translated by Halsted, Austin, Texas, U.S.A. 4th edition, 1892.]; even then, *they do not appear to have obtained the notice they deserved, until, in 1868, Beltrami unearthed the article in Crelle, and made it the theme of a brilliant interpretation.* [Emphasis added.]

There is no explicit reference in Dedekind's own writings to Lobachevsky or to non-Euclidean ideas; so one is left to wonder just how influential they might have been at all, in motivating or reinforcing Dedekind's commitment to arithmetization.

The only surmise that seems reasonable here, for want of evidence from within Dedekind's published references—which are ample on other topics, but silent on the matter of geometry—is that he would have learned his mistrust of geometric intuition from his own mentor, Gauss. There is an interesting allusion to Gauss by Bolzano, in the preface to his 1817 piece *Rein analytischer Beweis ...* . At p. 227 of Bolzano [1996c] we read

> [Gauss] had already presented us with a proof of [the] proposition [that between every two values of the unknown quantity, which give results of opposite sign, there must always lie at least one real root of the equation] in 1799;[fn] but it had, as he admitted, the *defect* that it proved a purely analytic truth on the basis of a *geometrical consideration* [Betrachtung]. But his two most recent proofs[fn] [in 1816—NT] are quite free of this *defect*; the *trigonometric functions* which occur in them can, and must, be understood in a purely analytical sense. [First and third emphases added.]

There is, however, one overarching irony about the suggestion here being contemplated—the suggestion that it might have been the development of non-Euclidean geometry that led to a mistrust of geometric intuition. Kagan (*ibid.*, at p. 55) writes

> It is ... noteworthy that the very construction of non-Euclidean geometry did not at all proceed along purely formal logical lines. This may seem very strange but intuition helped its creator in the same way

> as it did in the creation of classical geometry. And the one [*sic*] who clearly understood the process, could not fail to see that we could think not only in terms of the old, established space concepts, but also in terms of entirely new, radically different images ...

Kagan also notes (p. 59) that Lobachevsky employed his ideas from hyperbolic geometry to 'find the values of many indefinite integrals', upon which 'it was frequently possible to find also analytical ways which led to the same goal.' This was a case of *metabasis eis allo genos* if ever there was one.

Finally, it is worth noting that Lobachevskian (plane) geometry gained its final acceptance as a consistent system when Beltrami [1868] provided for it an interpretation *within Euclidean space*. The straight lines of Lobachevskian geometry were identified with certain curves on three-dimensional, 'pseudospherical' surfaces. Under this interpretation, all the postulates of Lobachevskian geometry were satisfied, including the non-Euclidean postulate to the effect that through any point p off a given line l there are exactly two lines, called the *extremals*, that do not meet l in any point, and between which all (the infinitely many) lines passing through p do not meet l either. (In some presentations of Lobachevskian geometry, only the extremals are called parallels of l. See, for example, Kagan [1957], at pp. 37–38.) This furnished a model-theoretic proof of the relative consistency of the two geometries: if three-dimensional Euclidean geometry is consistent, than so too is Lobachevskian plane geometry.

McCarty (personal correspondence) has cited

> the influence of the oft-noted essays by Riemann and Helmholtz on the prospects that geometry is an empirical and not an *a priori* science, as Kant supposed. If geometry turned out to be an empirical science, pure mathematicians thought, they should insist that its arguments, constructions, and methods play no role, or only a reduced role, in pure mathematics.

The issue on which Euclid's geometry disagrees with non-Euclidean geometries is the metric and curvature of space. This is a global *differentia*; mathematicians and physicists frequently speak of non-Euclidean geometries that are 'locally Euclidean'. The issue strikes the present author as orthogonal to the question whether one can rely on one's geometrical intuitions concerning the continuity of an idealized straight line. We think of any line-segment, no matter how short, as still infinitely divisible into ever-smaller segments. All one needs, in order to attain to the concept of continuity, is the idealized conception of a potentially infinite sequence of points $\gamma_0, \gamma_1, \ldots$ on a line-segment, with γ_n strictly to the left of γ_{n+1}, for every n, and with some point (a 'right limit point') strictly to the right of every γ_n. The principle of continuity is then to the effect that there is a leftmost right limit point—that is, a point strictly to the right of every γ_n such that no point strictly to the left of it has that property. (This will be developed in greater detail in Chapter 22.) In addition to this 'incrementalist' conception of bounded iterative selection of points, we need only the assumption that (short enough) line-segments can be bisected (with the usual idealized accuracy characteristic of Euclidean thought). It is important to stress why we can say 'short enough' here. These bisections, as will become clear in due course, are needed only in order to make sense of bicimal expansions after the 'bicimal point'—expansions which correspond to a sub-unit length. By choosing the unit small enough, one can ensure that one can treat it in Euclidean fashion: it will make sense to speak of bisecting it. Within a Euclidean framework, one can describe a ruler-and-compass construction whereby one can bisect a given line-segment $[a, b]$. But one can be more modest than that, and simply postulate that for every line-segment $[a, b]$ there is a unique point c (on $[a, b]$) such that the segments $[a, c]$ and $[c, b]$ are congruent (i.e., exactly as long as each other). This postulate will then deliver all the bisection points that one will need in order to construct a bicimal expansion to any number of places. We shall explain the role of these expansions in Chapter 22.

Note that bisection is just a special case of n-section, with $n = 2$. It is chosen for its simplicity and familiarity. It follows from a well-known theorem of Descartes in Euclidean geometry that n-section of a line-segment can be effected by ruler-and-compass construction, for any natural number n.[6]

Moreover, even if the metric is non-Euclidean, the iterated 'bisective' construction can be carried out provided only that it makes sense to speak of the midpoint of a finite line-segment; and, even in Lobachevsky's geometry, it does. See, for example, Smogorzhevsky [1976], §11, 'Measurement of Segments of Hyperbolic Straight Lines'.

But, the objector might ask, what about line-segments long enough to make a non-Euclidean metric something one has to worry about? The answer to this worry is that such segments are measured by the laying-on-end of a suitably short, idealized, measuring rod. This determines how many integral units of length lie between the endpoints of the segment (and before the sub-unit remainder, if any, has to be determined as a bicimal expansion by bisections). It was just this operational meaning of measurement of length that led Einstein to use the Lorentz transformations of spatial coordinates between the results of measurement undertaken within two different inertial frames, given the invariance (constancy) of the speed of light across all inertial frames. Indeed, the fundamental insight was furnished years earlier, in 1868, in a lecture by Hermann von Helmholtz to an audience in Göttingen. (See von Helmholtz [1971], translated into English as von Helmholtz [1876].) Helmholtz offered some insightful reflections on what one sees in a spherical mirror, if a person is using a measuring rod to measure the length of some extended thing in his vicinity. The measurer, the measuring rod, and the measured thing would all be subject to the same apparent distortions, as viewed by us. But the measurer would not be able, in principle, to learn from his measurements that that is how he, his rod, and the thing being measured appear

[6] See Hartshorne [2000], Theorem 13.2 at p. 122. The reader will recall how Edwin the Fractionator in Part III made use of this method of n-section, in order to cut a Slim Jim into eleven equal pieces.

to us. As von Helmholtz put it (*loc. cit.*, p. 316):

> ... I do not see how men in the mirror are to discover that their bodies are not rigid solids and their experiences good examples of the correctness of Euclid's axioms.

This was perhaps one of the earliest statements of the relativity of results of measurement to the frame of reference of the observer. The relativistic physicist has to operationalize in this now-familiar way the meaning of the statement 'the distance between point a and point b is r units of length' (where r is some real number, to within some degree of approximation). In so doing, the relativistic physicist is merely stressing how the method of measuring length is actually that of the Euclidean. It is precisely because the method remains the same (after the discovery of the constancy of the speed of light in all inertial frames) that the relativist abandons the Galilean transformations and adopts the Lorentzian ones. The method of measuring the length of a line-segment—the laying-on-end of (copies of) a standardized measuring rod of unit length—is invariant across choice of global geometry (and metric).

The eschewal of geometric intuition when doing real analysis has been explained by some by pointing out ways in which geometric intuition allegedly led its consulters astray in their mathematical thinking. Thus for example Felix Klein (Klein [1996a], at p. 966) claims that in the case of some of Gauss's reasoning

> space intuition had led to the too hasty assumption of the generality of certain theorems which are by no means general. Hence arose the demand for exclusively arithmetical methods of proof; nothing shall be accepted as part of science unless its rigorous truth can be clearly demonstrated by the ordinary operations of analysis.

Klein himself, however, is careful not to give up or jettison spatial intuition altogether. He believes that it can be refined. In its naive form it is 'largely a natural gift, which is unconsciously increased by minute study of one branch or other of science'. (p. 969) It is also 'always far in advance of logical reasoning and covers a wider field.' He then insists that 'Logical investigation is not in place until intuition has completed the task of idealization.'

The question, then, is how best to eliminate the risk of falsity or fallacy when resorting to intuition. It generates conjectures, and leading ideas for proofs. It generates counterexamples to faulty generalizations. So it is like a logical probe in both directions (validity of inferential transition, as well as invalidity thereof). It is an abstract faculty inchoately descrying symbolic or combinatorial structure, but also intimately connected with the digital-to-analog operation of the human senses—which is why it is so important for us in calculus, which began as the mathematics of our grasp of space and time, both of which were presumed to be continua.

Klein of course was writing well before the thorough, detailed proof-theoretic analysis afforded in the 1930s by the work of Gerhard Gentzen (Gentzen [1934,

1935]), which laid bare for the first time (in a natural fashion) the ultimate logical structure of the inferences and proofs that are actually carried out in mathematics. If Klein could have had the benefit of our own historical hindsight, there is no doubt but that he would have sought a 'logicist remedy' for the occasional problem of intuition-induced ailments of reasoning. He would have laid stress (as Hilbert did, in his re-axiomatization of Euclidean geometry) on the need to

1. make explicit every single one of one's premises for an argument;
2. reveal the exact logical structure within each premise, using only the permitted primitives of a strictly circumscribed extra-logical vocabulary;
3. ensure that every step of argument is in accordance with an explicitly stated rule (whether of the underlying logic, or of the theory being developed); which involves also the need to
4. ensure that definitions are faithfully 'unpacked' at appropriate junctures in the course of one's reasoning.

Whenever intuition leads one astray, it is because it makes one believe, over-hastily, that matters are in good logical order when in fact they are not. And if and when they are not, the methodological prescriptions just given would enable one to pinpoint precisely where one's reasoning had gone astray.[7]

The emerging point is subtle, and often overlooked in our all-too-anachronistic readings of foundational thinkers whose contributions antedate the major developments in mathematical logic in the 1920s and 1930s. The antidote to intuitional sloppiness (if it ever occurs) is symbolic-logical rigor. This means, first and foremost, the kind of formal exactitude that is now afforded by (say) Gentzenian systems of natural deduction. *That* is the methodological gold standard by which correctness of mathematical reasoning is to be judged. Note that one can achieve the requisite rigor while reasoning from premises involving geometrical primitives, provided only that those premises have been explained, argued for, and properly regimented in formal notation. There are a great many simple, obviously true axioms of a geometric kind that one could put forward, and that would be immediately evident to all mathematicians—as not only true of Euclidean straight lines but true also of any dimension susceptible of measurement

[7]There is an echo here of the view of Lambert [1786], as discussed by Detlefsen [2005], at p. 250. More recently, Burgess [2015], at p. 86, has expressed a consonant view:

> ... to oppose logicism is not to oppose rigor, whose requirements pertain to how one gets from postulates to theorems, not to where one gets the postulates from ... Hilbert as much as Poincaré saw the need for postulates suggested by intuition rather than logic, and Poincaré as much as Hilbert granted in principle the importance of excluding further appeal to intuition in proofs once the postulates have been set up.

Note, however, that this last remark is compatible with exercising one's *a priori* intuition in seeing one's way forward with an unfolding deduction in, say, real analysis, while yet ensuring that the rigorous but informal proof that results could be fully regimented as a purely symbolic Gentzenian natural deduction.

by real numbers. The great service rendered by formal logic is then to make our inferential transitions topic invariant. So, provided only that the starting points of a proof are accepted as justified, the result we arrive at as its conclusion will be just as acceptable.

In Voss [1908], we read the following, at pp. 97–98:[8]

> The knowledge of mathematicians too is unfinished work; questions always arise again and again, which are unanswered and appear to be unanswerable. But we are guided by the conviction, not yet disappointed, that reason must be able to answer even the questions whose motivation is drawn by reason exclusively from the realm that reason has created for itself.[fn]
>
> According to our contemporary insight we have to admit that the solution of the big questions that concern the origin of organic life and the expression of the same in experiences, ideas and thoughts—indeed, all expressions of any kind of mental life—is forever closed off from conceptual knowledge. We do not know, we will not know: we do not understand them and never will. But in Mathematics there is no ignorabimus; rather, there is only the certainty of a progress that overcomes all difficulties.

The footnote is as follows:[9]

> One can, however, raise the following question, without wishing in so doing to shake the moral conviction just stated.
>
> Let there be given a certain number of undefined symbols (undefined, because known to be unambiguous in their application to given objects) along with a certain number of uncontradictory postulates about the connections among these symbols. Must it now be the case,

[8] Author's translation of the following German original:

> Auch das Wissen des Mathematikers ist Stückwerk, immer aufs neue treten Fragen auf, die unbeantwortet sind, und unbeantwortbar scheinen. Aber uns leitet die bisher nie getäuschte Überzeugung, daß die Vernunft diejenigen Fragen, deren Veranlassung sie ausschließlich ihrem eigenen selbst geschaffenen Reiche entnimmt, auch zu beantworten fähig sein muß.[fn]
>
> Nach unserer gegenwärtigen Einsicht müssen wir zugeben, daß die Lösung der großen Fragen, welche den Ursprung des organischen Lebens und die Äußerungen desselben in Empfindungen, Vorstellungen und Gedanken, ja alle Äußerungen des geistigen Lebens überhaupt betreffen, unserer begrifflichen Erkenntnis auf immer beschlossen ist, ignoramus, ignorabimus: wir verstehen sie nicht und werden sie nie verstehen. Aber in der Mathematik gibt es kein ignorabimus, sondern nur die Gewißheit eines Fortschrittes, der alle Schwierigkeiten überwindet.

[9] Author's translation of the following German original:

> Man kann indessen die folgende Frage aufwerfen, ohne damit die angegebene moralische Überzeugung erschüttern zu wollen.

> of necessity, that any question that is posed with regard to those symbols or objects can be decided by means of a mathematical proof? One would be able to maintain this with certainty only if one presupposes that such a decision be possible on the basis of the laws of connections given by the postulates. Is this for example certain for every number-theoretic statement that is expressed empirically at first, but problematically? Must there be, for every well defined number, a method to decide its transcendental or algebraic nature? We do not have an answer to this, as one is accustomed to saying, 'in the contemporary state of knowledge'. One recognizes, however, from what has already been explained, that no logical ground is available for the given conviction; rather, that we have here a confidence based only on *experience*, without which, to be sure, no progressive development is possible at all.

This is impressively prescient on the part of Voss. He was explicitly anticipating the kind of incompleteness of number-theory that Gödel in due course established just over two decades later. Gödelian incompleteness caused consternation within a mathematical community not particularly persuaded that Voss's misgiving might be proved to be correct. Voss's reference to 'big questions' whose solutions are 'forever closed off from conceptual knowledge' was tacitly invoking the famous *Ignorabimusstreit* initiated in the 1860s by Emil du Bois Reymond. It was also a respectful demurral to the famous Hilbert—for it was the *Ignorabimus* motto to which Hilbert was emphatically opposed when he announced, in his famous address to the International Congress of Mathematicians in Paris in 1900,[10]

> This conviction that each and every mathematical problem is soluble is a powerful incentive to us in our work. We hear within us the constant call: *There is the problem. Seek its solution. You can find it*

Es sei eine gewisse Zahl nicht definierter (weil hinsichtlich ihrer Anwendung auf gegebene Objekte unzweideutig bekannter) Symbole und eine gewisse Zahl widerspruchsloser Postulate der Verknüpfung dieser Symbole gegeben. Muß nun notwendig jede Frage, welche hinsichtlich jener Symbole oder Objekte aufgeworfen wird, mittels eines mathematischen Beweises entschieden werden können? Mit Sicherheit wird man dies nur behaupten können, wenn man voraussetzt, daß diese Entscheidung auf Grund der durch die Postulate gegebenen Verknüpfungsgesetze möglich sei. Ist dies z. B. gewiß für jeden zahlentheoretischen Satz, der zunächst empirisch aber problematisch ausgesprochen wird? Muß es für jede bestimmt definierte Zahl eine Methode geben, ihre Transzendenz oder ihre algebraische Natur zu entscheiden? Eine Antwort hierauf besitzen wir, wie man zu sagen pflegt „bei dem gegenwärtigen Zustande der Wissenschaft" nicht. Man erkennt aber aus dem soeben Ausgeführten, daß ein logischer Grund für die angegebene Überzeugung *nicht* vorhanden ist, sondern daß hier nur ein auf die *Erfahrung* gestütztes Selbstvertrauen vorliegt, ohne welches allerdings überhaupt keine fortschreitende Entwicklung möglich ist.

Emphases in the original, by insertion of extra spaces between the letters of the words.

[10]For more details about Hilbert's role in the later stages of the *Ignorabimusstreit*, see [2007].

by pure reason, for in mathematics there is no Ignorabimus.

On the same theme, we have the following from Hilbert:[11]

> The continuum of real numbers is a system of things which are linked to one another by determinate relations, the so-called axioms. In particular, in place of the definition of real number by Dedekind cut, we have the two axioms of continuity, namely, the Archimedean axiom and the so-called completeness axiom. To be sure, the Dedekind cuts can then also be used to specify individual real numbers, but they do not provide the definition of the concept of real number. Rather, a real number is conceptually just a thing belonging to our system. [7] This grounding of the theory of the continuum is not at all opposed to intuition ⟦Anschauung⟧. The concept of extensive magnitude, as we derive it from intuition, is independent of the concept of number ⟦Anzahl⟧; and it is therefore thoroughly in keeping with intuition if we make a fundamental distinction between number and measuring-number ⟦Maßzahl⟧ or quantity.

[11]This is the English translation in Hilbert [1996], at p. 1118, of Hilbert [1922], at pp. 158–159. The original German is as follows:

> Das Kontinuum der reellen Zahlen ist ein System von Dingen, die durch bestimmte Beziehungen, sogenannte Axiome, miteinander verknüpft sind. Insbesondere treten an Stelle der Definition der reellen Zahl durch den Dedekindschen Schnitt die zwei Stetigkeitsaxiome, nämlich das Archimedische Axiom und das sogenannte Vollständigkeitsaxiom. Die Dedekindschen Schnitte können dann zwar auch zur Festlegung der einzelnen reellen Zahlen dienen, aber sie dienen nicht zur Definition des Begriffs der reellen Zahl. Vielmehr is begrifflich eine reelle Zahl eben ein Ding unseres Systems.
>
> Diese Begründung der Theorie des Kontinuums ist keineswegs im Gegensatz zur Anschauung. Der Begriff der extensiven Größe, wie wir ihn aus der Anschauung entnehmen, ist ein selbstständiger gegenüber dem Begriff der Anzahl, und es ist daher durchaus der Anschauung entsprechend, wenn wir Anzahl und Maßzahl oder Größe grundsätzlich unterscheiden.

Chapter 20

Impurities and Incompletenesses

Abstract

Contemporary foundationalists have examined extensively whether certain results in a branch of mathematics depend for their proof on principles governing notions not embedded in those results themselves. A pure proof of a theorem φ is one whose premises are axioms embedding only non-logical primitives that are embedded in φ. With reference to famous results in number theory (such as the Prime Number Theorem, Dirchlet's Theorem, and Fermat's Last Theorem) and to foundational results about Gödelian incompleteness of theories, it is questioned whether Bolzano was justified in insisting on purity of proof. The investigation therefore underscores, by tacit implication, the likelihood that any 'purely logical' re-capture of various mathematical theories is bound to be of rather limited extent. This lends heightened interest to the question of what, exactly, the 'purely logical' parts of these theories *are*.

Contemporary foundationalists have the benefit of a better grasp of the limitations of an Aristotelian or Bolzanoan axiomatic method that seeks to solve all mathematical problems stated in a given vocabulary by appeal only to axioms that are themselves stated in that same vocabulary. Twentieth-century mathematics is by and large a story of how such 'purity of method' is honored in the breach. A trenchant quote that underscores this is from G. H. Hardy, who, in 1921, expressed the following view to the Mathematical Society of Copenhagen:[1]

> It is rash to assert that a mathematical theorem cannot be proved in a particular way; but one thing seems quite clear. We have certain views about the logic of the theory; we think that some theorems, as we say, 'lie deep', and others nearer to the surface. If anyone produces an elementary proof of the prime number theorem, he will show that these views are wrong, that the subject does not hang together in the way we have supposed, and that it is time for the books to be cast aside and for the theory to be rewritten.

[1] See Hardy [1921] at pp. 549–550.

The Logic of Number. Neil Tennant, Oxford University Press. © Neil Tennant 2022.
DOI: 10.1093/oso/9780192846679.003.0020

As we shall see below, Hardy's choice of example is not altogether felicitous; but the viewpoint he is expressing continues to be widely held. Mathematicians still believe that certain results about, say, the real numbers, are to be had only by making an excursus into the containing system of the complex numbers. Therefore, the common suspicion goes, one cannot restrict one's theorizing efforts to 'within' the perspective of the contained structure. Instead, one has to step outside of it, and see aspects of it as 'firmed up' only by virtue of its inclusion within some wider containing system. As Jacques Hadamard put it:[2]

> It has been written that the shortest and best way between two truths of the real domain often passes through the imaginary one.

Two historical examples will illustrate this point. The Prime Number Theorem—Hardy's example above—was first proved by Hadamard [1896] and de la Vallée Poussin [1896] using non-elementary means. These were the proofs that Hardy would have had in mind. Only 53 years later, in 1949, was the first elementary proof found, by Erdős [1949] and Selberg [1949a]. As Colin McLarty has pointed out (personal correspondence)

> ... history did not go exactly as [Hardy] foresaw, since he more or less assumed that an elementary proof would also be *easier* than the analytic one, but he was quite right about the issues it would raise.
>
> When the elementary proof was found it did in fact re-create a good part of the subject, producing for example sieve methods. And some number theorists affirmed it was really an easier proof and did show the subject hangs together differently than the analytic types thought, and so we should scrap the analytic books. Had they gotten their way, Hardy would have been entirely confirmed. Others held that the elementary proof was not easier but actually more difficult and isolated from other important results, and so they said it effectively re-confirmed that the analytic approach hangs together better—and overall they won the day, on very much the same grounds as Hardy said would be decisive. Hardy was only wrong to suppose that an elementary proof once found would replace the analytic one.

Likewise, Dirichlet's Theorem—that there are infinitely many prime numbers in all arithmetic progressions with first term and difference coprime (see Dirichlet [1837])—was first proved by non-elementary means. Only much later were elementary proofs found, by Selberg [1949b] and Zassenhaus [1949]. One wonders what the situation will be with Fermat's Last Theorem—will Wiles's proof persist as the only one ever found, or will we find a wholly elementary proof for this result?

In this connection, note the 'Grand Conjecture' of Harvey Friedman:[3]

---

[2]See Hadamard [1945], at p. 123.

[3]See Friedman [1999]. See also Avigad [2003] at p. 258.

> Every theorem published in the Annals of Mathematics whose statement involves only finitary mathematical objects (i.e., what logicians call an arithmetical statement) can be proved in EFA. EFA is the weak fragment of Peano Arithmetic based on the usual quantifier free axioms for 0,1,+,x,exp, together with the scheme of induction for all formulas in the language all o[f] whose quantifiers are bounded. This has not even been carefully established for Peano Arithmetic. It is widely believed to be true for Peano Arithmetic, and I think that in every case where a logician has taken the time to learn the proofs, that logician also sees how to prove the theorem in Peano Arithmetic. However, there are some proofs which are very difficult to understand for all but a few people that have appeared in the Annals of Mathematics - e.g., Wiles' proof of FLT.

The resort to the complex number system in order to obtain results strictly about the reals is not, however, logically essential. True, the proofs that result from such an excursus into complex numbers can be short and elegant; but it should always be possible, in principle, to obtain the result about reals within the resources of real number theory itself, even if there may be blow-up in the length of such 'elementary' proof. The essential point is that, for example, various axiomatizations of first-order $Th(\mathbb{R}, +, ., 0, 1, >)$ are complete; likewise for $Th(\mathbb{C}, +, ., 0, 1, i, >_{\mathbb{R}})$.[4]

Within these complete theories, however, there is no way of identifying the natural numbers as a contained kind (among the reals). If the naturals were identifiable, then the theories in question would be afflicted by the Gödelian incompleteness phenomena. From our post-Gödelian perspective, Bolzano's insistence on purity of method appears to be even less justified than it would have been to a Hadamard or a Hardy.

There is a manifest tension arising from the immediately preceding considerations, when they are taken in conjunction with the Gödelian phenomena of incompleteness (and indeed: Π^0_1-incompleteness, at that). The tension is evident in Friedman's own work on both fronts. On the one hand, he conjectures that certain very deep, famous, and deductively 'distant' results are actually all to be had within the scope of a surprisingly weak system of arithmetical axioms. On the other hand, he has himself extended the Gödelian program to dizzying heights, in revealing that certain very strong large-cardinal assumptions need to be adjoined to ZFC in order to prove seductively simple-looking combinatorial conjectures of his own invention.

independence results concerning any system of axioms for mathematics become stronger when either or both of the following two conditions are met:

1. the sentence whose logical independence from the axioms is established is as elementary and intuitively graspable as possible;

[4] The classic paper is Tarski [1967]. The originally scheduled date of publication was 1940, but the printer's setting was destroyed 'as a result of war activities'. The author's page proofs survived. The work is reprinted in Tarski [1986]. See Theorems 2.1 and 3.3.

2. the mathematical system from which its independence is established is as strong as possible, both in terms of its all-encompassing nature and in terms of the existential strength of its axioms.

Beginning with Gödel's incompleteness theorem for first-order arithmetic,[5] logicians have been improving their independence results in stages. Gödel's independent sentence was extremely long and cumbersome, obtained by the method of coding syntax in arithmetic. It made no intuitively graspable arithmetical claim; rather, its interest lay in what it could be thought of as 'saying' (concerning itself) via the coding: to wit, 'I am unprovable in the present formal system.' And the formal system concerned was only that of *Principia Mathematica*. Gödel's result could, of course, be indefinitely generalized, in the sense that, given any extension of the system, one would be able to find yet another sentence independent of the extended system. But note that the choice of independent sentence depended on the system.

It is worth expanding here on the brief description of the 'semantical argument' for the truth of the independent Gödel sentence G that we set out earlier (p. 37 ff.). The peculiar nicety about Gödelian incompleteness of arithmetic is that the proof of the metatheorem itself furnishes an argument to the effect that the independent sentence is indeed *true* in the intended model $\mathbb{N}$ of the natural numbers. The independent sentence has the form

$$\forall n \mathcal{G}(n)$$

where $\mathcal{G}(n)$ is so constructed that, via the Gödel numbering, it 'says' that (i.e., it is interdeducible with the claim that) n is not the Gödel number of any proof, in the system, of the sentence $\forall n \mathcal{G}(n)$ itself. Thus, if the system is consistent, we have

$$\vdash \mathcal{G}(0), \vdash \mathcal{G}(1), \vdash \mathcal{G}(2), \ldots$$

whence (by soundness) we have

$$\mathcal{G}(0) \text{ is true}, \mathcal{G}(1) \text{ is true}, \mathcal{G}(2) \text{ is true}, \ldots$$

From 'outside' the system, one is therefore justified in inferring that

$$\forall n \mathcal{G}(n),$$

since 0, 1, 2, ... are all the individuals there are in the domain of $\mathbb{N}$. But this is precisely what Gödel's theorem shows to be unprovable within the system. The metatheorem states that, if consistent, the formal system under investigation cannot itself contain a proof of this last result.

The formal system could be extended, however, so as to enable us to codify within the extended system a formal proof of the formerly independent sentence. Such an extension could be effected by adopting a primitive truth predicate for

[5] See Gödel [1931].

the unextended language, thereby making available new instances, within the language thus extended, of the axiom scheme of mathematical induction.[6] Of course, because of the essential incompletability of formal arithmetic, this extended system will, in turn, be unable to settle the truth or falsity of yet another independent Gödel sentence. Nevertheless, the point is that each independent Gödel sentence, at any stage of formalization, succumbs to formal proof (in a suitably expanded sense) at the next stage. So the Gödel sentence for any particular formal system of arithmetic is clearly not a case of utterly verification-transcendent truth of a kind that a misguided anti-realist might seek to establish as existing, in opposition to the realist's adoption of the Principle of Bivalence.[7]

Gödel's first incompleteness theorem for arithmetic, then, is of no avail to anyone in search of a single absolutely undecidable sentence of arithmetic. So we can allay the extreme form of epistemic pessimism that the prospect of finding such a sentence might provoke. It would be a mistake, though, to switch to an untutored optimism in this regard. For there has been a succession of increasingly stronger independence results since Gödel's theorem, a brief overview of which would be in order here.

The next advance on the incompleteness front came when Gödel moved on from arithmetic (dealing with the most minimal set of Kroneckerian 'God-givens') to set theory (dealing with the most capacious universe possible for the accommodation of all of mathematics). Gödel and Cohen between them proved the independence of the Axiom of Choice (AC) and of the Continuum Hypothesis (CH) from the axioms of Zermelo–Fraenkel set theory (ZF). Gödel showed, in ZF, the truth of both AC and the Generalized CH in the so-called 'constructible universe' (which is definable in ZF). Cohen showed that CH can be falsified in a different kind of model for ZFC.[8] Here was the would-be all-encompassing theory, and here were two deep and interesting foundational claims shown to be independent of that theory. Indeed, at least one of them—AC—has good claim to be taken as an axiom, given how widespread are the appeals made to it (or to its equivalents *modulo* ZF) in mathematics at large. By Cohen's result, even ZFC fails to prove CH; and by Gödel's result ZFC fails to refute CH. More evidence of the baffling recalcitrance of CH comes from subsequent results showing that CH evades both proof and disproof within any extension of ZFC by large-cardinal axioms.

Looking at AC in relation to ZF, one can see a strong analogy between the situation with set theory and the situation with Euclidean geometry, concerning the Parallels Postulate in relation to Euclid's remaining postulates. In homage to Beltrami (see p. 225), we shall call such independence results *Beltramian*. They

[6]An alternative, 'less semantical' extension could be effected by simply adopting as a new axiom the consistency statement Con_S for whatever system S is being extended.

[7]We say that the anti-realist would be misguided in seeking to do this because it is incoherent, by the anti-realist's own lights, to say that it is possible that there be a counterexample to the Principle of Bivalence. There is an easy core proof of $\perp$ from $\Diamond\exists\varphi\neg(\varphi \vee \neg\varphi)$

[8]Gödel [1940] and Cohen [1963].

establish the independence, from the remaining axioms, of a mathematical statement seriously under consideration for adoption as an axiom—thereby underscoring the necessity of stating it as an axiom, if one is thus intellectually inclined.

After Gödel and Cohen accomplished this breakthrough foundational work in set theory, Paris and Harrington proved the first so-called 'natural independence result' in arithmetic.[9] They found a simple arithmetical statement, which had reasonably sophisticated but mathematically 'combinatorial' content, and showed that it was independent of Peano arithmetic (PA). The situation here was not quite Beltramian in the sense just introduced. The independent statement in question was not under consideration for adoption as an axiom; it was just thought to be a true conjecture which one would reasonably have expected eventually to admit of proof within the system PA.

More recently still, Friedman has accomplished what may be regarded as virtually the culmination of the lines (1) and (2) above.[10] He reveals an astonishing extent of incompleteness, even at the level of intuitively accessible, combinatorially-flavored statements about naturals and rationals (and finite vectors composed of them). Friedman has found an exceptionally simple, elementary statement φ about numbers, which is about functions on and into finite sets of vectors of integers. He has shown this sentence φ to be independent, not just of Zermelo–Fraenkel set theory with the Axiom of Choice (ZFC), but of its extension by certain large-cardinal existence axioms. In the present stage of development of Friedman's foundational program, φ is provable upon the additional postulation of the existence of yet larger cardinals (those which are 'k-subtle for all k'). Modulo ZFC, the sentence φ is equivalent to the consistency of these deciding cardinals. Nothing smaller will do for the purposes of settling the truth of φ. Friedman's results, to summarize, take the generic form

> Such-and-such combinatorial statement is equivalent, *modulo* a base theory such as EFA (exponential function arithmetic), to the consistency of (ZFC+ so-and-so large-cardinal hypothesis).

This appears to undermine Bolzano's insistence on purity of proof, in the absence of any further argument to the effect that the extant first principles of real analysis, including the principle of continuity, should be attainable only by arithmetical means. After all, if a simple combinatorial statement requires powerful set-theoretic axioms for its proof, might not some of the first principles of real analysis, for their 'founding justifications', require either higher set-theoretical axioms or axioms drawn from some different area of mathematics (such as geometry)? Remember that by Gödel's second incompleteness theorem, the consistency statement for (ZFC+ so-and-so large-cardinal hypothesis) is more powerful than (ZFC+ so-and-so large-cardinal hypothesis) itself—provided, of course, that the latter is consistent.

---

[9] Paris and Harrington [1977].

[10] Friedman [1998].

Friedman is confident that his program can be prosecuted even further. He conjectures that he will be able, with the methods he has already developed, to find an exceptionally simple number-theoretic claim ψ that would be immediately understood by any college-level algebra student; and that he will be able to show that ψ is decided only by postulating the largest cardinal ever considered, namely, that associated with an elementary embedding of the set-theoretic universe into itself. The existence of the latter cardinal is known to be inconsistent with ZFC, but not with ZF. The truth of ψ would thereby have been consigned to a region where even the best mathematicians no longer had any clear intuitions.

What might one make now of the suggestion from an anti-realist that the Friedman sentence ψ is perhaps an example of the sort of 'recognition-transcendent truth' (if it is true) (or 'recognition-transcendent falsity', if it is false) whose existence the Principle of Bivalence is supposed to secure? For, applying bivalence to Friedman's sentence ψ, the realist will say that either ψ is true, or $\neg\psi$ is true. If ψ is true, then, by Friedman's independence result, it cannot be recognized as true. On the other hand, if $\neg\psi$ is true, then, by that same result, it cannot be recognized as true. Either way, we get a recognition-transcendent truth—or so it would seem.

Nevertheless, despite the impressive nature of Friedman's present result, and the unsettling implications of its conjectured future strenghtening, it cannot be pressed into the sort of logico-philosophical service here that an anti-realist might think we need in order to establish that bivalence implies the existence of recognition-transcendent truths. The trouble is that we have no guarantee that the particular extension of Zermelo–Fraenkel set theory involved in Friedman's best possible independence result would have to be the 'last word' on the matter of a foundational starting-point on which to base eventual recognition of truth. We cannot second-guess what new sorts of axioms, or families of principle, might be devised or divined by mathematicians in the future, and appended to the current 'cardinal existence' extensions of Zermelo–Fraenkel set theory. After all, not too long ago even those cardinal existence axioms would not have been foreseen by the best mathematicians. The large-cardinal axioms gathered up and extended the impact of the earlier so-called reflection principles, which emerged only after set-theoretic foundationalists had pondered long and hard the overall structure of the cumulative hierarchy. Later still, the Axiom of Determinacy shed new light on the nature of the continuum (even if it also brought out tensions with other candidates for axiomhood). We have no way of foreclosing on future extensions of our collective intellectual insight. Who knows what new principle might not emerge within the next few years, and settle the truth-value of Friedman's 'most independent' (and simplest) sentence? The impressive character of his ultimate (but still only conjectured) independence result derives from the way it would appear to use up all our current intellectual resources in the specification of the system from which independence is proved; and also from the exceptionally simple character of the sentence shown thus to be independent. All that, however, still fails to make the desired logical transition available to the kind of anti-realist under consideration here: the transition, that is, from bivalence to the existence of recognition-transcendent truths.

The situation is even more complicated than the foregoing account would so far suggest. As mentioned above (p. 234), Friedman is also on record with the 'Grand Conjecture' to the effect that every number-theoretic result (such as Fermat's Last Theorem) that has been proved in the journal literature (for definiteness, before the end of the year 2000) is a theorem of EFA (exponential function arithmetic).

This conjecture would have made Hardy gasp. It highlights just how difficult it is to find the sorts of combinatorial statements that Friedman is proving equivalent, *modulo* EFA, to consistency statements for large-cardinal assumptions. On the other hand, Friedman's recent program of *strict* reverse mathematics holds out the prospect that we might be able to calibrate logical strengths of theories from disparate areas of mathematics (such as geometry and the theory of real closed fields), and produce results that would either reinforce or allay Bolzanoan misgivings about basing the foundations of one such theory on considerations drawn from the other.

The Bolzanoan could object that Friedman's equivalences are still ones that obtain between two sentences in the same vocabulary of arithmetic. It is just that the consistency statement is, logico-grammatically, highly complex, employing as it does an arithmetical predicate devised to encode provability in a formal system, via some system of Gödel-numbering. Even though that formal system is one of higher set theory, its provability predicate, and its consistency statement are nevertheless purely arithmetical. Indeed, the latter is Π^0_1—'of Goldbach type'.

This, however, responds only to the form of Friedman's result whereby

$$\text{EFA} \vdash \varphi \leftrightarrow \mathit{Con}(\text{ZFC} + \mathit{Large\ Cardinal\ Hypothesis}).$$

Friedman has established other forms of independence result that escape the envisaged Bolzanoan objection, such as

$$\text{ZFC} + \forall k\ \mathit{there\ exists\ a\ k\text{-}subtle\ cardinal} \vdash \varphi \quad \text{but} \quad \Delta \nvdash \varphi,$$

where Δ is any consistent subset of the theorems of

$$\text{ZFC} + \{\mathit{there\ exists\ a\ k\text{-}subtle\ cardinal} \mid 0 < k \in \omega\}$$

from which EFA can be derived.[11]

Such a result puts one in a position to say, rhetorically: So, you want to prove this nice, elegant, intuitively graspable combinatorially-flavored statement φ? Then you are going to *have* to make certain large-cardinal existence assumptions, because φ cannot be proved from any weaker assumptions.

[11] Friedman's Theorem 5.91 on p. 892 of Friedman [1998] is the only precursor in print of independence results of this last kind. In Theorem 5.91, because of the details of the independent statement φ (Friedman's 'Proposition *A* for #-decreasing'), the last part of the result had to read 'from which ZFC can be derived', rather than 'from which EFA can be derived'.

Chapter 21

The Concept of Real Number

Abstract

This chapter lays the conceptual groundwork that is necessary by way of prelude to the technical work that is to be undertaken in Chapter 22, where logically precise axioms are framed governing the orderings of points on directed lines. Here it is explained how reference (and commitment) to reals arises from the re-carving of contents of statements of dimensional measurement in terms of a unit, and a notion of congruence (or equality-of-magnitude). Thus one speaks of a dimension **D** (e.g., length; duration), unit-of-**D** (e.g., meter; second), **D*** (e.g., long), $\#_{\mathbf{D}}$ (e.g., the length of; the duration of), and $\cong_{\mathbf{D}}$ (e.g., exactly as long as; equal in duration to). There follows a survey of the different locutions we employ that appear to embed reference to reals, and a tabulation of the systematic similarities across various measurable dimensions (such as length, time, weight, etc.). The outcome of this study of systematic variations in expression of some same state of affairs (i.e., the outcome of measurement) is the formulation of Schema R for the reals. It is compared and contrasted with Schema N for the naturals and with Schema Q for the rationals. Schema R turns out to admit of proof (more precisely: proofs of all its instances) courtesy of introduction and elimination rules involving canonical statements of measurement and identity statements involving the real-number abstraction operator $\#_{\mathbf{D}}$ on one side, and a *de-dimensionalized* numerical term on the other side. The crux of this treatment by appeal to one's geometric intuition of the continuity of a (directed) line will be its painstaking description of how, in principle, to determine the aforementioned de-dimensionalized numerical representation. The considered choice here will be a (potentially infinite) bicimal expansion. The constructive character of such an expansion turns on the determinacy of the trichotomy of ordering of points on a directed line. The chapter argues, as Russell did, for the primacy of spatial measurement (that is, lengths of line segments). Measurement of lengths serves as the paradigm case of measurement in any dimension, for reasons that are expounded upon.

We aim here to reveal the thoroughly geometric, or logico-geometric, provenance of our concept of real number; and to provide a reconstructive, so-called 'logico-genetic' account, in the sense already explained (see pp. 50–52, 202), of the mathematical theory of real numbers. The account must also satisfy the four conditions of adequacy that we imposed in Chapter 5, on p. 55. The contention is that our concept of real number derives first and foremost—in a logically articulable way—from our conception of the magnitude (of lengths) of straight-line seg-

The Logic of Number. Neil Tennant, Oxford University Press.
DOI: 10.1093/oso/9780192846679.003.0021

ments, in terms of a chosen unit of length. The idea is fundamentally Euclidean—in the perfectly clear mathematical sense, with none of the connotations of intellectual inappositeness that it has acquired from the displacement of Newton's theory of physical space as Euclidean by Einstein's relativistic, non-Euclidean one. And the idea is intuitive rather than logical. We aim to round it out here while confining ourselves within the conceptual universe of the Euclidean geometer of one dimension.

The only occasions on which we shall have recourse to two dimensions will be (i) when we advert to the length of the diagonal of the unit square, in order to motivate the idea that (what turns out to be) an irrational number has to be taken in one's stride when one is a 'geometrizing logicist' about the reals; and (ii) when we bisect a line-segment in order to determine its midpoint. The ruler-and-compass construction for bisection invokes, of course, points off the line-segment in some same plane. The good news, however, for one who might worry that space is at best locally Euclidean, is that the method of bisection presupposes a planar rectangular region only as long as the segment to be bisected, and no wider than the segment is long—indeed, of any lesser but non-zero width. So one is entitled to choose an arbitrarily small width around the line whose sub-unit segments are being bisected (or k-sected, if one is employing a place notation with base k).

The most fundamental aspect that has to be ensured by any account of the reals is the continuity of the 'real line'. The real numbers may be thought of as points forming a line only because they (the real numbers) are intended as representations (with respect to an origin, a direction and a unit) of points on an oriented geometric line. And the *Ur*-intuition is that any geometric line is continuous. So naturally the real numbers will inherit this property, as representatives of points on a geometric line.

We therefore seek to express the *Ur*-intuition in thoroughly geometric terms. This will ensure that, when real numbers are eventually introduced as representatives of points on a geometric line, they (the real numbers) will themselves form a linearly ordered continuum. We have to earn the right so to regard the reals. We cannot blithely just assume that the reals form 'the real line'.

We must also display a geometric origin for addition and multiplication of real numbers (and also for subtraction and division). For addition, the fundamental geometric idea is the straight laying-on-end of finite line-segments. For multiplication, the fundamental geometric idea might be thought to be the formation of rectangles, whose areas can be determined from the lengths of their sides; but in fact one can make use of a different fundamental geometric idea which is more 'linear', involving successively larger multiples (results of layings-on-end) of successively longer line-segments. This idea, however, still invokes the method of bisection, so that it does after all involve recourse to two dimensions.

Like Frege,[1] we proceed from the natural numbers to the real numbers, without first securing the rational numbers as a 'stepping stone' species of mathemat-

[1] Frege's omission of the rationals is noted by Dummett [1991] at p. 246 and elsewhere.

ical objects out of which to 'construct' the reals. Once we have the reals, the rationals will of course 'drop out' as special ones among them—ones with finite, or recurring, (bicimal) expansions. But this defining feature of their expansions does not suffice to mark the rationals as constituting a different kind of mathematical object, especially as far as applications are concerned. For, reals (hence also: rationals) are (as both Newton and then Frege emphasized) ratios of magnitudes. It is also something of a justifying irony for the Fregean that even our best attempts actually to measure any particular value of a continuously variable magnitude can only ever result in a rational number, because of the practical impossibility of attaining absolute precision. (This predicament is one that Hilary Putnam has exploited in order to argue, in Putnam [1971], that the field of rational numbers actually suffices for scientific purposes.)

We seek hereby to illuminate the question of how and why the real numbers are applicable in the measurement of continuous magnitudes—geometric lengths being the paradigm case. By slightly catachrestic extension, the 'real line' can also be applied for the measurement of other unbounded linear continua within which one can fix an origin, a preferred direction, and a unit. Thus, for example, the dimension of time is taken to be real-measurable. One can fix any instant as the origin of one's system of temporal measurement; one usually takes the arrow of time pointing from the past to the future as giving the preferred direction; and one can fix a unit of temporal length via any one of a number of 'stably periodic' processes in nature.

We say that geometric length is nevertheless the paradigm case because in this case the measurements and comparisons that one needs to make can always be repeated, in order to confirm results or to attain greater precision. One cannot do that with any period of time whose duration has to be measured.

Geometric length also encompasses the negative magnitudes, because one is thinking of points on a directed line, in relation to a chosen origin. Half of them, as it were, will be to the left of the origin (negative), and half of them to the right (positive). This is in contrast with those dimensions of continuous magnitude, such as light intensity or absolute temperature, for whose measurement only the non-negative real numbers can feature (once a suitable unit for the dimension in question has been chosen).

This way of thinking about real numbers as representatives of extensive magnitudes within some linear continuum (primarily geometric lengths or distances), and with respect to an origin, a preferred direction or orientation, and a chosen unit, helps also to resolve the problem of how it can be that the natural number n is identical to the rational number n, which is in turn identical to the real number n; and how the rational number $\frac{p}{q}$ is identical to the real number $\frac{p}{q}$. We have already raised this (starting with our earlier discussion of Dirichlet on p. 58) as the problem of identity under embeddings. The naturals embed within the integers, which in turn embed within the rationals, which in turn embed within the reals:

$$\mathbb{N} \mapsto \mathbb{I} \mapsto \mathbb{Q} \mapsto \mathbb{R}.$$

And any natural number n *is*—in the metaphysical sense of identity, also known (non-punningly, here) as numerical identity—upon each such embedding, *itself* again. As we shall have occasion to remark again below, there is no pun intended in saying that one is talking, here, of what the philosopher calls numerical identity—being one and the same thing.[2] A natural number does not just have an 'integer counterpart', or a 'rational counterpart', or a 'real counterpart', under the embeddings in question. Rather, under these embeddings, each natural number n corresponds to itself. The problem is to explain how this is so. Obstacles to such an explanation arise when we say such things as that, *qua* integer, n 'is' the ordered pair $\langle n, 1\rangle$; and that, *qua* rational, n 'is' the ordered pair $\langle\langle n, 1\rangle, 1\rangle$; and that, *qua* real, n 'is' the Dedekind cut

$$\langle\{\rho \in \mathbb{Q} \mid \rho \leq n\}, \{\rho \in \mathbb{Q} \mid n < \rho\}\rangle$$

(where $\mathbb{Q}$ is the set of all rationals).

There are of course various alternative ways of defining cuts; no particular importance attaches to this one.

Note that the problem of explaining identity under embedding is not solved by the neo-Fregean abstractionist account of the reals in Shapiro [2000b]. In that account, the various new abstracta are abstracted from quite varying equivalence relations, and no attempt is made to ensure that the natural number n *is* the integer n, and *is* the real number n. Indeed, on p. 339 Shapiro confesses that he proposes 'to avoid the issue [of *identity* under embedding] here'. We must bear in mind that Shapiro's account of the reals, and his account of the rationals in Shapiro [2000a], are based on double-barreled abstraction principles. Strictly within the context of such principles, the study of Cook and Ebert [2005] draws pessimistic conclusions about the prospects of settling 'cross-sortal' identity claims of the form

$$@_1(P) = @_2(Q)$$

where P and Q are concepts, and $@_1$ and $@_2$ are abstraction operators featuring in second-order abstraction principles of the form

$$\forall X \forall Y(@(X) = @(Y) \Leftrightarrow E_{@}(X, Y)$$

involving operator-specific equivalence relations (among concepts) on the right-hand side. Nor do Cook and Ebert consider the rationals at all in their discussion of cross-sortal identities. The overall, and highly general, import of their considerations, however, confirms the view that double-barreled abstraction principles

[2] The use of the adjective 'numerical' in the abstract noun 'numerical identity' adverts to the idea that it is the kind of identity involved when one counts things in a (finite) collection. It is by employing the notion of numerical identity among the things in question that one will be able to determine how many of them there are—that is, their number. Fortunately, the same notion extends to the infinite case. One wants to be able to ignore the possibility of, say, uncountably many indiscernibles when determining the cardinality of a countably infinite set.

involving concepts cast no light at all on the issue raised above of identity of numbers under embeddings.

Perhaps Kronecker was right when he said that God gave us the integers (i.e., the naturals). We say 'perhaps' here because we have seen, in Part II, that the provenance of the naturals lies entirely within our logical faculties. The question that then has to be considered is whether God gave us those. But insofar as 'humankind did all the rest', we should want to say: humankind filled in all the rest, not that humankind came up with various type-raising constructions under which ones loses sight of the original God-given integers, as one makes room for all the rest.

What, then, is our recommended solution to the problem of identity under embeddings? We can assume a solution to the prior problem of the natural numbers as representing the outcomes of (discrete) counting of finite collections, which vouchsafes a conception of natural numbers as (dimensionless) logical objects. (This indeed has been accomplished in Constructive Logicism's earlier work.)

Let us suppose, then, that we have in hand an adequate theory of natural numbers, which explains, by implying all instances of Schema N, the applicability of natural numbers for the counting of finite collections of any kinds of individuable and re-identifiable objects whatsoever—including natural numbers themselves, if necessary. This theory in turn permits us to make use of inductive definitions on the natural numbers, so as (for example) to attain to the concept of a certain point x, say, on a geometric line, and to the right of the origin, lying (exactly) a certain whole number of units of length away from the origin. The real number that represents x by reference to that origin, that direction, and that unit, will then *be* the whole number n itself. It will not be, on our analysis, a cut of the rationals, or a class of co-convergent Cauchy sequences, or any other type-raising 'construction out of the natural numbers'. The natural number n *is* the real number n, period.

This insistence on (what philosophers would call) numerical identity (again, no pun intended) rules out also the stratagem of the reverse mathematician working in subsystems of so-called second-order arithmetic, which are really two-sorted first-order systems. In Simpson [1999], Remark I.4.1 on p. 11 is very revealing. It confesses to treating each (positive or negative) integer as a particular representative of the equivalence class (of (codes of) ordered pairs of natural numbers) that a Dedekindian, working in a set-theoretic context, would take as 'the' integer in question; and to treating each rational, similarly, as a representative of the equivalence class (of (codes of) ordered pairs of integers) that a Dedekindian would take as 'the' rational in question. What Simpson does not remark on, however, is that this stratagem of 'embedding' the naturals within the integers, and then in turn the integers within the rationals, puts the new creations at two removes from their Dedekindian conceivings. For, on the reverse mathematician's treatment, ordered pairs of naturals are coded as naturals—via the definition (*op. cit.*,

p. 9)

$$(m, n) = (m + n)^2 + m .$$

Thus rational numbers end up being identified with particular naturals. Moreover, any natural number k, *qua* rational, will be identified with some natural number other than k. This is to obliterate altogether the desired 'preservation of identity under injection' as one moves from the naturals to the integers, and from the integers to the rationals. By 'first-orderizing' what is usually (for the Dedekindian) a type-raising procedure, the reverse mathematician's coding methods leave us with an utter mangling of the underlying Platonic identities of these numbers. Only a perverse allegiance to structuralist prescriptions for re-construal can make sense of the result—of this way of 'creating' it from the raw materials of the naturals—being 'the' ordered field of the rationals.[3]

There is a final abstractive leap when we consider algebraic operations on, and ordering relations among, real numbers themselves, without an eye to the dimension of measurement that is always involved in actual applications of real numbers, whether explicitly or implicitly. The pure mathematician always seeks to abstract away from the situation(s) in which mathematical objects find application (in measurement). The termini of such abstractions are the entities within a pure mathematical structure. Here, the 'pure' structure $\mathbb{R}$ of real numbers is thought to consist of 'dimensionless' entities, just as is the 'pure' structure $\mathbb{N}$ of natural numbers (for the reasons essayed above). The members of $\mathbb{R}$ are abstract entities that are not spatial; not temporal; not massive; . . . . They are not lengths, not durations, not 'extensive magnitudes' (such as temperatures, energies, masses, densities etc.) of any kind.

The abstractive processes that take us to a conception of real numbers as (members of a) dimensionless (structure) are worth tracking by means of equivalences analogous to those supplied by Schema N above. The following sequence of segués among equivalent forms of expression effects such abstraction, beginning with mensurations in adverbial mode, and ending by re-formulating them in nominal mode:

> Point c lies three meters to the right of origin 0 (along line L).
>
> Line segment $[0, c]$ is three meters long.
>
> The length of line-segment $[0, c] = 3$ meters.
>
> The length of line-segment $[0, c]$ in meter-units $= 3$.

Compare:

> He died three years after he was born.

[3] The reader will recognize in our remarks about the arithmetizing method of reverse mathematics an echo of similar criticisms of set-theoretic foundationalism, with its various conventionally chosen set-surrogates for the different kinds of numbers (as exemplified in Suppes [1960]), that is to be found in Simons [1987], at pp. 29–30.

His life was three years long.

His lifespan = 3 years.

The duration of his life in years = 3.

In both the spatial case and the temporal case, the final form of expression is an identity statement in which, on the right-hand side, we have a pure-numerical representation, with mention of the relevant dimension, and of its unit, confined to the left-hand side.[4] In order to carry this essential feature over into the logical regimentations of these claims, they ought to be rendered along the following lines. First, we consider statements of length. Take the statement

The length of line-segment σ = 3 meters.

The natural regimentation of this is

$$\mathcal{L}(\sigma) = 3\mathbf{m},$$

or, rather more carefully,

$$\mathcal{L}(\sigma) = 3 \odot \mathbf{m}.$$

Here the binary symbol $\odot$ is not to be assumed to represent the usual binary operation of multiplication, whose arguments are taken to be co-members of the same field. Rather, $\odot$, as we have seen, needs a special definition, since it involves a number as one of its apparent 'arguments', and a dimensionalized magnitude as the other 'argument'. We first broached this 'operation' $\odot$ on p. 166, in a context exactly similar to this one; and we gave a rigorous inductive definition of contexts in which it occurs, in Chapter 16 (see Definition 9 on p. 182). It is important to remind the reader here of our caveat that preceded Definition 9. We are not conceiving of

$$t = n \odot \mu$$

as an identity statement on whose right-hand side is a singular term with $\odot$ as its dominant expression-forming term. Rather, we are conceiving of it as a ternary predication, in which the familiar symbol '=' is being press-ganged into unusual service. One can rewrite the 'identity', if necessary, as

$$F(t, n, \mu),$$

[4] *Cf.* Quine [1960] at p. 245:

> ... 'length in miles' is to be understood as true of this or that number relative to this and that body or region. Thus instead of 'length of Manhattan = 11 miles' we would now say 'length-in-miles of Manhattan = 11' (form F of $b = a$') or '11 is length-in-miles-of Manhattan' (form 'Fab').

But Quine does not press any further the interesting investigation of how best to regiment the logical form of the beefed-up left-hand sides of these equations of measurement (which have just a numeral on their right-hand sides).

in order to maintain logical hygiene. It says that t is dimensionally equal, or congruent, to any segment that results from n layings-on-end of segments of magnitude μ.

That said, we shall now be lazy and elide the wretched $\odot$. The reader must just remain mindful of what it really means when it is lurking in the background. In effect, physicists proceed in this manner all the time; so, then, can we.

On the right-hand side we are referring to '3 times a meter-unit', or '3 layings-on-end of one-meter segments' to say what the result of any length-measurement of the segment σ would be. The singular term '3**m**' wears its dimensionality on its sleeve; it is not a pure-numerical representation. A pure-numerical representation would be achieved only by 'de-dimensionalizing' the right-hand side:

> The length of line-segment σ in meter-units = 3.

The term 'The length of line-segment σ' is itself dimensionalized (with implicit reference to meter-units); the expression 'in meter-units' that then follows it (on the left-hand side of this last identity) serves to 'de-dimensionalize' that reference. One is, as it were, taking a 'metered quantity', and 'dividing through' by a meter-unit, so as to obtain a 'dimensionless', pure numerical result.

Compare Burgess and Rosen [1997], at pp. 77–78:

> ... by reconstruing or reparsing 'the mass of x is two grams' as 'the mass-in-grams of x is two', impure numbers can be avoided: only pure numbers are required for the measurement of intensive magnitudes (mass, charge) or extensive magnitudes (length, area, volume, duration), or positional magnitudes (spatial and temporal coordinates).

Burgess and Rosen do not, however, pursue the question of how precisely to regiment canonical measurement-statements with dimensionless reals on their right-hand sides.

All this is very much in the spirit of our quote from Newton at the outset.

Let us introduce the formal predicate '$x \cong_{\mathcal{L}} y$' to express the thought that x is exactly as long as y, or, as one can also say, 'of the same length' as y. A natural regimentation of

> The length of line-segment σ in meter-units = 3.

would be

$$\#_{\mathcal{L}}x(\sigma, x \cong_{\mathcal{L}} \mathbf{m}) = 3.$$

Another way of reading this formal sentence would be to say

> The number of meter-units (**m**s) that would be taken up in any measurement of the length of $\sigma = 3$,

where 'number' hearkens back to the initial '#', and 'length' to its subscript $\mathcal{L}$. So $\#_{\mathcal{L}}$ is not the natural number-abstraction operator # that we dealt with above, when counting how (finitely) many objects are in the extension of a sortal predicate. Its logico-linguistic category is different. Whereas # binds a variable x in a predicate $\Phi(x)$ to produce a singular term $\#x\Phi(x)$ denoting a natural number, the operator $\#_{\mathcal{L}}$ binds a variable x in a canonical unit-of-length-specifying predicate of the form '$x \cong_{\mathcal{L}} \mathbf{m}$', in association with a singular term σ denoting the object whose length is in question. An abstractive term of the form

$$\#_{\mathcal{L}}x(\sigma, x \cong_{\mathcal{L}} \mathbf{m}),$$

to be sure, denotes a real number, and indeed (in our example) a real number that happens also to be a natural number. The denotation of σ therein, however, must be an object that can have a length. This is much more exigent than the requirement, in the case of the natural-number term-abstraction operator #, that the predicates to which it may intelligibly be applied must be sortal predicates (i.e., predicates that supply a criterion of individuation and re-identification of the objects that fall under them). Many kinds of things finite collections of which can be counted with natural numbers are not things possessed of lengths—*a fortiori*, not possessed of lengths that can be measured, in terms of a unit of length, by real numbers. One obvious such kind of thing is: natural numbers.

The subscripting of # with $\mathcal{L}$ is very important, since it registers the fact that there is a unit of *length* with reference to which the measurement of length (now taken to be a real number) has to be carried out, in order for that real number to be a correct (dimensionless) representation of the length of the object σ in question, in terms of that unit.

So too with other dimensions. Take time, for example. Temporal segments, also known as periods or durations, are measured in terms of some unit-duration $\mathbf{y}$ (a year, say). (Note that '$\mathbf{y}$' is a name, not a variable.) Some 'point-event' marks the beginning of the period in question, and another point-event marks its end. In our earlier example, we took these to be the birth and the death, respectively, of some individual. Let his lifespan be the temporal segment λ. When we say

$\lambda = 3$ years

there is implicit dimensionality on the left-hand side that is matched by explicit dimensionality on the right-hand side. We can 'de-dimensionalize' by saying, equivalently,

The duration of λ in year-units = 3.

A natural regimentation of this statement would be

$$\#_{D}x(\lambda, x \cong_{D} \mathbf{y}) = 3,$$

where the binary predicate $\cong_{D}$ now represents equality-of-duration of two temporal periods. Another way of reading this formal sentence would be to say

> The number of year-units (**y**s) that would be taken up in any measurement of the duration of $\lambda = 3$.

So $\#_D$, like $\#_{\mathcal{L}}$, is not the number-abstraction operator # that we dealt with above. The operator $\#_D$ binds a variable x in a canonical unit-of-time-specifying predicate of the form '$x \cong_D \mathbf{y}$', in association with a singular term λ denoting the period of time whose duration (or, as one so easily says: length) is in question. An abstractive term of the form

$$\#_D x(\lambda, x \cong_D \mathbf{y}),$$

to be sure, denotes a real number, and indeed (in our example) a real number that happens also to be a natural number. The denotation of λ therein, however, must be a temporal period. Once again, this is much more exigent than the requirement, in the case of the natural-number term-abstraction operator #, that the predicates to which it may intelligibly be applied must be sortal predicates.

The subscripting of # with D is very important, since it registers the fact that there is a unit of *duration* with reference to which the measurement of duration (now taken to be a real number) has to be carried out, in order for that real number to be a correct (dimensionless) representation of the duration of the period λ in question, in terms of that unit.

In general, then, canonical statements of measurement take the form

$$\mathbf{dimension}(t) = r\ \mathbf{units\text{-}of\text{-}dimension}$$

where the term t denotes the object whose **dimension** is being measured. And canonical statements of measurement involving dimensionless real numbers on their right-hand sides take the 'de-dimensionalized' form

$$\#_{\mathbf{dimension}} x(t, x \cong \mathbf{unit\text{-}of\text{-}dimension}) = r$$

where the congruence relation $\cong$ is the appropriate one for the dimension concerned (sameness of length, or sameness of duration, in the preceding discussion).[5] But even with the right-hand side of such an identity statement 'de-dimensionalized', the left-hand side is nevertheless still freighted, twice over, with reference to the banished dimension.

Some further examples of statements with this regimented form are

> Her age in years = 12.
>
> His monthly net income in dollars = 4000.
>
> Her temperature in degrees Celsius = 38.
>
> His weight in pounds = 240.

[5]The captious reader might insist that we ought here to write '$\cong_{\mathbf{dimension}}$' instead of just '$\cong$'. We shall in effect do so in due course, upon abbreviating '**dimension**' to '**D**'. Note that this is not the 'D' that we have been using for *duration*.

The density of this stuff, in grams per cubic centimeter = 5.

The energy contribution of this snack in calories = 200.

The area of my living room in square feet = 400.

All our examples have involved real numbers that happen to be whole numbers (i.e., natural numbers). But of course the point of measurement by real numbers, in terms of a unit for the dimension involved, is to enjoy a continuum of possible values, even if in practice one can attain only fractional (i.e., rational) approximations thereof. In principle, one wishes to be able to make, and to reason with, assertions such as

The length of the diagonal of a unit square = $\sqrt{2}$,

and

The length of the circumference of a unit circle = 2π.

The way to introduce numbers as logical objects is to explain the truth-conditions of canonical statements of identity of numbers. Thus, Schema N for the natural numbers provided a conceptual route—a logico-genetic path—to those numbers as logical objects. And Schema Q did the same thing for the rational numbers. The analogous route to real numbers, however, is conceptually more complicated—to the point where direct intellectual access to the numbers in question as would-be 'logical objects' is compromised.

Our two forms of canonical statements of measurement—the one with dimension featuring adjectivally, and the other one with only a dimensionless real number on the right-hand side—are of course equivalent. This is expressed by our (now long overdue) Schema R, with **dimension** abbreviated to **D**, and **D*** being the correlative adjective:

Schema R: $\#_{\mathbf{D}}x(t, x \cong_{\mathbf{D}} \textbf{unit-of-D}) = r \dashv\vdash t$ is r units-of-**D** **D***.

Schema R is the closest conceptual approximation we can make, for the real numbers, to Schema N for the natural numbers. For any choice of dimension **D**, any real number r, and any object t, the corresponding instance of Schema R should be derivable within an adequate logico-genetic theory of the real numbers. And indeed it is—just as simply as was the case with Schema Q, which was derived by direct application of the introduction and elimination rules for $\mathfrak{F}$. The analogous rules for $\#_{\mathbf{D}}$ are as follows.

$$\#_{\mathbf{D}}\text{-I} \quad \frac{t \text{ is } r \text{ units-of-}\mathbf{D}\ \mathbf{D^*}}{\#_{\mathbf{D}}x(t, x \cong_{\mathbf{D}} \textbf{unit-of-D}) = r} \qquad\qquad \#_{\mathbf{D}}\text{-E} \quad \frac{\#_{\mathbf{D}}x(t, x \cong_{\mathbf{D}} \textbf{unit-of-D}) = r}{t \text{ is } r \text{ units-of-}\mathbf{D}\ \mathbf{D^*}}$$

With Schema R, as with Schema N and with Schema Q, it is immaterial whether we speak of biconditionals in the object language, or of interdeducibilities between their left- and right-hand sides. Also, because of commutativity, it matters not which 'side' is mentioned first. We shall now give some examples in which the truth-condition-specifying but number-non-committal side comes first, followed by the numerical identity whose truth-conditions are thereby furnished. Consider:

$$\text{this rod is 3 } \textbf{units-of-Length long}$$

$$\leftrightarrow$$

$$\#_{\mathbf{Length}}x(\text{this rod}, x \cong_{\mathbf{Length}} \textbf{unit-of-Length}) = 3.$$

Or, with the unit of length specified in more familiar fashion:

$$\text{this rod is 3 } \textbf{meters long}$$

$$\leftrightarrow$$

$$\#_{\mathbf{Length}}x(\text{this rod}, x \cong_{\mathbf{Length}} \textbf{meter}) = 3.$$

Disregard the fact that we happen to have used the whole number 3 in our example. The example could just as well have been

$$\text{this rod is } \sqrt{2} \textbf{ meters long}$$

$$\leftrightarrow$$

$$\#_{\mathbf{Length}}x(\text{this rod}, x \cong_{\mathbf{Length}} \textbf{unit-of-Length}) = \sqrt{2}$$

—or, to drive the point home even more forcefully,

$$\text{this rod is } \pi \textbf{ meters long}$$

$$\leftrightarrow$$

$$\#_{\mathbf{Length}}x(\text{this rod}, x \cong_{\mathbf{Length}} \textbf{unit-of-Length}) = \pi.$$

Any fluent English speaker, when given an English specification of the relevant dimension **D**, should have no trouble coming up with English expressions to play the roles of the relevant unit-of-**D**; the adjective or adjectival phrase **D***; the abstractive operator $\#_{\mathbf{D}}$; and the equivalence relation $\cong_{\mathbf{D}}$.

Some examples are

D	unit-of-**D**	**D***	$\#_{\mathbf{D}}$	$\cong_{\mathbf{D}}$
length	meter	long	the length of	exactly as long as
width	meter	wide	the width of	exactly as wide as
depth	meter	deep	the depth of	exactly as deep as
area	meter^2	in area	the area of	equal in area to
volume	cc	in volume	the volume of	equal in volume to
duration	second	long (!)	the duration of	equal in duration to
weight	pound	in weight	the weight of	weighs exactly the same as
mass	gram	in mass	the mass of	is exactly as massive as
density	gram/cc	dense	the density of	is exactly as dense as

We note, and set aside, the problem that some of these dimensions **D** (such as mass) can yield only non-negative real numbers.

Sometimes there are slightly better circumlocutions than what would be obtained by sticking rigorously to this table of substitutions. For example, the table advises one to say something like

$$\text{this pumpkin is } \pi \textbf{ pounds in weight}$$
$$\leftrightarrow$$
$$\#_{\textbf{weight}}x(\text{this pumpkin}, x \cong_{\textbf{weight}} \textbf{pound}) = \pi,$$

which, after elimination of symbolism, becomes the biconditional

$$\text{this pumpkin is } \pi \text{ pounds in weight}$$
$$\leftrightarrow$$
$$\text{the weight of this pumpkin, in pounds} = \pi.$$

It is nevertheless better to say something like

$$\text{this pumpkin weighs } \pi \text{ pounds}$$
$$\leftrightarrow$$
$$\text{the weight of this pumpkin, in pounds} = \pi.$$

Here, the adjectival phrase 'in weight'—the substituend for **D***—becomes the more felicitous verb 'weighs'. Similarly, rather than saying that some event is one hour in duration, one could simply say that it lasts one hour. These points about good English style affect only those sides of the biconditional instances of Schema R that specify truth-conditions in a number-non-committal way.

Let us now display our three Schemas together, so that we can be mindful of both similarities and differences among them. To enable such comparison, we write their number-committal identities on the left, and their number-non-committal equivalents on the right.

Schema N $\quad \#x\Phi x = \underline{n} \dashv\vdash \nabla_n x \Phi x$
Schema Q $\quad \mathfrak{F}x(t, x \cong_{\Phi} \textbf{whole } \Phi) = p:q \dashv\vdash q \odot t \cong_{\Phi} p \odot \textbf{whole } \Phi$
Schema R $\quad \#_{\mathbf{D}}x(t, x \cong_{\mathbf{D}} \textbf{unit-of-D}) = r \dashv\vdash t \text{ is } r \text{ units-of-}\mathbf{D}\ \mathbf{D}^*$

We are talking here, of course, about commitment to there being numbers of the respective kind—natural, rational, or real. Thus Schema N, for the natural numbers, has a right-hand side that is non-committal about naturals; Schema Q, for the rational numbers, has a right-hand side that is non-committal about rationals; and Schema R, for the real numbers, has a right-hand side that (despite appearances) is non-committal about reals. The right-hand side of Schema Q, to be sure, presupposes the existence of the naturals; but that is fine, since the existence of naturals has already been secured. Schema Q and Schema R employ similar-looking abstraction operators on their left-hand sides, forming terms designed to reveal the applicability in measurement of the kinds of (dimensionless) number that they respectively serve to introduce. One might summarize this by saying that Schema Q and Schema R are methodologically akin. Note how analogous are their derivations using the respective—and analogous—introduction and elimination rules for their respective abstraction operators $\mathfrak{F}$ and $\#_{\mathbf{D}}$.

But it is with Schema N that Schema Q is ontologically akin. For both of these Schemas enable the thinker who grasps them to attain to their respective kinds of numbers (natural and rational) in purely logical fashion, without recourse to intuition.

It is in the latter respect that Schema R most importantly breaks the mold set by Schema N and Schema Q. As we shall presently see, the determinability-in-principle of its being the case that t is r units-of-**D D*** requires recourse to *a priori, geometric* intuition. The insight that this (i.e., t's being r units-of-**D D***) is indeed a possibility-in-principle is not vouchsafed by the understanding alone, on a purely logico-conceptual basis. That being said, however, we can point out that from there on, Schema R (using its right-to-left direction) enables the speaker to attain to the dimensionless reals without further ado—in the same way that Schema Q furnishes in the case of the (dimensionless) rationals.

There is a second respect in which Schema R breaks the mold set by Schema N and Schema Q. Note that Schema N has the numeral '$\underline{n}$' on its left-hand side, while the (metalinguistic) subscript 'n' occurring on its right-hand side does not function as a numerical term for the speaker of the object language. And Schema Q has the numerical term '$p : q$' (denoting a rational) on its left-hand side, while the numerical terms q and p (denoting naturals) occur separately on its right-hand side, where the speaker of the object language would take those terms as referring to naturals. Note now how different Schema R is from its predecessors in this regard: we see the numerical term 'r' occurring both on its left-hand side and on its right-hand side. This is unlike what happens with the preceding Schemas. As a placeholder for a completable-in-principle numerical representation—as we shall see, an infinite bicimal expansion—'r' on the right-hand side really appears in a context that should be regimented as

$$t \text{ is } r\odot\text{unit-of-}\mathbf{D}\ \mathbf{D}^*.$$

It is the latter thought for which a thorough methodological explication will be provided—a thought which, when grasped, invites the re-carving that yields the (real-)numerical identity

$$\#_{\mathbf{D}}x(t, x \cong_{\mathbf{D}} \textbf{unit-of-D}) = r$$

on the left-hand side, in which, finally, the numerical term 'r' is ontologically committal.

The third and final respect in which Schema R breaks the mold set by Schema N and Schema Q is one of considerable philosophical importance. Consider what is involved in determining that the right-hand side of any of these Schemas happens in a particular instance to be true. With Schema N and Schema Q one can find one's way to the truth of the statement in question by constructive means.

With Schema R, by contrast, one will have to resort to non-constructive means. This is because with instances of Schema R, the right-hand side's truth-value determinability (in principle) is based on the Law of Trichotomy for the ordering of points on a geometric line. We shall have reason to investigate more closely whether this makes our account of the reals irredeemably 'classical', or 'bivalent', or 'non-constructive' in the sense that would be troublesome to the traditional mathematical intuitionist or constructivist.

Let us return now to our examination of Schema R in particular. The question arises: Can we interpret Schema R as a conceptual postulate (albeit in schematic form), the truth of whose instances is immediately recognizable, and which gives us unfettered intellectual access to real numbers as dimensionless entities? It would seem that the only way to justify an affirmative answer would be to state Schema R in an appropriately generalized form, with universal quantification over the dimensions **D** involved. This would yield something like

$$(R^{\forall}) \qquad \forall\mathfrak{D}[\#_{\mathfrak{D}}x(t, x \cong_{\mathfrak{D}} \textbf{unit-of-}\mathfrak{D}) = r \;\dashv\vdash\; t \text{ is } r \text{ units-of-}\mathfrak{D}\ \mathfrak{D}^*].$$

We have no clear grasp, however, of the totality of eligible instantiations of the quantifier $\forall\mathfrak{D}$. What *is* a 'dimension', in general? And, once one has an intelligible answer to this question, how does one in general attain a grasp, for arbitrary instance **D**, of the crucial notions unit-of-**D**, **D***, $\#_{\mathbf{D}}$ and $\cong_{\mathbf{D}}$?

We stand in need here of a paradigm instance **D**. If we can find just one such—call it $\mathbb{D}$—for which the notions unit-of-$\mathbb{D}$, $\mathbb{D}^*$, $\#_{\mathbb{D}}$ and $\cong_{\mathbb{D}}$ are well understood, then we can accept as an adequacy condition on our account that it should yield all possible instances of the biconditional, or interdeducibility

$$\#_{\mathbb{D}}x(t, x \cong_{\mathbb{D}} \textbf{unit-of-}\mathbb{D}) = r \;\dashv\vdash\; t \text{ is } r \text{ units-of-}\mathbb{D}\ \mathbb{D}^*.$$

From the paradigm case $\mathbb{D}$ we could then proceed to widen our conception of dimension, by seeing further dimensions D as isomorphic to $\mathbb{D}$, by virtue of their analogues unit-of-D, D^*, $\#_D$ and $\cong_D$. Only then will we be in a position to appreciate the truth of the explicitly generalized form $(R^{\forall})$ of Schema R. (A caveat is needed here: we shall have to be mindful that there are some dimensions of measurement that involve only non-negative real numbers. But that poses no great problem in principle.)

We stand in need, therefore, of a paradigm instance of dimension, by comparison with which other dimensions will prove to be isomorphs. We cannot attain directly to a conception of the real numbers as logical objects, and simultaneously account for their applicability in measurement of various objects (line-segments; temporal periods; etc.) within the relevant dimension and in terms of the relevant unit.

The way to a full understanding of the reals is via their primary application, which is the measurement of spatial length. We seek, therefore, to elucidate the truth- or assertability-conditions of statements of the form

$$\#_{\mathbf{Length}}x(\sigma, x \cong_{\mathbf{Length}} \textbf{unit-of-length}) = r,$$

where σ is a line-segment. Because of the obvious equivalence already discussed, it suffices to elucidate the truth- or assertability-conditions of statements of the form

$$\mathbf{Length}(\sigma) = r\ \mathbf{units\text{-}of\text{-}length}.$$

We shall do this in a way that reveals how the values of r form a linearly ordered, uncountable continuum; and that allows the standard algebraic operations to be performed on them. By analogy with the case of length-measurement the pure or 'dimensionless' real numbers can also find application in measurement within other dimensions, with respect to appropriate units. All this can be done without begging any questions about the curvature of space, or the choice of Euclidean over non-Euclidean geometry. Provided only that one can make sense of bisecting a line-segment (locally), one will have all the geometric resources needed for the genesis of the reals. Details will emerge below.

It is in connection with measurement of spatial length that we seem to have our most subtly developed intuitions. We are familiar with how we can attain greater precision by the simple process of magnifying our view—coming closer to an object so that it seems larger, or re-positioning ourselves so as to get a better view of it. There is no analogue of this for temporal durations. We can measure and re-measure the length of a given line-segment—something we cannot do in the case of a fixed period of time. We have strongly developed intuitions concerning spatial orientation (left-right; up-down; front-back) and an origin of constant convenience (here). We can move around in space, and change our orientation, so that a line-segment previously regarded as running from left to right *this way* can later be regarded as so running *the other way*. We can check the straightness of any 'physical line' by looking along it (with one eye) from one end. An ideally straight line-segment would look like an infinitesimal speck in these circumstances. We can see, and confirm by touch, the minutest discrepancy in length (at least on a 'human scale') between any two objects. Moreover, our conventional unit-fixing standards exploit the reliable rigidity of certain physical objects. It is no accident that we speak, metaphorically, of yardsticks and of benchmarks whenever the measurement of human prowess or performance is in question.

In the course of human history, great accuracy was obtained in spatial measurements long before it was attained in the measurement of time. Indeed, every chronometric method we know of involves keeping track of positions or levels of things in space—the level of sand in an hourglass; the length of what remains of a burning candle; the angle at which a shadow is cast on a sundial; the motion of a pendulum, and the induced rotary motion of the hour- and minute-hands on a clockface. These may be quaintly dated examples to adduce, in this day and age, when we can keep track also of the natural resonance frequency of the cesium atom (9,192,631,770 Hz), which is the basis of the cesium fountain atomic clock of the National Institute of Standards and Technology. But even with these more sophisticated methods of keeping track of time, we have to resort, ultimately, to our ability to track things in space. Compare Russell [1897], at p. 78: 'Time, force, and mass are alike measured by *spatial* correlates ... .' [Emphasis added.] In the context of this quote, Russell meant 'measurable only by' when he wrote 'measured by'. Later, at p. 156, *ibid.*, when discussing how the notion of congruence finds no purchase in the case of temporal, as opposed to spatial, measurement, Russell went on to remark

> No day can be brought into temporal coincidence with any other day, to show that the two exactly cover each other; we are therefore reduced to the arbitrary assumption that some motion or set of motions, given us in experience, is uniform. Fortunately, we have a large set of motions which all roughly agree; the swing of the pendulum, the rotation and revolution of the earth and the planets, etc.

and on p. 176 he stresses once more that

> ... the absence of free Mobility in time ... renders direct measurement of time impossible.

Russell indeed concludes that only spatial quantity can have its magnitude directly measured. Toward the end of Chapter III, §B, 'The Axioms of Metrical Geometry', he concludes (pp. 176–177):

> ... infinite divisibility, free mobility, and homogeneity are necessary for the possibility of measurement in *any* continuous manifold, and these, as we have seen, are equivalent to our three axioms. These axioms are necessary, therefore, not only for spatial measurement, but for all measurement. *The only manifold given in experience, in which these conditions are satisfied, is space.* All other exact measurement—as could be proved, I believe, for every separate case—is effected, as we saw in the case of time, by reduction to a spatial correlative. [Second emphasis added.]

Mathematicians' realization that the real numbers are not only dense in their ordering but also continuous relied first and foremost on the application of real numbers in the measurement of lengths of Euclidean line segments. It was by appeal to Pythagoras's Theorem applied to the diagonal of a square that $\sqrt{2}$ was appreciated as needed for the measurement of the length of a line-segment in terms of the unit supplied by the side of the square.

That $\sqrt{2}$ is not a ratio of two whole numbers came as a subsequent surprise. Ironically, this negative result can be proved entirely within Peano Arithmetic, whose axioms can be derived by the constructive logicist and are made true by the natural numbers *qua* logical objects. The theorem of Peano Arithmetic in question can be proved from those axioms using only Core Logic:[6]

$$\neg\exists m \exists n\; m \times m = ss0 \times (n \times n).$$

It is hard to imagine, though, how any mensuration-based discovery of irrational real numbers would have taken place without the exercise of geometric intuition and understanding. How could it be discovered, through the needs of measurement, by a disembodied Cartesian soul inhabiting only the dimension of time? What could convince such a soul that there must be a real number such as $\sqrt{2}$? Contrast this with the situation of the Euclidean geometer inhabiting three-dimensional space, who knows what the basic method of length-measurement is—the laying-on-end of copies of a chosen unit of length—and who takes as an axiom that every line-segment has a unique length.

The contrast in the previous paragraph is between a being inhabiting space and time, and a being inhabiting only time, and what they are able to discover about the reals from the way they apply them in measurement. The Dedekindian arithmetizer could, of course, say on behalf of the disembodied Cartesian soul—call her Marie—that Marie could grasp that the *cut* of the rationals into the left class of those that are negative or have squares less than 2, and the right class consisting of all the rest, will 'give' Marie $\sqrt{2}$. Moreover, Marie will be able to understand the usual proof of the irrationality of $\sqrt{2}$. The problem for the Dedekindian, however, will then be to explain how Marie so much as attains to a prior use of the rationals, for (approximate) measurement of durations in terms of some unit of temporal duration. It is not enough for Dedekind simply to presume that the rationals are available, for cuts to be performed on them. The logico-geneticist who insists on the condition of adequacy concerning an account of applicability will not be content with the predictable Dedekindian 'creation' of the rationals as (say) ordered pairs of integers, or even equivalence classes thereof. For that is yet another structuralist ploy that leaves the question of applicability untouched, or at least makes any attempt to answer it an afterthought to be tacked on to the account, rather than built in to the very characterization of the rationals themselves—*if* they are to be 'created' *en route* to the reals, rather than be allowed simply to 'drop out' as reals with a particular property that can be remarked on only strictly after we have established our entitlement to the reals themselves.

In our conceptual construction of the reals, it will turn out that the operation of bisecting a line-segment or an angle is fundamental. These are Euclidean ruler-and-compass constructions in the spatial case. But how would a disembodied Cartesian soul inhabiting only the dimension of time set about bisecting a given period of time? Once the period is specified, its later endpoint will have

[6]This should not strike any contemporary foundationalist as a surprise. We know that all Π^0_2 theorems of (classical) Peano Arithmetic are theorems of (intuitionistic) Heyting Arithmetic, which is based on the very same axioms. Moreover, we know that any intuitionistic consequence of a consistent set of sentences is deducible from it in Core Logic.

elapsed, and the period would have vanished into the irretrievable past, in principle inaccessible to the would-be bisector, or determiner of its midpoint (or, rather, of its mid-instant). As we shall see, the possibility of carrying out bisections is fundamental to the simplest numerical system for representing real numbers: the 'bicimal' system, which uses only zeroes and ones.

It is no accident that mathematicians always think of the real-number system in terms of 'the real *line*', and that any trichotomous ordering of mathematical entities is called *linear*. We place enormous reliance on spatial intuition, at the initial and foundational level, when we engage in the mathematics of the real numbers, and real differential calculus. And even when the dimension of time is involved alongside spatial dimensions, we appeal to diagrams and graphs within which one spatial axis is treated as the temporal one.

The terminology of geometric length also infects our description of temporal duration. *Span* is first and foremost a geometric notion, as in the span of a bridge; but then we also talk of life*spans*. We talk of the *length of time* it takes to complete a task. Waits are *long* or *short*. We prefer to say *There comes a point when I will wait no longer*, rather than *There comes an instant when my wait will endure no more*. One is hard put to find any sustained discussion of temporal matters that is not shot through with expressions of geometric origin.

Chapter 22

Geometric Concepts and Axioms

Abstract

The focus here is on countably infinite sequences of points on a directed (or oriented) line. The sequences are of various kinds, characterized in terms of the underlying ordering relation $\blacktriangleleft$ among points. Thus one has sequences that are left- (or right-) limited; $\blacktriangleleft$-increasing (or decreasing); monotonic; strictly increasing (or decreasing) to a plateau; convergent to a given point; bisective; Cauchy .... These are all geometric sequences, not sequences of numbers. A stock of various geometrical concepts are defined in terms of $\blacktriangleleft$ that will enable one to formulate intuitively obvious axioms governing $\blacktriangleleft$, expressed by quantifying over points and segments. Important among these concepts are those of the nth left- and nth-right bisection points of a closed segment of an oriented line. Some of the axioms have obvious 'reflected' counterparts, in which 'right' is exchanged with 'left'. For all but four of these axioms, their right- and left-versions are equivalent. Continuity of the line is captured by the axioms stating the existence of left- and of right-limits for, respectively, $\blacktriangleleft$-increasing sequences that are right-limited, and $\blacktriangleleft$-decreasing sequences that are left-limited. This form of continuity is both simpler and more obvious than ones offered by Hilbert, Tarski, and analysts employing Cauchy sequences. Along with the property of Archimedean measure (which is logically derivable from simple axioms laid down here), the limit axioms ensure that any segment can be measured in terms of any other segment chosen as a unit. The chapter closes with proofs of various results about infinite subsequences of infinite sequences; and brings into focus an important kind of bisective sequence called a funnel sequence.

Any line L can be oriented in either one of just two opposite ways. Upon a chosen orientation, it can be determined, of any two distinct points x and y on L, whether x is to the left, or to the right, of y. We write $x \sqsubset L$ for 'x is on L' and $x \blacktriangleleft_L y$ for 'x is to the left of y on L'. Under the opposite orientation of L, all such determinations would be reversed. When L is understood from the context, we shall write $\blacktriangleleft$ in place of $\blacktriangleleft_L$.

The relation $\blacktriangleleft$ is one that obtains among points on a line, on a given left-right orientation. It is a geometric relation, not an arithmetical (or, more generally, number-theoretic) one. It is geometric twice over, as it were: first, its two arguments are geometric (they are points); second, how they stand in relation to each other is also geometric.

The Logic of Number. Neil Tennant, Oxford University Press. © Neil Tennant 2022.
DOI: 10.1093/oso/9780192846679.003.0022

A point z on the line determined by x and y lies *between* x and y just in case

if $x \blacktriangleleft y$, then both $x \blacktriangleleft z$ and $z \blacktriangleleft y$; and

if $y \blacktriangleleft x$, then both $y \blacktriangleleft z$ and $z \blacktriangleleft x$.

Let L be an oriented line, and let x and y be any two spatial points on L such that $x \blacktriangleleft y$. The points x and y determine the *closed line-segment* $[x, y]$. (We shall suppress the commas whenever we can.) The points lying on $[xy]$ are its *endpoints* x and y and all points on L that lie between x and y. The *open line-segment* (xy) consists of all points on L between x and y. The open segment (xy) is exactly as long as the closed segment $[xy]$, since the endpoints have no length. A closed segment τ is the *minimal closure* of an open segment σ just in case every point on σ is a point on τ, and every point on τ is a point on every closed segment that contains every point on σ. Degenerate segments of the form $[zz]$ are a special case, and are obviously *shorter than* any non-degenerate segment $[xy]$:

$$\forall x \forall y \forall z (x \blacktriangleleft y \rightarrow [zz] \lhd [xy]).$$

Here, $\lhd$ is the ordering relation 'is shorter than' on line-segments. Segments can stand in this relation to each other even when they are segments of different lines. When two segments σ and τ are exactly as long as each other, we write $\sigma \cong \tau$. Of course, all degenerate segments have the same length:

$$\forall x \forall y \ [xx] \cong [yy].$$

Any point's position on an (oriented) line L is determined by its predecessors under the relation $\blacktriangleleft$. We can express this as follows, where the quantifications are over points on L:

$$\forall x \forall y (x = y \leftrightarrow \forall z (z \blacktriangleleft x \leftrightarrow z \blacktriangleleft y)).$$

The same claim holds under reflection, that is, under change of orientation of the line. There are two ways to express the reflected version. We can use '$x \blacktriangleright y$' synonymously with '$y \blacktriangleleft x$', i.e., subject to the axiom

$$\forall x \forall y (x \blacktriangleright y \leftrightarrow y \blacktriangleleft x),$$

and write the reflected version as

$$\forall x \forall y (x = y \leftrightarrow \forall z (z \blacktriangleright x \leftrightarrow z \blacktriangleright y)).$$

Alternatively, we could stick with the original symbol $\blacktriangleleft$ and write

$$\forall x \forall y (x = y \leftrightarrow \forall z (x \blacktriangleleft z \leftrightarrow y \blacktriangleleft z)).$$

These last two claims are interdeducible *modulo* the axioms just stated.

It follows that there is exactly one minimal closure of an open segment (xy). It is obtained by adding the endpoints x and y to (xy), so as to obtain $[xy]$.

When we use the notation $[xy]$ to denote a segment on an oriented line, it is to be understood that (where the determination has been made) the point x is to the left of the point y. But there are occasions when such determination has not been made, or can be ignored. It is useful to have a notation that works in these cases. We shall use $\lfloor x, y \rfloor$ to denote the segment consisting of x, y and all points between x and y, without the presupposition that x is to the left of y. Thus $\lfloor x, y \rfloor$ really means

$$[min_{\blacktriangleleft}\{x, y\}, max_{\blacktriangleleft}\{x, y\}]$$

Here, $min_{\blacktriangleleft}\{x, y\}$ is defined as

$$\iota z((z = x \wedge x \blacktriangleleft y) \vee (z = y \wedge y \blacktriangleleft x)),$$

while $max_{\blacktriangleleft}\{x, y\}$ is likewise defined as

$$\iota z((z = x \wedge y \blacktriangleleft x) \vee (z = y \wedge x \blacktriangleleft y)).$$

Segments (open or closed) are ordered by the relation 'σ is longer than τ', which we shall abbreviate as $\tau \lhd \sigma$. The relation $\lhd$ is trichotomous: given any two segments σ and τ, exactly one of the following holds: $\sigma \lhd \tau$; $\tau \lhd \sigma$; or $\sigma \cong \tau$.

Suppose σ is a closed segment of an oriented line L. One can perform the operation of laying a copy of σ end-to-end on the line L, beginning at any point z of L. The operation is carried out to the right of z, so its result cannot be a point to the left of z. The point on L reached from z by iterating this operation n times is denoted

$$\Lambda(z, \sigma, n)$$

and is defined inductively as follows:

$$\Lambda(z, \sigma, 0) = z;$$

$$\Lambda(z, \sigma, n+1) \quad = \quad \iota w(\Lambda(z, \sigma, n) \blacktriangleleft_L w \ \wedge \ [\Lambda(z, \sigma, n), w] \cong \sigma).$$

The definite descriptive term on the right-hand side of this last identity is secured a denotation by the principle of **Segmental finitude** stated on p. 272.

In general, if n copies of σ are laid end-to-end and rightwards beginning at the point z, the result is a point v on L to the right of z such that $[zv]$ is exactly n times as long as σ:

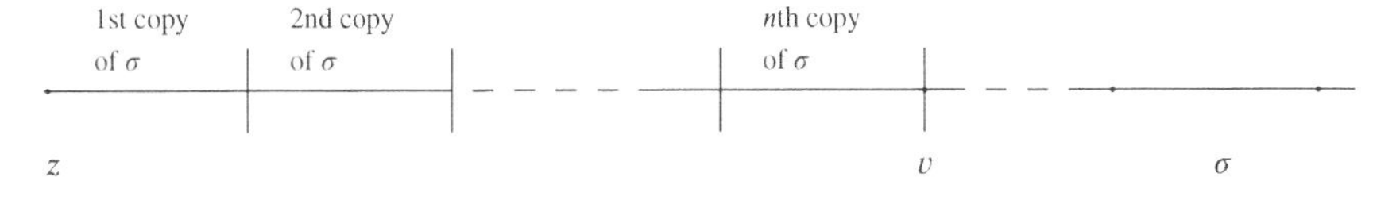

This point v is $\Lambda(z, \sigma, n)$.

Suppose that a unit of length has been determined. That is, we have chosen two distinct points a and b—it does not matter how 'close together' they might be—and have stipulated that the line-segment $[ab]$ is the unit of length.

The length—in terms of the chosen *unit* of length—of any line-segment $[xy]$ can in principle be determined, no matter how 'far apart' x and y might be. One uses the method just described of 'laying on end' copies of the unit segment, beginning (say) at the point x, taken to lie to the left of y. Some finite whole number n, say, of such copies will take one rightwards, on the line-segment $[xy]$, to some point z on $[xy]$ that lies within a unit length, and not to the right, of the point y.[1] The point z might be identical to y; if not, then z lies to the left of y. The number n might be 0:

If z coincides with y, then there is no residual segment $[zy]$ of any positive length. But if there is a residual segment $[zy]$ of positive length, then the unit segment will be longer than it. In this case, therefore, *the length of* $[zy]$ (which we have yet to define) will be some non-zero proportion ψ of the unit length $(0 < \psi < 1)$.

Here we are in partial agreement with Bigelow [1988], at p. 65:

> Real numbers are proportions: and that is why real numbers are entities of a completely different level from natural numbers.

Bigelow's second conjunct, however, would preclude a solution to the problem of identity under embeddings. And this is a problem that we are seeking to solve. That Bigelow does not seek to solve this problem is confirmed at p. 80, where he writes

> Eudoxus did not think of ratios or proportions as 'numbers'. On my account, they are indeed quite different sorts of things from the *natural numbers*. Yet proportions are, I claim, numbers of a different sort: real numbers.

We return to consider the case where the length of $[xy]$ is n units of length augmented by ψ units of length. Usually one suppresses the specification of the unit length, and says, less carefully, that the length of $[xy]$ 'is' the real number $n + \psi$. But we need to be mindful here of the unit in question. The length of $[xy]$ in our diagram is

n units of length $\oplus$ the proportion ψ of a unit of length.

[1] The intuitive and *a priori* truth being relied upon here is that the Euclidean line is Archimedean; and its being so will be secured in due course by the axiom of **Archimedean measure** on p. 278.

We are 'adding' *mensurated segments* here. That is why we use the unfamiliar but suggestive symbol $\oplus$ for this operation. It can be read as 'augmented by'. Note that the same result can be written as

$$(n + \text{the proportion } \psi) \text{ units of length,}$$

where the addition sign + has its usual sense, as addition of (dimensionless) numbers.

A *rational fraction* is a ratio of the form $\frac{p}{q}$ where p and q are natural numbers and $p < q$. There is no *a priori* reason to assume that *all proportions are rational fractions*. The *a priori* proof that the diagonal of a unit square has a length that exceeds the unit by an irrational fraction is conclusive justification for the *denial* of the italicized claim. It was only the unfounded Pythagorean dogma that 'the world is made out of whole numbers' that made the discovery of this proof a surprising one.

The role of the natural numbers n for the counting of finite collections has already been fixed. It suffices, therefore, to inquire after only how one might confer a sense on a sub-unit proportion like ψ, as a real number that lies strictly between 0 and 1. To repeat: not all proportions are rational fractions of the unit length.

The unit segment, once chosen, has its left endpoint conventionally labeled as 0, and its right endpoint conventionally labeled as 1. We shall be considering 'the' unit segment as containing 0 but not containing 1. So we shall denote it as $[0,1)$. We shall describe below how to determine ψ as a bicimal expansion for a certain point c within the unit segment. That point c is the unique point x within the unit segment such that $[0, x]$ is exactly as long as $[zy]$. (The reader is reminded of the diagram on p. 264.) The existence and uniqueness of c are guaranteed by the principle of **Segmental finitude** stated on p. 272. The bicimal expansion for c is generated by repeated bisections of ever shorter segments of the unit segment, chosen with an eye to the point c. We shall call the bicimal expansion in question $\mathfrak{b}(c)$. This bicimal expansion $\mathfrak{b}(c)$ is then taken as our numerical representation of the proportion ψ. In Chapter 23 we show how to construct bicimal expansions for geometric points lying in the unit interval.

Suppose that we are given a closed segment $[xy]$ on an oriented line, on which $x \blacktriangleleft y$. We define the nth *left-bisection point* of $[xy]$ inductively as follows:

$$B^{\blacktriangleleft}(0, [xy]) = y;$$

$$B^{\blacktriangleleft}(n+1, [xy]) = \text{ the midpoint of } [x, B^{\blacktriangleleft}(n, [xy])].$$

Abbreviate $B^{\blacktriangleleft}(n, [xy])$ as $^{n}[xy]$ The picture is then as follows.

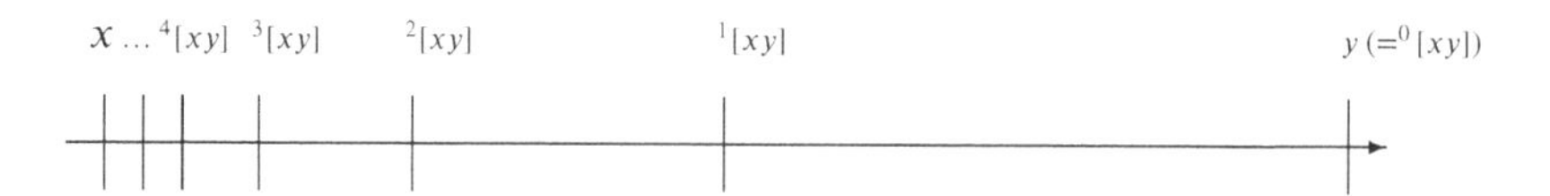

There is a corresponding definition of the nth *right-bisection point* of $[xy]$:

$$B^{\blacktriangleright}(0, [xy]) = x;$$

$$B^{\blacktriangleright}(n+1, [xy]) = \text{ the midpoint of } [B^{\blacktriangleright}(n, [xy]), y].$$

Abbreviate $B^{\blacktriangleright}(n, [xy])$ as $[xy]^n$. The picture is then as follows.

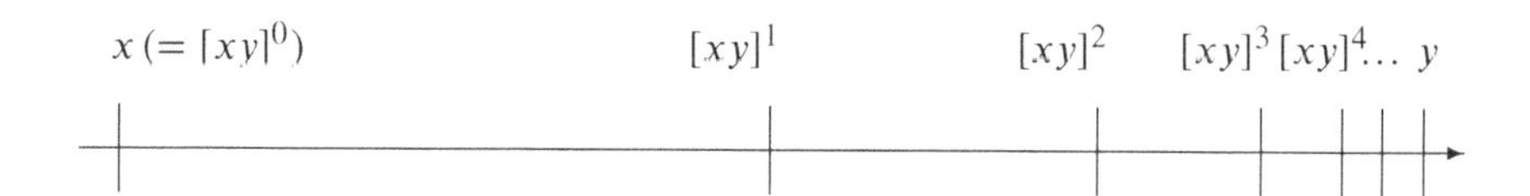

The midpoint of a line-segment σ is determined by a Euclidean ruler-and-compass construction:

> Taking in turn each endpoint of σ as center, draw a circle with radius exactly as long as σ. Draw the line-segment τ connecting the points of intersection of those two circles. The desired midpoint of σ is the point of intersection of τ with σ.

Note that the specification 'exactly as long' in this recipe for construction is not necessary; but it works. The radii of the circles must be longer than half of the segment σ. Indeed, one can use two intersecting arcs of the same radius on one side of σ, and another two intersecting arcs of a different radius on the other side of σ, provided only that both radii are longer than half of the segment σ.

We shall in due course state a principle of **Bisectability**: given a segment, and any point between its endpoints, we can get to the left of that point by 'bisecting the segment to the left' at most finitely many times. This of course has its 'reflected' companion: given a segment, and any point between its endpoints, we can get to the right of that point by 'bisecting the segment to the right' at most finitely many times.

An infinite sequence $\gamma_0, \gamma_1, \ldots$ of points on L can be treated as a mapping γ from natural numbers to points on L.

Such sequences are therefore countable, and their members are ordered (within the sequence), enjoying the order-type of the natural numbers in *their* natural ordering. Sequences afford a natural formalization of countable collections whose members are enumerated, or constucted, one by one in that natural order. In the case at hand, we shall be concentrating first and foremost on sequences of geometric points on a directed line. But of course in general the members of a sequence can be other kinds of object—perhaps even natural numbers. Later on we shall be considering also sequences whose members are certain kinds of slightly more complicated numerical representations. But for the time being, our focus will be on geometric points as members of our sequences.

Definition 11.
A sequence $\gamma_0, \gamma_1, \ldots$ *is* right-limited *just in case* $\exists c \forall n\ \gamma_n \blacktriangleleft c$.

Definition 12.
A sequence $\gamma_0, \gamma_1, \ldots$ *is* left-limited *just in case* $\exists c \forall n\ c \blacktriangleleft \gamma_n$.

Definition 13.
A sequence $\gamma_0, \gamma_1, \ldots$ *is* ($\blacktriangleleft$-)increasing
if and only if
$\forall n\ \gamma_n \blacktriangleleft \gamma_{n+1}$;
and it is ($\blacktriangleleft$-)decreasing
if and only if
$\forall n\ \gamma_{n+1} \blacktriangleleft \gamma_n$.[2]
Note that by 'increasing' we mean strictly *increasing; and similarly for 'decreasing'.*

We shall take as an intuitive starting point our ready appreciation of the fact that

> any infinite, right-limited, increasing sequence of points (on a directed line) has a **leftmost right limit point**—that is, a point to the right of all of them, such that any point to the left of **it** is to the left of one of them (hence also: to the left of all but finitely many of them).

The situation is very easy to visualize. Imagine a line running from your left to your right. Imagine an infinite sequence of points on this line, all of them to your left. Imagine that each point in the sequence is to the left of its immediate successor. It is then obvious—is it not?—that there is a point on the line, to the right of every point in the sequence, but such that any point to the left of it is to the left of some point (hence to the left of all subsequent points) in the sequence:

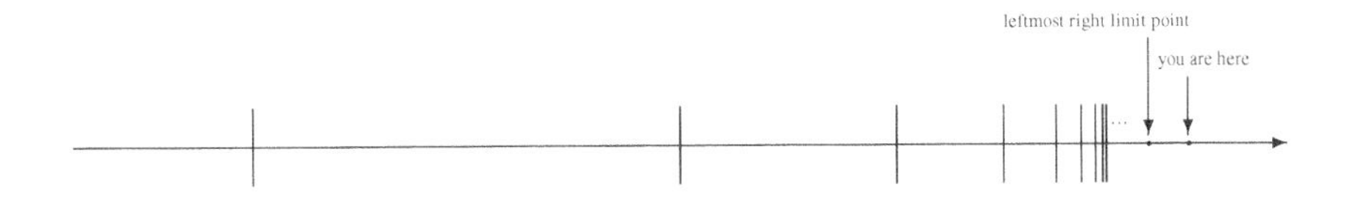

[2]Here we follow the terminology of Mendelson [1973], p. 216.

Anyone who understands the admittedly rather complex quantificational structure of this claim should grasp its truth immediately. Anyone who hesitates or fails to grasp its truth must do so because of their lack of mastery of the quantificational expressions, and not because they do not apprehend, intuitively, the continuity of a line. Given time and coaching, they should come to appreciate that what they intuitively apprehend does find precise expression in the quantified statement.

Our claim above that every infinite, right-limited, increasing sequence of points (on a directed line) has a leftmost right limit point would deserve to be classified by Huntington as an *axiom* rather than a *postulate*. Huntington [1902], in footnote (†) on p. 264, speaks of a 'usual distinction' (one, alas, of which logicians and mathematicians seem subsequently to have lost sight): he uses 'postulate' to mean 'a proposition the acceptance of which is demanded or agreed upon as a basis for future reasoning', and reserves 'axiom' to mean 'a *self-evident* proposition, requiring no formal demonstration to prove its truth, but *received and accepted as soon as mentioned*' (emphases added). Here, we relax slightly this latter demand, on Huntington's part, for such impressive intellectual alacrity. The reflections on meanings of expressions, and on intended abstract structures or interpretations, that may be called for before *a priori* insight into truth is attained, can require both time and coaching. The reader will find a foreshadowing of our geometric *axiom* in Huntington's fifth *postulate* (*loc. cit.*, p. 267) formulated in terms of his primitive binary operation $\circ$, in terms of which he defines the relation $<$.[3] This relation-symbol $<$ for Huntington, however, was not intended by him to represent the geometric relation '... is strictly to the left of ...' holding between points on a Euclidean line. His fifth postulate enjoys the same logical macro-structure as our axiom; and Huntington attributes his postulate to Weierstraß.[4]

The foregoing statement of (the existence of) leftmost right limits (for right-

[3]Huntington defines $a < b$ as short for $\exists y\, a \circ y = b$; and defines $a \leq b$ as short for $a < b \vee a = b$. He then expresses his fifth postulate as follows.

> If S is any infinite sequence of elements (a_k), such that
>
> $$a_k < a_{k+1},\ a_k < c \qquad (k = 1, 2, 3, \ldots)$$
>
> (where c is some fixed element), then there is one and only one element A having the following two properties:
>
> 1°) $a_k \leq A$ whenever a_k belongs to S;
>
> 2°) if y and A' are such that $y \circ A' = A$, then there is at least one element of S, say a_r, for which $A' < a_r$.

[4]Some other points of contrast with Huntington's postulates for 'absolute continuous magnitudes' are deserving of comment. Huntington was approaching the topic as an algebraist, and was concerned to provide a consistent, categorical set of postulates not necessarily aimed at characterizing ***geometric* continua.** His group-operation symbol $\circ$ admitted, for example, of interpretation as multiplication in the reals greater than 1 (*loc. cit.*, p. 268 *supra*). That it also admitted of interpretation as addition in the positive reals is neither here nor there. For, the former interpretation suffices to show that he was not (self-confessedly at least) aiming to express any intuition as to what the continuity of an oriented Euclidean line consists in. The latter aim, however, is absolutely central to our own account.

limited sequences) has its geometrically reflected companion:

> any infinite, left-limited, decreasing sequence of *points* (on a directed line) has a **rightmost left limit point**—that is, a point to the left of all of *them*, such that any point to the right of **it** is to the right of one of *them* (hence also: to the right of all but finitely many of *them*):

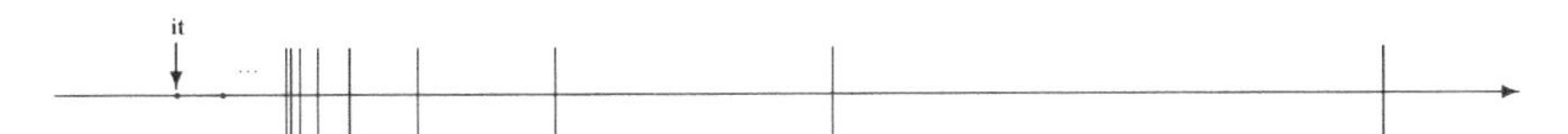

Note that right-limited strictly increasing and left-limited strictly decreasing sequences never attain their limits—that is, the limit point in question is distinct from each member of the sequence.

These intuitive starting points will be formalized below as the axioms **Right limits for ◀** and **Left limits for ◀**. They are, in the present author's view, the most succinct and obvious statements of the continuity of the geometric line.

The statement of **Right limits for ◀** says that every increasing and right-limited infinite sequence of points on L has a leftmost right limit point. As a geometric postulate, this would have been intuitively acceptable to Euclid had he been asked to reflect on it. And it was certainly implicit in Eudoxus's and Archimedes's method of exhaustion. The same holds for the corresponding statement of **Left limits for ◀**, which says that every decreasing and left-limited infinite sequence of points on L has a rightmost left limit point. We have chosen our expressions of continuity so as to render continuity obvious and intuitive.

Contrast this with the approach of Forster [2001], whose **Vollständigkeits-Axiom** (p. 41) is to the effect that in the system of real numbers every Cauchy-sequence converges. As Forster then immediately concedes, this axiom 'ist nicht besonders anschaulich' ('is not very intuitive').

The reader will recall Dedekind's foundational thought above:

> *jede Größe, welche beständig, aber nicht über alle Grenzen wächst, muß sich gewiß einem Grenzwert nähern* ... .
>
> every quantity that grows constantly, but does not do so beyond all limits, must certainly approach a limiting value ... .

This thought is exactly captured by **Right limits for ◀**. And, as Dedekind rightly surmised,

> *dieser... Satz kann gewissermaßen als ein hinreichendes Fundament für die Infinitesimalanalysis angesehen werden.*
>
> this statement can certainly be regarded as a sufficient foundation for infinitesimal analysis.

For the 'non-strict' cases we have the following terminology. A sequence $\gamma_0, \gamma_1, \ldots$ is said to be ($\blacktriangleleft$-)*non-decreasing* if and only if for all n, either γ_n coincides with γ_{n+1} or $\gamma_n \blacktriangleleft \gamma_{n+1}$; and it is ($\blacktriangleleft$-)*non-increasing* if and only if for all n, either γ_n coincides with γ_{n+1} or $\gamma_{n+1} \blacktriangleleft \gamma_n$. A sequence is *monotonic* if and only if it is either non-decreasing or non-increasing.

For non-decreasing but right-limited sequences we have the following close analogue of the axiom **Right limits for $\blacktriangleleft$**. The changes are marked by underlining:

> *any infinite, non-decreasing sequence of points (on a directed line) all to the left of some point has a right limit point—that is, a point not to the left of any of* them, *such that any point to the left of* it *is to the left of one of* them *(hence also: to the left of all but finitely many of* them*).*

Likewise, for non-increasing but left-limited sequences we have the following close analogue of the axiom **Left limits for $\blacktriangleleft$**:

> *any infinite, non-increasing sequence of points (on a directed line) all to the right of some point has a left limit point—that is, a point not to the right of any of* them, *such that any point to the right of* it *is to the right of one of* them *(hence also: to the right of all but finitely many of* them*).*

We have certain clear and distinct intuitions about points, lines, segments and the relations $\blacktriangleleft$ and $\lhd$, which can be captured by certain axioms, to be stated below. These axioms aim to convey a clear and determinate idea of the structure of a Euclidean straight line, rather than the geometric structure of the Euclidean plane or of Euclidean three-dimensional space. The choice of primitive concepts for the framing of these axioms is perhaps novel. From our logico-geneticist point of view, we help ourselves to the countably infinite progression of the ('standard') natural numbers, presumed to be secured by an antecedent logicist characterization, and therefore available for the characterization of infinite sequences of points on a line. Certain important axioms below provide for the existence, on the line, of limit-points for certain infinite sequences of points satisfying appropriate conditions. This idea would not have been novel or foreign to Euclid himself.

These 'limit axioms' are not employed by Hilbert [1899], in his famous re-axiomatization of Euclidean geometry. Hilbert employed instead, as his continuity condition, a maximality principle that is not even framed in the object-language of the geometrical theorizing at hand. Rather, it is a sort of model-theoretic comment—at best formalizable in the metalanguage, or at second-order—on the range of admissible interpretations of the remaining axioms (which aim to characterize features of the space other than its continuity). In Hilbert [1950] at p. 15, it is rendered thus:

> Axiom of Completeness.[fn] (*Vollständigkeit*): To a system of points, straight lines, and planes, it is impossible to add other elements in such a manner that the system thus generalized shall form a new geometry obeying all of the five groups of axioms. In other words, the elements of geometry form a system which is not susceptible of extension, if we regard the five groups of axioms as valid.

The ∀∃-re-axiomatization of 2-D and 3-D Euclidean geometry by Tarski [1959] also eschewed these 'limit axioms'. Tarski exploited the primitives of *point*, *betweenness*, and *congruence* (of segments, i.e., of pairs of points). Importantly, Tarski sought to capture continuity (at first order) by means of an axiom schema involving two schematic letters Φ and Ψ. The schema in effect expresses Dedekind's cut principle for points on the line (compare our discussion on p. 206), with the 'left class' consisting of the points satisfying Φ, and the 'right class' consisting of the points satisfying Ψ.

With these remarks about possible precursors by way of preparatory background, we proceed now to offer our own direct axiomatization of *a priori*, directly intuited, geometric properties of the Euclidean line.

The quantifications using the variables x, y, z and w are over the points on an oriented line L. The quantifications using the variables ρ, σ, τ and ω are over closed segments of L.

When we use the notation $[xy]$ to denote a segment on an oriented line, it is to be understood that (where the determination has been made) the point x is to the left of the point y. But there are occasions when such determination has not been made, or can be ignored. It is useful to have a notation that works in these cases. Recall the one we introduced on p. 263. We use $\lfloor x, y \rfloor$ to denote the segment consisting of x, y and all points between x and y, without the presupposition that x is to the left of y.

Segments (open or closed) are ordered by the relation 'σ is longer than τ', which we are regimenting as $\tau \lhd \sigma$. The relation $\lhd$ is trichotomous: given any two segments σ and τ, exactly one of the following holds: $\sigma \lhd \tau$; $\tau \lhd \sigma$; or $\sigma \cong \tau$.

The 'uniqueness quantifier' $\exists_1$ is defined as follows (for φ with x free and at none of its free occurrences within the scope of a quantifier prefix involving the variable y):

$$\exists_1 x\, \varphi \equiv_{df} \exists x(\forall y(x = y \leftrightarrow \varphi^x_y))$$

Here now (and at long last) are *our* axioms governing the geometric notions that we are taking as primitive, or have rigorously defined. Remember that these axioms concern only points on a given (directed, or oriented) geometric *line*. We can come to know they are true *a priori*, by both reflecting on their logical structure (for whose precise articulation the neo-Euclidean owes thanks to Weierstraß) and by exercising our pure (Kantian) spatial intuition.

Anti-symmetry of ◀	$\forall x \forall y(x \blacktriangleleft y \rightarrow \neg\, y \blacktriangleleft x)$.
Transitivity of ◀	$\forall x \forall y \forall z((x \blacktriangleleft y \wedge y \blacktriangleleft z) \rightarrow x \blacktriangleleft z))$.

Trichotomy of $\blacktriangleleft$	$\forall x \forall y(x = y \vee (x \blacktriangleleft y \vee y \blacktriangleleft x))$.
Density of $\blacktriangleleft$	$\forall x \forall y(x \blacktriangleleft y \rightarrow \exists z(x \blacktriangleleft z \wedge z \blacktriangleleft y))$.
Right unboundedness of $\blacktriangleleft$	$\forall x \forall y(x \blacktriangleleft y \rightarrow \forall z \exists_1 w(z \blacktriangleleft w \wedge [zw] \cong [xy]))$.
Right limits for $\blacktriangleleft$	$\forall \gamma : \mathbb{N} \mapsto L\, [((\forall n\, \gamma_n \blacktriangleleft \gamma_{n+1}) \wedge \exists x \forall n\, \gamma_n \blacktriangleleft x) \rightarrow$ $\exists y(\forall n\, \gamma_n \blacktriangleleft y \wedge \forall z(z \blacktriangleleft y \rightarrow \exists n\, z \blacktriangleleft \gamma_n))]$.
Segmental finitude right	$\forall x \forall \sigma \exists_1 y(x \blacktriangleleft y \wedge [xy] \cong \sigma)$.
Bisectability left	$\forall x \forall y \forall z((x \blacktriangleleft y \wedge y \blacktriangleleft z) \rightarrow \exists n B^{\blacktriangleleft}(n, [xz]) \blacktriangleleft y)$.
Reflexivity of $\cong$	$\forall \rho\, \rho \cong \rho$.
Symmetry of $\cong$	$\forall \rho \forall \sigma(\rho \cong \sigma \rightarrow \sigma \cong \rho)$.
Transitivity of $\cong$	$\forall \rho \forall \sigma \forall \tau((\rho \cong \sigma \wedge \sigma \cong \tau) \rightarrow \rho \cong \tau)$.
Anti-symmetry of $\lhd$	$\forall \rho \forall \sigma(\rho \lhd \sigma \rightarrow \neg \sigma \lhd \rho)$.
Discrepancy for $\lhd$	$\forall \rho \forall \sigma(\rho \lhd \sigma \rightarrow \neg \sigma \cong \rho)$.
Transitivity of $\lhd$	$\forall \rho \forall \sigma \forall \tau((\rho \lhd \sigma \wedge \sigma \lhd \tau) \rightarrow \rho \lhd \tau)$.
Trichotomy of $\lhd$	$\forall \rho \forall \sigma(\rho \cong \sigma \vee (\rho \lhd \sigma \vee \sigma \lhd \rho))$.
Density of $\lhd$	$\forall \rho \forall \sigma(\rho \lhd \sigma \rightarrow \exists \tau(\rho \lhd \tau \wedge \tau \lhd \sigma))$.
Null case for $\lhd$	$\forall x \forall y\, [xx] \cong [yy]$.
Minima for $\lhd$	$\forall x \forall \rho\, ([xx] \cong \rho \vee [xx] \lhd \rho)$.
Segmental distinction	$\forall x \forall y \forall z((x \blacktriangleleft y \wedge y \blacktriangleleft z) \rightarrow [yz] \lhd [xz])$.
	$\forall x \forall y \forall z((x \blacktriangleleft y \wedge y \blacktriangleleft z) \rightarrow [xy] \lhd [xz])$.

Inferentialist digression (rendering the Axiom of Right Limits inferentially).

Definition 14. *Nt means 't is a natural number'.*

Definition 15. $\blacktriangleleft$ *is the left-right linear ordering of the points on a left-right directed geometric line. Thus one may read '$x \blacktriangleleft y$' as 'the point x is to the left of the point y'.*

The axiom of **Trichotomy** for the ordering relation $\blacktriangleleft$ may be expressed inferentially as follows:

$$\dfrac{\begin{array}{c}\overline{u \blacktriangleleft v}^{(i)} \\ \vdots \\ \bot/\psi\end{array} \quad \begin{array}{c}\overline{u = v}^{(i)} \\ \vdots \\ \bot/\psi\end{array} \quad \begin{array}{c}\overline{v \blacktriangleleft u}^{(i)} \\ \vdots \\ \bot/\psi\end{array}}{\bot/\psi}{\scriptstyle (i)} \; .$$

When this rule is applied, the conclusion is the sentence ψ if at least one of the three subconclusions is ψ; otherwise, it is $\bot$.

The axiom of **Anti-symmetry** for the ordering relation $\blacktriangleleft$ may be expressed inferentially as follows:

$$\frac{u \blacktriangleleft v \quad v \blacktriangleleft u}{\bot} \; .$$

Throughout this discussion, γ will be a mapping from the natural numbers to points on a left-right directed geometric line. It determines a countably infinite sequence of points

$$\gamma(0), \gamma(1), \gamma(2), \ldots ,$$

which we shall render in the conventional way as

$$\gamma_0, \gamma_1, \gamma_2, \cdots .$$

The enumeration of points γ_i need not (for the time being, at least) respect any constraints in terms of the ordering $\blacktriangleleft$. The line will be assumed fixed for the rest of the discussion.

A useful pasigraph is

$$\blacktriangleleft\!|x(\gamma_x, u),$$

meaning that the sequence γ is bounded to the right by the point u. Its introduction rule is

$$\blacktriangleleft\!|\text{-I} \qquad \dfrac{\begin{array}{c}\overline{Na}^{(i)}\\ \vdots \\ \gamma_a \blacktriangleleft u\end{array}}{\blacktriangleleft\!|x(\gamma_x, u)}{}^{(i)} \qquad \text{where } a \text{ is parametric} ,$$

to which there corresponds the following elimination rule:

$$\blacktriangleleft\!|\text{-E} \qquad \dfrac{\blacktriangleleft\!|x(\gamma_x, u) \quad Nt}{\gamma_t \blacktriangleleft u} .$$

Observation 1. *The inference* $\dfrac{\blacktriangleleft\!|x(\gamma_x, u)}{\exists! u}$ *is derivable:*

$$\dfrac{\dfrac{\blacktriangleleft\!|x(\gamma_x, u) \quad \overline{N0}}{\gamma_0 \blacktriangleleft u}}{\exists! u} .$$

A second useful pasigraph is the one that will encode 'the sequence γ gets to the right of the point t (on the line)':

$$\vec{\blacktriangleleft}\, x(\gamma_x, t) .$$

Its introduction rule is

$$\vec{\blacktriangleleft}\text{-I} \qquad \dfrac{Nu \quad t \blacktriangleleft \gamma_u}{\vec{\blacktriangleleft}\, x(\gamma_x, t)} ,$$

to which there corresponds the following elimination rule:

$$\vec{\blacktriangleleft}\text{-E} \qquad \dfrac{\vec{\blacktriangleleft}\, x(\gamma_x, t) \qquad \begin{matrix} \underbrace{\overline{Na}^{\,(i)} \ , \ \overline{t \blacktriangleleft \gamma_a}^{\,(i)}} \\ \vdots \\ \theta \end{matrix}}{\theta}{\scriptstyle (i)} \qquad \text{where } a \text{ is parametric} \ .$$

Observation 2. *The inference* $\dfrac{\vec{\blacktriangleleft}\, x(\gamma_x, u)}{\exists! u}$ *is derivable:*

$$\dfrac{\vec{\blacktriangleleft}\, x(\gamma_x, t) \qquad \dfrac{\overline{u \blacktriangleleft \gamma_a}^{\,(1)}}{\exists! u}}{\exists! u}{\scriptstyle (1)} \ .$$

Lemma 41. $\dfrac{\vec{\blacktriangleleft}\, x(\gamma_x, u) \qquad \blacktriangleleft\!\mid x(\gamma_x, u)}{\bot}$.

Proof.

$$\dfrac{\vec{\blacktriangleleft}\, x(\gamma_x, u) \qquad \dfrac{\dfrac{\blacktriangleleft\!\mid x(\gamma_x, u) \qquad \overline{Na}^{\,(1)}}{\gamma_a \blacktriangleleft u}{\scriptstyle \blacktriangleleft\mid\text{-E}} \qquad \overline{u \blacktriangleleft \gamma_a}^{\,(1)}}{\bot}}{\bot}{\scriptstyle (1)\ \vec{\blacktriangleleft}\text{-E}}$$

□

A third useful pasigraph is

$$\overset{\rightsquigarrow}{\blacktriangleleft}\, x(\gamma_x, t) ,$$

which will encode 'the sequence γ gets arbitrarily close from the left to the point t (on the line)'—that is, 'the sequence γ gets to the right of any point to the left of t':

Its introduction rule is

$$\overset{\rightsquigarrow}{\blacktriangleleft}\text{-I} \qquad \dfrac{\exists! t \qquad \begin{matrix} \overline{a \blacktriangleleft t}^{\,(i)} \\ \vdots \\ \vec{\blacktriangleleft}\, x(\gamma_x, a) \end{matrix}}{\overset{\rightsquigarrow}{\blacktriangleleft}\, x(\gamma_x, t)}{\scriptstyle (i)} \qquad \text{where } a \text{ is parametric} \ ,$$

to which there corresponds the following two-part elimination rule:

$$\overset{\rightsquigarrow}{\blacktriangleleft}\text{-E} \qquad \dfrac{\overset{\rightsquigarrow}{\blacktriangleleft}\, x(\gamma_x, t) \qquad u \blacktriangleleft t}{\vec{\blacktriangleleft}\, x(\gamma_x, u)} \qquad \dfrac{\overset{\rightsquigarrow}{\blacktriangleleft}\, x(\gamma_x, t)}{\exists! t} \ .$$

Lemma 42. $$\frac{u \blacktriangleleft v \quad \blacktriangleleft\!|\, x(\gamma_x, u) \quad \overset{\rightsquigarrow}{\blacktriangleleft}\, x(\gamma_x, v)}{\bot}$$

Proof.
$$\cfrac{\cfrac{\overset{\rightsquigarrow}{\blacktriangleleft}\, x(\gamma_x, v) \quad u \blacktriangleleft v}{\overset{\rightarrow}{\blacktriangleleft}\, x(\gamma_x, u)}\,\overset{\rightsquigarrow}{\blacktriangleleft}\text{-E} \qquad \blacktriangleleft\!|\, x(\gamma_x, u)}{\bot}\,\text{L41}$$

□

Theorem 1. $$\frac{\blacktriangleleft\!|\, x(\gamma_x, u) \quad \overset{\rightsquigarrow}{\blacktriangleleft}\, x(\gamma_x, v) \quad \blacktriangleleft\!|\, x(\gamma_x, v) \quad \overset{\rightsquigarrow}{\blacktriangleleft}\, x(\gamma_x, u)}{u = v}$$

Proof. Suppose, first, that $u \blacktriangleleft v$. Lemma 42 tells us that that supposition, with the first two of the four premises above, leads to absurdity. Suppose, second, that, that $v \blacktriangleleft u$. Lemma 42 tells us that that supposition, with the last two of the four premises above, leads to absurdity. By **Trichotomy** of $\blacktriangleleft$ it now follows from those four premises that $u = v$. Formally:

$$\cfrac{\cfrac{\overset{(1)}{\overline{u \blacktriangleleft v}} \quad \blacktriangleleft\!|\, x(\gamma_x, u) \quad \overset{\rightsquigarrow}{\blacktriangleleft}\, x(\gamma_x, v)}{\bot}\,\text{L42} \qquad \cfrac{}{u = v}\,(1) \qquad \cfrac{\overset{(1)}{\overline{v \blacktriangleleft u}} \quad \blacktriangleleft\!|\, x(\gamma_x, v) \quad \overset{\rightsquigarrow}{\blacktriangleleft}\, x(\gamma_x, u)}{\bot}\,\text{L42}}{u = v}\,(1)$$

□

Theorem 1 guarantees the *uniqueness* of any point t satisfying the two conditions

$$\blacktriangleleft\!|\, x(\gamma_x, t) \;\text{ and }\; \overset{\rightsquigarrow}{\blacktriangleleft}\, x(\gamma_x, t)\,,$$

if such t should exist. We shall in due course formulate a simple condition on γ that will make the *existence* of such t intuitively self-evident.

Let us now introduce our key pasigraph, a variable-binding one that forms singular terms from functional ones:

$$\Lambda x \gamma_x\,.$$

This is to be understood (when it denotes) as 'the leftmost right limit point of the sequence γ'. Its introduction rule tells one how to infer a canonical identity statement with this pasigraphic term on one side:

$$\Lambda\text{-I} \qquad \frac{\blacktriangleleft\!|\, x(\gamma_x, t) \quad \overset{\rightsquigarrow}{\blacktriangleleft}\, x(\gamma_x, t)}{t = \Lambda x \gamma_x}\,,$$

to which there corresponds the following two-part elimination rule:

$$\Lambda\text{-E}_1 \qquad \frac{t = \Lambda x \gamma_x}{\blacktriangleleft\!|\, x(\gamma_x, t)} \qquad\qquad \Lambda\text{-E}_2 \qquad \frac{t = \Lambda x \gamma_x}{\overset{\rightsquigarrow}{\blacktriangleleft}\, x(\gamma_x, t)}\,.$$

Let us see now what the existence of $\Lambda x\gamma_x$ secures.

Theorem 2. $\dfrac{\exists!\Lambda x\gamma_x}{\blacktriangleleft\!|\,x(\gamma_x,\Lambda x\gamma_x)}$ $\qquad$ $\dfrac{\exists!\Lambda x\gamma_x}{\overset{\leadsto}{\blacktriangleleft}\,x(\gamma_x,\Lambda x\gamma_x)}$

Proof.

$$\dfrac{\exists!\Lambda x\gamma_x \qquad \dfrac{\dfrac{\dfrac{}{a=\Lambda x\gamma_x}{\scriptstyle(1)}}{\blacktriangleleft\!|\,x(\gamma_x,a)} \qquad \dfrac{}{a=\Lambda x\gamma_x}{\scriptstyle(1)}}{\blacktriangleleft\!|\,x(\gamma_x,\Lambda x\gamma_x)}}{\blacktriangleleft\!|\,x(\gamma_x,\Lambda x\gamma_x)}{\scriptstyle(1)} \qquad \dfrac{\exists!\Lambda x\gamma_x \qquad \dfrac{\dfrac{\dfrac{}{a=\Lambda x\gamma_x}{\scriptstyle(1)}}{\overset{\leadsto}{\blacktriangleleft}\,x(\gamma_x,a)} \qquad \dfrac{}{a=\Lambda x\gamma_x}{\scriptstyle(1)}}{\overset{\leadsto}{\blacktriangleleft}\,x(\gamma_x,\Lambda x\gamma_x)}}{\overset{\leadsto}{\blacktriangleleft}\,x(\gamma_x,\Lambda x\gamma_x)}{\scriptstyle(1)}$$

□

We promised a simple condition on γ that would make the existence of its left-most right limit $\Lambda x\gamma_x$ intuitively self-evident. To this end we now furnish the pasigraph

$$\blacktriangleleft x\,\gamma_x$$

to mean that γ is strictly increasing. It is governed by the following introduction rule:

$$\blacktriangleleft\text{-I} \qquad \dfrac{\begin{array}{c}\dfrac{}{Na}{\scriptstyle(i)}\\ \vdots \\ \gamma_a \blacktriangleleft \gamma_{a+1}\end{array}}{\blacktriangleleft x\,\gamma_x}{\scriptstyle(i)} \qquad \text{where } a \text{ is parametric} \;,$$

to which there corresponds the following elimination rule:

$$\blacktriangleleft\text{-E} \qquad \dfrac{\blacktriangleleft x\,\gamma_x \quad Nt}{\gamma_t \blacktriangleleft \gamma_{t+1}} \;.$$

The axiom **Right Limits for** $\blacktriangleleft$ can now be stated inferentially as follows:

$$\dfrac{\blacktriangleleft x\,\gamma_x \quad \blacktriangleleft\!|\,x(\gamma_x,u)}{\exists!\Lambda x\gamma_x} \;.$$

Note that the supposition $\blacktriangleleft x\,\gamma_x$ makes this axiom, intuitively, utterly compelling: any *strictly increasing* sequence of points $\gamma_0 \blacktriangleleft \gamma_1 \blacktriangleleft \gamma_2 \blacktriangleleft \ldots$, all of which lie to the left of some bound u, has a left-most bound, which we denote by $\Lambda x\gamma_x$.

Corollary 1. $\dfrac{\blacktriangleleft x\,\gamma_x \quad \blacktriangleleft\!|\,x(\gamma_x,u)}{\overset{\leadsto}{\blacktriangleleft}\,x(\gamma_x,\Lambda x\gamma_x)}$.

Proof. By **Right Limits for** $\blacktriangleleft$ and Theorem 2. □

End of inferentialist digression

Let us return now to the conventional axiomatic way of doing things. Corresponding to each axiom above involving the black- and/or white-triangular relational expressions $\blacktriangleleft$ and $\lhd$—except for **Null case for** $\lhd$ and **Minima for** $\lhd$—is its *left-right reflection*, which results from replacing $\blacktriangleleft$ and $\lhd$ with the reversed symbols $\blacktriangleright$ and $\rhd$ respectively:

Anti-symmetry of $\blacktriangleright$	$\forall x \forall y(x \blacktriangleright y \rightarrow \neg\, y \blacktriangleright x)$.
Transitivity of $\blacktriangleright$	$\forall x \forall y \forall z((x \blacktriangleright y \wedge y \blacktriangleright z) \rightarrow x \blacktriangleright z))$.
Trichotomy of $\blacktriangleright$	$\forall x \forall y(x = y \vee (x \blacktriangleright y \vee y \blacktriangleright x))$.
Density of $\blacktriangleright$	$\forall x \forall y(x \blacktriangleright y \rightarrow \exists z(x \blacktriangleright z \wedge z \blacktriangleright y))$.
Left unboundedness of $\blacktriangleright$	$\forall x \forall y(x \blacktriangleright y \rightarrow \forall z \exists_1 w(z \blacktriangleright w \wedge [zw] \cong [xy]))$.
Left limits for $\blacktriangleright$	$\forall \gamma : \mathbb{N} \mapsto L[((\forall n\, \gamma_n \blacktriangleright \gamma_{n+1}) \wedge \exists x \forall n\, \gamma_n \blacktriangleright x) \rightarrow$ $\exists y(\forall n\, \gamma_n \blacktriangleright y \wedge \forall z(z \blacktriangleright y \rightarrow \exists n\, z \blacktriangleright \gamma_n))]$.
Segmental finitude left	$\forall x \forall \sigma \exists_1 y(x \blacktriangleright y \wedge [xy] \cong \sigma)$.
Bisectability right	$\forall x \forall y \forall z((x \blacktriangleright y \wedge y \blacktriangleright z) \rightarrow \exists n B^{\blacktriangleright}(n, [xz]) \blacktriangleright y)$.
Anti-symmetry of $\rhd$	$\forall \rho \forall \sigma(\rho \rhd \sigma \rightarrow \neg \sigma \rhd \rho)$.
Discrepancy for $\rhd$	$\forall \rho \forall \sigma(\rho \rhd \sigma \rightarrow \neg \sigma \cong \rho)$.
Transitivity of $\rhd$	$\forall \rho \forall \sigma \forall \tau((\rho \rhd \sigma \wedge \sigma \rhd \tau) \rightarrow \rho \rhd \tau)$.
Trichotomy of $\rhd$	$\forall \rho \forall \sigma(\rho \cong \sigma \vee (\rho \rhd \sigma \vee \sigma \rhd \rho))$.
Density of $\rhd$	$\forall \rho \forall \sigma(\rho \rhd \sigma \rightarrow \exists \tau(\rho \rhd \tau \wedge \tau \rhd \sigma))$.
Segmental distinction	$\forall x \forall y \forall z((x \blacktriangleright y \wedge y \blacktriangleright z) \rightarrow [yz] \rhd [xz])$.
	$\forall x \forall y \forall z((x \blacktriangleright y \wedge y \blacktriangleright z) \rightarrow [xy] \rhd [xz])$.

The reader can verify that this replacement results, in several cases, in a new axiom that is equivalent to the old one, *modulo* one or both of the meaning postulates

$$\forall x \forall y\; (x \blacktriangleleft y \leftrightarrow y \blacktriangleright x);$$

$$\forall \rho \forall \sigma\; (\rho \lhd \sigma \leftrightarrow \sigma \rhd \rho).$$

But with four of our axioms, this is not the case. The right- and left-versions of **Unboundedness**, **Limits**, **Segmental finitude** and **Bisectability** are not, respectively, equivalent to one another. So the process of left-right reflection in generating axioms is needed in order to obtain a set of axioms that characterizes the geometric line in such a way as to ensure that its internal structure is essentially the same regardless of its left-right orientation.

Lemma 43. $\dfrac{t \blacktriangleleft u \quad u \blacktriangleleft v \quad v \blacktriangleleft w}{[uv] \lhd [tw]}$

Proof. By two applications of **Segmental distinction** and one of **Transitivity of** $\lhd$. □

Lemma 44. $$\frac{[tw]\cong[uw] \qquad t\blacktriangleleft w \qquad u\blacktriangleleft w}{t=u}$$

Proof. By the uniqueness provision of **Segmental finitude**. □

Lemma 45. $$\frac{t\blacktriangleleft u \qquad t\blacktriangleleft v \qquad u\blacktriangleleft w \qquad [tv]\cong[uw]}{v\blacktriangleleft w}$$

Proof. We need to rule out the possibility that $v = w$ and the possibility that $w\blacktriangleleft v$. Then by **Trichotomy of $\blacktriangleleft$** we shall have our result. The *reductio* of the assumption $v = w$ is as follows:

$$\dfrac{\dfrac{\dfrac{[tv]\cong[uw] \quad v=w}{[tw]\cong[uw]} \qquad \dfrac{t\blacktriangleleft v \quad v=w}{t\blacktriangleleft w} \qquad u\blacktriangleleft w}{t=u}\,\text{L44} \qquad t\blacktriangleleft u}{\bot}$$

The *reductio* of the assumption $w\blacktriangleleft v$ is as follows:

$$\dfrac{\dfrac{t\blacktriangleleft u \quad u\blacktriangleleft w \quad w\blacktriangleleft v}{[uw]\lhd[tv]}\,\text{L43} \qquad [tv]\cong[uw]}{\bot}$$

where the last step is by **Discrepancy**. □

The statement of **Archimedean measure for $\blacktriangleleft$** says that any segment $[xy]$ can, beginning at the point x, and with an eye to any point z to the right of x, be laid rightwards, end-to-end, finitely many times—say, n times, so as to reach a point (namely $\Lambda(x,[xy],n)$) which lies to the right of z. No point can be more than finitely many copies of a given segment away from a given point, no matter how short the given segment may be.

Digression. The continuity of the Euclidean line is not grasped by way of generalizing from empirical experience. Rather, it is appreciated both imaginatively and *a priori*, and helps to constitute our empirical experience (particularly our visual perception of bodies moving smoothly in space). To be sure, empirical experience has been best accommodated, in our combination of conjectured physical laws and geometry of physical space, by giving up the metrical part of the Euclidean account of space, and adopting in its stead a non-Euclidean one. This has happened both with the theory of special relativity and with the theory of general relativity. Nevertheless, the *a priori* intuitive grasp of the Euclidean line as continuous survives the replacement of Euclidean physical geometry by a non-Euclidean one. Indeed, our intuitive grasp of the continuity of lines in a non-Euclidean geometry involves the same resources as it does in the Euclidean case, deployed in the same fashion.

We have not (yet) 'gone granular' in our theorizing about the structure of space or of spacetime, in the way that Russell once surmised could well happen (recall p. 209), if our empirical experience might thereby be better explained. But even if we did thus go granular, our *a priori* intuitive grasp of the Euclidean line would survive. It is an intellectually robust *abstract* picture, transcending the vicissitudes involved in settling on the correct (topology and) geometry of *physical* space, or spacetime. *A priori* Euclideanism (and Archimedeanism) about 'the' straight line is undisturbed by this one extreme, namely that of possibly contrary (or otherwise devilishly difficult to accommodate) empirical experience.

At the other extreme, as it were, is the contention that the sum total of our empirical experience (thus far, at least) severely underdetermines the structure of physical space, and the structure of any line therein. This is particularly so with the presumed finitude of the distance between any two points (such a distance being able to be exceeded by some finite multiple of any chosen unit length). Thus Fenstad [1985], at p. 289:

> Is the Archimedian axiom a "true" geometric fact? What is given in our immediate experience is a limited part of the geometric line with at most a finite number of points marked on it, representing, e.g., the result of some physical measurement. The rest is an extension, ideal or real.

The point that Fenstad was concerned to make is that (for all we know, from our empirical experience thus far) the structure of a line in physical space might well be that of the hyperreal line, of Abraham Robinson's nonstandard analysis. For all we know, spatial lines really do have their spatial points so tightly squeezed together that, in among the 'real' ones (i.e., the ones that would enjoy real numbers as their numerical coordinates) there would be hyperreals differing from them only by infinitesimals. (A positive infinitesimal is a hyperreal number that is not identical to 0, but which is strictly less than any positive real number.) Fenstad concludes his paper by asserting (p. 300)

> ... the geometric line is not a pointset: The geometric line is an object in its own right, it is not to be "explained away". The line acts as support for pointsets. And we are free to create different pointsets on the line for different purposes.

The purposes, however, have to be independently established as worthwhile. On the one hand, with Occam's Razor glinting in the background, one would need arresting reason to 'create' the pointset of hyperreals on any line in physical space. On the other hand, as far as the Euclidean line of *a priori* intuition is concerned, there is simply no room for either infinitesimals or their infinite reciprocals (should we be intent on coördinatizing). For those infinite reciprocals would violate the Archimedean axiom, in which the natural number n is understood to be a standard one.

End of Digression.

Our statement above of **Archimedean measure for** $\blacktriangleleft$ spoke of laying a segment *right*wards end-to-end. There is, of course, a corresponding 'reflected' version of Archimedean measure that involves laying segments *left*wards end-to-end.

Theorem 3 (Archimedean measure for $\blacktriangleleft$**).**
$\forall x \forall y(x \blacktriangleleft y \rightarrow \forall z(x \blacktriangleleft z \rightarrow \exists n(z \blacktriangleleft \Lambda(x, [xy], n))))$.

Proof. Suppose $a \blacktriangleleft b \blacktriangleleft c$. Abbreviate $\Lambda(a, [ab], n)$ as γ_n. Obviously

$$\forall n\, \gamma_n \blacktriangleleft \gamma_{n+1}.$$

We seek to show $\exists n \quad c \blacktriangleleft \gamma_n$. Suppose for *reductio* that $\neg\exists n \quad c \blacktriangleleft \gamma_n$. Then by **Trichotomy of** $\blacktriangleleft$ we have

$$\forall n\ (\gamma_n = c \vee \gamma_n \blacktriangleleft c).$$

Let m be an arbitrary natural number, and suppose $\gamma_m = c$. Then $c \blacktriangleleft \gamma_{m+1}$, contradicting $\neg\exists n\ c \blacktriangleleft \gamma_n$. So

$$\forall n\ \gamma_n \blacktriangleleft c,$$

whence

$$\exists x \forall n\, \gamma_n \blacktriangleleft x.$$

So we have

$$(\forall n\, \gamma_n \blacktriangleleft \gamma_{n+1}) \wedge \exists x \forall n\, \gamma_n \blacktriangleleft x.$$

Recall **Right limits for** $\blacktriangleleft$:

$$\forall \gamma : \mathbb{N} \mapsto L[((\forall n\, \gamma_n \blacktriangleleft \gamma_{n+1}) \wedge \exists x \forall n\, \gamma_n \blacktriangleleft x)$$

$$\rightarrow \exists y(\forall n\, \gamma_n \blacktriangleleft y \wedge \forall z(z \blacktriangleleft y \rightarrow \exists n\, z \blacktriangleleft \gamma_n))].$$

By $\rightarrow$-Elimination, we infer

$$\exists y(\forall n\, \gamma_n \blacktriangleleft y \wedge \forall z(z \blacktriangleleft y \rightarrow \exists n\, z \blacktriangleleft \gamma_n)).$$

So, assume for $\exists$-Elimination that d is a witness to this existential:

$$\forall n\, \gamma_n \blacktriangleleft d \wedge \forall z(z \blacktriangleleft d \rightarrow \exists n\, z \blacktriangleleft \gamma_n).$$

By **Segmental finitude** we can choose a unique point e so that $e \blacktriangleleft d$ and $[ed] \cong [ab]$. So $\exists n\ e \blacktriangleleft \gamma_n$. Assume for $\exists$-Elimination that k is a witness to this existential: $e \blacktriangleleft \gamma_k$. Now we have

$$e \blacktriangleleft d \qquad e \blacktriangleleft \gamma_k \qquad \gamma_k \blacktriangleleft \gamma_{k+1} \qquad [ed] \cong [\gamma_k \gamma_{k+1}].$$

But then by Lemma 45 we have $d \blacktriangleleft \gamma_{k+1}$. Contradiction. □

Definition 16. *Let* $\gamma_0, \gamma_1, \ldots$ *be* any *sequence of geometric points. Then we say that this sequence* converges to the point c *just in case*

$$\forall n\, \exists m\, \forall i > m\ \lfloor \gamma_i, c \rfloor \lhd [0, \frac{1}{2^n}].$$

Lemma 46. *If* $\gamma_0, \gamma_1, \ldots$ *converges to* c_1 and *converges to* c_2, *then* $c_1 = c_2$. *That is, the existence of a point of convergence guarantees its uniqueness.*

Proof. Left to the reader as an exercise. □

Definition 17. *Suppose that* $\phi : \mathbb{N} \mapsto \mathbb{N}$ *is total, one-one, and non-decreasing. Let* f *be a total function on* $\mathbb{N}$, *i.e., a sequence of objects. Define* f^ϕ *by setting* $f^\phi(n)$ *to be* $f(\phi(n))$, *for every* n. *Clearly,* f^ϕ *is that infinite subsequence of* f *that consists of just those members* $f(n)$ *of* f*—in the order in which they appear in the sequence* f*—whose indices* n *are in the range of* ϕ.

Lemma 47. *If* f *converges to point c, then so does any subsequence* f^ϕ.

Proof. Left to the reader as an exercise. □

Definition 18. *Let* Ω *be any predicate satisfied by infinitely many natural numbers, i.e., such that* $\forall m\, \exists k > m\ \Omega(k)$. *Define* $c_\Omega : \mathbb{N} \mapsto \mathbb{N}$ *inductively as follows:*

$$c_\Omega(0) = \textit{the least } i \textit{ such that } \Omega(i);$$

$$c_\Omega(n+1) = \textit{the least } i > c_\Omega(n) \textit{ such that } \Omega(i).$$

The function c_Ω is total and one-one. In order to prove totality, one needs to establish the existence of the least i such that $\Omega(i)$, and also, for each n, the existence of the least $i > c_\omega(n)$ such that $\Omega(i)$. For this, we have to invoke the least number principle, which is a classical consequence of the principle of mathematical induction.

$f^{c_\Omega}(n)$ is that infinite subsequence of f that consists of just those members $f(n)$ of f—in the order in which they appear in the sequence f—whose indices n have the property Ω.

Consider the following instance of the Law of Excluded Middle:

$$\forall m\, \exists k > m\, \forall n > k\ R(fn, fk) \quad \vee \quad \neg \forall m\, \exists k > m\, \forall n > k\ R(fn, fk).$$

Here, R is any two-place predicate, and f is a total function on $\mathbb{N}$. In other words f is a sequence. At present it is not important to know what kind of things are in the sequence f (that is, it is not important to know what things form the range of f). All that matters, at this stage, is that R is a relation that can hold among such things.

The right-hand disjunct classically logically implies

$$\exists m\, \forall k{>}m\, \exists n{>}k\, \neg R(fn, fk).$$

The proof is as follows. Note that the steps marked (5), (4) and (1) are applications of *Classical Reductio ad Absurdum*, involving Δ_0-, Σ^0_1- and Σ^0_3-sentences respectively.

$$
\begin{prooftree}
\AxiomC{$\overline{c{>}b}^{(6)}$}
\AxiomC{$\overline{\neg R(fc, fb)}^{(5)}$}
\BinaryInfC{$\exists n{>}b\, \neg R(fn, fb)$}
\AxiomC{$\overline{\neg \exists n{>}b\, \neg R(fn, fb)}^{(4)}$}
\BinaryInfC{$\bot$}
\RightLabel{(5)}
\UnaryInfC{$R(fc, fb)$}
\RightLabel{(6)}
\UnaryInfC{$\forall n{>}b\, R(fn, fb)$}
\AxiomC{$\overline{b{>}a}^{(3)}$}
\BinaryInfC{$\exists k{>}a\, \forall n{>}k\, R(fn, fk)$}
\AxiomC{$\overline{\neg \exists k{>}a\, \forall n{>}k\, R(fn, fk)}^{(2)}$}
\BinaryInfC{$\bot$}
\RightLabel{(4)}
\UnaryInfC{$\exists n{>}b\, R(fn, fb)$}
\RightLabel{(3)}
\UnaryInfC{$\forall k{>}a\, \exists n{>}k\, R(fn, fk)$}
\UnaryInfC{$\exists m\, \forall k{>}m\, \exists n{>}k\, R(fn, fk)$}
\AxiomC{$\overline{\neg \exists m\, \forall k{>}m\, \exists n{>}k\, R(fn, fk)}^{(1)}$}
\BinaryInfC{$\bot$}
\RightLabel{(2)}
\UnaryInfC{$\exists k{>}a\, \forall n{>}k\, R(fn, fk)$}
\UnaryInfC{$\forall m\, \exists k{>}m\, \forall n{>}k\, R(fn, fk)$}
\AxiomC{$\neg \forall m\, \exists k{>}m\, \forall n{>}k\, R(fn, fk)$}
\BinaryInfC{$\bot$}
\RightLabel{(1)}
\UnaryInfC{$\exists m\, \forall k{>}m\, \exists n{>}k\, \neg R(fn, fk)$}
\end{prooftree}
$$

The classical mathematician can therefore assert the classical logical truth

$$\forall m\, \exists k{>}m\, \forall n{>}k\, R(fn, fk) \;\vee\; \exists m\, \forall k{>}m\, \exists n{>}k\, \neg R(fn, fk).$$

On the assumption, on the one hand, that

$$\text{(i)} \qquad \forall m\, \exists k{>}m\, \forall n{>}k\, R(fn, fk),$$

set $\Omega(k) \equiv_{df} \forall n > k\;\, R(fn, fk)$. Assumption (i) entails that there are infinitely many natural numbers k such that $\Omega(k)$. For this choice of Ω, the subsequence f^{c_Ω} of f is such that

$$\forall k\;\, R(f^{c_\Omega}(k+1), f^{c_\Omega}(k)),$$

whence, by $\vee$-Introduction, we have

$$\forall k\;\, R(f^{c_\Omega}(k+1), f^{c_\Omega}(k)) \;\vee\; \forall k\; \neg R(f^{c_\Omega}(k+1), f^{c_\Omega}(k)).$$

By existential generalization, we now conclude

$$\text{(iii)} \qquad \exists \phi : \mathbb{N} \overset{1\text{-}1}{\mapsto} \mathbb{N}(\forall k\;\, R(f^{\phi}(k+1), f^{\phi}(k)) \;\vee\; \forall k\; \neg R(f^{\phi}(k+1), f^{\phi}(k))).$$

On the assumption, on the other hand, that

$$\text{(ii)} \qquad \exists m\, \forall k{>}m\, \exists n{>}k\, \neg R(fn, fk),$$

set $\Theta(k) \equiv_{df} \exists n > k \ \neg R(fn, fk)$. Assumption (ii) entails that there are infinitely many natural numbers k such that $\Theta(k)$. Let **m** be the least m such that $\forall k > m \ \Theta(k)$.

Now define $d_\Theta : \mathbb{N} \mapsto \mathbb{N}$ inductively as follows:

$$d_\Theta(0) = 1 + \text{the least } i \text{ such that } \forall k > i \ \Theta(i);$$

$$d_\Theta(n+1) = \text{the least } i > d_\Theta(n) \text{ such that } \neg R(f(i), f(d_\Theta(n))).$$

The function d_Θ is total and one-one. Again, the proof of totality will involve appeal to the least number principle.

f^{d_Θ} is an infinite subsequence of f. Moreover, we have

$$\forall k \ \neg R(f^{d_\Theta}(k+1), f^{d_\Theta}(k)),$$

whence, by $\vee$-Introduction, we have

$$\forall k \ R(f^{d_\Theta}(k+1), f^{d_\Theta}(k)) \ \vee \ \forall k \ \neg R(f^{d_\Theta}(k+1), f^{d_\Theta}(k)).$$

By existential generalization, we once again conclude

$$\text{(iii)} \quad \exists \phi : \mathbb{N} \overset{1\text{-}1}{\mapsto} \mathbb{N}(\forall k \ R(f^\phi(k+1), f^\phi(k)) \ \vee \ \forall k \ \neg R(f^\phi(k+1), f^\phi(k))).$$

Since we have shown also that either (i) or (ii) holds, it follows that (iii) holds outright. That is, Classical Logic plus the least number principle together ensure the truth of the following result.

Theorem 4. *Any infinite sequence f has an infinite subsequence f^ϕ that is either a 'positive R'-chain, or a 'negative R'-chain.*

Suppose that a unit segment [0,1] has been fixed (on the oriented line L). For $n > 0$ and for odd k, $0 < k < 2^n$, it is clear what point lying strictly between 0 and 1 is denoted by the convenient algebraic term $\frac{k}{2^n}$. The midpoint of [0,1] is $\frac{1}{2}$, i.e., $\frac{1}{2^1}$. The midpoint of $[0, \frac{1}{2}]$ is $\frac{1}{4}$, i.e., $\frac{1}{2^2}$. The midpoint of $[\frac{1}{2}, 1]$ is $\frac{3}{4}$, i.e., $\frac{3}{2^2}$. And so on. Such points, which are constructible from the unit segment by repeated bisections, are called *bisective points*.

A sequence $\gamma_0, \gamma_1, \ldots$ of geometric points on a line is said to be *Cauchy* if and only if

$$\forall n \, \exists m \, \forall i > m \, \forall j > m \ \lfloor \gamma_i, \gamma_j \rfloor \lhd [0, \frac{1}{2^n}].$$

Note the equivalence of this condition with the usual one, whose geometrized version is

$$\forall \tau([0,0] \lhd \tau \ \rightarrow \ \exists m \ \forall i > m \ \forall j > m \ \lfloor \gamma_i, \gamma_j \rfloor \lhd \tau),$$

with the initial universal quantification being over segments. We remind the reader that we are being scrupulous in keeping our treatment geometric. That is why we avoid using the usual Cauchy condition, whose expression is number-theoretic:

$$\forall \epsilon (0 < \epsilon \rightarrow \exists m \, \forall i > m \, \forall j > m \ \mid \gamma_i - \gamma_j \mid < \epsilon),$$

with the points γ_i and γ_j already regarded as points on the real line, that is, as real numbers.

Strictly speaking, a Cauchy-sequence theorist might object here that the points in question are usually thought of as rational numbers, hence as points lying on the rational line, not on the real line—the aim of the Cauchy enterprise being to obtain the irrational real numbers as limits of Cauchy sequences of rationals. This objection, however, only serves to highlight an important difference between such an approach and the approach being pursued here. For we are seeking to attain to a proper conception of the real numbers as representatives of lengths of segments of oriented lines. On that approach, the distinction between rational and irrational numbers, though it can be made, is of no great significance. Indeed, seeing some sort of conceptual Rubicon between the rationals and the irrational reals is an impediment to seeing the reals for what they (really) are.

Lemma 48. *Every Cauchy sequence $\gamma_0, \gamma_1, \ldots$ is bounded above and below—that is, it is right-limited and left-limited.*

Proof. We have

$$\forall n \, \exists m \, \forall i > m \, \forall j > m \, \lfloor \gamma_i, \gamma_j \rfloor \lhd [0, \frac{1}{2^n}].$$

Hence, instantiating with respect to 0,

$$\exists m \, \forall i > m \, \forall j > m \, \lfloor \gamma_i, \gamma_j \rfloor \lhd [0, 1].$$

Let m_0 be the least m such that

$$\forall i > m \, \forall j > m \, \lfloor \gamma_i, \gamma_j \rfloor \lhd [0, 1].$$

It follows that

$$\forall j > m_0 \, \lfloor \gamma_{m_0+1}, \gamma_j \rfloor \lhd [0, 1].$$

Consider now the point r, say, which lies one unit segment to the *right* of point γ_{m_0+1}. This point r lies to the right of all points γ_j, for $j > m_0$. Take now the rightmost point among

$$\gamma_0, \gamma_1, \ldots, \gamma_{m_0}, r$$

and choose some point—call it $\mathbf{r}$—to the right of it. Then $\mathbf{r}$ lies to the right of *every* point in the sequence $\gamma_0, \gamma_1, \ldots$. So this sequence is right-limited.

Now consider the point l, say, which lies one unit segment to the left of point γ_{m_0+1}. This point l lies to the left of all points γ_j, for $j > m_0$. Take now the leftmost point among

$$\gamma_0, \gamma_1, \ldots, \gamma_{m_0}, l$$

and choose some point—call it $\mathbf{l}$—to the left of it. Then $\mathbf{l}$ lies to the left of *every* point in the sequence $\gamma_0, \gamma_1, \ldots$. So the sequence is left-limited. □

Lemma 49. *Suppose that $\gamma_0, \gamma_1, \ldots$ is a Cauchy sequence. Suppose that the function $\phi : \mathbb{N} \mapsto \mathbb{N}$ is total, one-one, and non-decreasing (i.e., $\forall n\, \phi n \geq n$). Suppose that the subsequence γ^{ϕ} converges to point c. Then $\gamma_0, \gamma_1, \ldots$ converges to point c.*

Proof. We use the abbreviation $R(x, y, n)$ for $\lfloor x, y \rfloor \lhd [0, \frac{1}{2^n}]$. The following is then a derivable geometric inference:

$$\frac{R(v, t, n+1) \qquad R(v, u, n+1)}{R(t, u, n)} \,.$$

This is because the bisective point $\frac{1}{2^{n+1}}$ is the midpoint of the segment $[0, \frac{1}{2^n}]$; and we can derive the geometric inference

$$\frac{\lfloor v, t \rfloor \lhd [p, r] \qquad \lfloor v, u \rfloor \lhd [p, r] \qquad [p, r] \cong [r, s]}{\lfloor t, u \rfloor \lhd [p, s]} \,.$$

The third premise says that r is the midpoint of $[p, s]$. And of course this premise is a theorem-by-definition in the case at hand:

$$[0, \frac{1}{2^{n+1}}] \cong [\frac{1}{2^{n+1}}, \frac{1}{2^n}],$$

since the bisective point $\frac{1}{2^{n+1}}$ is defined to be the midpoint of the segment $[0, \frac{1}{2^n}]$. The third premise can accordingly be suppressed in the inference that is the sole *geometric* move in the formal proof of the lemma that is displayed in landscape mode in Appendix B, and which otherwise contains quantifier manipulations and simple inferences about the ordering of the natural numbers. □

Definition 19. *The* quasi-minimization operator $\mu_x[m, P(x)]$ *for natural numbers m and predicates $P(x)$ on the natural numbers is defined as follows:*

$$\mu_x[m, P(x)] \begin{cases} = \textit{the least natural } i > m \textit{ such that } P(i), \textit{ if } \exists k > m\, P(k) \\ \textit{is undefined if } \neg\exists k > m\, P(k) \end{cases}$$

If there are infinitely many natural numbers satisfying the predicate P—that is, if $\forall k \exists n > k\ P(n)$—then $\mu_x[m, P(x)]$ will be defined for every m. The proof of this uses the least-number principle, which is a classical consequence of the principle of mathematical induction.

Example. $\mu_x[m, x \text{ is prime}]$ is defined for every m, and its first few values are:

$$\mu_x[0, x \text{ is prime}] = 2$$

$$\mu_x[1, x \text{ is prime}] = 2$$
$$\mu_x[2, x \text{ is prime}] = 3$$
$$\mu_x[3, x \text{ is prime}] = 5$$
$$\mu_x[4, x \text{ is prime}] = 5$$
$$\mu_x[5, x \text{ is prime}] = 7$$
$$\mu_x[6, x \text{ is prime}] = 7$$
$$\vdots$$

Suppose that $\mathcal{X}$ is a set of points and that $\gamma = \gamma_0, \gamma_1, \ldots$ is an infinite sequence of points, at least one of which is in $\mathcal{X}$. Equipped with the quasi-minimization operator, we inductively define the following non-decreasing function $\lambda_\gamma^\mathcal{X}$ on the natural numbers:

$$\lambda_\gamma^\mathcal{X}(0) = 0;$$

$$\lambda_\gamma^\mathcal{X}(n+1) = \begin{cases} \mu_x[\lambda_\gamma^\mathcal{X}(n), \gamma_x \in \mathcal{X}], & \text{if this exists;} \\ \lambda_\gamma^\mathcal{X}(n) \text{ otherwise} \end{cases}$$

Example. Suppose $\gamma_n \in \mathcal{X}$ just in case n is prime. Then the first few values of the function $\lambda_\gamma^\mathcal{X}$ are as follows:

$$\lambda_\gamma^\mathcal{X}(0) = 0$$
$$\lambda_\gamma^\mathcal{X}(1) = 2$$
$$\lambda_\gamma^\mathcal{X}(2) = 3$$
$$\lambda_\gamma^\mathcal{X}(3) = 5$$
$$\lambda_\gamma^\mathcal{X}(4) = 7$$
$$\lambda_\gamma^\mathcal{X}(5) = 11$$
$$\lambda_\gamma^\mathcal{X}(6) = 13$$
$$\vdots$$

That is, $\lambda_\gamma^\mathcal{X}(n)$ (for $n > 0$) is the nth prime.

Definition 20. *The $\mathcal{X}$-subsequence of γ, denoted $\gamma^\mathcal{X}$, can now be defined by stipulating that (for all n) we have*

$$\gamma_n^\mathcal{X} = \gamma_{\lambda_\gamma^\mathcal{X}(n+1)}$$

Example. Suppose as in the last example that $\gamma_n \in \mathcal{X}$ just in case n is prime. Then the first few members of the sequence $\gamma^{\mathcal{X}}$ are as follows:

$$\gamma_0^{\mathcal{X}} = \gamma_2$$
$$\gamma_1^{\mathcal{X}} = \gamma_3$$
$$\gamma_2^{\mathcal{X}} = \gamma_5$$
$$\gamma_3^{\mathcal{X}} = \gamma_7$$
$$\gamma_4^{\mathcal{X}} = \gamma_{11}$$
$$\gamma_5^{\mathcal{X}} = \gamma_{13}$$
$$\gamma_6^{\mathcal{X}} = \gamma_{17}$$
$$\vdots$$

Note that since γ can contain repetitions (in the sense that we can have $\gamma_i = \gamma_j$ for distinct i and j), so too can $\gamma^{\mathcal{X}}$.

Our geometric axioms **Right limits for ◀** and **Left limits for ◀** speak of *limit* points, which are 'approached', respectively, from the *left* by infinitely *increasing*, or from the *right* by infinitely *decreasing*, sequences of points. (Remember that we are talking about points on a directed line, so that 'increasing' means 'moving to the right', and 'decreasing' means 'moving to the left'.) With Cauchy sequences, however, the points can 'bounce around', or 'oscillate', without any steady leftwards or rightwards drift. We wish to reserve the terminology of a *limit* point for sequences that approach such limit points of theirs steadily from one side or the other, and which do not bounce around or oscillate. So for Cauchy sequences, we shall use the earlier terminology *point of convergence* rather than 'limit point'; and we shall speak of a (Cauchy) sequence as *converging to* a particular point (when it does).

We have purposely (but not perversely) left open, until now, the question whether every Cauchy sequence of geometric points does indeed converge (to a geometric point). Those who have a clear geometric intuition to the effect that such sequences do converge are to be congratulated for their perspicuity. For the present author submits that one can be intuitively certain about the truth of the two axioms **Right limits for ◀** and **Left limits for ◀**, without (yet) having conclusive grounds for the proposition that every Cauchy sequence of geometric points converges to a geometric point. As testimony for the defence, we simply submit the quote from Forster on p. 269, which concedes as much. For the logicogenetic theorizer, there is still some logical work to do, before one is warranted in asserting Cauchy-convergence in the geometric case.

Theorem 5. *Every Cauchy sequence of geometric points on a directed line converges.*

Proof. Recall Theorem 4: *any* infinite sequence f—whether Cauchy or not—has an infinite subsequence f^{ϕ} that is either a 'positive R'-chain, or a 'negative R'-chain. So, let R be $\blacktriangleleft$. Then *every* infinite sequence f has an infinite subsequence f^{ϕ} that is either (i) strictly increasing, or (ii) (by Trichotomy) non-increasing.

Now we argue by cases (i) and (ii), appealing to the further assumption that f is Cauchy. Given that f is Cauchy, by Lemma 48, f has a right limit (that is, f is 'bounded above') and a left limit (that is, f is 'bounded below'). And so too does any subsequence of f.

Case (i): Suppose that f^{ϕ} is strictly increasing. f^{ϕ} also has a right limit. Hence by **Right limits for** $\blacktriangleleft$, f^{ϕ} has a leftmost right limit point. Call this point c. Obviously f^{ϕ} converges to c. But then by Lemma 49, the Cauchy sequence f converges to c also.

Case (ii): Suppose that f^{ϕ} is non-increasing. Then one can extract from f^{ϕ} either (a) a strictly decreasing sequence f_1, or (b) a sequence f_2 that strictly decreases until it reaches a point that recurs.

In case (a), the sequence f_1 has a left limit. Hence by **Left limits for** $\blacktriangleleft$, f_1 has a rightmost left limit point. Call this point c. Obviously f_1 converges to c. But f_1 is a subsequence of f. Hence by Lemma 49, the Cauchy sequence f also converges to c.

In case (b), f_2 obviously converges to its recurring point. Call this point d. But f_2 is a subsequence of f. Hence by Lemma 49, the Cauchy sequence f also converges to d. □

This completes the proof of Theorem 5. Note that it has been proved on the basis of the much more intuitively secure geometric principles **Right limits for** $\blacktriangleleft$ and **Left limits for** $\blacktriangleleft$. The general principle of Cauchy convergence need not be taken as an axiomatic starting point in a logico-genetic account of the real numbers.

Thus far our terminology has been standard, except for the stress on *geometric* points, rather than on real numbers conceived as 'points on the real line'. Now we introduce an unusual concept.

Definition 21. *An infinite sequence of bisective points* $\gamma_0, \gamma_1, \ldots$ *on L is a* bisective sequence *if and only if*

$$\forall n\, \forall k > n\ \lfloor \gamma_n, \gamma_k \rfloor \lhd [0, \frac{1}{2^n}].$$

Lemma 50. *Every bisective sequence is Cauchy.*

Proof. Left to the reader as an exercise. □

Indeed, one could say that a bisective sequence is 'Cauchy with a vengeance'.

Note that there are bisective sequences that are not monotonic—for example, any bisective sequence with the initial segment

$$0, \frac{1}{4}, \frac{1}{8}, \frac{3}{16}, \frac{3}{16}, \frac{11}{64}, \frac{23}{128}, \ldots .$$

$\frac{1}{2}$

0

(This is an initial segment of a sequence, not of a geometric line.)

Non-monotonicity is already exhibited within the initial segment displayed. Note too that points can be repeated within a bisective sequence (such as the point $\frac{3}{16}$ in this example). There is no requirement that consecutive points within a bisective sequence be geometrically distinct.

Both monotonic and non-monotonic bisective sequences can be *eventually constant*, such as the sequence

$$0, \frac{1}{4}, \frac{1}{8}, \frac{3}{16}, \frac{3}{16}, \frac{11}{64}, \frac{23}{128}, \frac{23}{128}, \frac{23}{128}, \frac{23}{128}, \frac{23}{128}, \ldots .$$

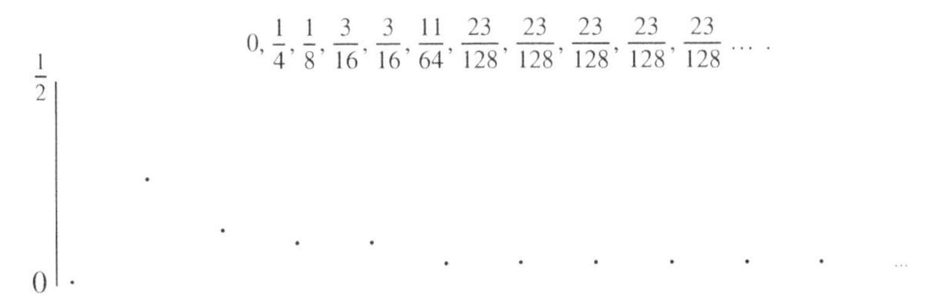

Definition 22. *A sequence $\gamma_0, \gamma_1, \ldots$ of points on a directed line is said to be* strictly increasing to a plateau *if and only if*

$$\exists k(\forall i\, \forall j(i < j < k \rightarrow \gamma_i \blacktriangleleft \gamma_j) \wedge \forall m > k\; \gamma_k = \gamma_m).$$

A sequence $\gamma_0, \gamma_1, \ldots$ of points on a directed line is said to be strictly decreasing to a plateau *if and only if*

$$\exists k(\forall i\, \forall j(i < j < k \rightarrow \gamma_j \blacktriangleleft \gamma_i) \wedge \forall m > k\; \gamma_k = \gamma_m).$$

A sequence that strictly increases to a plateau is a special case of a non-decreasing sequence. Likewise, a sequence that strictly decreases to a plateau is a special case of a non-increasing sequence. In each case the sequence has its plateau-value as its limit point. So the sequence actually attains its limit.

Lemma 51. *Any bisective sequence contains an infinite subsequence that is either strictly increasing, or strictly increasing to a plateau, or strictly decreasing, or strictly decreasing to a plateau.*

Proof. Left as an exercise for the reader. □

Definition 23. *Given any Cauchy sequence $\gamma = \gamma_0, \gamma_1, \ldots$ of geometric points on an oriented line L, we can define the 'upper class' $\mathcal{U}_\gamma$ and the 'lower class' $\mathcal{L}_\gamma$ of points involved in γ as follows:*

$$\gamma_i \in \mathcal{U}_\gamma \quad \leftrightarrow \quad \exists m > i\ \forall k > m(\gamma_k \blacktriangleleft \gamma_i \vee \gamma_k = \gamma_i)$$

$$\gamma_i \in \mathcal{L}_\gamma \quad \leftrightarrow \quad \exists m > i\ \forall k > m(\gamma_i \blacktriangleleft \gamma_k \vee \gamma_k = \gamma_i)$$

Thus $\mathcal{U}_\gamma$ consists of those points in γ that are succeeded (within γ) by at most finitely many points to the *right* of them (on the oriented line L); and $\mathcal{L}_\gamma$ consists of those points that are succeeded by at most finitely many points to the *left* of them. Note that both $\mathcal{U}_\gamma$ and $\mathcal{L}_\gamma$ are *classes* or *sets* of points, not *sequences* of points. Their union $(\mathcal{U}_\gamma \cup \mathcal{L}_\gamma)$ is the *range* of the sequence γ, thought of as a mapping from the natural numbers to geometric points on L.

For the statement of the remaining results of this section, γ is a Cauchy sequence of geometric points on an oriented line L, unless stated otherwise.

Lemma 52. *$\mathcal{U}_\gamma$ and $\mathcal{L}_\gamma$ have at most one point in common.*

Lemma 53. *Suppose c is in $\mathcal{U}_\gamma$ and in $\mathcal{L}_\gamma$. Then*

$$\exists n\ \forall m > n\ \gamma_m = c,$$

and both $\mathcal{U}_\gamma$ and $\mathcal{L}_\gamma$ are finite.

Lemma 54. *Suppose both $\mathcal{U}_\gamma$ and $\mathcal{L}_\gamma$ are finite. Then there is a unique point c common to both, and*

$$\exists n\ \forall m > n\ \gamma_m = c.$$

Lemma 55. *Suppose $\mathcal{U}_\gamma$ and $\mathcal{L}_\gamma$ have no point in common. Then either $\mathcal{U}_\gamma$ is infinite or $\mathcal{L}_\gamma$ is infinite. (Note that this is an inclusive disjunction: it could be the case that both $\mathcal{U}_\gamma$ and $\mathcal{L}_\gamma$ are infinite.)*

Lemma 56. *Suppose $\mathcal{U}_\gamma$ is infinite. Then $\mathcal{U}_\gamma$ has no leftmost point (in the sense of the ordering relation $\blacktriangleleft$ of points on the oriented line L); and obviously also $\gamma^{\mathcal{U}_\gamma}$ has no leftmost point.*

Lemma 57. *Suppose $\mathcal{L}_\gamma$ is infinite. Then $\mathcal{L}_\gamma$ has no rightmost point (in the sense of the ordering relation $\blacktriangleleft$ of points on the oriented line L); and obviously also $\gamma^{\mathcal{L}_\gamma}$ has no rightmost point.*

Suppose $\mathcal{L}_\gamma$ is infinite. The infinite sequence $\gamma^{\mathcal{L}_\gamma}$ (which is a subsequence of γ) need not be monotonic—in particular, it need not be non-decreasing. From this sequence $\gamma^{\mathcal{L}_\gamma}$, however, one can extract a *strictly increasing* subsequence $(\gamma^{\mathcal{L}_\gamma})\uparrow$. Moreover, the leftmost right limit point of $(\gamma^{\mathcal{L}_\gamma})\uparrow$ will be the point of convergence of the original Cauchy sequence γ itself.

Suppose $\mathcal{U}_\gamma$ is infinite. The infinite sequence $\gamma^{\mathcal{U}_\gamma}$ (which is a subsequence of γ) need not be monotonic—in particular, it need not be non-increasing. From this sequence $\gamma^{\mathcal{U}_\gamma}$, however, one can extract a *strictly decreasing* subsequence $(\gamma^{\mathcal{L}_\gamma})\downarrow$. Moreover, the rightmost left limit point of $(\gamma^{\mathcal{U}_\gamma})\downarrow$ will be the point of convergence of the original Cauchy sequence γ itself.

Suppose both $\mathcal{L}_\gamma$ and $\mathcal{U}_\gamma$ are infinite. Suppose that the point of convergence c of γ occurs in γ itself—perhaps even infinitely often. Ironically, c will be in neither $\mathcal{L}_\gamma$ nor $\mathcal{U}_\gamma$. *But* c will be the leftmost right limit point of $(\gamma^{\mathcal{L}_\gamma})\uparrow$ and will also be the rightmost left limit point of $(\gamma^{\mathcal{U}_\gamma})\downarrow$.

Example. Let γ be the following Cauchy sequence of bisective points:

$$\frac{1}{2}, \frac{3}{4}, \frac{1}{2}, \frac{1}{4}, \frac{1}{2}, \frac{5}{8}, \frac{1}{2}, \frac{3}{8}, \frac{1}{2}, \frac{9}{16}, \frac{1}{2}, \frac{7}{16}, \frac{1}{2}, \frac{17}{32}, \frac{1}{2}, \frac{15}{32}, \frac{1}{2}, \frac{33}{64}, \frac{1}{2}, \frac{31}{64}, \frac{1}{2}, \frac{65}{128}, \frac{1}{2}, \frac{63}{128}, \frac{1}{2}, \ldots$$

whose oscillating graph can be pictured as follows. Members of the upper class $\mathcal{U}_\gamma$ are shown as little circles, and members of the lower class $\mathcal{L}_\gamma$ are shown as little crosses. The natural numbers (the indices of the members of the sequence) can be thought of as laid along the horizontal axis; the unit interval is represented by the vertical line. Thus, in interpreting the sequence in this graphical way, for 'rightmost' we must think 'uppermost', and for 'leftmost' we must think 'bottom-most'. That is, the ordering relation $x \blacktriangleleft y$ of geometric points holds just in case x is *below* y on the vertical unit segment in the diagram.

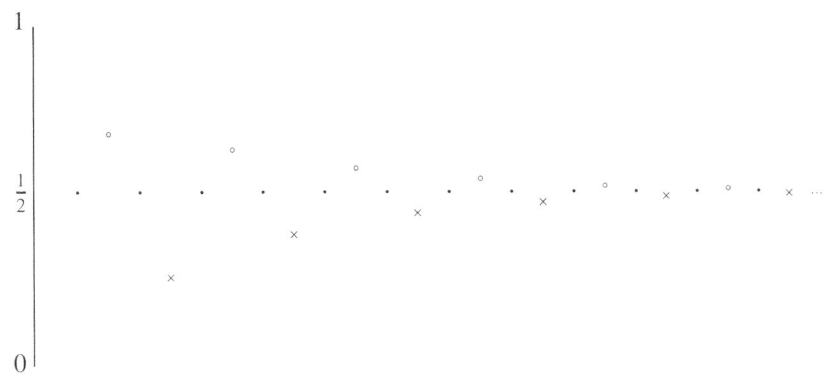

In this example, the (sub)sequences $\gamma^{\mathcal{L}_\gamma}$ and $\gamma^{\mathcal{U}_\gamma}$ happen to be monotonic. Indeed, $\gamma^{\mathcal{L}_\gamma}$ is strictly increasing, and $\gamma^{\mathcal{U}_\gamma}$ is strictly decreasing. Thus we have both $(\gamma^{\mathcal{L}_\gamma})\uparrow = \gamma^{\mathcal{L}_\gamma}$ and $(\gamma^{\mathcal{U}_\gamma})\downarrow = \gamma^{\mathcal{U}_\gamma}$. But, as remarked earlier, this is not always the case. The following example involves only a slight permutation of an initial segment of the previous one:

$$\frac{1}{2}, \frac{5}{8}, \frac{1}{2}, \frac{3}{8}, \frac{1}{2}, \frac{3}{4}, \frac{1}{4}, \frac{1}{2}, \frac{1}{2}, \frac{9}{16}, \frac{1}{2}, \frac{7}{16}, \frac{1}{2}, \frac{17}{32}, \frac{1}{2}, \frac{15}{32}, \frac{1}{2}, \frac{33}{64}, \frac{1}{2}, \frac{31}{64}, \frac{1}{2}, \frac{65}{128}, \frac{1}{2}, \frac{63}{128}, \frac{1}{2}, \ldots$$

Here, neither $\gamma^{\mathcal{L}_\gamma}$ nor $\gamma^{\mathcal{U}_\gamma}$ is monotonic. Indeed, in this example $\gamma^{\mathcal{L}_\gamma}$ is not even non-decreasing, and $\gamma^{\mathcal{U}_\gamma}$ is not even non-increasing. Hence $(\gamma^{\mathcal{L}_\gamma})\uparrow$ (which is obtained by omitting the point represented by the lowest cross) is a *proper* subsequence of $\gamma^{\mathcal{L}_\gamma}$, and $(\gamma^{\mathcal{U}_\gamma})\downarrow$ (which is obtained by omitting the point represented by the highest little circle) is a *proper* subsequence of $\gamma^{\mathcal{U}_\gamma}$.

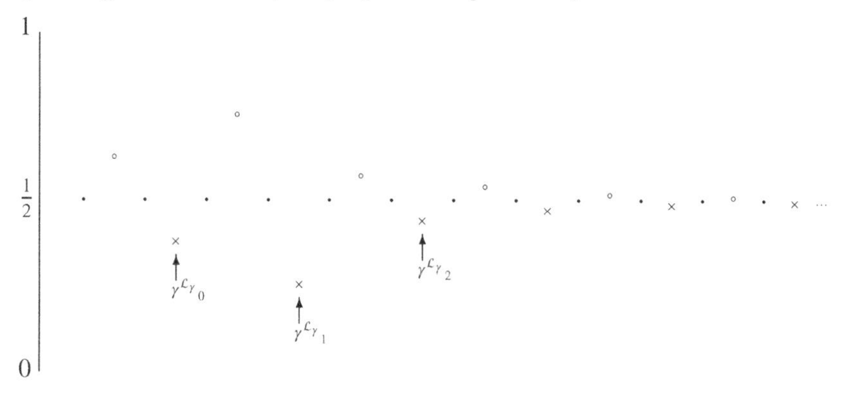

The diagram suggests clearly how the strict subsequences $(\gamma^{\mathcal{L}_\gamma})\uparrow$ and $(\gamma^{\mathcal{U}_\gamma})\downarrow$ are to be obtained from $\gamma^{\mathcal{L}_\gamma}$ and $\gamma^{\mathcal{U}_\gamma}$ respectively. We shall focus just on $(\gamma^{\mathcal{L}_\gamma})\uparrow$.

Set $(\gamma^{\mathcal{L}_\gamma})\uparrow_0 = \gamma^{\mathcal{L}_\gamma}{}_0$. Then define $(\gamma^{\mathcal{L}_\gamma})\uparrow_{n+1}$ to be $\gamma^{\mathcal{L}_\gamma}{}_k$, where k is the least index $i > n$ for which $\gamma^{\mathcal{L}_\gamma}{}_n \blacktriangleleft \gamma^{\mathcal{L}_\gamma}{}_i$. In the last example, it is easy to see that $(\gamma^{\mathcal{L}_\gamma})\uparrow_1 = \gamma^{\mathcal{L}_\gamma}{}_2$.

Cauchy sequences contain too much clutter for our theoretical purposes. The points in the *upper* class of a Cauchy sequence do not necessarily form a non-*in*creasing subsequence. And the points in the *lower* class of a Cauchy sequence do not necessarily form a non-*de*creasing subsequence. Moreover, a Cauchy sequence can contain points that are neither in its upper class nor in its lower class. This means that the theory of convergence for Cauchy sequences requires one to extract subsequences, and regard certain points within it as irrelevant, for the purpose of identifying its convergence point with the limit point that is guaranteed by either one of our geometric axioms **Right limits for $\blacktriangleleft$** or **Left limits for $\blacktriangleleft$**. The ideal situation would be one in which we are always working with (or can handily find) the kinds of sequences to which these two geometric axioms directly apply.

As it happens, Cauchy sequences are too general for an ideally smooth development of a theory of real numbers as bicimal (or, more generally, k-mal, for any $k \geq 2$) representations of geometric points (on a directed line with an origin and a unit segment). We need a less general notion that is nevertheless general enough. The notion in question is that of a *funnel sequence*.

By way of intuitive motivation: a funnel sequence is a special kind of bisective sequence. We have already described bisective sequences as 'Cauchy with a vengeance' because of the exigent requirement of a certain rate of convergence that is imposed upon them. Beyond index n, any two members of a bisective sequence $\gamma_0, \gamma_1, \ldots$ must be separated by less than one 2^n-*th* part of a unit segment. (Moreover, each γ_i must itself be a bisective point as defined above.)

We have seen, however, that even a bisective sequence can have the drawbacks just noted above for Cauchy sequences in general. We seek now to overcome these drawbacks by securing the result that every point in a sequence of the desired kind—a funnel sequence—will be in the union of its upper and lower classes. To take an earlier example, consider once again the bisective sequence we pictured thus:

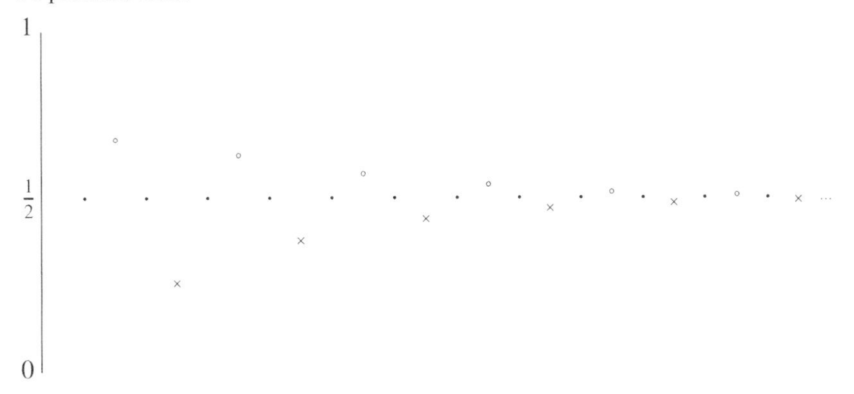

This is not a funnel sequence. This is because the black dots do not belong to either the upper class (little circles) or the lower class (little crosses) of the sequence. The *funnel* that needs to be discerned consists of just the circles and the crosses.

Definition 24. *A bisective sequence* $\gamma_0, \gamma_1, \ldots$ *of points on a directed line is a* funnel sequence *just in case*

$$\forall i(\neg\exists j > i\ \gamma_j \blacktriangleleft \gamma_i \vee \neg\exists j > i\ \gamma_i \blacktriangleleft \gamma_j).$$

Lemma 58. *Let* $\gamma_0, \gamma_1, \ldots$ *be a funnel sequence. Then for all* i

$$\gamma_i \in \mathcal{U}_\gamma \leftrightarrow \neg\exists j > i\ \gamma_i \blacktriangleleft \gamma_j$$

and

$$\gamma_i \in \mathcal{L}_\gamma \leftrightarrow \neg\exists j > i\ \gamma_j \blacktriangleleft \gamma_i.$$

Lemma 59. *Let* $\gamma_0, \gamma_1, \ldots$ *be a funnel sequence. Suppose there is some* i *such that both* $\neg\exists j > i\ \gamma_j \blacktriangleleft \gamma_i$ *and* $\neg\exists j > i\ \gamma_i \blacktriangleleft \gamma_j$. *Let* k *be the least such* i. *Suppose* $\gamma_k = c$. *Then for all* $m > k$ *we have* $\gamma_m = c$.

Lemma 60. *Let $\gamma_0, \gamma_1, \ldots$ be a funnel sequence. Then $\gamma^{\mathcal{L}_\gamma}$ is a non-decreasing funnel sequence, and $\gamma^{\mathcal{U}_\gamma}$ is a non-increasing funnel sequence.*

Lemma 61. *Let $\gamma_0, \gamma_1, \ldots$ be a funnel sequence. Then the right limit point of $\gamma^{\mathcal{L}_\gamma}$ and the left limit point of $\gamma^{\mathcal{U}_\gamma}$ are identical to* $\lim(\gamma)$.

Lemma 61 allows us to use either one of $\gamma^{\mathcal{L}_\gamma}$ and $\gamma^{\mathcal{U}_\gamma}$ to determine the limit of γ itself. Remember that $\gamma^{\mathcal{L}_\gamma}$ is non-decreasing and $\gamma^{\mathcal{U}_\gamma}$ is non-increasing. In light of this we ought to choose a particular one of $\gamma^{\mathcal{L}_\gamma}$ and $\gamma^{\mathcal{U}_\gamma}$ to do duty for γ; and we do so by considering how the limit point of γ stands in relation to the origin 0. The reason for our choice is that we want to use non-decreasing sequences of bisective points to determine bicimal expansions for positive real numbers (corresponding to geometric points c such that $0 \blacktriangleleft c$), and we want to use non-increasing sequences of bisective points to determine bicimal expansions for negative real numbers (corresponding to geometric points c such that $c \blacktriangleleft 0$).

Definition 25. **0** *is the infinite sequence such that for all i $\mathbf{0}(i) = 0$.*

Definition 26. *Let $\gamma_0, \gamma_1, \ldots$ be a funnel sequence. (Remember that the γ_i are points on a directed line, with origin* 0.*)*

$$\overline{\gamma} =_{df} \begin{cases} \gamma^{\mathcal{L}_\gamma} \text{ if } 0 \blacktriangleleft lim(\gamma); \\ \gamma^{\mathcal{U}_\gamma} \text{ if } lim(\gamma) \blacktriangleleft 0 \\ \mathbf{0} \text{ if } lim(\gamma) = 0. \end{cases}$$

Corollary 2. *Let $\gamma_0, \gamma_1, \ldots$ be a funnel sequence. Then $lim(\overline{\gamma}) = lim(\gamma)$.*

Chapter 23

Bicimals

Abstract

In this chapter one finally arrives at the natural logicist's proposed method of numerical representation of real numbers. The chosen method is of bicimal (rather than decimal) expansions, since it is so elegant and straightforward. It also makes the correspondence between expansions and sets of natural numbers pellucid. The central aim is to show that any point in the open unit segment is represented by a (possibly infinite) *unique canonical bicimal expansion*. In doing so one draws only on the conceptual resources available to the Euclidean that were developed in Chapter 22, and one uses only effective Euclidean constructions. We show how to generate the expansion for any point in a unit interval (whose left endpoint is the origin) of a directed straight line. The process involves finding the midpoints of each successive interval (chosen in an orderly way), and determining whether the point in question is to the left of, to the right of, or identical to, the midpoint. The first case generates a 1; the second case generates a 0; and in the case of identity, the construction ceases.

The use of decimal expansions to represent real numbers is now in our mathematical marrow. But the same job can be accomplished by using only the digits 0 and 1, and 'counting to base 2'. Decimal expansions are then replaced by bicimal expansions. Thus the rational number

$$\frac{1}{2} \ (= \frac{1}{2^1})$$

is represented as the bicimal expansion

$$.1$$

rather than by the decimal expansion

$$.5 \ (= \frac{5}{10^1}).$$

The rational number $\frac{3}{4}$ is represented as the bicimal expansion

$$.11 \quad (= \frac{1}{2^1} + \frac{1}{2^2}),$$

The Logic of Number. Neil Tennant, Oxford University Press. © Neil Tennant 2022.
DOI: 10.1093/oso/9780192846679.003.0023

rather than by the decimal expansion

$$.75 \qquad (= \frac{7}{10^1} + \frac{5}{10^2}).$$

The rational number $\frac{5}{8}$ is represented as the bicimal expansion

$$.101 \qquad (= \frac{1}{2^1} + \frac{0}{2^2} + \frac{1}{2^3}),$$

rather than by the decimal expansion

$$.625 \qquad (= \frac{6}{10^1} + \frac{2}{10^2} + \frac{5}{10^3}).$$

These examples should suffice to convey to the reader the idea behind bicimal expansions.

We need to show that any point in the open unit segment is represented by a (possibly infinite) unique canonical bicimal expansion. And our demonstration of this fact will draw only on conceptual resources available to the Euclidean.

> **Given** a point c in the open *line-segment of unit length*, a.k.a. the *unit segment*:

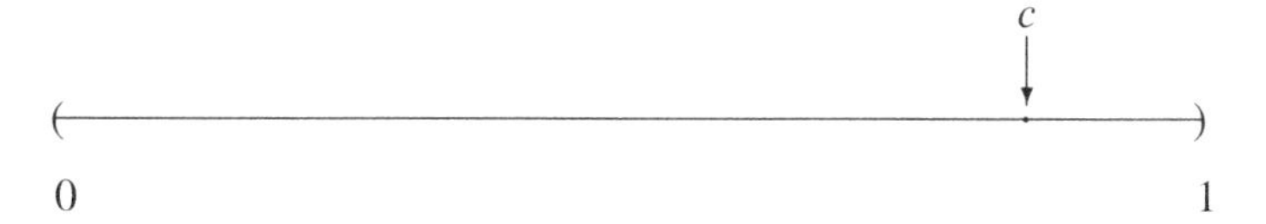

> **Problem:** Generate the bicimal representation $\mathfrak{b}(c)$ of the point c, by means of *effective Euclidean constructions*.

Call the given open unit segment I_0. This is the 0-th segment of our construction process. Our recipe for constructing $\mathfrak{b}(c)$, which we are about to lay out, will involve keeping track of segments $I_0, I_1^c, I_2^c, \ldots$. (Those after I_0 will depend on c.) I_1^c will be a subsegment of I_0; and for every $n \geq 1$, we shall have that I_{n+1}^c is a subsegment of I_n^c. Indeed, each successor segment will be either the *left open half-segment*, or the *right open half-segment*, of its predecessor. Exactly how this transpires will emerge below.

We begin at *Stage 0* of the construction process. We *bisect* the segment I_0:

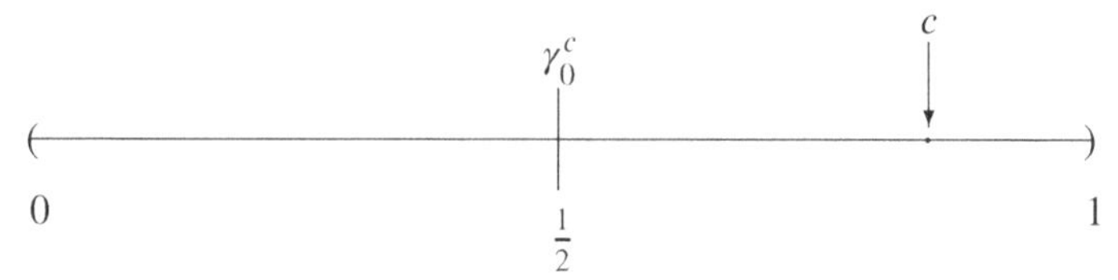

The new bisection point $\frac{1}{2}$ will be called the *0-th bisection point*, or γ_0^c.

Comment. Bisection is an effective Euclidean construction, which can be carried out by means of ruler and compass. We are talking here of an idealized process, involving perfect precision. The moving compass 'pencil point' draws an arc of no width. Such arcs intersect, if they do, at geometric points—that is, points of no spatial extension. Points can be connected by perfectly straight line-segments of no width.

Now we must determine where c lies in relation to the 0-th bisection point γ_0^c. **Trichotomy** tells us there are exactly three possibilities, and by **Anti-symmetry** these are mutually exclusive:

$$c \blacktriangleleft \gamma_0^c; \qquad c = \gamma_0^c; \qquad \gamma_0^c \blacktriangleleft c.$$

Comment. Given any two points c and d on an oriented line-segment, that have been constructed by effective Euclidean means, it is an effective Euclidean decision as to whether $c \blacktriangleleft d$, or $c = d$, or $d \blacktriangleleft c$.

In the example at hand, we have

$$\gamma_0^c \blacktriangleleft c.$$

The *1st digit* of our sought bicimal expansion $\mathfrak{b}(c)$ for c is therefore 1. Accordingly, we write

$$\mathfrak{b}(c) = \ .1 \ldots$$

without yet knowing what digits will follow in the 2nd and later places.

Note that c lies in the right open half-segment $(\frac{1}{2}, 1)$ of I_0. Accordingly, we set

$$I_1^c = (\tfrac{1}{2}, 1).$$

Now we enter *Stage 1* of our construction process. We bisect the segment I_1^c (which is the only segment for which we continue to provide a line-segment in the diagram below):

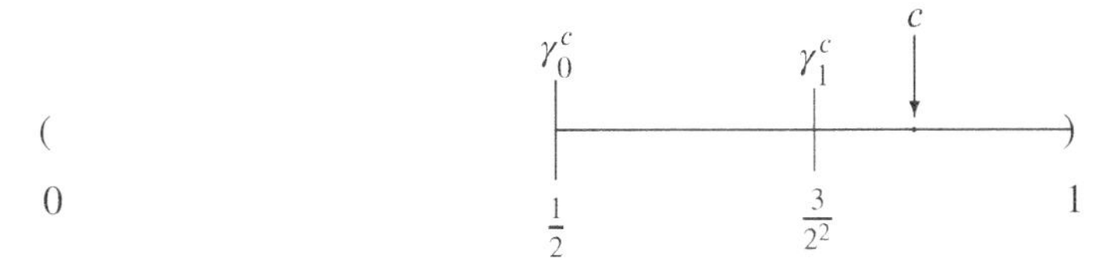

The new bisection point $\frac{3}{2^2}$ will be called the *1st bisection point determined by* c, or γ_1^c.

Now we must determine where c lies in relation to γ_1^c. As before, there are exactly three, mutually exclusive, possibilities:

$$c \blacktriangleleft \gamma_1^c; \qquad c = \gamma_1^c; \qquad \gamma_1^c \blacktriangleleft c.$$

In the example at hand, we have

$$\gamma_1^c \blacktriangleleft c.$$

The *2nd digit* of our sought bicimal expansion $\mathfrak{b}(c)$ for c is therefore 1. Accordingly, we write

$$\mathfrak{b}(c) = .11\ldots$$

without yet knowing what digits will follow in the 3rd and later places.

Note that c lies in the right open half-segment $(\gamma_1^c, 1)$ of I_1. Accordingly, we set

$$I_2^c = (\gamma_1^c, 1).$$

Now we enter *Stage 2* of our construction process. We bisect the segment I_2^c (which is the only segment for which we continue to provide a line-segment below):

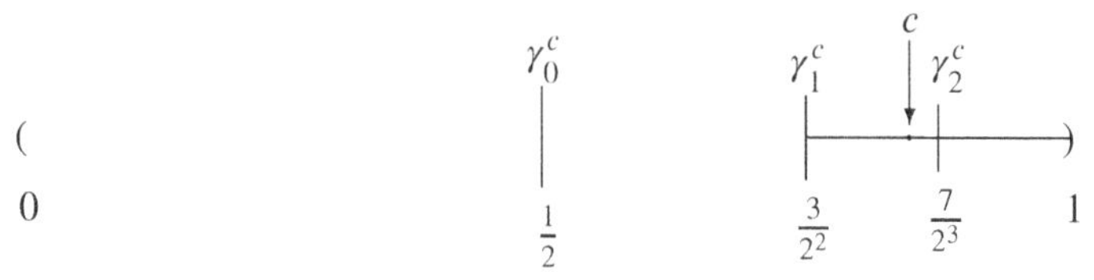

c

$\gamma_0^c \qquad \gamma_1^c \qquad \gamma_2^c$

$0 \qquad \frac{1}{2} \qquad \frac{3}{2^2} \qquad \frac{7}{2^3} \qquad 1$

The new bisection point $\frac{7}{2^3}$ will be called the *2nd bisection point determined by* c, or γ_2^c.

Now we must determine where c lies in relation to γ_2^c. There are the—by now familiar—three mutually exclusive possibilities

$$c \blacktriangleleft \gamma_2^c; \qquad c = \gamma_2^c; \qquad \gamma_2^c \blacktriangleleft c.$$

In the example at hand, we have

$$c \blacktriangleleft \gamma_2^c.$$

The *3rd digit* of our sought bicimal expansion $\mathfrak{b}(c)$ for c is therefore 0. Accordingly, we write

$$\mathfrak{b}(c) = .110\ldots$$

without yet knowing what digits will follow in the 4th and later places.

Note that c lies in the left open half-segment (γ_1^c, γ_2^c) of I_2. Accordingly, we set

$$I_3^c = (\gamma_1^c, \gamma_2^c).$$

Now we enter *Stage 3* of our construction process. We bisect the segment I_3^c (which is the only segment for which we continue to provide a line-segment below):

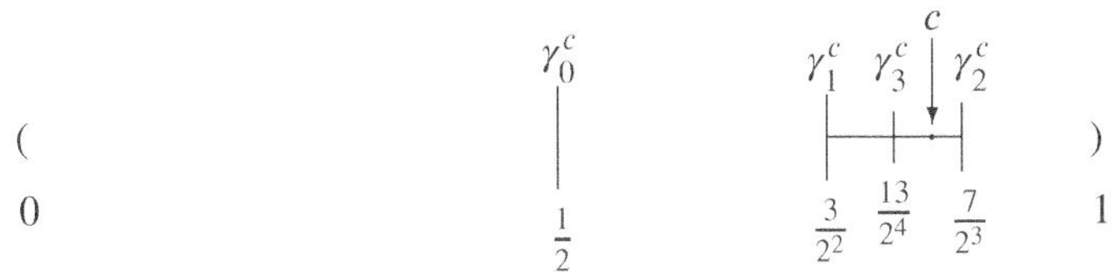

γ_0^c $\quad \gamma_1^c \quad \gamma_3^c \quad c \quad \gamma_2^c$

$($ $\qquad 0 \qquad \frac{1}{2} \qquad \frac{3}{2^2} \qquad \frac{13}{2^4} \qquad \frac{7}{2^3} \qquad 1 \qquad)$

The new bisection point $\frac{13}{2^4}$ will be called the *3rd bisection point determined by* c, or γ_3^c.

Now we must determine where c lies in relation to γ_3^c. The three mutually exclusive possibilities are

$$c \blacktriangleleft \gamma_3^c; \qquad c = \gamma_3^c; \qquad \gamma_3^c \blacktriangleleft c.$$

In the example at hand, we have

$$\gamma_3^c \blacktriangleleft c.$$

The *4th digit* of our sought bicimal expansion $\mathfrak{b}(c)$ for c is therefore 1. Accordingly, we write

$$\mathfrak{b}(c) = \ .1101\ldots$$

without yet knowing what digits will follow in the 5th and later places.

Note that c lies in the right open half-segment (γ_3^c, γ_2^c) of I_3. Accordingly, we set

$$I_4^c = (\gamma_3^c, \gamma_2^c).$$

It is unnecessary to illustrate the construction process any further. The diagram will become too crowded; and the reader will lose patience. The pattern that has emerged is as follows.

> At Stage n we define γ_n^c as the bisection point of segment I_n^c.
>
> > If $\gamma_n^c \blacktriangleleft c$, then we write 1 in the nth place of the bicimal expansion $\mathfrak{b}(c)$ for c, and we define I_{n+1}^c to be the right half open segment of I_n^c.
> >
> > If $c \blacktriangleleft \gamma_n^c$, then we write 0 in the nth place of the bicimal expansion $\mathfrak{b}(c)$ for c, and we define I_{n+1}^c to be the left half open segment of I_n^c.

Both these conditions have been illustrated in the construction process carried out above. But what happens if c coincides with γ_n^c? We take care of such an eventuality as follows:

> If $c = \gamma_n^c$, then we write 1 in the nth place of the bicimal expansion $\mathfrak{b}(c)$ for c, and we define I_{n+1}^c to be the right half open segment of I_n^c.

This ensures that any multiple of the reciprocal of a power of 2 has infinitely many consecutive zeroes in its bicimal expansion. For, given the foregoing definition of I_{n+1}^c as the right half open segment of I_n^c (when c coincides with γ_n^c), the recipe for construction will keep supplying zeroes thereafter, since c will always be to the left of the ensuing bisection points $\gamma_{n+1}, \gamma_{n+2}, \ldots$.

It follows that we never have the bicimal expansion $\mathfrak{b}(c)$ for c looking like this, with a terminal 0 followed only by 1s:

$$. \ldots 0\underbrace{111\ldots}_{\text{all 1s}}$$

Instead, the expansion would come out as

$$. \ldots 1\underbrace{000\ldots}_{\text{all 0s}}$$

In particular, we never have the bicimal expansion

$$\underbrace{.111\ldots}_{\text{all 1s}}$$

For that would correspond to 1, or rather

$$1.\underbrace{000\ldots}_{\text{all 0s}}$$

which is the right endpoint of the closed segment [0,1], hence not in the open segment (0,1).

A *canonical* bicimal expansion is one with no terminal 0—that is, there is no place within the expansion after which one encounters only 1s. Our method of repeated bisection of the open unit segment ensures that to each of its points there corresponds a unique canonical bicimal expansion. (Strictly speaking, our construction works also with the left-closed unit segment [0,1). For the geometric point 0 our recipe would then construct the bicimal expansion .00000... , which is canonical.) Henceforth we suppress the adjective 'canonical' unless it is needed for argumentative purposes.

Chapter 24

Uncountability

Abstract

This chapter shows that one can meet the one remaining condition of adequacy that has been imposed on any account of the real numbers—that of demonstrating their uncountability. It rigorously examines the method inherent in Cantor's proof of the uncountability of the reals. The proof takes subtly different forms, depending on whether one is conceiving of the reals as bicimals (as is the case here), or as the one-one corresponding sets of natural numbers. There is also the general set-theoretic form, establishing that every set has strictly more subsets than members. A careful investigation is undertaken of how the 'shape' or 'line of argument' in each of these diagonalization proofs is respectively regimented as a formal deduction. The method of diagonalization is so elementary in its existential and methodological presuppositions that it should be completely convincing to all stripes of mathematician contemplating the question of how many reals there are—including those not committed to the existence of any completed infinite totality, let alone a completed *uncountably* infinite totality. Even the ontologically conservative Kroneckerian, who is committed to no more than the individual natural numbers (and not to the totality they form), and who employs only constructive deductive reasoning, can see that there must be uncountably infinitely many reals, if they exist. This philosophical conclusion is based on the formally rigorous regimentation of the Cantorian reasoning by diagonalization, in free Core Logic.

The reader will recall from Chapter 5 (see p. 56) that one of our four main conditions of adequacy for a natural-logicist account of the real numbers is that the account should reveal that there are uncountably many real numbers. It is to be expected that Cantorian diagonalization will be involved somehow. Indeed it is—and in perhaps the most direct and economical way, when one is working with bicimals as representing the reals.

In order rigorously to examine the method of Cantor's proof of the uncountability of the reals, it will be useful to look at the subtly different forms it takes, in connection with two ways of thinking of the reals, and in connection with sets in general.

First, one can deal directly, and right away, with the reals as *bicimals*, and show that there are uncountably many of them. Recall that a bicimal representing a real number is generated by the geometric determinacy of successive Yes/No

The Logic of Number. Neil Tennant, Oxford University Press. © Neil Tennant 2022.
DOI: 10.1093/oso/9780192846679.003.0024

answers to two questions. The first of these is the question 'Is the given target point identical to the most recently determined bisection point?'. If the answer is Yes, then the value of the bicimal at that stage is determined to be 1, and all further values will be 0. If, however, the answer is No, then the second question has to be raised: 'Is the given target point to the left or to the right of the most recently determined bisection point?'. If the answer is 'to the left', then the value of the bicimal at that stage is determined to be 0; whereas if the answer is 'to the right', then the value of the bicimal at that stage is determined to be 1. Whichever of these is the case—to the left or to the right—a new bisection point of the 'residual interval' has to be determined so that the generation of 0s and 1s can be continued. Geometric reality dictates the answers, at every stage, to the two kinds of question raised. The resulting bicimal sequence of 0s and 1s for the target point is therefore 'geometrically effectively enumerable'.

Second, one can reconceptualize bicimals as corresponding one-one with sets of natural numbers, and show that there are uncountably many of the latter. The one-one correspondence is obvious: the set of natural numbers corresponding to a given bicimal $\mathfrak{b}$ has n as a member just in case $\mathfrak{b}(n) = 1$. Moreover—and this will emerge as important in further philosophical discussion below—these corresponding sets of natural numbers, thanks to the properties of the bicimals themselves, are listed in the increasing order of their members. Accordingly, membership in the set $\mathfrak{b}_N$ of naturals corresponding to the bicimal $\mathfrak{b}$ is 'geometrically effectively decidable'. For any natural number k, to determine whether $k \in \mathfrak{b}_N$, all one has to do is determine $\mathfrak{b}(k)$; if this value is 0, then $k \notin \mathfrak{b}_N$, whereas if this value is 1, then $k \in \mathfrak{b}_N$.

Third, one can generalize this second form of proof so as to deal with sets in general: one shows that every set has more subsets than members.

By regimenting these three respective forms of 'diagonal proof' in free Core Logic, using the respective vocabularies that are called for, one can see exactly what is rigorously established in each case, and attain an important insight: the uncountability phenomenon is stable across different combinations of ontological and methodological views. Even the constructivist who eschews the strictly classical inferences of classical logic, and who in addition will not commit to the existence of any infinite totality (including even that of the natural numbers themselves), can appreciate, on the basis of the formal proofs we shall furnish, that there must be uncountably many real numbers.

Let us deal now with the first case, involving bicimals. This is the setting that makes it obvious why the method has come to be known as the 'diagonal' method.

In due course we give an informally rigorous proof (Theorem 6) that there are uncountably infinitely many bicimals. But first we provide a governing definition, and a few further remarks about the universal acceptability and impact of Cantor's reasoning.

Definition 27. *A* bicimal *is an infinite sequence of 0s and 1s. Thus we render a* *bicimal* $\mathfrak{b}$ *as taking the 'list form'*

$$\mathfrak{b}_0, \mathfrak{b}_1, \mathfrak{b}_2, \ldots$$

where for every natural number n

$$\textit{either } \mathfrak{b}_n = 0 \textit{ or } \mathfrak{b}_n = 1.$$

A bicimal may be thought of as a function that is defined on all and only natural numbers, and whose only values are 0 and 1. Thus each entry $\mathfrak{b}_n$ in the list form of $\mathfrak{b}$ that we have just displayed is the value $\mathfrak{b}(n)$ of the function $\mathfrak{b}$ on the argument n.

Note that the modern mathematician's standard way of saying that $\mathfrak{b}$ is such a function is to write

$$\mathfrak{b} : \mathbb{N} \mapsto \{0, 1\},$$

or

$$\mathfrak{b} : \omega \mapsto \{0, 1\}.$$

This form of expression usually presupposes that $\mathbb{N}$ (or ω) is the completed totality of natural numbers. It presupposes also that the pair set $\{0, 1\}$ exists—which, to be sure, is a much tamer existential commitment.

Either one of the foregoing is just one way—the most conventional one for the contemporary mathematician at home in ZF—of conceiving of a bicimal as a thing, or an object, in one's mathematical ontology. The mathematician might be thinking of $\mathbb{N}$ as the completed totality of natural numbers where these are conceived of as *sui generis*; or she might be thinking of ω as the completed totality (at rank $V_{\omega+1}$ in the cumulative hierarchy of pure sets) of the finite von Neumann ordinals, which are the set theorist's usual surrogates for the natural numbers. Indeed, the two casts of mathematical mind—the one that regards the natural numbers as *sui generis*, and the one that regards them as finite von Neumann ordinals—enjoy a kind of confluence in agreement if they say that the function in question is the completed totality of ordered pairs of the form $\langle n, \mathfrak{b}(n)\rangle$, where n is a natural number (however conceived) and each $\mathfrak{b}(n)$ is either 0 or 1 (and that value is the only one for the given n). Either way, on the conception of a function as a set of ordered pairs constituting a many-one relation, the mathematician is committed to the existence of a completed or potentially infinite totality.

Whichever is her cast of mind concerning just the natural numbers themselves, the mathematician has to be able to reify, or hypostasize, bicimals in order to be able to raise the important question

How many bicimals are there?

Note that this question is about how many completed or potentially infinite totalities of a certain circumscribed kind there 'happen' to be. This 'happening', of course, is not a contingent one. It could not have been, or be, otherwise. It is a Platonic necessity, albeit potentially an intellectually elusive one.

We wish to maintain that there is a shared and robust commonality of conception (of bicimals) among all mathematicians, whatever their differentiating ideological or ontological commitments might be regarding infinite totalities as completed or merely potential. They can all conceive of and think about bicimals in their respective trademark ways. This is so whether they are (at one end of the scale) constrained 'Koneckerian constructivists' making do with what human thinkers can make out of the divine gift of the natural numbers, or (at the other end of the scale) committed 'infinitarian Platonists' who are happy to embrace a cumulative hierarchy of sets extending well beyond the hereditarily finite pure sets. The only stripe of mathematician who has no place at the table, to discuss the question raised, is the strict finitist.

We contend here that Cantor's method of diagonalization is *so elementary* in its existential and methodological presuppositions that it should be completely convincing to all stripes of mathematician contemplating the question of how many bicimals there are. The answer that should be uniformly convincing is that there are uncountably infinitely many of them. And this answer can be deduced, and advanced, even by a thinker who is not committed to the existence of any completed infinite totality—let alone a completed uncountably infinite totality.

The (wrong) answer that there are only countably infinitely many bicimals takes the following form:

> There is a 'master' list of bicimals
>
> $$\mathfrak{b}^0, \mathfrak{b}^1, \mathfrak{b}^2, \ldots$$
>
> on which every bicimal appears, i.e., such that
>
> $$\forall \text{ bicimal } \mathfrak{b}\ \exists m\ \mathfrak{b} = \mathfrak{b}^m.$$

Note that this alleged master list is, in effect, a countably infinite list of countably infinite lists (of 0s and 1s). So, depicting the latter lists as proceeding horizontally across the page, and the former master list of lists as proceeding vertically down the page, the claim under consideration (for *reductio ad absurdum*) is that there is a vertical list of horizontal lists like this:

$$\begin{array}{l}
\mathfrak{b}^0(0), \mathfrak{b}^0(1), \mathfrak{b}^0(2), \ldots \\
\mathfrak{b}^1(0), \mathfrak{b}^1(1), \mathfrak{b}^1(2), \ldots \\
\mathfrak{b}^2(0), \mathfrak{b}^2(1), \mathfrak{b}^2(2), \ldots \\
\vdots \\
\mathfrak{b}^n(0), \mathfrak{b}^n(1), \mathfrak{b}^n(2), \ldots \\
\vdots
\end{array}$$

that contains every bicimal as one of its horizontal rows.

Given any countable 'master' list like the foregoing, of bicimals—call such a list $\mathfrak{b}$—we can define as follows a so-called *diagonal bicimal* for it—call it $\delta_{\mathfrak{b}}$. From now on, however, we suppress the subscript $\mathfrak{b}$ and simply render the diagonal bicimal as

$$\delta = \delta_0, \delta_1, \delta_2, \ldots .$$

δ is defined as follows:

$$\forall n \begin{cases} \delta_n = 0 \text{ if } (\mathfrak{b}^n)_n = 1; \\ \delta_n = 1 \text{ if } (\mathfrak{b}^n)_n = 0. \end{cases}$$

An alternative, *inferentially schematic*, formulation of this definition of δ would be

Definition 28. $\dfrac{(\mathfrak{b}^n)_n=1}{\delta_n=0} \qquad \dfrac{(\mathfrak{b}^n)_n=0}{\delta_n=1}$

The diagonal δ is definitely a bicimal. It assigns to each natural number n either the value 0 or the value 1. Moreover, it does so in a way that is

(i) at least as determinate and constructively given[1] as the supposed master list of bicimals; and
(ii) at least as determinate and constructively given as each and every one of the bicimals appearing in the supposed master list.

For any natural number n, the bicimal δ will have its first n digits (0s and/or 1s) determined within a finite time. This is because one can generate, in a finite time, the initial segments of length n of the first n members of the master list. Thereafter one changes the nth digit of the n bicimal in the master list in order to obtain the nth digit of the bicimal δ that is 'under construction'.

Theorem 6. [Cantor on bicimals]
There can be no countable list of all bicimals.

Proof. For *reductio ad absurdum*, suppose there is a countably infinite 'master' list

$$\begin{array}{c} \mathfrak{b}^0 \\ \mathfrak{b}^1 \\ \mathfrak{b}^2 \\ \vdots \end{array}$$

that contains all bicimals. Its diagonal bicimal δ is itself a bicimal. It would therefore follow, as a consequence of our *reductio* supposition, that δ appears as

[1] We use 'constructive' here in the usual sense among practicing mathematicians. That is, one is able to specify a real number by means of sufficiently (but finitely) many places in k-mal place notation, to get within an arbitrary margin of accuracy to the real number that is the limit of the 'whole series'. In the context of our considerations, this limit will be approached 'from below', since the progressively longer initial segments of the bicimal being generated are non-decreasing.

one of the bicimals on the master list. That is, the following existential claim would hold:

$$\exists m\ \delta = \mathfrak{b}^m . \tag{24.1}$$

Suppose, then, (for existential elimination) that δ appears on the master list as $\mathfrak{b}^i$. So we have

$$\delta = \mathfrak{b}^i . \tag{24.2}$$

Since $\mathfrak{b}^i$ is a bicimal, it follows from Definition 27 that

$$\text{either}\ \ \mathfrak{b}^i(i) = 0\ \ \text{or}\ \ \mathfrak{b}^i(i) = 1 .$$

We now argue by cases.

First case: suppose that

$$\mathfrak{b}^i(i) = 0 .$$

Then by definition of the construction of δ we have

$$\delta(i) = 1 .$$

This contradicts (24.2). This is because a necessary condition for the identity or functions is that they assign the same value to any argument.[2]

Second case: suppose that

$$\mathfrak{b}^i(i) = 1 .$$

Then by definition of the construction of δ we have

$$\delta(i) = 0 ,$$

again contradicting (24.2).

By $\vee$-Elimination we now have contradiction following from (24.2). But (24.2) is our parametric assumption of $\exists$-Elimination. So contradiction follows from the existential (24.1) above.

The *reductio ad absurdum* is now complete. There can be no countably infinite master list of all countably infinite lists of 0s and 1s. □

In order to regiment this informally rigorous proof of the bicimals' uncountability into a formally rigorous one, it serves our purposes well to avail ourselves of some further formal rules, which allow the natural logicist to 'atomicize' the formal proof as much as possible. Recall that the monadic sortal predicate Nx

[2]That is (in the direction needed for our deductive purposes here), for any two functions f and g defined on the natural numbers,

$$f = g\ \Rightarrow\ \forall i\ f(i) = g(i) .$$

means 'x is a natural number', and that the Constructive Logicist has already 'logicized' it (see Part II).

Rules of inference for $\mathbb{B}(\mathfrak{b})$
('$\mathfrak{b}$ is a bicimal')

$$\mathbb{B}\text{-I} \qquad \dfrac{\begin{array}{c} \overline{Na}^{\,(i)} \\ \vdots \\ \mathfrak{b}(a)=0 \vee \mathfrak{b}(a)=1 \end{array}}{\mathbb{B}(\mathfrak{b})}{\scriptstyle (i)} \qquad \text{where } a \text{ is parametric}$$

$$\mathbb{B}\text{-E} \qquad \dfrac{\mathbb{B}(\mathfrak{b}) \quad Nt \quad \begin{array}{c} \overline{\mathfrak{b}(t)=0}^{\,(i)} \\ \vdots \\ \psi \end{array} \quad \begin{array}{c} \overline{\mathfrak{b}(t)=1}^{\,(i)} \\ \vdots \\ \psi \end{array}}{\psi}{\scriptstyle (i)}$$

Rules of inference governing identity between bicimals

The identity statement $\mathfrak{b}=\mathfrak{b}'$ for *bicimals* $\mathfrak{b}$, $\mathfrak{b}'$ is governed by the following rules:

$$\mathbb{B}_{=}: \quad \dfrac{\begin{array}{c} \overline{Na}^{\,(i)} \\ \vdots \\ \mathfrak{b}(a)=\mathfrak{b}'(a) \end{array}}{\mathfrak{b}=\mathfrak{b}'}{\scriptstyle (i)} \quad \text{where } a \text{ is parametric} \qquad\qquad \mathbb{B}^{=}: \quad \dfrac{\mathfrak{b}=\mathfrak{b}' \quad Nt}{\mathfrak{b}(t)=\mathfrak{b}'(t)}$$

Rules of inference for $\mathcal{L}\mathbb{B}(\beta)$
('β is a countably infinite list of bicimals')

$$\mathcal{L}\mathbb{B}\text{-I} \qquad \dfrac{\begin{array}{c} \overline{Na}^{\,(i)} \\ \vdots \\ \mathbb{B}(\beta(a)) \end{array}}{\mathcal{L}\mathbb{B}(\beta)}{\scriptstyle (i)}$$

$$\mathcal{L}\mathbb{B}\text{-E} \qquad \dfrac{\mathcal{L}\mathbb{B}(\beta) \quad Nt}{\mathbb{B}(\beta(t))}$$

Extra rule of inference in addition to $\mathcal{L}\mathbb{B}$-I and $\mathcal{L}\mathbb{B}$-E, for
'β is a countably infinite list of *all* bicimals'

$$\omega\forall:\quad \dfrac{\mathbb{B}(\mathfrak{b}) \qquad \begin{array}{c}\underbrace{\overline{\mathfrak{b}=\beta(a)}^{\,(i)}\ ,\ \overline{Na}^{\,(i)}}\\ \vdots\\ \psi\end{array}}{\psi}\,(i) \qquad \text{where } a \text{ is parametric}$$

Here now is the fully formal proof promised:

$$\dfrac{\mathbb{B}(\delta) \qquad \dfrac{\dfrac{\mathbb{B}(\delta)\quad \overline{\delta=\mathfrak{b}^a}^{\,(2)}}{\mathbb{B}(\mathfrak{b}^a)} \quad \overline{Na}^{\,(2)} \quad \dfrac{\dfrac{\dfrac{\dfrac{\overline{\delta=\mathfrak{b}^a}^{\,(2)}\quad \overline{Na}^{\,(2)}}{\delta(a)=\mathfrak{b}^a(a)}\mathbb{B}{=} \quad \overline{\mathfrak{b}^a(a)=0}^{\,(1)}}{\delta(a)=0} \quad \dfrac{\overline{\mathfrak{b}^a(a)=0}^{\,(1)}}{\delta(a)=1}\text{D28}}{0=1}}{\bot} \quad \dfrac{\dfrac{\dfrac{\dfrac{\overline{\delta=\mathfrak{b}^a}^{\,(2)}\quad \overline{Na}^{\,(2)}}{\delta(a)=\mathfrak{b}^a(a)}\mathbb{B}{=} \quad \overline{\mathfrak{b}^a(a)=1}^{\,(1)}}{\delta(a)=1} \quad \dfrac{\overline{\mathfrak{b}^a(a)=1}^{\,(1)}}{\delta(a)=0}\text{D28}}{0=1}}{\bot}}{\bot}(1)\ \mathbb{B}\text{-E}}{\bot}(2)\ \omega\forall$$

This is a *reductio* with $\mathbb{B}(\delta)$ as sole undischarged *sentential* assumption. It is not, however, a *reductio of* $\mathbb{B}(\delta)$; for we have already convinced ourselves of the truth of $\mathbb{B}(\delta)$. The target of the *reductio* is the *inferential* assumption $\omega\forall$. This is the inference rule used at the final step. It gives expression to the false claim that

$$\mathfrak{b}^0, \mathfrak{b}^1, \mathfrak{b}^2, \ldots$$

is a countably infinite list of all bicimals.

Let us now look at Cantor's reasoning in the context of sets in general. For a fully rigorous exposition we need to state formally the free-logical rules for the set-abstraction operator in set theory. Before doing so, however, we take this opportunity to emphasize an important philosophical and methodological point: the natural-deduction rules below characterize the logic of sets. They incur no ontological commitment to any sets whatsoever. All they do is capture the analytic connections among predication, set-existence, and set-membership.

A set-abstraction term is formed by means of a dominant occurrence of the variable-binding abstraction operator $\{x|\ldots x\ldots\}$. This operator may be applied to a formula Φ to form the set-abstraction term $\{x|\Phi\}$ if, but only if, the variable x enjoys a free occurrence in Φ.

The rule of introduction (in free logic) for the variable-binding abstraction operator that forms set-terms from predicates is

$$
\{\ \}\mathrm{I}\qquad
\begin{array}{ccc}
\underbrace{{}^{(i)}\overline{\exists!a}\ ,\ \overline{\Phi^x_a}^{(i)}} & & \overline{a\in t}^{(i)}\\
\vdots & & \vdots\\
a\in t & \exists!t & \Phi^x_a\\
\hline
\multicolumn{3}{c}{t=\{x|\Phi\}}
\end{array}{}^{(i)}
$$

, where a is parametric.[3]

Note how the canonical conclusion

$$t=\{x|\Phi\}$$

of { }I has t on its left-hand side, as a placeholder for any singular term whatsoever, including the parameters (conventionally a, b, c, ...) that can be used for reasoning involving existentials and universals.

The elimination rules corresponding to the introduction rule for { } are the following three, each one employing the canonical identity statement

$$t=\{x|\Phi\}$$

as its major premise (to the left, immediately above the inference stroke). The minor premises (or subproofs) of the first and third rules correspond, respectively, to the first and third immediate subproofs of the introduction rule. This is a convincing sign that the elimination rules are in harmony with the introduction rule that begets them. Bear in mind that the major premise $t=\{x|\Phi\}$ stands proud in any application of an elimination rule for { }.

$$
\{\ \}\mathrm{E}_1\qquad \frac{t=\{x|\Phi\}\quad \exists!v\quad \Phi^x_v}{v\in t}
$$

$$
\{\ \}\mathrm{E}_2\qquad \frac{t=\{x|\Phi\}}{\exists!t}
$$

$$
\{\ \}\mathrm{E}_3\qquad
\begin{array}{ccc}
 & & \overline{\Phi^x_v}^{(i)}\\
 & & \vdots\\
t=\{x|\Phi\} & v\in t & \theta\\
\hline
\multicolumn{3}{c}{\theta}
\end{array}{}^{(i)}
$$

The rule { }E_1 has an atomic conclusion, so it is not necessary to parallelize it for the purposes of Core Logic. This is because no atomic conclusion can feature as the major premise of any elimination.[4]

[3] Note that since $\in$ is an *atomic* binary predicate, the assumption $a\in t$ in the rightmost subordinate proof implies $\exists!a$ (by the Rule of Atomic Denotation—see p. 12.). So is it not necessary to have $\exists!a$ as a further dischargeable assumption in that subordinate proof.

[4] Recall that a signal feature of proofs in Core Logic is that major premises of eliminations stand proud, with no proof-work above them.

The rule { }E_2 is a special case of the Rule of Atomic Denotation.

The rule { }E_3 needs to be parallelized, in order to avoid having non-trivial proof-work above Φ^x_v should it happen to stand as the major premise of an elimination.

Definition 29.

$$x \subseteq y \equiv_{df} \forall z(z \in x \rightarrow z \in y)$$

Definition 30.

$$\{\varphi(x)|\psi(x)\} =_{df} \{x|\varphi(x) \wedge \psi(x)\}$$

Observation 3. *The definiendum in Definition 30 can be read felicitously as 'the set of all* φ*s that* ψ*'. When* $\varphi(x)$ *takes the form* $x \in X$*, the reading is the familiar 'the set of all* x *in* X *such that* $\psi(x)$*'. More formally:*

$$\{x \in X|\psi(x)\} =_{df} \{x|x \in X \wedge \psi(x)\}$$

We shall prove rigorously a handful of lemmas that will find application in our regimentation of Cantorian 'diagonal' reasoning about sets.

Lemma 62. $$\dfrac{v \in \{x|\Phi x \wedge \Psi x\}}{\Phi v}$$

Proof.

$$\dfrac{\dfrac{v \in \{x|\Phi x \wedge \Psi x\}}{\exists!\{x|\Phi x \wedge \Psi x\}} \qquad \dfrac{{}^{(2)}\overline{a = \{x|\Phi x \wedge \Psi x\}} \quad \dfrac{v \in \{x|\Phi x \wedge \Psi x\} \quad {}^{(2)}\overline{a = \{x|\Phi x \wedge \Psi x\}}}{v \in a} \quad \dfrac{\overline{\Phi v \wedge \Psi v}^{\,(2)} \quad \overline{\Phi v}^{\,(1)}}{\Phi v}{\scriptstyle (1)}}{\Phi v}{\scriptstyle (2)\ \{\ \}\text{-}E_3}}{\Phi v}{\scriptstyle (3)}$$

□

Lemma 63. $$\dfrac{t = \{\varphi x|\psi x\}}{\forall y(y \in t \rightarrow \varphi y)}$$

Proof.

$$\dfrac{\dfrac{\dfrac{\dfrac{\dfrac{\overline{a \in t}^{\,(1)} \quad t = \{\varphi x|\psi x\}}{a \in \{\varphi x|\psi x\}}}{a \in \{x|\varphi x \wedge \psi x\}}{\scriptstyle \text{D30}}}{\varphi a}{\scriptstyle \text{L62}}}{a \in t \rightarrow \varphi a}{\scriptstyle (1)}}{\forall y(y \in t \rightarrow \varphi y)}$$

□

Lemma 64. $\dfrac{t \in \{x \in X \,|\, \psi(x)\}}{\psi(t)}$

Proof. By Lemma 62, via Definition 30. □

Lemma 65. $\dfrac{t = \{x \in X \,|\, \psi(x)\}}{t \subseteq X}$

Proof.

$$\cfrac{\cfrac{\cfrac{\cfrac{\cfrac{\overline{a \in t}^{(1)} \quad t = \{x \in X \,|\, \psi(x)\}}{a \in \{x \in X \,|\, \psi(x)\}}}{a \in X}\,\text{L62}}{a \in t \rightarrow a \in X}\,(1)}{\forall z(z \in t \rightarrow z \in X)}}{}$$

i.e., $t \subseteq X$

□

Lemma 66. $\dfrac{\exists!\{x|\Phi x\} \quad \exists! t \quad \Phi t}{t \in \{x|\Phi x\}}$

Proof.

$$\cfrac{\exists!\{x|\Phi x\} \qquad \cfrac{\overline{a = \{x|\Phi x\}}^{(1)} \qquad \cfrac{\overline{a = \{x|\Phi x\}}^{(1)} \quad \exists! t \quad \Phi t}{t \in a}\,\{\,\}\text{E}_1}{t \in \{x|\Phi x\}}}{t \in \{x|\Phi x\}}\,(1)$$

□

We now state and prove Cantor's Theorem for set theory. It concerns sets in general, and is not particularly focused on either the naturals or the reals.

Theorem 7. [Cantor on sets in general]
For no set X does any function map to each subset of X some member of X.

Proof. Let X be any set. Suppose, for the main *reductio ad absurdum*, that f is a function mapping to each subset of X some member of X. Suppose the set

$$\{x \in X \,|\, x \notin f(x)\}$$

exists. Call it D:

$$D = \{x \in X \,|\, x \notin f(x)\}\,.$$

Then, by Lemma 65, we have $D \subset X$. By supposition, there is some $d \in X$ such that $D = f(d)$. (Note that it is not required that d be unique in this regard.)

Suppose, for subsidiary *reductio*, that

$$d \in f(d),$$

i.e.,

$$d \in \{x \in X \mid x \notin f(x)\}.$$

Then by Lemma 64

$$d \notin f(d).$$

Thus

$$d \notin f(d), \tag{24.3}$$

independently of the *reductio* assumption that $d \in f(d)$.

But now by Lemma 66, since $d \in X$, we have, from this fact, along with the existence of $\{x \in X \mid x \notin f(x)\}$ and (24.3),

$$d \in \{x \in X \mid x \notin f(x)\},$$

i.e.,

$$d \in f(d).$$

Contradiction. □

So: no function maps to each subset of X some member of X. *A fortiori*, there cannot be any 1-1 relation between all the members of X and all the subsets of X—because such a relation would provide a function of the kind shown to be impossible.

Note that this proof does not require that one be able to form the power set of X, i.e., the set of all subsets of X. It shows the impossibility, for any set X, of a relation $\varphi(x, y)$ purporting to represent a function from some (not necessarily: all) of the members of X to all the subsets of X, i.e., a relation $\varphi(x, y)$ for which the following conditions would hold:

$\forall x \forall y \forall z((\varphi(x, y) \wedge \varphi(x, z)) \rightarrow y = z)$	φ is single-valued, i.e., a function
$\forall y(y \subseteq X \rightarrow \exists x(x \in X \wedge \varphi(x, y)))$	Every subset of X is borne φ by a member of X

Nota bene: We make no use, in our *reductio*, of any assumption to the effect that the function φ is everywhere defined on X, or that φ is 1-1.

We now construct a completely formal proof of the inconsistency of the last two displayed sentences within the (free) core logic of sets. We shall use the inferential method. Our proofs will involve only literals, and existential statements of the form $\exists!t$. We shall use the inferential rule stated below, which involves only atomic sentences (including one that counts as atomic in the context, involving the defined predicate $\subseteq$). This rule will serve as the 'main *reductio* assumption' in the proof of Cantor's Theorem for sets in general. The sentential expression of the *reductio* assumption would be

'φ is onto all subsets of X, from members of X.'

Here now is the inferential rule, in natural-deduction terms, that expresses this thought:

$$\Omega : \quad \dfrac{t \subseteq X \qquad \begin{array}{c} \underbrace{\overline{t = \varphi a}^{\,(i)} \;,\; \overline{a \in X}^{\,(i)}} \\ \vdots \\ \psi \end{array}}{\psi}\,(i)$$

The existential parameter a may occur only where explicitly indicated.

Note that we write $t = \varphi a$ instead of $t = \iota y \varphi a y$. Then we regiment the foregoing informal reasoning in the free core logic of sets, using the rules already stated.

Proof. **(of Theorem 7, fully regimented)**
First we define the proof Π as follows.

$$\begin{array}{c} \underbrace{D=\{x\in X|x\notin fx\}\;,\; d\in X\;,\; D=fd} \\ \Pi \\ d\in\{x\in X\,|\,x\notin fx\} \end{array} \quad =_{df}$$

$$\dfrac{\dfrac{D=\{x\in X\,|\,x\notin fx\}}{\exists!\{x\in X\,|\,x\notin fx\}}\,\text{RAD} \qquad \dfrac{d\in X}{\exists! d} \qquad \dfrac{d\in X \qquad \dfrac{\dfrac{\dfrac{\dfrac{D=\{x\in X\,|\,x\notin fx\} \qquad \dfrac{D=fd \quad \overline{d\in fd}^{\,(1)}}{d\in D}\,{=}\text{Sub}}{d\in\{x\in X\,|\,x\notin fx\}}\,{=}\text{Sub}}{d\notin fd}\,\text{L64} \qquad \overline{d\in fd}^{\,(1)}}{\bot}}{d\notin fd}\,(1)}{d\in X\wedge d\notin fd}}{d\in\{x\in X\,|\,x\notin fx\}}\,\text{L66, Defn.30}$$

Then we embed two copies of Π to form the proof Σ as follows.

$$\Sigma : \quad \dfrac{\exists!\{x\in X|x\notin fx\} \qquad \dfrac{\dfrac{\overline{D=\{x\in X|x\notin fx\}}^{\,(4)}}{D\subseteq X}\,\text{L65} \qquad \dfrac{\dfrac{\begin{array}{c}\underbrace{\overline{D=\{x\in X|x\notin fx\}}^{\,(4)}\,,\,\overline{d\in X}^{\,(3)}\,,\,\overline{D=fd}^{\,(3)}} \\ \Pi \\ d\in\{x\in X|x\notin fx\}\end{array}}{d\notin fd}\,\text{L64} \qquad \dfrac{\dfrac{\overline{D=\{x\in X|x\notin fx\}}^{\,(4)} \quad \begin{array}{c}\underbrace{\overline{D=\{x\in X|x\notin fx\}}^{\,(4)}\,,\,\overline{d\in X}^{\,(3)}\,,\,\overline{D=fd}^{\,(3)}} \\ \Pi \\ d\in\{x\in X|x\notin fx\}\end{array}}{d\in D} \qquad \overline{D=fd}^{\,(3)}}{d\in fd}\,{=}\text{Sub}}{\bot}}{\bot}\,(3)\,\Omega}{\bot}\,(4)$$

□

Despite the fact that bicimals correspond one-one so obviously with sets of naturals (as explained above), the diagonal proof-method that deals with reals as bicimals does not translate straightforwardly into one that deals with reals as sets of naturals. Instead, the diagonal proof-method for the latter has to follow rather slavishly the line of argument (regimented by Σ above) for Cantor's Theorem concerning sets in general. Details to warrant this claim will emerge below. We shall see how Cantor's Theorem in the foregoing general form for sets 'specializes down' to the natural numbers. This is the case even though we do not take $\mathbb{N}$ for X; instead, we simply speak in general of sets of naturals without undertaking any commitment to the set $\mathbb{N}$ itself—let alone to its power set.

Theorem 8. [Cantor on sets of naturals]
No function maps to each set of naturals a natural.

Proof. Suppose, for *reductio ad absurdum*, that there is a function φ that maps to each set of naturals a natural. Formally:

$$\exists\varphi\forall z(\forall x(x \in z \rightarrow Nx) \rightarrow \exists y(Ny \wedge \varphi(y) = z)). \tag{24.4}$$

Let f be such a function. Thus we have

$$\forall z(\forall x(x \in z \rightarrow Nx) \rightarrow \exists y(Ny \wedge f(y) = z)).$$

Consider the set

$$D^f \ =_{df} \ \{x|Nx \wedge x \notin f(x)\}$$

of natural numbers. Note that D^f *is* a set of natural numbers, *should it exist*. Let us assume it does exist. Then the free core logician can instantiate $\forall z$ with respect to D^f. By { }-Elim and $\wedge$-Elim we would have further that

$$\forall x(x \in D^f \rightarrow Nx).$$

From our *reductio* supposition (24.4) concerning f, it follows by $\forall$-Elim (instantiating z with D^f) and $\rightarrow$-Elim that

$$\exists y(Ny \wedge f(y) = D^f).$$

For the purposes of $\exists$-Elim, let d be an arbitrary natural number such that

$$Nd \wedge f(d) = D^f.$$

Hence we have both

$$Nd$$

and

$$f(d) = D^f.$$

Note that by definition of D^f we have

$$f(d) = \{x|Nx \wedge x \notin f(x)\}. \quad (24.5)$$

Suppose for subsidiary *reductio* that

$$d \in f(d),$$

i.e., by (24.5)

$$d \in \{x|Nx \wedge x \notin f(x)\}.$$

Then by { }-Elim and $\wedge$-Elim, it follows that

$$d \notin f(d).$$

Thus we have

$$d \notin f(d) \quad (24.6)$$

discharging the subsidiary *reductio* assumption that $d \in f(d)$. The subsidiary *reductio* is now complete.

But now, since Nd, we have

$$Nd \wedge d \notin f(d),$$

whence by Lemma 66 and the assumed fact that $\exists!d$ we have

$$d \in \{x|Nx \wedge x \notin f(x)\}. \quad (24.7)$$

Substituting in (24.7) by (24.5), we conclude that

$$d \in f(d).$$

This contradicts the earlier conclusion

$$d \notin f(d)$$

reached above.

The *reductio* of our main supposition (24.4) is now complete.

No function maps to each set of naturals a natural. □

What we have given is a proof meeting the standard of 'informal rigor'. The overall logical result that it establishes is the impossibility that the 'diagonal set' $\{Nx|x \notin fx\}$ exist if f assigns to every set of naturals a natural.

Consider now the philosophical implications of this, before we regiment the proof fully in our Core Logic of sets. The free core logician is theorizing about sets, but is at the extraordinarily innocent stage where no ontological commitments to any set(s) of any kind have been incurred. To be sure, he has committed himself earlier to the naturals numbers, individually, as logical objects *sui generis*, satisfying the predicate N. But he has not yet committed himself to the existence of a *totality* of natural numbers, either in the form $\{x|Nx\}$ or in the form of ω, the set of all finite von Neumann ordinals, which is ZF's gold standard as the first, and countable, infinity. Nevertheless, the core logician who is theorizing about sets only analytically, on the basis of the introduction and elimination rules for the set-abstraction operator, is fully apprised of the explosive Cantorian consequence of combining either one of the outright existential claims $\exists!\{x|Nx\}$ or $\exists!\omega$ with even a very tame form of *Aussonderung*, or Separation:

$$\frac{\exists! X}{\exists!\{x \in X | \Phi x\}}\ , \text{ where } \Phi \text{ is a } \Sigma^0_1 \text{ predicate.}$$

This Markovian condition on Φ would be met by the predicate $x \notin fx$ on any construal of how a set of naturals, and a function f defined on naturals, might be 'given' to a constructivist. But in the context of the natural logicist's theorizing about the reals, and in light of our remarks on p. 302 about 'geometric effective decidability', the restriction on Separation could be ultimately tame: Φ would be 'geometrically' Δ^0_1.

The explosive Cantorian consequence is that as soon as one commits oneself to the existence of countably infinitely many things, one is forced to acknowledge that there will be uncountably infinitely many things of a 'new' kind of which one takes oneself to have some comprehending grasp—bicimals, say, or sets of naturals. One cannot stop at a merely countable infinity. If one wishes to assign a cardinality, in due course, to the sorts of things of which there are uncountably many more than there are naturals, then it will have to be an uncountable cardinality. The chastening lesson, offered by the likes of a Kroneckerian constructivist, for whom the totality of naturals does not exist, but who can perfectly well follow the foregoing Cantorian reasoning, is *See? What did I tell you? Yonder lie dragons!'*.

We turn now to give a completely formal proof of Cantor's Theorem for sets of naturals. Once again we shall use an inferential rule that will serve as the 'main *reductio* assumption' in the formal proof. The sentential expression of the *reductio* assumption would be

'the function φ is onto all sets of naturals, from naturals.'

The inferential rule, in natural-deduction terms, that expresses this thought is as follows:

$$\Xi\ :\quad \frac{\forall y(y \in t \to Ny) \qquad \begin{array}{c} \overbrace{\overline{t = \varphi a}^{\,(i)}\ ,\ \overline{Na}^{\,(i)}} \\ \vdots \\ \psi \end{array}}{\psi}\,{}^{(i)}$$

where the existential parameter a may occur only where explicitly indicated.

We now re-write our earlier formal proof with Nx in place of $x \in X$.

Proof. **(of Theorem 8, fully regimented)**
We define a proof Π that will be embedded twice in the final proof Σ.

$$\begin{array}{c}\underbrace{D=\{Nx|x\notin fx\},\ Nd,\ D=fd}\\ \Pi\\ d\in\{Nx\mid x\notin fx\}\end{array}\quad =_{df}$$

$$\dfrac{\dfrac{D=\{Nx\mid x\notin fx\}}{\exists!\{Nx\mid x\notin fx\}}\,{\scriptstyle \mathrm{RAD}}\qquad \dfrac{Nd}{\exists!d}\qquad \dfrac{Nd\qquad \dfrac{\dfrac{\dfrac{\dfrac{D=\{Nx\mid x\notin fx\}\qquad \dfrac{D=fd\quad \overline{d\in fd}^{\,(1)}}{d\in D}\,{\scriptstyle =\mathrm{Sub}}}{d\in\{Nx\mid x\notin fx\}}\,{\scriptstyle =\mathrm{Sub}}}{d\notin fd}\,{\scriptstyle \mathrm{L64}}\qquad \overline{d\in fd}^{\,(1)}}{\bot}}{d\notin fd}\,{\scriptstyle (1)}}{Nd\wedge d\notin fd}}{d\in\{Nx\mid x\notin fx\}}\,{\scriptstyle \mathrm{L66,\ Defn.30}}$$

Now we embed two copies of Π to form the proof Σ as follows.

$$\Sigma\ :\quad \dfrac{\exists!\{Nx|x\notin fx\}\qquad \dfrac{\dfrac{\overline{D=\{Nx|x\notin fx\}}^{\,(4)}}{\forall y(y\in D\rightarrow Ny)}\,{\scriptstyle \mathrm{L63}}\qquad \dfrac{\dfrac{\begin{array}{c}\underbrace{\overline{D=\{Nx|x\notin fx\}}^{\,(4)},\ \overline{d\in X}^{\,(3)},\ \overline{D=fd}^{\,(3)}}\\ \Pi\\ d\in\{Nx|x\notin fx\}\end{array}}{d\notin fd}\,{\scriptstyle \mathrm{L64}}\qquad \dfrac{\dfrac{\overline{D=\{Nx|x\notin fx\}}^{\,(4)}\qquad \begin{array}{c}\underbrace{\overline{D=\{Nx|x\notin fx\}}^{\,(4)},\ \overline{d\in X}^{\,(3)},\ \overline{D=fd}^{\,(3)}}\\ \Pi\\ d\in\{x\in X|x\notin fx\}\end{array}}{d\in D}\qquad \overline{D=fd}^{\,(3)}}{d\in fd}\,{\scriptstyle =\mathrm{Sub}}}{\bot}}{\bot}\,{\scriptstyle (3)\exists}}{\bot}\,{\scriptstyle (4)}$$

□

Chapter 25

Back to Bicimals

Abstract

This chapter picks up the threads of the discussion in Chapter 23 of bicimal expansions for points on a line. There is a natural way of ordering such expansions. One defines a progressive matrix as a list of non-decreasing bicimals. Every progressive matrix β has a *characteristic bicimal expansion*, which will be called β_∞. The matrix β of bicimal expansions $\beta_1, \beta_2, \ldots$ for a strictly increasing sequence of points $\gamma_1, \gamma_2, \ldots$ is a progressive matrix. The expansion β_∞ is that for the right limit point of the point-sequence $\gamma_1, \gamma_2, \ldots$. It is shown that every canonical bicimal expansion α corresponds to the limit point of an increasing sequence of points $\gamma_1, \gamma_2, \ldots$, where each γ_i is the point whose bicimal representation is given by the first n digits of α (followed thereafter by 0s). Distinct geometric points receive distinct bicimal expansions. To every bicimal expansion there corresponds a unique point, namely, the limit of the increasing sequences of points that correspond to the ever longer 'finite truncations' of that bicimal expansion. To distinct bicimal expansions there correspond distinct such limit points. The author wraps up and hangs his spurs after explaining the operation of addition on (dimensionless) real numbers in terms of a notion of addition-of-line-segments as the *ur*-operation, in geometric intuition.

Lemma 67. *There are at most countably many non-canonical bicimal expansions.*

Proof. By definition, a non-canonical bicimal expansion $\mathfrak{b}$ is one for which

$$\exists n \forall m \geq n \; \mathfrak{b}[m] = 1\,.$$

Let $\underline{\mathfrak{b}}$ be the least n such that $\forall m \geq n \; \mathfrak{b}[m] = 1$. Then the non-canonical bicimal expansions $\mathfrak{b}$ correspond one-one with their finite truncations $.\mathfrak{b}[0]\,\mathfrak{b}[1]\,\ldots\,\mathfrak{b}[\underline{\mathfrak{b}}]$. There are at most countably many of these latter objects. Hence there are countably many non-canonical bicimal expansions. □

Corollary 3. *There are uncountably many canonical bicimal expansions.*

Proof. Immediate from Theorem 6 and Lemma 67. □

The Logic of Number. Neil Tennant, Oxford University Press. © Neil Tennant 2022.
DOI: 10.1093/oso/9780192846679.003.0025

Bicimal expansions can be ordered as follows (we suppress the initial punctuation points). Here, α and β are arbitrary bicimal expansions (finite or infinite).

$$0\alpha < 1\beta$$
$$0\alpha < 0\beta \text{ if } \alpha < \beta$$
$$1\alpha < 1\beta \text{ if } \alpha < \beta$$

So, given two bicimal expansions, one orders them by comparing their digits, beginning with the first. At the first discrepancy between digits at a place, the bicimal expansion with 1 at that place is the greater of the two.

Suppose that g is a function mapping positive integers to 0 or 1. We denote by $\overrightarrow{g(n)}$ the obvious bicimal expansion of length n:

$$.\ g(1) \ldots g(n)$$

Let β be a computable function that maps each natural number $i \geq 1$ to a computable function β_i, which in turn maps each natural number $n \geq 1$ to 0 or 1. This means that we have an infinite matrix ϕ_{ij} ($= \beta_i(j)$; $1 \leq i, j$) where in the i-th row the j-th entry ϕ_{ij} is 0 or 1.

Suppose now that for $i, j \geq 1$ we have $\overrightarrow{\beta_i(j)} \leq \overrightarrow{\beta_{i+1}(j)}$. That is, as one descends within the jth column, the row-wise bicimal expansions of length j (which terminate in that column) never decrease. A matrix satisfying this condition will be called a *progressive* matrix.

Example of a progressive matrix:

	1	2	3	4	5	...
β_1	0	0	0	0	0	...
β_2	0	0	0	0	1	...
β_3	0	1	0	1	1	...
β_4	1	0	1	0	1	...
β_5	1	0	1	1	0	...
β_6	1	1	0	0	0	...
β_7	1	1	1	0	1	...
$\vdots$	$\vdots$	$\vdots$	$\vdots$	$\vdots$		

Define now a *quasi-minimization operator* $\nu_x[m, P(x)]$ for natural numbers m and predicates $P(x)$ on the natural numbers:

$$\nu_x[m, P(x)] \begin{cases} = \text{the least natural } i \geq m \text{ such that } P(i), \text{ if } \exists k \geq m\ P(k); \\ \text{is undefined if } \neg\exists k \geq m\ P(k) \end{cases}$$

Equipped with this quasi-minimization operator ν, we inductively define, for a matrix β of the kind we have been considering, the following non-decreasing function λ_β on the natural numbers:

$$\lambda_\beta(0) = 1;$$

$$\lambda_\beta(n+1) = \begin{cases} \nu_x[\lambda_\beta(n), \beta_i(x) = 1], & \text{if this exists;} \\ \lambda_\beta(n) \text{ otherwise} \end{cases}$$

In the foregoing example,

$$\lambda_\beta(1) = 4$$

$$\lambda_\beta(2) = 6$$

$$\lambda_\beta(3) = 7$$

but for values of n greater than 3 there is not enough information in the diagram to determine $\lambda_\beta(n)$.

Every progressive matrix β has a *characteristic bicimal expansion*, called β_∞, defined as follows. First, we give an inductive definition of a *provisional* function β^*_∞

$$\beta^*_\infty[1] = \begin{cases} 1 \text{ if } \exists i \ \beta_i(1) = 1 \\ 0 \text{ if } \forall i \ \beta_i(1) = 0 \end{cases}$$

$$\beta^*_\infty[n+1] = \begin{cases} 1 \text{ if } \exists i \geq \lambda_\beta(n) \ \beta_i(n) = 1 \\ 0 \text{ if } \forall i \geq \lambda_\beta(n) \ \beta_i(n) = 0 \end{cases}$$

The recipe for determining the nth digit in the bicimal expansion β^*_∞ involves using $\lambda_\beta(n)$ as a 'counter' that tells us, in effect, that we need only look at the $\lambda_\beta(n)$-th and subsequent rows of the matrix β. If in the nth column we find, in one of those rows, the digit 1, then $\lambda_\beta(n+1)$ is set to be the index of the first such row. Thereafter, one need only look at *that* row, and subsequent ones, in order to determine the $(n+1)$-th digit of the expansion β^*_∞.

Thus far we have defined only the *provisional* function β^*_∞. Now we complete our definition of β_∞ by stipulating that β_∞ is identical to β^*_∞ if there is no terminal 0 in β^*_∞; otherwise, the sequence 011111... beginning with the terminal 0 is to be replaced by 100000... . This ensures that β_∞ is a canonical bicimal expansion.

Observation 4. *Let β be a progressive matrix. For every n, for every $i \geq \lambda_\beta(n)$, β^*_∞ agrees with β_i on the first n places.*

Observation 5. *Let α be a canonical bicimal expansion and let α^i be the digit in the ith place of α. Define a matrix β by setting its ith row β_i to be the 'ith truncation' of α, namely*

$$\alpha^1 \ldots \alpha^i 00000 \ldots$$

Then β is progressive and $\beta_\infty = \beta^*_\infty = \alpha$.

Observation 5 guarantees that every canonical bicimal expansion α corresponds to the limit point γ of an increasing sequence of points $\gamma_1, \gamma_2, \ldots$, where each γ_i is the point whose bicimal representation is given by the first n digits of α (followed thereafter by 0s).

Note that β_∞ can be rational, and β_∞ need not lie in the open unit segment. Both these points are illustrated by the progressive matrix whose ith row is the bicimal expansion for $(2^i - 1)/2^i$:

	1	2	3	4	5	...
β_1	1	0	0	0	0	...
β_2	1	1	0	0	0	...
β_3	1	1	1	0	0	...
β_4	1	1	1	1	0	...
β_5	1	1	1	1	1	...
$\vdots$	$\vdots$	$\vdots$	$\vdots$	$\vdots$		

With this matrix β we have $\beta^*_\infty = .11111\ldots$, whence $\beta_\infty = 1.00000\ldots$.

Suppose now that we are given a 'Euclidean constructible' sequence of points

$$\gamma_1, \gamma_2, \ldots$$

on the unit segment, in such a way that for $m \geq 1$ we have $\gamma_m \blacktriangleleft \gamma_{n+1}$:

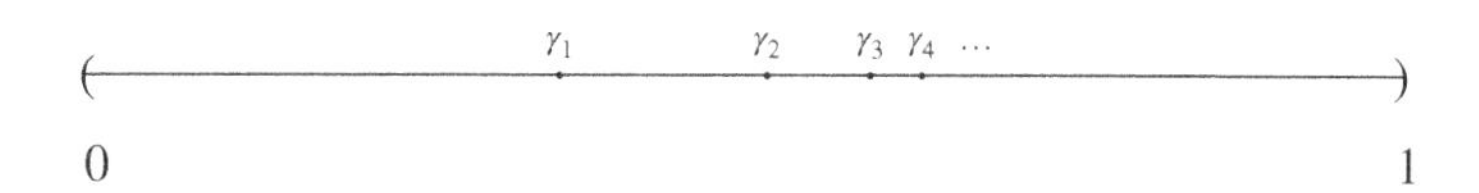

For each $i \geq 1$ we can carry out our construction of a bicimal expansion β_i for γ_i. We can register our progress by recording, for each stage j of the expansion process, the j-th digit that we have generated:

Stage j	1	2	3	4	...
β_i	1	0	1	1	...

Note that the row β_i for γ_i serves as the sequence of digits in the bicimal expansion of γ_i. Only the initial point is missing. So β_i in this example is .1011... . Note further that it follows easily, from the requirement that for $m \geq 1$, $\gamma_m \blacktriangleleft \gamma_{n+1}$, that the matrix β whose ith row is the sequence β_i of digits in the bicimal expansion for γ_i is progressive. For, in general, if point c is to the left of point d, then at any finite stage n the nth digit in the bicimal expansion constructed for c will be no greater than the nth digit in the bicimal expansion constructed for d. This follows from our recipe, using only Euclidean conceptual materials, for constructing the bicimal expansion for a given point in the unit segment.

The matrix of bicimal expansions $\beta_1, \beta_2, \ldots$ for the points $\gamma_1, \gamma_2, \ldots$ is therefore a progressive matrix. Call it β. It follows that the infinite bicimal expansion β_∞ is determined in accordance with the definition that we have provided above. We take β_∞ as the bicimal expansion for the right limit point, or least upper bound, of the increasing sequence of points $\gamma_1, \gamma_2, \ldots$ in the unit segment.

That such a limit point exists is a matter of geometric intuition, as stated in **Right limits for ◀**. First, a right limit point has this property: it is to the right of each point in the (monotonically) increasing sequence that it limits. Second, no point to the left of it has the property in question—such a point would be to the left of some point in the sequence (and therefore also lie to the left of all subsequent points in the sequence).

Now a geometric point (in a unit segment) is not itself the corresponding bicimal expansion. Rather, the point is to be supplied with its bicimal expansion as its numerical representative in a system of numerical representation. And that numerical representative is determined *modulo* the unit segment as the unit of measurement for spatial distances. Naturally the system of numerical representation must supply representatives that stand in numerical relations that correspond to the geometrical relations among the points that they represent. But the geometric points must not, on pain of conceptual confusion, be identified with their numerical representations. (That would be to make a 'category mistake', in Gilbert Ryle's sense.)

Geometric points on an oriented line are ordered by the intuitively grasped geometric relation ◀; while bicimal expansions are ordered by the numerically definable relation <. If we have two points c and c' with associated representatives (i.e., bicimal expansions) β and β', then the following condition must be satisfied:

$$c \blacktriangleleft c' \;\Leftrightarrow\; \beta < \beta'$$

The left-to-right direction should be clear from our recipe for construction of bicimal expansions:

> For, if $c \blacktriangleleft c'$, then there will come a first stage in the bisection process (generating the bicimal expansions β and β') when the newly created bisection point either (i) coincides with c; or (ii) lies between c and c'; or (iii) coincides with c'.
>
> In case (i), both β and β' will acquire the entry 1. *But* in all subsequent stages, the entries for β will be 0; while we know by **Bisectability** that eventually β' will acquire another entry 1.
>
> In cases (ii) and (iii), β will immediately acquire the entry 0 and β' will acquire the entry 1.
>
> It follows that at some first stage of discrepancy, the bicimal expansion β for c will have a 0 entry, while the bicimal expansion β' for c'

> will have a 1 entry. And that will guarantee that $\beta < \beta'$.

For the right-to-left direction the argument is as follows:

> Suppose $\beta < \beta'$. Find the place n where β and β' have their first discrepant digits, i.e., where β has 0 and β' has 1. Up to this stage the two expansion-processes would have produced the same bisection points $\gamma_1^{c,c'}, \ldots, \gamma_{n-1}^{c,c'}$. Consider the bisection point $\gamma_n^{c,c'}$ ($=\gamma_n$, for short) created at the nth stage of the process and with respect to which the discrepant nth-place digits of the respective bicimal expansions are determined. Since the expansion β has 0 at the nth place, it follows that $c \blacktriangleleft \gamma_n$. And, since the expansion β' has 1 at the nth place, it follows that either (i) γ_n coincides with c', or (ii) $\gamma_n \blacktriangleleft c'$. In case (i), we have $c \blacktriangleleft c'$. In case (ii), by transitivity of $\blacktriangleleft$, we have $c \blacktriangleleft c'$.

Moreover: suppose we have any $\blacktriangleleft$-increasing sequence of points $\gamma_1, \gamma_2, \ldots$ in the unit segment. These have their associated numerical representatives (i.e., bicimal expansions) $\beta_1, \beta_2, \ldots$. The right limit point γ of $\gamma_1, \gamma_2, \ldots$ exists, where this notion of limit is defined by reference to the geometric relation $\blacktriangleleft$. We have shown how to construct the bicimal expansion β_∞, which is intended to be our numerical representative for the right limit point γ. It needs to be shown, therefore, that

> β_∞ is the least upper bound, with reference now to the ordering relation $<$ of bicimal expansions, of the $<$-increasing sequence $\beta_1, \beta_2, \ldots$.

And this can indeed be shown.

> First, each bicimal row β_i in the progressive matrix is exceeded (by reference to the ordering $<$ of bicimal expansions) by β_∞. This much is clear from the recipe for constructing β_∞. No row β_i agrees at every place with β_∞, on pain of contradicting the monotonic increases as we go down the rows in the matrix. Nor does any row β_i agree with β_∞ up to some place at which β_i has 1 where β_∞ has 0. Rather, every β_i has, at some first place of discrepancy with β_∞, the digit 0 where β_∞ has 1. So the bicimal expansion β_∞ exceeds each bicimal row β_i of the $<$-increasing sequence of bicimal rows within the progressive matrix..
>
> Second, suppose that α is a canonical bicimal expansion (i.e., one with no terminal 0) and $\alpha < \beta_\infty$. We need to show that for some i, $\alpha < \beta_i$. So suppose for *reductio* that for no i do we have $\alpha < \beta_i$. At the first place (say the nth) of discrepancy between α and β_∞, α has 0 where β_∞ has 1. But if α is not less than *any* β_i then every β_i, for $i \geq \lambda_\beta(n)$, has 0 at that place. Hence by construction β^*_∞ has 0 at the nth place.
>
> If β_∞ agrees with β^*_∞ at the nth place, then β_∞ has 0 at the nth place. Contradiction. So β_∞ does not agree with β^*_∞ at the nth place.

> Therefore from the nth place onwards the expansion β^*_∞ is 011111... (whence from the nth place onwards the expansion β_∞ is 100000...). It follows by Observation 4 that α, in order not to be less than any γ_i, must have the digit 1 from the $(n+1)$th place onwards. But this contradicts the supposition that α is a canonical bicimal expansion.

We have now established a one-one correspondence between geometric points in the open unit segment, and bicimal expansions. For we have shown how to determine, for any such point c, its unique canonical bicimal expansion $\mathfrak{b}(c)$. Distinct geometric points receive distinct bicimal expansions. And to every bicimal expansion there corresponds a unique point, namely, the limit of the increasing sequences of points that correspond to the ever longer 'finite truncations' of that bicimal expansion. To distinct bicimal expansions there correspond distinct such limit points.

This one-one correspondence preserves the respective orderings $\blacktriangleleft$ and $<$, and also preserves the respective results of taking limits of increasing sequences. It should further come as no surprise that it preserves also the algebraic operations that are naturally definable on either side of the correspondence—addition, multiplication, subtraction, and division—when we deal with a whole geometric line within which a unit segment is identified, and allow integers to precede the bicimal point.

We have described the construction of bicimal expansions as numerical representations for geometric points on an open unit segment of an oriented line. But what about the points on that line that do not lie within that unit segment? How are they to be assigned their numerical representations (*modulo* the unit constituted by that segment)?

The answer follows from our earlier discussion of the laying-on-end of copies of the unit segment. The starting point for this process will always be the point called 0, namely the left endpoint of the chosen unit segment. On the assumption that the point c for which we are seeking a numerical representation is to the right of 0, we lay copies of the unit segment [0,1] end-to-end rightwards, keeping a count of how many are laid down until we reach a stage where the right endpoint (call it d) of the nth copy of the unit segment [0,1] either coincides with c or falls to the left of c, with the segment $[dc]$ shorter than the unit segment [0,1]. (This point d is the point $\Lambda(0,[0,1],n)$ in our earlier notation.) The former case results in a measurement of exactly n units of length for the point c. The latter case will leave an excess proportion ψ of the unit segment, resulting in a measurement of $(n+\psi)$ units of length for c. The great mistake of Pythagoras was to maintain dogmatically that this proportion ψ of the unit segment will always be a (rational) fraction.

If c lies to the left of 0, the same procedure is followed, but the result has a minus sign in front of it. Going rightwards produces positive results, going leftwards produces negative ones.

The number n is represented by a finite sequence of 0s and 1s in binary notation. Write that sequence down, and write a punctuation point (the 'bicimal point') after it. We have seen how to carry out an effective Euclidean construction of a bicimal expansion for the segment $[dc]$. Write that bicimal expansion down immediately after the bicimal point. (Of course one cannot actually write down an infinite sequence of 0s and 1s. But one can imagine doing so. And one can, in principle, write down the first k digits of such an expansion, for any k.) The result is the numerical representation, in bicimal notation, of the point c's remove to the right from 0, in terms of the chosen unit segment $[0,1]$ as the unit of length.

Henceforth we shall interpret $\mathfrak{b}(c)$ as the canonical bicimal representation of an arbitrary point c of an oriented line with distinguished points 0 and 1.

We have not yet said anything about the algebraic operations, such as addition, that can be carried out on segments, or on mensurated segments, or on real numbers themselves. Here we shall consider only the operation of addition.

One can 'add' line-segments by laying them end-to-end so as to form a new line-segment. Famously, Proposition II of Book I of Euclid's *Elements* gives the recipe for constructing a segment with a given point as an endpoint, which is exactly as long as a given segment. The recipe can be generalized so as to allow one to construct the required segment, on a given line, with a given point on that line as an endpoint.

Suppose one is given two distinct line-segments σ and τ, and a line L (not necessarily containing either σ or τ). Let c be any point on L. The aforementioned construction allows one to lay end-to-end on L, starting at the point c, two distinct line-segments exactly as long, respectively, as σ and τ, so as to create a new line-segment of L. The construction is to produce its copy of σ rightwards beginning at c, followed by a copy of τ rightwards beginning at the rightmost endpoint of the copy of σ that has just been laid down. Relative to L and c, this rightwards laying-on-end-to-end of the segments σ and τ produces a unique result, which we may denote in Polish notation as

$$\boxplus(c, L, \sigma, \tau)$$

or in the more customary infix notation as

$$\sigma \boxplus_L^c \tau.$$

If point c is on oriented line L and point d is on oriented line K, then

$$\sigma \boxplus_L^c \tau \cong \sigma \boxplus_K^d \tau.$$

Moreover,

$$\sigma \boxplus_L^c \tau \cong \tau \boxplus_K^d \sigma$$

and

$$\sigma \boxplus_L^c \tau = \tau \boxplus_L^c \sigma.$$

So this addition of line-segments is commutative. The operation is also associative:

$$(\sigma \boxplus_L^c \tau) \boxplus_L^c \rho \cong \sigma \boxplus_K^d (\tau \boxplus_K^d \sigma)$$

and

$$(\sigma \boxplus_L^c \tau) \boxplus_L^c \rho = \sigma \boxplus_L^c (\tau \boxplus_L^c \sigma).$$

This algebraic operation $\boxplus$ (parametrized by a line and by a point thereon) displays two of the most important properties of addition, commutativity and associativity, even though we have not yet said anything about *lengths*, let alone *mensurated lengths* (that is, lengths rendered in terms of some chosen unit of length). What is lacking, of course, is a *unique* additive identity, even when c and L have been fixed. There are infinitely many candidates for 'being a zero' with respect to the operation $\boxplus_L^c$—take any degenerate interval of the form $[d, d]$. But none of these can be singled out as *the* natural choice for the zero element.

The operation $\boxplus_L^c$ dwells entirely within the geometric realm, which has, in addition to the (logical) relation of identity on geometric entities, only the ordering relation $\lhd$ among line-segments, the equivalence relation $\cong$ among line-segments, and the relation $\blacktriangleleft$ among points on oriented lines. (It is a cruel expository irony that the philosopher would usually stress the nature of this identity relation by calling it *numerical* identity.) The present author submits that this notion $\boxplus$ of addition of line-segments is the *ur*-operation, in intuition, from which the operation of addition on (dimensionless) real numbers arises. Let us see how the operation comes to be such, and how it acquires a unique zero.

Suppose now that σ and τ are not *arbitrary*, *undirected* line-segments, but are, rather, arbitrary *directed* segments *of the oriented line* L. Thus, if a and b are points on L, the segment $[a, b]$ is the reversal (in direction) of the segment $[b, a]$. If $a \blacktriangleleft b$, we can say that the segment $[a, b]$ is *directed rightwards* on L, while the segment $[b, a]$ is *directed leftwards* on L. The laying-on-end method of construction is now to produce its copy of σ in the direction of σ beginning at c (which, remember, is a point on L), followed by a copy of τ in the direction of τ beginning at the terminal point of the copy of σ that has just been laid down. Relative to L and c, this *directed* laying-end-to-end of the segments σ and τ produces a unique *directed* segment, which we may denote in infix notation as

$$\sigma \underline{+}_L^c \tau.$$

As before, the operation is commutative and associative. Moreover, the operation must be total on directed segments of L. It must produce a result—a directed segment—on the inputs $[a, b]$ and $[b, a]$. This will be the unique zero that was lacking earlier: the degenerate segment [0,0]. It has all the required properties of an additive identity:

$$\sigma \underline{+}_L^c [0, 0] = \sigma$$

$$[0, 0] \underline{+}_L^c \sigma = \sigma$$

We do not yet, however, have unique additive inverses for directed segments. To be sure, the directed segment $[b, a]$ serves as *an* additive inverse for the directed segment $[a, b]$:

$$[a, b] \underline{+}^{c}_{L} [b, a] = [0, 0] \ ;$$

but so too would any other directed segment of L that is exactly as long as $[b, a]$ and that has the same direction as $[b, a]$.

In the previous section we showed how to add together any two directed segments of an oriented line L, where the result of the operation of addition was a directed segment beginning at the origin. That operation of addition, though it had a natural zero, did not, however, furnish unique additive inverses. Now we refine the operation so that the segments that are its inputs also begin at the origin. This allows one to reconceive the addition operation as one performed on the 'other endpoints' of the directed segments in question, rather than on the whole segments themselves.

Let a 'master line' M be fixed, with a distinguished point, called 0 (and also called 'the origin'), and with a given orientation. Under that orientation, and in relation to the origin, we can define—without recourse to numbers—a genuine additive operation on geometric points a and b on M:

$$a \dot{+}^{0}_{M} b \equiv_{df} \iota x(x \sqsubset M \ \wedge \ [0, x] = [0, a] \underline{+}^{0}_{M} [0, b]),$$

where $\underline{+}^{0}_{M}$ is the operation of addition of directed segments discussed in the previous section.

The operation $\dot{+}^{0}_{M}$ is commutative and associative, and has the origin 0 as its natural zero. Moreover it furnishes unique additive inverses, insofar as the following geometric result can be proved:

$$\forall x(x \sqsubset M \rightarrow \exists_{1} y(y \sqsubset M \ \wedge \ x \dot{+}^{0}_{M} y = 0)).$$

The stage is now set for us to explain how real numbers themselves may come to be added together, and to appreciate how this explanation itself is thoroughly geometric in its conceptual materials. We keep in mind our oriented master line M with its origin 0, and we consider only points on M. Choose now another point on M to the right of 0, and call it 1 (or 'unity'). We saw earlier how to construct an infinite canonical bicimal expansion $\mathfrak{b}(c)$ for any point c in the open unit segment (0,1), and then how to construct a bicimal representation $\mathfrak{b}(d)$ for an arbitrary point d of M by using finitely many digits 0 and 1 in front of the bicimal point, and with an initial minus sign if $d \blacktriangleleft 0$.

Our question now is this: for arbitrary points a and b of M, what is

$$\mathfrak{b}(a \dot{+}^{0}_{M} b)?$$

In one sense, the answer is easy: $\mathfrak{b}(a \dot{+}^{0}_{M} b)$ is simply the bicimal representation, which can be determined by our earlier recipe, for the point $a \dot{+}^{0}_{M} b$ of M, which in turn can be determined geometrically from the directed segments $[0, a]$ and $[0, b]$ of $\boldsymbol{M}$.

So the real question is: Can the bicimal representation $\mathfrak{b}(a \dot{+}^0_M b)$ be determined in a rule-governed way from the bicimal representations $\mathfrak{b}(a)$ and $\mathfrak{b}(b)$? The answer is affirmative: we can define the 'plain old' operation $+$ of *numerical* addition so that we can eventually prove that

$$\mathfrak{b}(a) + \mathfrak{b}(b) = \mathfrak{b}(a \dot{+}^0_M b).$$

Moreover, although the operation $+$ will reveal itself to be *intrinsically numerical* (in a sense that will emerge), it will nevertheless be the case that the truth of the equation just stated is best appreciated by a geometric understanding of what is involved.

Consider the ith truncations of

$$\mathfrak{b}(a) = a_1 \; a_2 \; \dots ,$$

and of

$$\mathfrak{b}(b) = b_1 \; b_2 \; \dots ,$$

for $i \geq 1$ (and where each entry of the form a_k or b_k is either 0 or 1):

$$\begin{array}{lcllllllll}
\mathfrak{b}(a)_1 & = & a_1 & 0 & 0 & 0 & 0 & 0 & 0 & \dots \\
\mathfrak{b}(a)_2 & = & a_1 & a_2 & 0 & 0 & 0 & 0 & 0 & \dots \\
\mathfrak{b}(a)_3 & = & a_1 & a_2 & a_3 & 0 & 0 & 0 & 0 & \dots \\
 & \vdots & & & & & & & &
\end{array}$$

$$\begin{array}{lcllllllll}
\mathfrak{b}(b)_1 & = & b_1 & 0 & 0 & 0 & 0 & 0 & 0 & \dots \\
\mathfrak{b}(b)_2 & = & b_1 & b_2 & 0 & 0 & 0 & 0 & 0 & \dots \\
\mathfrak{b}(b)_3 & = & b_1 & b_2 & b_3 & 0 & 0 & 0 & 0 & \dots \\
 & \vdots & & & & & & & &
\end{array}$$

We are going to define the bicimal expansion $\mathfrak{b}(a) + \mathfrak{b}(b)$ in terms of these truncations. The method is obvious. We first define the infinite sequence of sums of truncations of increasing but equal length:

$$\begin{array}{c}
\mathfrak{b}(a)_1 + \mathfrak{b}(b)_1 \\
\mathfrak{b}(a)_2 + \mathfrak{b}(b)_2 \\
\mathfrak{b}(a)_3 + \mathfrak{b}(b)_3 \\
\vdots
\end{array}$$

These sums will form the rows of a progressive matrix β. Then we take the canonical bicimal expansion β_∞.

So, first we need to define the bicimal expansion that results from adding two equally long truncations. Let the expansion c that is to be equal to $\mathfrak{b}(a)_k + \mathfrak{b}(b)_k$, i.e., to

$$a_1 \ldots a_k \, 0\,0\,0\,0\,0\,0 \ldots + b_1 \ldots b_k \, 0\,0\,0\,0\,0\,0 \ldots$$

be defined algorithmically as follows. This is a computational recipe in pseudocode that spells out in complete detail how to add two finite bicimal expansions of equal length.

for $m > k$ set $c_m = 0$;

enter NON-CARRY MODE;

set COUNTER $= k$ and **do** the following **until** COUNTER $= 1$:

if $a_{\text{COUNTER}} = 0$ then:

if $b_{\text{COUNTER}} = 0$ then:

if in NON-CARRY MODE, then:

set $c_{\text{COUNTER}} = 0$;
remain in NON-CARRY MODE;
set COUNTER $= k - 1$; but

if in CARRY MODE, then:

set $c_{\text{COUNTER}} = 1$;
enter NON-CARRY MODE;
set COUNTER $= k - 1$

if $b_{\text{COUNTER}} = 1$ then:

if in NON-CARRY MODE, then:

set $c_{\text{COUNTER}} = 1$;
remain in NON-CARRY MODE;
set COUNTER $= k - 1$; but

if in CARRY MODE, then:

set $c_{\text{COUNTER}} = 0$;
remain in CARRY MODE;
set COUNTER $= k - 1$

but

if $a_{\text{COUNTER}} = 1$ then:

if $b_{\text{COUNTER}} = 0$ then:

if in NON-CARRY MODE, then:

set $c_{\text{COUNTER}} = 1$;
remain in NON-CARRY MODE;
set COUNTER $= k - 1$; but

if in CARRY MODE, then:

set $c_{\text{COUNTER}} = 0$;
remain in CARRY MODE;
set COUNTER $= k - 1$

if $b_{\text{COUNTER}} = 1$ then:

if in NON-CARRY MODE, then:

set $c_{\text{COUNTER}} = 0$;
enter CARRY MODE;
set COUNTER $= k - 1$; but

if in CARRY MODE, then:

set $c_{\text{COUNTER}} = 1$;
remain in CARRY MODE;
set COUNTER $= k - 1$

When COUNTER $= 0$:

if in CARRY MODE, then:

set $c_{\text{COUNTER}} = 1$; and
End;

but

if in NON-CARRY MODE, then:

set $c_{\text{COUNTER}} = 0$; and
End

The 'zero-th' place of the resulting bicimal expansion is of course the place immediately before the 'bicimal point'. This is to allow for the sum of two bicimal expansions less than unity to exceed unity. (Such a sum cannot, however, exceed 2.)

The 'sums of ever-longer truncations'

$$\mathfrak{b}(a)_1 + \mathfrak{b}(b)_1$$

$$\mathfrak{b}(a)_2 + \mathfrak{b}(b)_2$$

$$\mathfrak{b}(a)_3 + \mathfrak{b}(b)_3$$

$$\vdots$$

form the rows of a progressive matrix β. They are bicimal expansions representing bisective points $c_1, c_2, \ldots$. (We naturally extend the definition of a bisective point so as to cover such points to the right of 1.) Moreover, the sequence $c_1, c_2, \ldots$ is bisective and non-decreasing. And its limit point is represented by the canonical bicimal expansion β_∞.

We have therefore succeeded in defining the bicimal expansion $\mathfrak{b}(a) + \mathfrak{b}(b)$, given the bicimal expansions $\mathfrak{b}(a)$ and $\mathfrak{b}(b)$.

This modest resting place, dear reader, is as far as this logical sherpa chooses to go. There are no impossibly steep slopes ahead to the summit of real algebra. The rest of the journey, as a mathematician would say, is 'merely technical'.

Appendix A

Proof of the Non-Compossibility Theorem

Metatheorem 1.

It is impossible that the following seven conditions hold:

1. L is an eligible language
2. Δ is a set of L-sentences
3. $\mathfrak{M}$ is an infinite L-model of Δ
4. every element of $\mathfrak{M}$ is denoted by some L-term
5. every L-model of Δ is isomorphic to $\mathfrak{M}$
6. S is a sound proof-system for the L-operators
7. for any name a not in L, if $\Delta \cup L^a$ has no model, then there is an S-proof of $\perp$ from $\Delta \cup L^a$

Proof. Suppose (1)-(7) hold. We shall derive a contradiction.

Definition 31. *When a model $\mathfrak{M}$ makes a sentence φ true, we write $\mathfrak{M} \Vdash \varphi$. When a model $\mathfrak{M}$ makes every sentence φ in a set Δ of sentences true, we write $\mathfrak{M} \Vdash \Delta$.*

Extend L by adding a new name a. Suppose, for a subsidiary *reductio ad absurdum*, that $\Delta \cup L^a$ has a model. Call this model $\mathfrak{N}$. Recall that the sentence $\exists!a$ is in L^a. So $\mathfrak{N} \Vdash \exists!a$. Thus, the new name a denotes an individual in $\mathfrak{N}$. Call that denotation α:

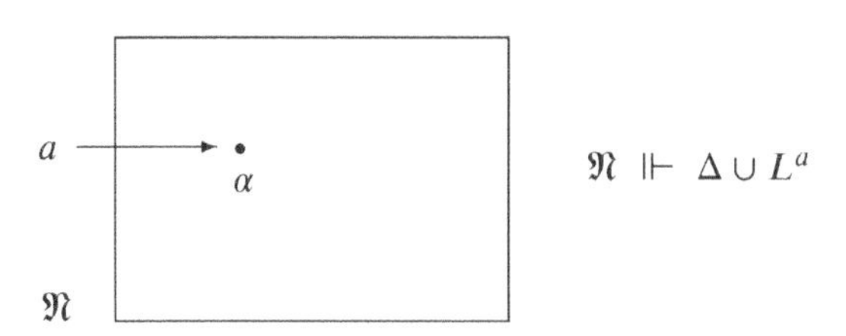

Let $\mathfrak{N}_L$ be the restriction of $\mathfrak{N}$ to the language L:

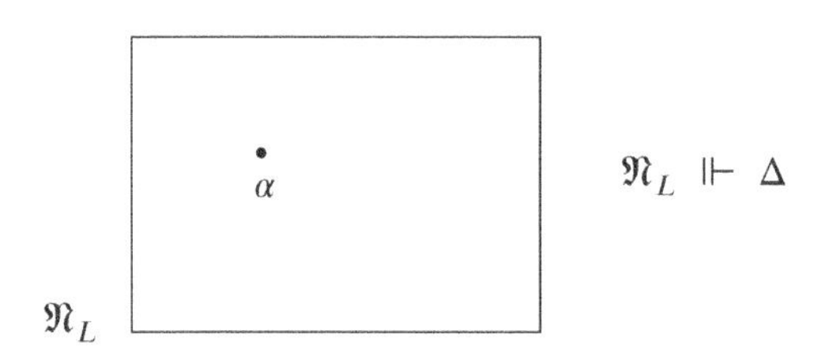

$\mathfrak{N}_L$ is a model of Δ. Hence by (5), $\mathfrak{N}_L$ is isomorphic to $\mathfrak{M}$. That is, there is a 1-1, structure-preserving mapping from $\mathfrak{N}_L$ onto $\mathfrak{M}$. Call the mapping ϕ:

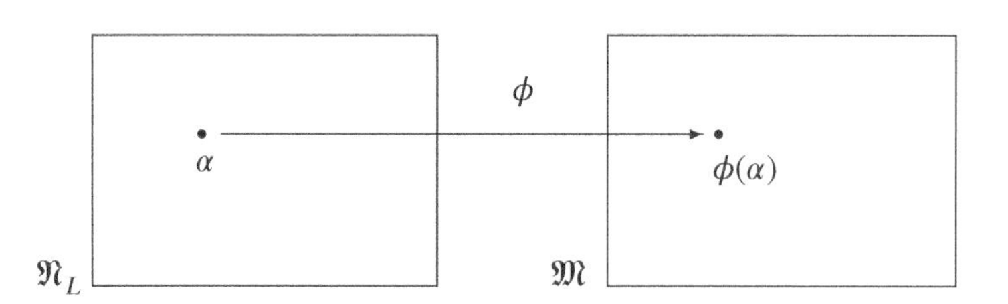

By (4), the individual $\phi(\alpha)$ is denoted in $\mathfrak{M}$ by some L-term t:

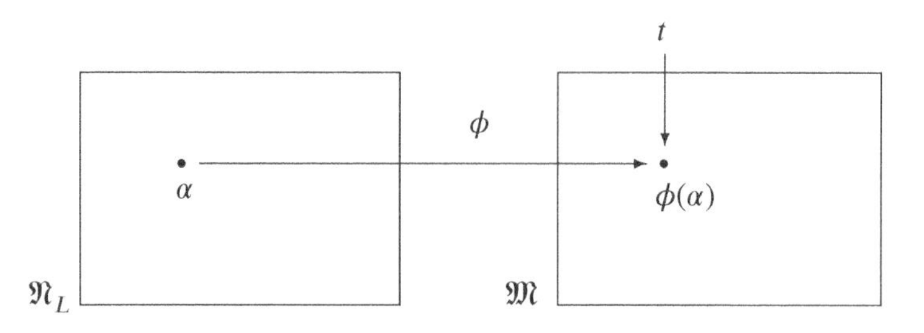

By the isomorphism ϕ between $\mathfrak{N}_L$ and $\mathfrak{M}$, the individual α is denoted in $\mathfrak{N}_L$, *hence also in* $\mathfrak{N}$, by that same term t:

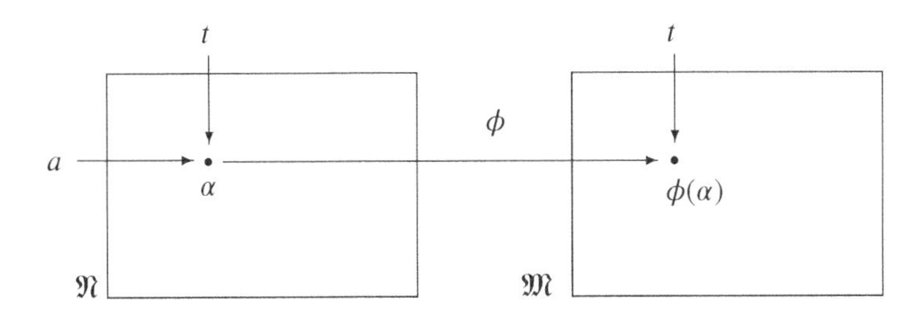

So $\mathfrak{N} \Vdash a = t$. But $\mathfrak{N}$ is a model of $L^a_{\neq}$. So $\mathfrak{N} \Vdash \neg a = t$. Contradiction. It follows that $\Delta \cup L^a$ has no model. (This ends the subsidiary *reductio ad absurdum*.)

It now follows by (7) that there is an S-proof of $\perp$ from $\Delta \cup L^a$. Let Π be the proof of $\perp$ in question. Π has the form

$$\begin{array}{c} \Theta, \Xi \\ \Pi \\ \perp \end{array},$$

where the undischarged assumptions of Π form a finite set $\Theta \cup \Xi$, with $\Theta \subseteq \Delta$ and $\Xi \subseteq L^a$.

Note that $\Delta \cup \{\exists!a\}$ has a model. (Let the name a denote any individual in $\mathfrak{M}$.) So by (6) there is no S-proof of $\perp$ from $\Delta \cup \{\exists!a\}$. Hence Ξ contains at least one member of $L^a_{\neq}$, but only finitely many such. Suppose these are $\neg a = t_1, \ldots, \neg a = t_k$. Let the respective denotations of the terms $t_1, \ldots, t_k$ in the domain of $\mathfrak{M}$ be $\alpha_1, \ldots, \alpha_k$:

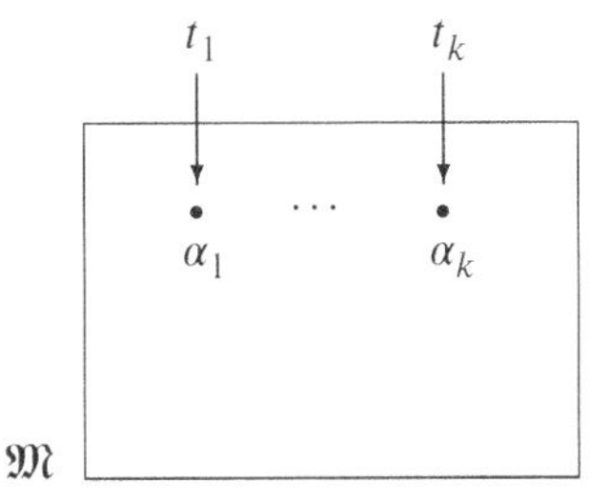

Since $\mathfrak{M}$ is infinite (by (3)), there is an individual in the domain of $\mathfrak{M}$ that is not denoted by any of the terms $t_1, \ldots, t_k$. Let β be such an individual:

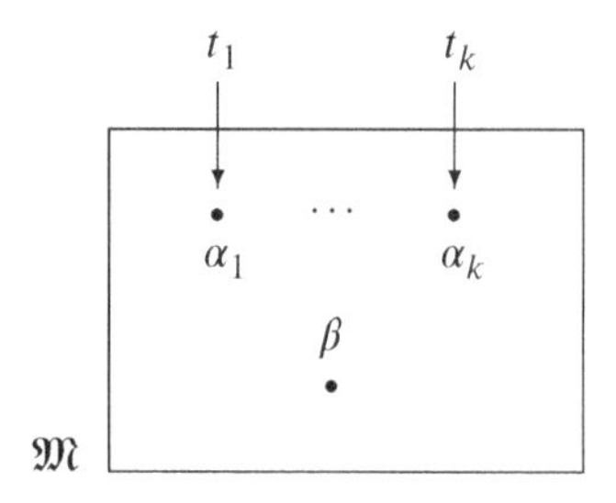

Extend the model $\mathfrak{M}$ of Δ by making the name a denote β. Call the extended model $\mathfrak{M}_a^\beta$:

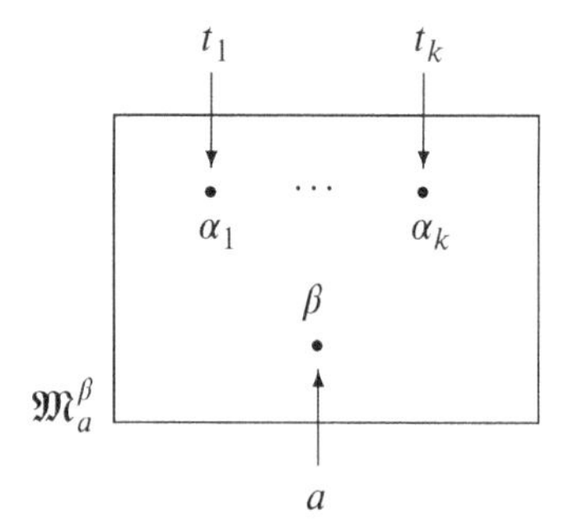

Since $\Theta \subseteq \Delta$, $\mathfrak{M}$ is a model of Θ. Moreover, $\mathfrak{M}_a^\beta$ interprets L exactly the way $\mathfrak{M}$ does. So $\mathfrak{M}_a^\beta$ is a model of Θ:

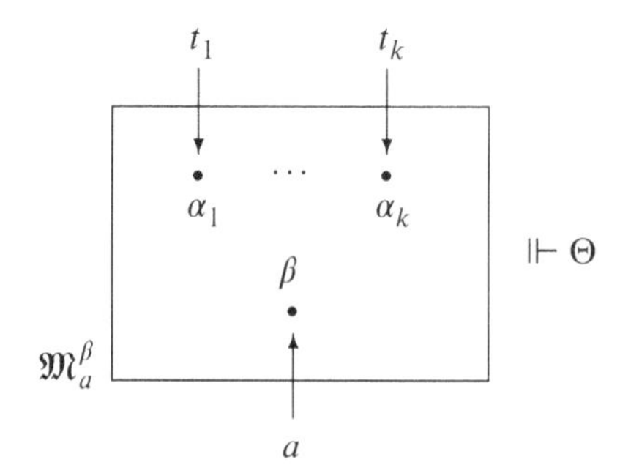

By choice of β, each of the non-identities $\neg a = t_1, \ldots, \neg a = t_k$ is true in $\mathfrak{M}_a^\beta$. So too is $\exists!a$. Hence $\mathfrak{M}_a^\beta$ is a model of Ξ as well:

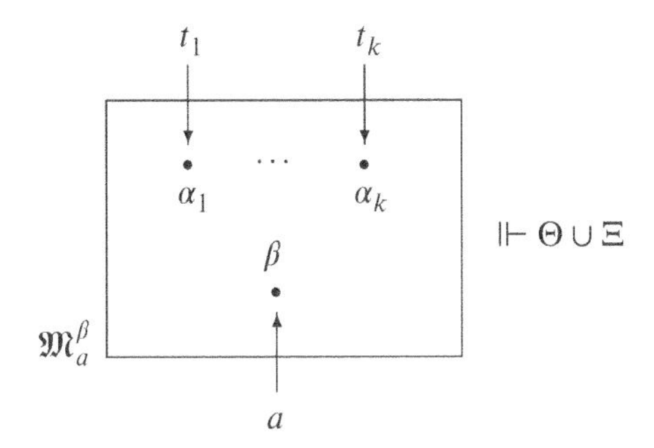

So $\mathfrak{M}_a^\beta$ makes true the premises of the proof Π:

$$\begin{array}{c}\Theta, \Xi \\ \Pi \\ \bot\end{array} \quad .$$

By (6), the proof Π is sound. Hence the conclusion of Π is true in $\mathfrak{M}_a^\beta$. But the conclusion of Π is $\bot$, which is false in every model. Contradiction.

We have reduced (1)-(7) to absurdity.

Appendix B

Formal Proof of a Geometric Inference

On the following page is a very wide formal proof of Lemma 49, rotated 90 degrees so as to (just) fit. Recall the discussion on p. 285 of our entitlement to the geometric inference marked by a dagger.

$$
\dfrac{\dfrac{\dfrac{\begin{array}{c}\gamma \text{ is Cauchy:}\\ \forall n\,\exists k\,\forall i>k\,\forall j>k\;R(\gamma_i,\gamma_j,n)\end{array}}{\exists k\,\forall i>k\,\forall j>k\;R(\gamma_i,\gamma_j,d+1)} \quad \dfrac{\dfrac{\begin{array}{c}\gamma^{\phi} \text{ converges to } c:\\ \forall n\,\exists k\,\forall i>k\;R(\gamma_{\phi i},c,n)\end{array}}{\exists k\,\forall i>k\;R(\gamma_{\phi i},c,d+1)} \quad \dfrac{\dfrac{{\scriptstyle(4)}\dfrac{}{\exists! k_1} \quad {\scriptstyle(3)}\dfrac{}{\exists! k_2}}{\exists!\max(k_1,k_2)} \quad \dfrac{\dfrac{\dfrac{{\scriptstyle(4)}\dfrac{}{\exists! k_1} \quad {\scriptstyle(3)}\dfrac{}{\exists! k_2}}{\exists\imath\, i>\max(k_1,k_2)} \quad \dfrac{\dfrac{\dfrac{{\scriptstyle(2)}\dfrac{}{b>\max(k_1,k_2)}}{b>k_1} \quad \dfrac{\dfrac{\dfrac{}{\phi a\geq a} \quad \dfrac{{\scriptstyle(1)}\dfrac{}{a>\max(k_1,k_2)}}{a>k_1}}{\phi a>k_1} \quad \dfrac{}{\forall i>k_1\,\forall j>k_1\;R(\gamma_i,\gamma_j,d+1)}{\scriptstyle(4)}}{\forall j>k_1\;R(\gamma_{\phi a},\gamma_j,d+1)}}{R(\gamma_{\phi a},\gamma_b,d+1)} \quad \dfrac{\dfrac{\dfrac{}{a>\max(k_1,k_2)}{\scriptstyle(1)}}{a>k_2} \quad \dfrac{}{\forall i>k_2\;R(\gamma_{\phi i},c,d+1)}{\scriptstyle(3)}}{R(\gamma_{\phi a},c,d+1)}}{R(\gamma_b,c,d)}{\scriptstyle\dagger}}{R(\gamma_b,c,d)}{\scriptstyle(1)}}{\forall j>\max(k_1,k_2)\;R(\gamma_j,c,d)}{\scriptstyle(2)}}{\exists k\,\forall j>k\;R(\gamma_j,c,d)}{\scriptstyle(3)}}{\exists k\,\forall j>k\;R(\gamma_{\phi i},c,d)}{\scriptstyle(4)}}{\exists k\,\forall j>k\;R(\gamma_j,c,d)}}{\begin{array}{c}\forall n\,\exists k\,\forall j>k\;R(\gamma_j,c,n)\\ \text{i.e., } \gamma \text{ converges to } c\end{array}}
$$

Bibliography

Jeremy Avigad. Number theory and elementary arithmetic. *Philosophia Mathematica*, 11(3):257–284, 2003.

E. T. Bell. Review of Richard Dedekind's *Gesammelte mathematische Werke*. *Bulletin of the American Mathematical Society*, 36(9):611–612, 1930.

John L. Bell. Frege's Theorem in a Constructive Setting. *Journal of Symbolic Logic*, 64(2):486–488, 1999.

E. Beltrami. Saggio di interpretazione della geometria non-euclidea. *Giornale di Matematiche*, 6:284–312, 1868.

Paul Benacerraf. What numbers could not be. *Philosophical Review*, 74(1):47–73, 1965.

Paul Benacerraf. Recantation *or* Any old ω-sequence would do after all. *Philosophia Mathematica (3)*, 4:184–189, 1996.

Vieri Benci and Mauro Di Nasso. Numerosities of labelled sets: a new way of counting. *Advances in Mathematics*, 173(1):50–67, 2003.

John Bigelow. *The Reality of Numbers: A Physicalist's Philosophy of Numbers*. Clarendon Press, Oxford, 1988.

Bernard Bolzano. *Beyträge zu einer begründeteren Darstellung der Mathematik*. Caspar Widtmann, Prag, 1810.

Bernard Bolzano. *Rein analytischer Beweis des Lehrsatzes, dass zwischen je zwei Werten, die ein entgegengesetztes Resultat gewähren, wenigstens eine reelle Wurzel der Gleiching liege*. Gottlieb Haase, Prag, 1817.

Bernard Bolzano. *Dr. Bernard Bolzanos Paradoxien des Unendlichen, herausgegeben aus dem schriftlichen Nachlasse des Verfassers von Dr. Fr. Prihonsky*. Reclam, Leipzig, 1851.

Bernard Bolzano. *Funktionenlehre* (ed. Karel Rychlik). Königliche Böhmische Gesellschaft der Wissenschaften, Prag, 1930.

Bernard Bolzano. *Beyträge zu einer begründeteren Darstellung der Mathematik*. Wissenschaftliche Buchgesellschaft, Darmstadt, 1974.

Bernard Bolzano. A. Preface to considerations on some objects of elementary geometry. In William Ewald, editor, *From Kant to Hilbert: A Source Book in the Foundations of Mathematics, Volume I*, pages 172–174. Clarendon Press, Oxford, 1996a.

Bernard Bolzano. Contributions to a Better-Grounded Presentation of Mathematics. In William Ewald, editor, *From Kant to Hilbert: A Source Book in the Foundations of Mathematics, Volume I*, pages 174–224. Clarendon Press, Oxford, 1996b.

Bernard Bolzano. Purely analytic proof of the theorem that between any two values which give results of opposite sign there lies at least one real root of the equation. In William Ewald, editor, *From Kant to Hilbert: A Source Book in the Foundations of Mathematics, Volume I*, pages 225–248. Clarendon Press, Oxford, 1996c.

George Boolos. Is Hume's Principle analytic? In Richard Heck, editor, *Language Thought and Logic: Essays in Honour of Michael Dummett*, pages 245–261. Clarendon Press, Oxford, 1997.

David Bostock. *Logic and Arithmetic, Volume 2: Rational and Irrational Numbers*. Clarendon Press, Oxford, 1979.

John P. Burgess. *Fixing Frege*. Princeton University Press, Princeton, 2005.

John P. Burgess. *Rigor & Structure*. Oxford University Press, Oxford, 2015.

John P. Burgess and Gideon Rosen. *A Subject with No Object: Strategies for Nominalistic Interpretation of Mathematics*. Clarendon Press, Oxford, 1997.

Georg Cantor. Ein Beitrag zur Mannigfaltigkeitslehre. *Journal für die reine und angewandte Mathematik*, 84:242–258, 1878.

Rudolf Carnap. Der Raum: Ein Beitrag zur Wissenschaftslehre. *Kant-Studien Ergänzungsheft*, 56:1–87, 1922.

Augustin-Louis Cauchy. *Cauchy's Cours d'Analyse: An Annotated Translation*, by Robert E. Bradley and C. Edward Sandifer. Springer, Dordrecht, 2009.

Paul J. Cohen. The independence of the continuum hypothesis. I. *Proceedings of the National Academy of Sciences, U.S.A.*, 50(6):1143–1148, 1963.

Julian C. Cole. Mathematical domains: Social constructs? In Bonnie Gold and Roger Simons, editors, *Proof and Other Dilemmas: Mathematics and Philosophy*, pages 109–128. Mathematics Association of America, Washington, DC, 2008.

Julian C. Cole. Creativity, Freedom, and Authority: A New Perspective On the Metaphysics of Mathematics. *Australasian Journal of Philosophy*, 87(4):589–608, 2009.

Roy T. Cook and Philip A. Ebert. Abstraction and Identity. *Dialectica*, 59(2): 121–139, 2005.

C.-J. de la Vallée Poussin. Recherches analytiques la théorie des nombres premiers. *Ann. Soc. scient. Bruxelles*, 20:183–256, 1896.

Richard Dedekind. *Stetigkeit und Irrationale Zahlen.* Vieweg & Sohn, Braunschweig, 1872.

Richard Dedekind. *Essays on the Theory of Numbers,* tr. Wooster Woodruff Beman. Open Court Publishing Company, Chicago, 1901.

Richard Dedekind. Was sind und was sollen die Zahlen? In Robert Fricke, Emmy Noether, and Öystein Ore, editors, *Richard Dedekind: Gesammelte Mathematische Werke, Dritter Band*, pages 335–391. Vieweg & Sohn, Braunschweig, 1932.

Richard Dedekind. Continuity and Irrational Numbers. In William Ewald, editor, *From Kant to Hilbert: A Source Book in the Foundations of Mathematics, Volume II*, pages 765–779. Clarendon Press, Oxford, 1996a.

Richard Dedekind. Was sind und was sollen die Zahlen? In William Ewald, editor, *From Kant to Hilbert: A Source Book in the Foundations of Mathematics, Volume II*, pages 787–833. Clarendon Press, Oxford, 1996b.

William Demopoulos and Peter Clark. The Logicism of Frege, Dedekind, and Russell. In Stewart Shapiro, editor, *The Oxford Handbook of Philosophy of Mathematics and Logic*, pages 129–165. Oxford University Press, New York, 2005.

Michael Detlefsen. Formalism. In Stewart Shapiro, editor, *The Oxford Handbook of Philosophy of Mathematics and Logic*, pages 236–317. Oxford University Press, New York, 2005.

Michael Detlefsen. Purity as an Ideal of Proof. In Paolo Mancosu, editor, *The Philosophy of Mathematical Practice*, pages 179–197. Oxford University Press, New York, 2008.

Lejeune Dirichlet. Beweis des Satzes, dass jede unbegrenzte arithmetische Progression, deren erstes Glied und Differenz ganze Zahlen ohne gemeinschaftlichen Factor sind, unendlich viele Primzahlen enthählt. *Abhandlungen der Königlich Preussischen Akademie der Wissenschaften*, 48:45–81, 1837.

P. G. Lejeune Dirichlet. *Vorlesungen über Zahlentheorie*. Vieweg & Sohn, Braunschweig, 1894.

Michael Dummett. *Frege: Philosophy of Mathematics*. Harvard University Press, Cambridge, Massachusetts, 1991.

P. Erdős. Démonstration élémentaire du théorème sur la distribution des nombres premiers. *Scriptum*, 1, Centre Mathématique, Amsterdam:199–220, 1949.

Euclid. *The Thirteen Books of Euclid's Elements,* translated from the text of Heiberg by Sir Thomas L. Heath, Second Edition, Volume I. Dover Publications, Inc., New York, 1956.

William Ewald. Introductory note to Gauss on Non-Euclidean Geometry. In William Ewald, editor, *From Kant to Hilbert: A Source Book in the Foundations of Mathematics, Volume I*, pages 296–299. Clarendon Press, Oxford, 1996a.

William Ewald. Bernard Bolzano (1781–1848). In William Ewald, editor, *From Kant to Hilbert: A Source Book in the Foundations of Mathematics, Volume I*, pages 168–174. Clarendon Press, Oxford, 1996b.

Solomon Feferman. Conceptions of the Continuum. *Intellectica*, 51(1):169–189, 2009.

Jens Erik Fenstad. Is Nonstandard Analysis Relevant for the Philosophy of Mathematics? *Synthese*, 62(2):289–301, 1985.

Otto Forster. *Analysis 1, 6. verbesserte Auflage*. Vieweg, Braunschweig/Wiesbaden, 2001.

Abraham A. Fraenkel. Der Begriff "definit" und die Unabhängigkeit des Auswahlsaxioms. *Sitzungsberichte der Preussischen Akademie der Wissenschaften, Physikalisch-mathematische Klasse*, XXI:253–257, 1922.

Craig G. Fraser. History of Mathematics in the Eighteenth Century. In Roy Porter, editor, *The Cambridge History of Science, Volume 4: Eighteenth-Century Science*, pages 305–327. Cambridge University Press, Cambridge, 2003.

Gottlob Frege. *Begriffsschrift, eine der arithmetischen nachgebildete Formelsprache des reinen Denkens*. Louis Nebert, Halle, 1879.

Gottlob Frege. *Die Grundlagen der Arithmetik: eine logisch mathematische Untersuchung uber den Begriff der Zahl*. Georg Olms Verlagsbuchhandlung, Hildesheim, 1884; reprinted 1961.

Gottlob Frege. *Grundgesetze der Arithmetik. I. Band*. Georg Olms Verlagsbuchhandlung, Hildesheim, 1893; reprinted 1962.

Gottlob Frege. *Grundgesetze der Arithmetik. II. Band.* Georg Olms Verlagsbuchhandlung, Hildesheim, 1903; reprinted 1962.

Harvey Friedman. FOM: grand conjectures. *fom*, http://cs.nyu.edu/pipermail/fom/1999-April/003014.html, 1999.

Harvey M. Friedman. Finite Functions and the Necessary Use of Large Cardinals. *Annals of Mathematics, Second Series*, 148(3):803–893, 1998.

Harvey M. Friedman. Interpretations, According to Tarski. Nineteenth Annual Tarski Lectures, *Interpretations of Set Theory in Discrete Mathematics and Informal Thinking*. Lecture 1. *Downloadable from http://www.math.osu.edu/ friedman/manuscripts.html*, 2007.

Carl Friedrich Gauss. On the Metaphysics of Mathematics. In William Ewald, editor, *From Kant to Hilbert: A Source Book in the Foundations of Mathematics, Volume I*, pages 293–296. Clarendon Press, Oxford, 1996.

Gerhard Gentzen. Untersuchungen über das logische Schliessen. *Mathematische Zeitschrift*, I, II:176–210, 405–431, 1934, 1935. Translated as 'Investigations into Logical Deduction', in *The Collected Papers of Gerhard Gentzen*, edited by M. E. Szabo, North-Holland, Amsterdam, 1969, pp. 68–131.

Kurt Gödel. Die Vollständigkeit der Axiome des logischen Funktionenkalküls. *Monatshefte für Mathematik und Physik*, 37:349–360, 1930.

Kurt Gödel. Über formal unentscheidbare Sätze der Principia Mathematica und verwandter Systeme I. *Monatshefte für Mathematik und Physik*, 37:173–198, 1931.

Kurt Gödel. *The Consistency of the Continuum Hypothesis and of the Generalized Continuum-Hypothesis with the Axioms of Set Theory.* Princeton University Press, Princeton, New Jersey, 1940.

Ivor Grattan-Guinness. *The Norton History of the Mathematical Sciences: The Rainbow of Mathematics.* W. W. Norton & Co., New York, 1997.

J. Hadamard. Sur la distribution des zéros de la fonction $\zeta(s)$ et ses conséquences arithmétiques. *Bull. Soc. math. France*, 24:199–220, 1896.

Jacques Hadamard. *The Psychology of Invention in the Mathematical Field.* Dover Publications, Inc. (copyright 1945, Princeton University Press), New York, 1945.

P. Hajek and P. Pudlak. *Metamathematics of First-Order Arithmetic.* Perspectives in Mathematical Logic. Springer, Berlin, 1998.

Bob Hale. *Abstract Objects.* Blackwell, Oxford, 1987.

Bob Hale. Reals by Abstraction. *Philosophia Mathematica*, 8:100–123, 2000.

Bob Hale. Definitions of Numbers and their Applications. In Philip A. Ebert and Marcus Rossberg, editors, *Abstractionism: Essays in Philosophy of Mathematics*. Oxford University Press Scholarship Online, DOI:10.1093/acprof:oso/9780199645268.003.0017, 2016.

Bob Hale and Crispin Wright. *The Reason's Proper Study: Essays towards a Neo-Fregean Philosophy of Mathematics*. Clarendon Press, Oxford, 2001.

G. H. Hardy. Goldbach's Theorem. In *Collected Papers, Vol. I*. Clarendon Press, Oxford, 1921.

L. A. Harrington, M. D. Morley, A. Ščedrov, and S. G. Simpson. Introduction. In L. A. Harrington, M. D. Morley, A. Ščedrov, and S. G. Simpson, editors, *Harvey Friedman's Research on the Foundations of Mathematics*, pages vii–xii. North Holland, Amsterdam, 1985.

W. D. Hart. Review of *Anti-realism and Logic: Truth as Eternal*. *Journal of Symbolic Logic*, 54(4):1485–1486, 1989.

Robin Hartshorne. *Geometry: Euclid and Beyond*. Springer, New York, 2000.

William S. Hatcher. *Foundations of Mathematics*. W. B. Saunders Co., Philadelphia, 1968.

Richard J. Heck. The development of arithmetic in Frege's Grundgesetze der Arithmetik. *The Journal of Symbolic Logic*, 58:579–601, 1993.

David Hilbert. *Grundlagen der Geometrie*. B. G. Teubner, Leipzig, 1899.

David Hilbert. *Grundlagen der Geometrie*. B. G. Teubner, Leipzig, 1903.

David Hilbert. Neubegründung der Mathematik. Erste Mitteilung. In David Hilbert, editor, *Gesammelte Abhandlungen, Dritter Band*, pages 41–52. Chelsea Publishing Company, Reprint, New York, 1922.

David Hilbert. *The Foundations of Geometry*, authorized translation by E. J. Townsend. The Open Court Publishing Company, La Salle, IL, 1950.

David Hilbert. *Foundations of Geometry*. Translated from the 10th German edition by Leo Unger. Revised by Paul Bernays. Open Court, La Salle, Illinois, 1971.

David Hilbert. The New Grounding of Mathematics. First Report. In William Ewald, editor, *From Kant to Hilbert: A Source Book in the Foundations of Mathematics, Volume II*, pages 1115–1134. Clarendon Press, Oxford, 1996.

D. Hilbert and W. Ackermann. *Grundzüge der Theoretischen Logik*. Springer, Berlin, 1928.

D. Hilbert and W. Ackermann. *Grundzüge der Theoretischen Logik, 2. Auflage*. Springer, Berlin, 1938.

D. Hilbert and W. Ackermann. *Principles of Mathematical Logic*. Chelsea Publishing Co., New York, 1950.

Edward V. Huntington. A Complete Set of Postulates for the Theory of Absolute Continuous Magnitude. *Transactions of the American Mathematical Society*, 3(2):264–279, 1902.

Daniel Isaacson. Arithmetical Truth and Hidden Higher-Order Concepts. *Studies in Logic and the Foundations of Mathematics*, 122:147–169, 1987.

V. Kagan. *N. Lobachevsky and His Contribution to Science*. Foreign Languages Publishing House, Moscow, 1957.

Akihiro Kanamori. *The Higher Infinite. Large Cardinals in Set Theory from their Beginnings*. Perspectives in Mathematical Logic. Springer, Berlin, 1994.

Philip Kitcher. *The Nature of Mathematical Knowledge*. Oxford University Press, Oxford, 1983.

Christian Felix Klein. The Arithmetizing of Mathematics. In William Ewald, editor, *From Kant to Hilbert: A Source Book in the Foundations of Mathematics, Volume II*, pages 965–971. Clarendon Press, Oxford, 1996a.

Christian Felix Klein. On the Mathematical Character of Space-Intuition and the Relation of Pure Mathematics to the Applied Sciences. In William Ewald, editor, *From Kant to Hilbert: A Source Book in the Foundations of Mathematics, Volume II*, pages 958–965. Clarendon Press, Oxford, 1996b.

J. H. Lambert. Theorie der Parallellinien. *Magazin für reine und angewandte Mathematik*, 2:137–164, 1786. Reprinted in P. Stäckel and F. Engel, eds., *Theorie der Parallellinien von Euclid bis auf Gauss*, Teubner, Leipzig, 1895.

Johann Heinrich Lambert. Mémoire sur quelques propriétés remarquables des quantités transcendentes circulaires et logarithmiques. *Histoire de l'Académie Royale des Sciences et des Belles-Lettres de Berlin*, 17:265–322, 1768.

M. Lange. What Makes a Scientific Explanation Distinctively Mathematical? *British Journal for Philosophy of Science*, 64:485–511, 2013.

Oystein Linnebo. Introduction. *Synthese*, 170:321–329, 2009.

Nikolai Lobachevsky. On the Principles of Geometry. *Kazan Messenger*, pages 25–28, 1829.

Nikolai Lobachevsky. Géométrie imaginaire. *Journal für die reine und angewandte Mathematik*, 17:295–320, 1837.

Nikolai Lobachevsky. *Geometrische Untersuchungen zur Theorie der Parallellinien*. F. Fincke, Berlin, 1840.

Nikolai Lobachevsky. *Pangéométrie ou précis de géométrie fondée sur une théorie générale et rigoureuse des parallèles*. Kazan: Universitet, 1856.

J. R. Lucas. *The Conceptual Roots of Mathematics: An Essay on the Philosophy of Mathematics*. Routledge, New York, 2000.

Paolo Mancosu. *Abstraction and Infinity*. Oxford University Press, Oxford, 2016.

Elliott Mendelson. *Number Systems and the Foundations of Analysis*. Academic Press, London, 1973.

Isaac Newton. *Arithmetica Universalis, 2nd edition*. (1st edition in Latin, 1707.) Longman, London, 1728.

Marco Panza. The Twofold Role of Diagrams in Euclid's Plane Geometry. *Synthese*, 186(1):55–102, 2012.

J. Paris and L. Harrington. A Mathematical Incompleteness in Peano Arithmetic. In Jon Barwise, editor, *Handbook of Mathematical Logic*, pages 1133–1142. North-Holland, Amsterdam, 1977.

Charles Parsons. Frege's Theory of Number. In Max Black, editor, *Philosophy in America*, pages 180–203. Cornell University Press, Ithaca: New York, 1965.

Charles Parsons. *Mathematical Thought and Its Objects*. Harvard University Press, Cambridge, MA, 2008.

Giuseppe Peano. I Fondamenti dell'Arithmetica. *Formulaire de mathématiques, Turin, Bocca Frères*, II(2):VIII, 1–15, 1898.

Ioseph Peano. *Arithmetices Principia: Nova Methodo Exposita*. Augustae Taurinorum: Ediderunt Fratres Bocca, Rome, 1889.

G. Peano. Sur une courbe, qui remplit toute une aire plane. *Mathematische Annalen*, 36(1):157–160, 1890.

Dag Prawitz. *Natural Deduction: A Proof-Theoretical Study*. Almqvist & Wiksell, Stockholm, 1965.

Hilary Putnam. *Philosophy of Logic*. Harper and Row, New York, 1971.

W. V. O. Quine. *Word and Object*. M.I.T. Press, Cambridge, MA, 1960.

Willard Van Orman Quine. *Methods of Logic, 2nd edition.* Holt, Rinehart and Winston, New York, 1972.

J. B. Rosser. Extensions of Some Theorems of Gödel and Church. *The Journal of Symbolic Logic*, 1(3):87–91, 1936.

Ian Rumfitt. Singular Terms and Arithmetical Logicism. *Philosophical Books*, 44(3):193–219, 2003.

Bertrand Russell. *An Essay on the Foundations of Geometry*. Dover Publications, Inc., New York, 1897.

Bertrand Russell. On Denoting. *MInd*, n.s. 14(56):479–493, 1905.

Bertrand Russell. *Introduction to Mathematical Philosophy*. George Allen and Unwin Ltd., London, 1919.

Matthias Schirn. Introduction: Frege on the Foundations of Arithmetic and Geometry. In Matthias Schirn, editor, *Frege: Importance and Legacy*, pages 1–42. de Gruyter, Berlin; New York, 1996.

Peter Schroeder-Heister. A Natural Extension of Natural Deduction. *Journal of Symbolic Logic*, 49:1284–1300, 1984.

A. Selberg. An Elementary Proof of the Prime-Number Theorem. *Annals of Mathematics*, 50(2):305–313, 1949a.

Atle Selberg. An Elementary Proof of Dirichlet's Theorem About Primes in an Arithmetic Progression. *Annals of Mathematics*, 50(2):297–304, 1949b.

Stewart Shapiro. *Thinking about Mathematics: The Philosophy of Mathematics*. Oxford University Press, New York, 2000a.

Stewart Shapiro. Frege meets Dedekind: a Neologicist Treatment of Real Analysis. *Notre Dame Journal of Formal Logic*, 41(4):335–364, 2000b.

Stewart Shapiro and Alan Weir. 'Neo-Logicist' Logic is Not Epistemically Innocent. *Philosophica Mathematica*, 8:160–189, 2000.

Peter M. Simons. Frege's Theory of Real Numbers. *History and Philosophy of Logic*, 8(1):25–44, 1987.

Stephen G. Simpson. Partial Realizations of Hilbert's Program. *The Journal of Symbolic Logic*, 53:349–363, 1988.

Stephen G. Simpson. *Subsystems of Second Order Arithmetic*. Perspectives in Mathematical Logic. Springer, Berlin, 1999.

Stephen G. Simpson. The Gödel Hierarchy and Reverse Mathematics. In Solomon Feferman, Charles Parsons, and Stephen G. Simpson, editors, *Gödel: Essays for his Centennial*, pages 109–127. Cambridge University Press, Cambridge, 2010.

Stephen G. Simpson. Foundations of Mathematics: An Optimistic Message. In R. Kahle and M. Rathjen, editors, *The Legacy of Kurt Schütte*, pages 401–414. Springer, Berlin, 2020.

A. S. Smogorzhevsky. *Lobachevskian Geometry*. Mir Publishers, Moscow, 1976.

Craig Smoryński. Nonstandard Models and Related Developments. In L. A. Harrington, M. D. Morley, A. Šc̆edrov, and S. G. Simpson, editors, *Harvey Friedman's Research on the Foundations of Mathematics*, pages 179–229. North Holland, Amsterdam, 1985.

Ernest Snapper. The Three Crises in Mathematics: Logicism, Intuitionism, and Formalism. *Mathematics Magazine*, 52(4):207–216, 1979.

Florian Steinberger. What Harmony Could and Could Not Be. *Australasian Journal of Philosophy*, 89(4):617–639, 2011.

Patrick Suppes. *Axiomatic Set Theory*. Van Nostrand, New York, 1960.

W. W. Tait. Finitism. *The Journal of Philosophy*, 78(9):524–546, 1981.

Alfred Tarski. The Concept of Truth in Formalized Languages. In J. H. Woodger, editor, *Logic, Semantics, Metamathematics*, pages 152–278. Clarendon Press, Oxford, 1933 in Polish.

Alfred Tarski. What is Elementary Geometry? In Leon Henkin, Patrick Suppes, and Alfred Tarski, editors, *The Axiomatic Method, with Special Reference to Geometry and Physics. Proceedings of an International Symposium held at the University of California, Berkeley, December 26, 1957–January 4, 1958. Studies in Logic and the Foundations of Mathematics*, pages 16–29. North-Holland, Amsterdam, 1959.

Alfred Tarski. *The Completeness of Elementary Algebra and Geometry*. Institute Blaise Pascal, Paris, iv+50 pp., 1967.

Alfred Tarski. *Collected Papers, Vol. 4, 1958–1979, edited by S. R. Givant and R. N. McKenzie*. Birkhäuser, Basel, 1986.

Neil Tennant. *Natural Logic*. Edinburgh University Press, Edinburgh, 1978.

Neil Tennant. Intentionality, Syntactic Structure and the Evolution of Language. In Christopher Hookway, editor, *Minds, Machines and Evolution*, pages 73–103. Cambridge University Press, Cambridge, 1984a.

Neil Tennant. Constructive Logicism: An Adequate Theory of Number. *Minutes of the University of Cambridge Moral Sciences Club*, October 23rd, 1984 (by Roger Teichman; lodged in the University Library, Cambridge), 1984b.

Neil Tennant. Conventional Necessity and the Contingency of Convention. *Dialectica*, 41:79–95, 1987a.

Neil Tennant. *Anti-Realism and Logic: Truth as Eternal*. Clarendon Library of Logic and Philosophy, Oxford University Press, 1987b.

Neil Tennant. *Autologic*. Edinburgh University Press, Edinburgh, 1992.

Neil Tennant. Intuitionistic Mathematics Does Not Need *Ex Falso Quodlibet*. *Topoi*, 13:127–133, 1994.

Neil Tennant. The Necessary Existence of Numbers. *Noûs*, 31:307–336, 1997a.

Neil Tennant. *The Taming of The True*. Oxford University Press, Oxford, 1997b.

Neil Tennant. Deductive versus Expressive Power: A Pre-Gödelian Predicament. *Journal of Philosophy*, XCVII(5):257–277, 2000.

Neil Tennant. Ultimate Normal Forms for Parallelized Natural Deductions, with Applications to Relevance and the Deep Isomorphism between Natural Deductions and Sequent Proofs. *Logic Journal of the IGPL*, 10(3):1–39, 2002a.

Neil Tennant. Deflationism and the Gödel Phenomena. *Mind*, 111:551–582, 2002b.

Neil Tennant. Review Essay on Bob Hale and Crispin Wright, *The Reason's Proper Study*. *Philosophia Mathematica*, 11(2):226–241, 2003.

Neil Tennant. A General Theory of Abstraction Operators. *The Philosophical Quarterly*, 54(214):105–133, 2004.

Neil Tennant. Mind, Mathematics and the *Ignorabimusstreit*. *British Journal for the History of Philosophy*, 15(4):745–773, 2007.

Neil Tennant. Natural Logicism via the Logic of Orderly Pairing. In Sten Lindström, Erik Palmgren, Krister Segerberg, and Viggo Stoltenberg-Hansen, editors, *Logicism, Intuitionism, Formalism: What Has Become of Them?*, pages 91–125. Synthese Library, Springer Verlag, 2009.

Neil Tennant. *What Are the Reals, Really?* (unpublished ms., assigned reading at The Ohio State University for Autumn 2011 Graduate Seminar on Neo-Logicism). 2010.

Neil Tennant. Cut for Core Logic. *Review of Symbolic Logic*, 5(3):450–479, 2012a.

Neil Tennant. *Changes in Mind: An Essay on Rational Belief Revision*. Oxford University Press, Oxford, 2012b.

Neil Tennant. Parts, Classes, and *Parts of Classes*: an Anti-Realist Reading of Lewisian Mereology. *Synthese*, 190(4):709–742, 2012c.

Neil Tennant. Cut for Classical Core Logic. *Review of Symbolic Logic*, 8(2): 236–256, 2015.

Neil Tennant. Pythagoras Meets Peano. *Unpublished ms. downloadable from author's webpage https://u.osu.edu/tennant.9/*, 2016.

Neil Tennant. *Core Logic*. Oxford University Press, Oxford, 2017.

Neil Tennant. On Tarski's Axiomatization of Mereology. *Studia Logica*, Online first: https://doi.org/10.1007/s11225–018–9819–3, 2018.

Neil Tennant. Frege's Class Theory and the Logic of Sets. In Thomas Piecha and Kai Wehmeier, editors, *Peter Schroeder-Heister on Proof-Theoretic Semantics*, pages XXX–XXX. Springer, Berlin, forthcoming.

Roberto Torretti. Nineteenth Century Geometry. In Edward N. Zalta, editor, *Stanford Encyclopedia of Philosophy*. The Metaphysics Research Lab, Center for the Study of Language and Information, Stanford University, Stanford, CA 94305-4115. URL=<http://plato.stanford.edu/entries/geometry-19th/#LobGeo/>. First published Mon Jul 26, 1999; substantive revision Wed Jan 13, 2010.

M. van Atten. Kant and Real Numbers. In Peter Dybjer, Sten Lindström, Erik Palmgren, and Göran Sundholm, editors, *Epistemology versus Ontology: Essays on the Philosophy and Foundations of Mathematics in Honour of Per Martin-Löf*, pages 3–23. Springer, Dordrecht, 2012.

Peter van Inwagen. The New Anti-Metaphysicians. *Proceedings and Addresses of the American Philosophical Association*, 83(2):45–61, 2009.

Achille Varzi. Mereology. In Edward N. Zalta, editor, *The Stanford Encyclopedia of Philosophy*. Metaphysics Research Lab, Stanford University, winter 2016 edition, 2016.

Hermann von Helmholtz. The Origin and Meaning of Geometrical Axioms. Translated by Edmund Atkinson. *Mind, o.s.*, 1(3):301–321, 1876.

Hermann von Helmholtz. Über den Ursprung und die Bedeutung der geometrischen Axiome. In Herbert Hörz and Siegfried Wollgast, editors, *Philosophische Vorträge und Aufsätze*, pages 187–217. Akademie Verlag, Berlin, 1971.

Ferdinand von Lindemann. Über die Zahl π. *Mathematische Annalen*, 20(2): 213–225, 1882.

A. Voss. *Über das Wesen der Mathematik: Rede gehalten am 11. März 1908 in der öffentlichen Sitzung der K. Bayerischen Akademie der Wissenschaften.* B. G. Teubner, Leipzig, 1908.

H. Weber. Leopold Kronecker. *Jahresbericht der Deutschen Mathematiker-Vereinigung*, 2:5–31, 1891–1892.

K. Weierstraß. Über continuirliche Functionen eines reellen Arguments, die für keinen Werth des letzteren einen bestimmten Differentiialquotienten besitzen (Gelesen in der Konigl. Akademie der Wissenschaften am 18. Juli 1872.). In *Mathematische Werke, Band 2 (1895)*, pages 71–74. Mayer & Müller, 1872.

Crispin Wright. *Frege's Conception of Numbers as Objects*. Aberdeen University Press, Aberdeen, 1983.

Crispin Wright. Reply to Dummett. In Mathias Schirn, editor, *Philosophy of Mathematics Today*, pages 389–406. Clarendon Press, Oxford, 1998.

Crispin Wright. Is Hume's Principle Analytic? *Notre Dame Journal of Formal Logic*, 40(1):6–30, 1999.

Crispin Wright. Neo-Fregean Foundations for Real Analysis: Some Reflections on Frege's Constraint. *Notre Dame Journal of Formal Logic*, 41(4):317–334, 2000.

Hans Zassenhaus. Über die Existenz von Primzahlen in arithmetischen Progressionen. *Commentarii Mathematici Helvetici*, 22:232–259, 1949.

E. Zermelo. Untersuchungen über die Grundlagen der Mengenlehre. I. *Mathematische Annalen*, 65:261–281, 1908.

Index